Achieving Democracy

Achieving Democracy

Democratization in Theory and Practice

Edited by

Mary Fran T. Malone

continuum

The Continuum International Publishing Group
80 Maiden Lane, New York, NY 10038
The Tower Building, 11 York Road, London SE1 7NX

www.continuumbooks.com

ISBN: 978-1-4411-9179-3 (hardcover)
         978-1-4411-8182-4 (paperback)

Library of Congress Cataloging-in-Publication Data
Achieving democracy: democratization in theory and practice / [edited]
by Mary Fran T. Malone.
p. cm.
Includes bibliographical references and index.
ISBN-13: 978-1-4411-9179-3 (hardcover : alk. paper)
ISBN-10: 1-4411-9179-8 (hardcover : alk. paper)
ISBN-13: 978-1-4411-8182-4 (pbk. : alk. paper)
ISBN-10: 1-4411-8182-2 (pbk. : alk. paper)
1. Democratization. 2. Democracy. I. Malone, Mary Fran T. II. Title.

JC423.A249 2011
321.8–dc22
                                                            2011004344

Typeset by Newgen Imaging Systems Pvt Ltd, Chennai, India
Printed and bound in the United States of America

To
Donna and Warren Brown

Contents

Contents **ix**

List of Contributors

Dinorah Azpuru is an associate professor of political science at Wichita State University in Kansas and a member of the Scientific Support Group of the Latin American Public Opinion Project at Vanderbilt University. She has published extensively on issues of democratization, post-conflict societies, and public opinion in Latin America. Her articles have appeared in the *Journal of Democracy, Orbis,* and *Latin American Politics and Society,* among others.

Paolo Dardanelli is a lecturer in European and comparative politics at the University of Kent. His research investigates the evolving connections between statehood, nationality, and democracy. He is the author of *Between Two Unions: Europeanisation and Scottish Devolution* and of articles in *Political Studies, Party Politics, Regional and Federal Studies,* and *Nations and Nationalism,* among others.

Paul Fritz is an assistant professor in the department of political science at Hofstra University. He specializes in international security studies, international relations theory, and US foreign and defense policy. His interest in German democratization stems from a larger research project that examines the notion of prudence in victory, or how victorious states manage defeated great powers.

Ewa Golebiowska is an associate professor of political science at Wayne State University, specializing in political psychology and political behavior. Her articles have appeared in numerous journals, including the *Journal of Politics, Political Behavior,* and *International Journal of Public Opinion Research.* Reflective of her broad interests in attitudes toward civil rights and liberties, Golebiowska has written about ethnic and religious tolerance in Poland, support for the rights of Polish political dissenters, as well as attitudes toward women in Polish politics.

Nicoletta F. Gullace is an associate professor of history at the University of New Hampshire. Her research focuses on the expansion of citizenship in Great Britain. She is the author of *The Blood of Our Sons: Men, Women, and the Renegotiation of British Citizenship during the Great War.*

Mary Alice Haddad is an assistant professor of government at Wesleyan University. She is author of *Politics and Volunteering in Japan: A Global Perspective, Making Democracy Real in Japan*, and articles in journals such as *Comparative Political Studies, Democratization, Journal of Asian Studies*, and *Nonprofit and Voluntary Sector Quarterly*.

Jonathan Hiskey is associate professor of political science at Vanderbilt University. His research focuses on the consequences of Latin America's uneven political and economic transitions over the past 30 years, with a particular interest in Mexico. Hiskey also studies migration, and the political implications of large scale emigration for the communities left behind.

Laura Dudley Jenkins is an associate professor of political science at the University of Cincinnati. She is author of *Identity and Identification in India: Defining the Disadvantaged*. Her research focuses on social justice policies in the context of culturally diverse democracies, such as India.

Marvin P. King, Jr. is assistant professor in the department of political science at the University of Mississippi. He has authored articles in journals such as the *National Political Science Review, Journal of Black Studies*, and *Publius*, which examine race and politics in the United States.

Alynna J. Lyon is an associate professor in the department of political science at the University of New Hampshire. Her research focuses on international organizations, multilateralism, peacekeeping, and American foreign policy.

Mary Fran T. Malone is an assistant professor in the department of political science at the University of New Hampshire. She specializes in Latin American politics and democratization, focusing in particular on the impact of crime on citizens' political attitudes and behavior.

Stephanie McLean received her Ph.D. in political science at the University of Pittsburgh in 2006, where she examined the impact of race on political attitudes and behavior in the United States. She has extended her study of public opinion to include Canadian politics, and currently analyzes public opinion data for the Canadian Prime Minister's office.

Harita Patel is a graduate student in the department of political science at the University of Cincinnati. Her research examines identity and politics in India, Pakistan, and Kashmir.

Emily Rodio is a lecturer in the department of political science at St. Joseph's University. Her research focuses on South Africa's Truth and Reconciliation Commission and its impact on the democratization process. In a recent publication in the *International Journal of Human Rights*, she also examines transnational human rights activism.

Mitchell A. Seligson is the Centennial Professor of Political Science and Professor of Sociology at Vanderbilt University. He founded, and directs the Latin American Public Opinion Project, which conducts the Americas-Barometer surveys that currently cover over 20 countries in the Americas. His research on democratization and Latin American politics has appeared in over 140 articles, 14 books, and more than 35 monographs and occasional papers.

Marlene K. Sokolon is associate professor of political science at Concordia University in Montreal, Canada. Her main area of specialization is ancient Greek political thought, but she has wider interests in the history of political ideas, political emotions, and the contribution of poetry and literature to political conceptualizations. She is the author of several publications including the book *Political Emotions: Aristotle and the Symphony of Reason and Emotion*.

Jeannie Sowers is an assistant professor in the department of political science at the University of New Hampshire. Her research focuses on the intersections between politics and environment in the Middle East. She has published on the politics of water, conservation, climate change, and pollution, particularly in Egypt. Sowers's publications include articles in *Climatic Change* and *The Journal of Environment and Development*.

Acknowledgments

In 2007, I received a grant to organize the Saul O Sidore lecture series for the 2007–08 academic year at the University of New Hampshire. Together with the Center for the Humanities, I arranged for a group of scholars and practitioners to come to campus to share their thoughts on democracy, both at home and abroad. I learned a great deal from the presentations and discussions of these scholars, and this lecture series serves as the basis of this book. I am so very grateful to the Saul O Sidore Foundation for providing the opportunity for the lecture series, as well as to Burt Feintuch, Mimi Winder, and Mary Jo Alibrio for providing guidance and assistance throughout the year. I am very thankful that Ellen Cohn suggested I continue my collaboration with these scholars and practitioners in the form of an edited volume. I am also grateful for the practical advice I received from Jon Hurwitz, based upon his own editing experiences. Jon Hurwitz, along with Mitchell Seligson, also provided a great deal of inspiration for this project. From them I learned not just about political science, but also about being a good teacher. If I have channeled just a little bit of their energy and passion for teaching into this volume, the students reading it will undoubtedly benefit.

This work has also been enriched by the contributions of Madelaine Georgette, the artist who painted *Going to Vote IV*, which graces the cover. *Going to Vote IV* was inspired by the first all-race elections in South Africa, in April 1994, and is therefore a fitting as well as beautiful image for this book. Several other people worked hard to improve the quality of this collection. My editor, Marie-Claire Antoine, provided valuable assistance at all stages of the manuscript preparation. My graduate and undergraduate assistants, Sophia Weeks, Elizabeth Kyriacou, Richard Barney, and Christina Ladam, pored over the pages to account for all references and minimize all errors. A series of reviewers read this manuscript in part, or in full, and offered very valuable insights: Warren Brown, Uwe Serdült, Elisabeth Armstrong, Ash Narain Roy, Siddhartha Baviskar, Christine Malone-Rowe, and Stacy VanDeveer. I would like to thank these reviewers, as well as the anonymous reviewers that provided such valuable feedback at the early planning stages of the project. My thanks also go to my supportive colleagues in the Department of Political Science and the Justice Studies Program at the University of New Hampshire. Of course, all of us would be lost without the expert guidance of our administrative staff, particularly Marcie Anderson, Deborah Briand, and Janis Marshall.

This book has also benefited greatly from the assistance of two very energetic, yet quite small, research assistants. While Sonia and Eva Barth-Malone sometimes had trouble reaching my mailbox and the photocopier, they nevertheless were eager to help me in the carrying of books and papers, and interrupted several playground sessions to accompany me to the library. I am grateful to my parents, Martin and Christine Malone, as well as to my sister and nephew, Christine Malone-Rowe and Anthony Berenato, for providing such wonderful extra childcare assistance when these two little researchers tired of such tasks. It is much easier to spend time writing when I know my girls are having the time of their lives at Grandmom and Grandpop's famous beach house. Additional thanks go to the teachers and staff of Live and Learn Early Learning Center in Lee, NH, as well as to the director, Johanna Booth-Miner. I never had to feel guilty about going to work, as I knew my girls were in such caring and creative hands.

While working on this project, I have also been incredibly fortunate to have had wonderful support from a group of working mothers. Frequently, snow days and childhood illnesses do not respect publishing deadlines. On those occasions, when I have been about to drop the ball on the endless juggling of family and work, I have been rescued by other moms who have been so eager to help. Many, many thanks to this amazing and generous group of working moms: Lisa Baglione, Roslyn Chavda, Alynna Lyon, Kerry Palombaro, Cristal Partis, Jo Porter, Sharyn Potter, Rachel Rouillard, Mary Schwarzer, and Jeannie Sowers.

My husband, Sascha Barth, has also been so generous about helping me with this project and pushing me when I most needed it. His very valuable advice of "more typing and less talking, Malone" very frequently is the exact motivation I need. Sascha graciously puts his own career on hold to help me with mine and treats my work with the same care as his own. I thank him for all of his support, as well as for being patient about waiting for a book to be dedicated to him (although I promise that is coming soon).

Finally, I would like to thank Donna and Warren Brown, to whom this book is dedicated. Every day, Donna and Warren uphold the values and practices that make me love my job so much. Throughout their four decades at the University of New Hampshire, they have helped create an environment that welcomes the creation and active exchange of ideas—the ultimate goal of a university. Donna has worked diligently to create opportunities for students and professors to collaborate on research projects, and many of my favorite memories of working at the University of New Hampshire have been through her programs. Warren will forever go down in history for working so hard for so little thanks as department chair. One of the reasons I have been able to write this book is because Warren worked tirelessly to find resources, create opportunities, provide advice, and supply a great deal of encouragement for his colleagues. As Donna and Warren prepare for their retirement, I am sure they have spent a great deal of time thinking about their years at the University of New Hampshire. There are many measures of a successful academic career—awards, titles, books, articles, interviews. Perhaps one of the most valuable, yet overlooked, is the number of colleagues from all over the university who wish you would reconsider your retirement plans, and miss you when you move on.

Foreword

Mitchell A. Seligson
Centennial Professor of Political Science and Director of
the Latin American Public Opinion Project (LAPOP), Vanderbilt University

Why should we care about democracy? Aren't most countries democratic, and won't they stay that way? If you are asking yourself these questions as you begin this book, you are like the great majority of people in the United States, a country that has been democratic at least since 1789. We tend to think of democracy as the normal state of affairs, with regular elections, protection of free speech, the unfettered right to demonstrate, and freedom from arbitrary arrest, among other civil liberties long enjoyed by Americans. But when we look out across the seas we find a very different picture. Many nations still suffer under the yoke of dictatorship, while others have only recently emerged from dictatorial rule. In still others, nascent democracies are being severely challenged, limiting democracy to elections alone, while most other freedoms, including the right to form political parties, are nonexistent.

If we think further, we might also want to reexamine our own experiences with democracy. Was the United States really a democracy in 1789, even though the Founding Fathers called it a democracy? After all, women couldn't vote, and Afro-Americans were not counted as citizens. Indeed, property and other qualifications for voting restricted the electorate to a tiny minority in most states. So was the United States a democracy in 1789, and if not, was it in 1919 when the Nineteenth Amendment finally gave women the right to vote, or was it in 1965 when the National Voting Rights Act finally outlawed discrimination that had de facto disenfranchised most Afro-Americans living in the South? Throughout this entire period the United States was called, and considered itself to be, a democracy; yet, by contemporary standards, in those earlier periods it was at best only a partial democracy, or limited democracy. The point is that our notions of democracy have evolved and expanded, and we today have a higher standard for a democratic country than we did in the past.

This book is one that will allow you to reflect on those questions by looking at the experiences of countries worldwide and over time. As you read through the excellent chapters that follow, you will begin to realize that much of what you thought about democracy needs to be reexamined. One thing that becomes clear as you read through the historical chapters is that "democracy" does not mean the same thing at all times and all places. This point does not refer to the bizarre Orwellian terminology employed by the Soviet Union, which regularly held "elections" in which the winning candidate garnered 99 percent of the vote. That so-called "people's democracy" was not a democracy at all, but the dictatorship of a tiny ruling group that held an iron grip on the lives of Soviet citizens. So, the labeling of "democracy" in that case was meaningless. But this illustration brings out a very important lesson in your effort to understand what democracy means. As you will see in this book when the authors discuss their definitions of democracy, in order for elections to be meaningful, they have to be *competitive*; no competition, no democracy. As Adam Przeworski, one of the leading thinkers on the subject, has often told us, democracy means the institutionalization of uncertainty. This means that in a political system where the outcomes of elections are always known before they take place, democracy does not exist. Uncertainty, however, does not mean instability, far from it. Indeed, it is the uncertainty of the outcomes of elections that gives hope to those who were defeated in their efforts to win office, knowing they will be able to return to the "battlefield" another day to contest those same positions. Uncertainty helps *reduce* political instability, not only by giving hope to the defeated, but by serving as a restraint on those who win office, since they cannot be confident, the way dictators often are, that they will rule "forever." The defeated minority is almost certain to become a ruling majority sometime down the line.

Legitimate debate over the meaning of the term "democracy" comes largely from variation in its definition over time. To understand this, readers should pay close attention to the chapters in Section 1. There, Professor Malone, editor of this volume, and her coauthor, Professor Sokolon, elegantly trace for you the history of the development of democracy since the Greeks. As they show, democracy in Athens coexisted with slavery, and only an estimated 10 percent of the population were citizens. As already noted, the United States called itself a democracy in 1789, even though much of the "demos" (the people) were excluded from the right to vote. But in the eighteenth century our notions of democracy were much more restricted than they are today. Thus, while today we use the same word, "democracy," that we used in 1789, we do not consider voting limitations by gender, race, or ethnicity to be legitimate. In Chapter 2, Professors Hiskey and Lyon show that democracy may play many important functions, and help explain why democracy is so much more desirable than dictatorship. For example, they discuss its role in promoting human rights, economic development and, perhaps most importantly, of preventing wars. Democracy does not do all good things, but it seems to limit wars and, most important, it limits state abuse of citizens' human rights.

As you read Section 2, you will look at the early cases of what we can call "modern democracies," namely those of Great Britain, reviewed by Professor Gullace, the United States, by Professor King and Dr. McLean, and Switzerland, studied by Professor Dardanelli. In each of these early cases, citizens struggled against monarchies, royalties, or those who would promote slavery. These struggles were painted with a wide brush over longer periods of time. Modern democracies were not born all of a piece; they were constructed slowly as they tested the different institutional forms that would allow for popular participation, the demos, while also allowing the state to be effective in its basic responsibilities of defense, taxation, and providing for the common good. In this period, a "political culture" of democracy arose, enabling and facilitating the long-term stability of democracy.

In Section 3, you will read of the democracies in the so-called "second wave," namely the cases of Germany, examined by Professor Fritz, Japan, studied by Professor Haddad, and India, examined by Professor Jenkins and Ms. Patel. This is a hugely diverse set of countries, and their leaders came to democracy with the experience of the "first-wave" countries firmly in mind. They did not have to invent brand new solutions to the problems of representation, rule of law, judicial review, and central–local control. Rather, these new democracies had to sort out what they could learn from the existing cases and borrow what they thought would work in their particular region of the world, discarding the rest.

In Section 4 you will look at the most recent wave, the "third wave" of democracy. There, Professor Malone provides information on Chile, Professor Golebiowska on Poland, and Professor Rodio on South Africa. These more recent cases face a new set of challenges related to globalization, migration, the environment, and worldwide plagues such as AIDS.

Democracy continues to evolve and spread throughout the world. However, one wonders if there are parts of the world where democracy will not take hold, and whether things can be done to nudge along the process of democratization. These questions are tackled in Section 5, where Professor Sowers looks at the Middle East, a region that until recently seemed singularly unattracted to the appeals (and benefits noted by Hiskey and Lyon) of democracy. Will the Middle East democratize, or will it remain stuck in an authoritarian trap? Prof. Azpuru makes clear that things can be done to promote democracy, as her data show that foreign assistance programs by the

United States government have had a significant impact on the development of democracy in many regions of the world.

Thus, you are about to embark on an adventure that spans the centuries as it spans the globe. This collection of outstanding, original essays will open your eyes to many important issues in the comparative study of democracy.

Section 1

Introduction to Democratic Development

Nelson Mandela casts his historic vote in South Africa's first multiracial election in 1994.
Photo courtesy of the UN/Chris Sattlberger

1

Democracy's March through History

Marlene K. Sokolon and Mary Fran T. Malone

At the end of the twentieth century, the world was more democratic than it had ever been. Not only did more countries boast democratic governments, but more people within these countries were full-fledged democratic citizens. Furthermore, these democratic citizens enjoyed political rights and civil liberties that were wider in scope than ever. Observers appraised this democratic status quo with a great deal of optimism. Democracy was clearly on the march. In the eighteenth century only a handful of countries had dusted off ancient democratic practices to shape their own political development. By the end of the twentieth century, the majority of countries in the world had done so. The international community increasingly encouraged the laggards to catch up; democracy was considered the ultimate goal of political reform.

Several watershed moments sustained this optimism. Democracy had spread to the most unlikely of places. In 1990, Nelson Mandela emerged triumphant from his South African prison after 27 years, poised to win his decades-long fight for equal rights for all South Africans. In 1994, photographers took aerial view photographs of South Africans lining up for miles to vote in the first multiracial election in the country's history. Journalists interviewed black South Africans in their eighties, overjoyed to vote for the first time. The first multiracial election made Mandela's dream of a rainbow nation a reality; after his landslide victory, he led the long-divided country through an era of reconciliation.

In places like Eastern Europe, the world watched in awe as citizens successfully took to the streets to protest their political exclusion and government repression. In 1956, tanks crushed such protests. In 1989, protests successfully toppled communism. Germany hosted the most dramatic event, as the Berlin Wall crumbled and East Germans eagerly embraced the democratic governance of their counterparts to the west. Those who tried to stand in the way of change, such as Romania's Nicolae Ceauşescu, were crushed. Indeed, as authoritarian leaders searched vainly for the Soviet tanks and military power that had long sustained them, they discovered to their dismay that the Soviet Union was also unable to ward off democracy's spread. The political liberalization of the late 1980s culminated in the implosion of the Soviet Union and the democratization of many of its former republics. Russia, the heart of the Soviet Union, freely elected its first president in 1991.

China proved to be a sobering exception to this trend, opening fire on democracy protestors in the infamous Tiananmen Square Massacre of 1989. Still, this horrific setback was soon overshadowed by democratic milestones in other regions. In Central America, peace accords ended decades of civil war and dictatorship, and elections ushered in an era of democratic governance. Costa Rica was no longer the region's exception, as its neighbors also began to settle disputes in the ballot box instead of on the battlefield. In South America, democracy's march caught up with longstanding dictators like Chile's Augusto Pinochet, whose grip on power proved no match for elections, and he soon joined the ranks of other discarded dictators like those of Argentina, Brazil, Uruguay, and Bolivia. In Nigeria, Africa's most populous country, the death of military leader General Sani Abacha led his replacement to call for elections, not the military, to replace him. Democracy's global spread led many to believe it would only be a matter of time before authoritarian rule would be relegated to an historical note. Even in China, people were optimistic that an economic boom and growing, educated middle class would pave the way for democratic reform.

A decade into the twenty-first century, memories of these watershed moments have dimmed. Some democracies have remained steadfast despite challenges, while others have weakened. In notable cases like Russia, democratic gains have been reversed. Such events most certainly temper optimism, but a review of history tells us that democratic reversals are not unique. Historically, democracy has proceeded in ebbs and flows, and waves of democracy are followed by waves of reversal. Democratization is a dynamic process (Markoff 1996; Tilly 2007). To understand current trends in political development, this chapter reviews democracy's historical footprints. It examines early democratic practices like those of ancient Greece, and explains how these practices adapted to fit other regions and time periods.

As we trace democracy's path through history, numerous problems emerge. Perhaps the thorniest issue is deciding when a country can be considered democratic. De Tocqueville famously penned *Democracy in America* in the early 1800s, aiming to determine why democracy proved viable in the United States but not in his home country of France. Still, given the large number of Americans who faced enslavement at that time, democracy in the United States was a far cry from what we think of today when we use the term democracy. Markoff discusses this problem of defining democracy, stating:

> I believe the central reason scholars have found it so difficult to agree on which countries at which particular moments in history are democratic is that the definition of democracy is not under the control of scholars. Democracy has been continually defined and redefined by the people challenging government in the streets and fields and by the powerholders writing new laws and constitutional documents. . . . Democracy is not some fixed set of procedures that, once achieved, remains in place unaltered. (Markoff 1996, xvi–xvii)

This review of democratic history does not provide a final, unequivocal solution to this problem. Rather, it identifies the origins of some principles and practices closely linked with today's conceptualization of democracy, and highlights the ways in which these principles and practices have evolved and adapted over time.

Athenian democracy

Most tourists visiting Athens spend at least some time on the Acropolis admiring the Parthenon, a temple dedicated in 438 BCE to Athena, the patron goddess of the city. In many respects, it symbolizes the "Golden Age" of Athens, the height of Athenian cultural and imperial power. Fewer tourists, though, may notice a gently sloping hill less than a mile west of the Acropolis. Although the exact date is uncertain, probably sometime late in the sixth century BCE, Athenians began to use this sacred hill, the Pnyx, as the meeting place of the People's Assembly. Sitting on this hill, citizens deliberated and voted on all political measures, including matters of war and peace, or expenditures like funding the building of the Parthenon. It was here, on this now unassuming site, that Athenian democracy was born. Today, all that remains on the natural amphitheatre incline of the Pnyx is a flat stone platform with a modest flight of stairs and a small sign to mark the probable location of the *bema* (or speaker's corner), where Themistocles, Pericles, and other famous leaders, or any common citizen, addressed their peers on all the major issues of their day.

In Greek, democracy or *dēmokratia* literally means rule or power (*kratos*) by the common people (*dēmos*). In practice, the label democracy was used to differentiate a type of rule or political organization in which the people held ultimate power from other kinds of systems, such as oligarchies or tyrannies. Oligarchies (*oligarchia*), or rule of the few (*oligos*), were the most common form of political organization in ancient Greece. Although the oligarchic rulers were wealthy, their political power was based on their lineage. Originally in Greece, the term tyrant was not pejorative, but simply described a method of acquiring one-man power: kingship (*basileus*) was power inherited through lineage, and tyranny (*tyrannos*) was the rule of one man, good or bad, who acquired power by force or any means other than birth. After the last Athenian tyrants were removed in 510 BCE, tyranny began to take on a negative connotation, especially when ancient philosophers, such as Plato and Aristotle, began to use the term to describe, not the means of acquiring power, but unjust and self-interested rule (Plato 1968, 575a–79e; Aristotle 1985, 1289a25–b1).

Unlike today, in ancient Greece the term democracy signified a kind of rule or a type of political system, not the basis for legitimate political authority, or for the protection of political values, such as individual and human rights (Dunn 2006, 15). This means Athenian democracy did not reflect many principles associated with our understanding of contemporary liberal democracy. We cannot, for example, look to Athenian democracy as the birthplace of the idea of universal natural equality; as in every other ancient society, the Athenian economy relied heavily on a large slave population. Nor did the Athenian system uphold universal adult suffrage. In Athens, only male citizens over the age of 20 were allowed to participate in political deliberation and decision making. This meant Athenian women, children, slaves, and metics (resident foreigners) could not participate in politics.

This status did not mean, as is commonly thought, that women were not "citizens" in the contemporary sense of being excluded from the community. In fact, for much of the democratic period in Athens, male citizenship was based on having both a citizen mother and father. The status of women was similar to that of minors today; they were valuable members of the community, but could not vote and were under the legal protection of their guardian (*kyrios*). The Greek term for citizenship—*politeia*—stressed not only full legal status but also a life of active participation in the *polis*. Athenian democracy was distinguished from other political systems because this participatory life included all male citizens regardless of their wealth or status. Thus, the Greek word *polis*, which is generally translated into "city-state," did not really indicate a "state" in the sense of a governing body or geopolitical territory; instead, it referred to the small, male, kin-based, and culturally homogenous political community that traced its roots back to mythological times (Manville 1990, 7–13).

Despite these differences, Athenian democracy did reflect several democratic practices and principles familiar to contemporary audiences. First, Athenian democracy was a highly developed political system constantly evolving to meet new political challenges and pressures. In this way, it was similar to our contemporary democracies that also evolve and, for example, only relatively recently have adopted universal suffrage. Second, Athenian democracy upheld a long-standing commitment to the rule of law, although this commitment was not limited to democratic government (as oligarchic governments also could be restrained by law) (Coleman 2000, 24). The Greek word for law—*nomos*—means not only positive law or legal enactments, but also cultural practices, such as a respect for and duty to uphold moral and religious principles. Athens ensured all citizens knew the laws by "publishing," or inscribing them, on stone pillars in public places. It also ensured law was supreme, since special courts allowed any citizen to bring cases against the decisions of the magistrates. The principle of equality before the law (*isonomia*) guaranteed that no citizen was above the law, that all citizens were treated equality before the law, and that all citizens could participate in making judgments to ensure the rule of law. [1]

The belief in *isonomia* stresses equality (*isos*), a third principle fundamental to Athenian democracy that is reflected in contemporary democracy (Coleman 2000, 28–30). As discussed, for the ancient Greeks, equality did not mean equality of opportunity or universal natural equality; rather, the defining characteristic of democracy meant political and legal equality among those who actively participated in the *polis*. The most significant type of equality in Athens was the principle of equality of speech in the Assembly (*isēgoria*), which guaranteed any citizen the right to speak or address the Assembly during debate. In addition, the Athenians had a concept of "free speech" (*parrhēsia*) that meant ancient Athenians valued open and honest speech in public settings, such as the Assembly and marketplace (Saxonhouse 2006, 97). Although the ancient understanding of equality was not universal, in comparison to many contemporary democratic institutions it stressed equal and open access to political deliberation for all citizens, not just elites. Fourthly, similar to contemporary democracy, the Athenians highly valued the principle of freedom (*eleutheria*), which safeguarded the right of each citizen to engage fully in the life of the city, and ensured the people's independence from elite oligarchic or tyrannical rule (Coleman 2000, 34–37; Woodruff 2005, 61–79).

History and development of democracy in Athens

Democracy in Athens lasted roughly two hundred years, typically dated from the reforms of Cleisthenes in 508/7 BCE to the final defeat by the Macedonians in 318 BCE. As with most political systems, democracy in Athens did not have a definitive founding moment; it evolved from pre-existing political organizations over a period of several centuries. The existence of popular assemblies can be traced to the eighth century BCE. In Homer's *Iliad,* for example, there is a scene where the kings consult an assembly of average soldiers.[2] In Athens, the People's Assembly (*ekklēsia*) was the most important political decision-making institution (Thorley 1996, 32–34).[3] As discussed, all citizens had the right to speak openly on all topics for discussion, and voting was based on a simple majority by a show of hands. The Assembly met approximately 40 times per year; quorum consisted of the first 6,000 eligible citizens who arrived on Pnyx hill. Scholars are not sure why this number was quorum, although the fact that Pnyx means close, squashed, or packed together might indicate that this was as many people as the hill could hold. If sufficient numbers of citizens did not arrive for the day's business, it was common practice for magistrates to rope off the area from the Pnyx to the marketplace (*agora*) and usher citizens directly into the Assembly. If too many showed up, then the same rope system would be used to close off the area (Woodruff 2005, 33).

Another milestone of political development was the unification of the geopolitical territory of the urban center of Athens and the surrounding countryside of Attica. Although not large by modern nation–state standards, this unified territory of Athens (land area approximately half the size of Delaware) made it one of the largest *poleis* in Greece (Thorley 1996, 1).

This large territory corresponded to a sizeable population consisting of a few large landholders, but mostly numerous small property owners and hired laborers. From the defeat of the Persians in 480 BCE, Athens maintained a large navy that depended for rowers upon the service of these small property owners and laborers. This reliance for the city's defense on the poorer classes, rather than on the more wealthy cavalry or infantry, created pressure to expand political rights to the poor. It is difficult to estimate population, but most scholars suggest that in the mid-fifth century there were probably about 40,000–45,000 male citizens eligible for political participation, with a total population of women, children, metics, and slaves of 200,000–300,000.

Modern scholarship also reveals that for most of Athenian history—despite a mythological claim to have been ruled by kings—the *polis* was ruled by oligarchs through the Areopagus Council, which met on the a rocky outcrop northwest of the Acropolis. This Council's membership was restricted to the most powerful aristocratic families. From earliest times, the Areopagus Council did have to put forth proposals for a vote to an Assembly of all large property-owners. The first substantial steps to a democratic political system began with the establishment of the rule of law. The first written Athenian legal code, attributed to a man named Dracon, appeared in 621 BCE. Although his punishments were reputed to be ruthless (the English word draconian is derived from his name), ironically his only proscription to survive rather leniently prescribes exile for unpremeditated killing (Thorley 1996, 10).

Dracon's code was reformed by Solon in 594/3 BCE. Solon's reforms were widespread, including both economic restructuring, such as debt relief and the cancellation of debt-bondage, and political reforms, such as the reorganization of the class system by wealth, and not pure lineage. In later years, this political restructuring set in motion the larger democratic expansion to the poor. His reforms also expanded eligibility for the positions of the nine chief and judicial officers (*archons*) to wealthy, but non-noble, citizens. He also introduced the Council of 400 (*boulē*) as a check on the Areopagus Council. Solon's Council had strict wealth requirements, but it did function as an executive with the power to set the agenda for discussion in the Assembly. By Solon's time, the Assembly may already have begun to include the lowest class of poor citizens.

Most significantly, Solon introduced the principle of accountability for political officials by establishing the People's Court (*dikastēria*). This court gave all propertied classes, including the poorest, the right to take legal action (Coleman 2000, 25–27). In addition, all citizens were eligible to form the juries of this court, which essentially worked as a court of appeal. This meant any citizen, no matter how rich or poor, could charge another citizen with an offense. It also meant any citizen could take legal action against the decisions of magistrates and members of the Areopagus Council, or against political leaders who proposed illegal propositions in the Assembly. There were various courts for different types of offenses, and the seriousness of the charge determined the size of the jury, which ranged from 201 to 501 members. We know, for example, that the trial of the philosopher Socrates in 399 BCE was before a jury of 501 members. Ancient Athens had no professional legal system, which meant accusers and defendants both were given equal time to make their own speeches before their jury. The jury then voted, without deliberation, by indicating guilty or not guilty by means of a voting disk.

The ancient Athenians began to call their system a democracy sometime after Cleisthenes reformed Solon's system in 508/7 BCE. Most scholars think Cleisthenes introduced his reforms to win the support of the *dēmos*—the people—against his oligarchic rivals; yet, his proposals seriously undermined the power of the oligarchs. His most significant reform was to reorganize the traditional associations of kinship and patron relationships into ten new political tribes (*phylai*), which were subdivided into 140 regional units (demes). This reorganization undercut the concentrated oligarchic power by ensuring each tribe consisted of demes from all regions: the coast, the hills, and the city. By Cleisthenes's time, the People's Assembly had evolved into the most powerful political body, and any male citizen over 20 was eligible to speak and vote on all political decisions.

Cleisthenes also expanded the executive Council (*boulē*) to 500 members, but with continuing property qualifications. Members of the Council were chosen by a lottery system from the ten political tribes for a 1-year appointment. The main function and power of the Council of 500 was to prepare the agenda, draft proposals for discussion and vote in the Assembly, and receive foreign ambassadors (Thorley 1996, 28–32). It was also in charge of implementing policy decisions and, although there was not much of a bureaucracy, it did direct the small number of mostly slaves who worked as civil secretaries. After their 1-year term of office, members of the Council were held accountable for their actions by a process called *euthynai* (a setting straight). This process included not only submitting financial reports for investigation by official inspectors, but guaranteed the right of any citizen to prosecute managerial offenses before the People's Court. Finally, as a check on powerful leadership Cleisthenes introduced ostracism, which allowed the people to exile any political leader for ten years through a mechanism of voting on pieces of pottery (*ostraka*). Although ostracisms were rare, one of the most famous examples occurred in 471 BCE, when Themistocles, the great Athenian general responsible for the defeat of Persia, went into exile. Piles of *ostraka* with his name inscribed can be seen today at the Agora Museum in Athens.

Additional reforms expanded Athenian democracy. Sometime after the victory of Marathon in 490 BCE, the selection of the nine chief magistrates (*archons*) was changed to a lottery system. Importantly, in 462/1 BCE, Ephialtes introduced a reform that transferred most of the remaining legal and supervisory power of the oligarchic Areopagus Court to the Popular Courts. The Areopagus Court remained responsible for certain religious offenses and murder trails, but all other legal power transferred to the democratic court system (Staveley 1972, 23–26). Pericles also significantly expanded political participation in 450/1 BCE, when he introduced pay for those serving on the Popular Courts, the Council, and as magistrates. Since membership in the Council and magistrate positions was supposed to be restricted to those sufficiently wealthy enough to afford infantry armor, this reform indicates that by Pericles's time the rule excluding the poorer citizens was routinely ignored.

Democracy in Athens waxed and waned over the next century. Pericles died of the plague early in the Peloponnesian War between Athens and its oligarchic rival, Sparta. This war placed a great deal of pressure on the democracy. After several defeats, in 411 BCE the Assembly voted to abandon democratic rule in hopes of allying with the Persian king against Sparta. For one year, an oligarchic council ruled the city until democratic forces overthrew it. In 404 BCE, Sparta defeated Athens and appointed a group of wealthy citizens, known as the Thirty Tyrants, to replace democratic rule. The Thirty Tyrants suspended the rule of law and used their power to rule by terror, ruthlessly executing all opposition. They were overthrown one year later by a rebel group of democratic exiles, who restored and reformed the democracy. The triumphant former exiles reformed the selection of jury panels, for example, from the first-come system to a lottery; they expanded public payment to include attending the Assembly and, around 340 BCE, certain religious-political events, such as the great theater festivals.

At the same time, however, the new rulers tempered radical democracy by restoring administrative authority over magistrates and granting wider judicial powers to the old Areopagus Court. In roughly 403 BCE, a special court (*nomothetai*) was established to limit the creation of new laws; the Council and Assembly held preliminary discussions and proposed legislation, but this special court had the final say on the creation of any new laws.

Also around this time, the city began to elect, rather than choose by lot, all magistrates responsible for fiscal management. Thus, the Athenians came to consider expertise essential for those responsible for the city's funds, rather than the principle that everyone could rule. Athenian democracy continued to flourish and functioned without much interruption for much of the fourth century BCE, until it was destroyed, not from internal decline, but by defeat in war. In 318 BCE, Athens attempted to revolt against the expanding Macedonian Empire, but finally was starved into accepting an oligarchic system and the end of its democratic form of government (Coleman 2000, 21–22).

Democracy after Greece

After the collapse of Athenian democracy in the fourth century BCE, demo-cratic practices were rare until the late eighteenth century CE. One reason for this absence is that the term itself fell into disrespect as it came to mean "mob rule," or tyranny of the majority. Aristotle (1984, 1160b), for example, describes democracy as a political system in which the people rule not for the common good, but for their own private self-interest. It was not until the late seventeenth century that democracy slowly began to shed its negative connotation (Dunn 2006, 59).

Even rarer than the use of the term democracy are examples of Athenian institutions of direct or radical democracy. Again, until the late eighteenth century, most political systems were ruled by what the Greeks would have called kingships or oligarchies. Although never called democracy, other political systems often reflected certain principles and institutional prac-tices similar to Athenian democracy. Since Polybius in the third century, for example, tradition categorized the republican period of Rome as similar to Aristotle's mixed political system that incorporated democratic elements. The Romans themselves never used the word democracy to describe their political system. After the overthrow of their kings and establishment of the authority of the Senate, the Romans called their system a republic, because it concerned *res publica* or public matters. The Roman political system was highly complex. It had some institutional features delegating power or rule to common citizens (*plebs*), who were distinguished from the aristocratic *patricians*, not necessarily by wealth, but by birth (Staveley 1972, 121–33). Certain kinds of propositions, such as changes to the law or declaring war, had to be brought by the magistrates to a plebian assembly called the *comitia centuriata*. All magistrates had to be elected either by this assembly or another plebian assembly organized by tribes (*comitia tributa*). The *plebs* also had their own magistrates, called tribunes, who for a period of time could propose laws to the people's assembly without the Senate's approval. In general, however, the Roman Republic was more oligarchic than democratic. The most important political institution and deliberative body in Rome was not the people's assembly but the Senate. All magisterial positions (other than the *plebs'* tribunes) and membership in the Senate were restricted to the aristocratic class. Significantly, the *plebian* assemblies did not have the power of initiative and could only ratify but not alter proposals (Botsford 1968, 173). Most significantly, the *comitia centuriata* was not a one-man, one-vote system; it arranged the people into voting blocs that highly favored the wealthy (and disenfranchised the poorest class).

While rare, there are other ancient examples of rule of the people. One of the closest relatives to Greek democracy was the Old Icelandic Common-wealth. Possibly as early as 930, a national assembly called an *Althing* was established as a public forum for all free men, which set up a common code of laws (Johannesson 1974, 46–74). Until it was disbanded by Denmark in 1800, the *Althing* met at annual intervals as a festival and forum for all important announcements and speeches. Early on, in place of an official standing executive, there was a position of law-speaker, whose duties included the memorization and proclamation of the law code and presiding at the assembly. There were also several chieftains who, in effect, represented smaller groups of free farmers. The chieftaincies were held like private property and could be inherited, sold, shared, or confiscated; free men had to declare their alliance to a chieftain once a year, but were free to change alliances every year (Byock 2002, 9–11). Chieftains sat on the Court of Legislature and Courts of Justice, which also included panels of judges drawn from the freemen who acted as juries.

Other examples of democratic practices emerged in northern Italy as early as the eleventh century. Medieval communes developed in cities, such as Pisa, Milan, and Florence, and some lasted until the fourteenth century. These medieval communes originated as defensive alliances of urban citizens, and many had popular assemblies in which the less powerful guilds of merchants won some participation in government. Still, most scholars see the real power in this turbulent and violent period as wielded by the oligarchy of nobility and major guilds (Marks 1963, 77).

From the fifteenth through eighteenth centuries, the Swiss cantons and city governments also manifested some democratic qualities and principles. As a form of local government, the organization of the political system varied significantly from canton to canton, but many cantons had a forum that allowed for direct consultation, deliberation, and participation by eligible (adult male) citizens (Tilly 2007, 70; Tilly 2004, 169). Scholars (Rokkan 1999, 247) argue that the Swiss were able to build on this long tradition of participation, which provided a foundation for a new (both conceptually and institutionally) modern liberal democratic state.

The Long Century

What is most significant about the irregularity of democracy until the modern era is not simply the infrequency of this form of government, but the discontinuous tradition of democracy from ancient to modern times (Coleman 2000, 22). Previous isolated examples aside, democratic practices lay dormant for the most part until the late eighteenth century. At this time, in Belgium and the Netherlands, reformers started to use the term "democratic" positively, to describe a political system they hoped to create (Markoff 1996, 2). In a few countries, the processes of political liberalization gradually culminated into some type of popular participation in governance on a national scale. This ushered in the "Long Century," which refers to the time of tremendous economic, social, and political change—from 1760 through the early 1900s (Goldblatt 1997).

The Industrial Revolution drove many of these changes. Starting in Britain in the mid 1800s, the Industrial Revolution transformed economic production, and technological innovations irrevocably altered the ways in which people communicated, traveled, and lived. New socioeconomic groups emerged, and many of them flocked from the countryside to the cities. From Britain, the Industrial Revolution and its accompanying transformations spread to France and the United States. In all three cases, new socioeconomic groups, particularly the economically powerful bourgeoisie, put pressure on their respective states and fundamentally altered historic state–society relations. This process did not necessarily result in democracy, however. In France, tensions between the state and its people culminated in the French Revolution (1789–93), which established "one of history's most influential models of democratic development" (Tilly 2007, 33). Sweeping away the aristocracy, the revolution replaced the king with a popularly elected parliament. Revolutionary extremism, civil war, and Napoleon's dictatorship curtailed this democratic trial, but the French experiment with democracy inspired political reformers in other countries. France, itself, would return to these democratic roots in the late 1800s under the Third

Republic, which upheld many democratic practices but still maintained limitations on suffrage until 1945 (Tilly 2007).[4]

Political reformers in the United States found much to admire in European and particularly French philosophy, and used these ideals as a rallying cry against British colonial rule. Many of the American colonies already practiced some democratic norms; indeed, the Fundamental Orders of Connecticut are considered to be one of the first written constitutions of modern democracy (Huntington 1991, 15). In the aftermath of the American Revolution and independence from Britain, American reformers sought to institute democratic governance on a much larger, national scale. The democracy that emerged provided protections for citizens' rights, the election of national leaders, and extensive institutional mechanisms for holding officials accountable. Still, the new democracy maintained broad limitations on suffrage, and slavery persisted. By 1828, the abolition of property qualifications allowed more than half of white men to vote. The American Civil War (1861–65) finally abolished slavery and, in 1870, the Fifteenth Amendment to the US Constitution expanded suffrage to all adult men (although in practice many states undermined voting rights). With women's suffrage guaranteed in 1920, the US Constitution finally pledged universal adult suffrage; however, particularly in the South, a series of mechanisms prevented black Americans from voting until 1965.

In a very different way, the French Revolution also fostered democratic gains in Britain. The revolution's violence and subsequent instability frightened British elites, leading them to pursue political concessions with popular sectors to ward off more violent and sweeping revolutionary changes. The British concessions reverberated around the world, as overseas colonies also adopted reforms. Indeed, some British colonies went further than the mother country, as New Zealand became the first country to allow all adults to vote in 1893.

France, the United States, and Britain were the most visible cases of what Huntington (1991) calls the first wave of democracy. A "wave" describes a "group of political changes happening close together in time in different countries" (Markoff 1996, 1). For the nineteenth century, Huntington relaxes the definition of democracy to include any country that allowed 50 percent of adult males to vote and was governed by an executive who maintained either "majority support in an elected parliament" or was victorious in periodic popular elections (Huntington 1991, 16). Even with this relaxed definition, very few countries were democratic prior to World War I (1914–18). On this short list, Huntington counts the United States, Switzerland, France,

Italy, Argentina, Finland, Sweden, Norway, and Great Britain and some of its colonies (Huntington 1991, 13–18).

World War I greatly accelerated the process of democratization (Goldblatt 1997). In its wake, more countries began to call themselves democracies, and this label increasingly designated full universal adult suffrage. In particular, the victors of World War I were staunch supporters of democratic governance. One of the most ardent advocates, American president Woodrow Wilson, embarked on an ambitious plan to promote democracy throughout the countries of war-torn Europe, viewing democracy as a valuable tool to curb aggressive states. Wilson believed citizens of democratic countries would be reluctant to bear the brunt of war. Consequently, they would thwart their leaders' bellicose intentions, preferring to channel conflict through institutions and to resolve problems through the rule of law rather than military might. President Wilson launched a crusade to make the world "safe for democracy." The successor states of defeated empires were transformed into parliamentary governments with democratic constitutions, and

Table 1.1 First wave of democracy and its reversal

Viable democracies	Reversed democracies
Australia	Austria
Canada	Argentina
Chile	Belgium
Finland	Colombia
Iceland	Czechoslovakia
Ireland	Denmark
New Zealand	Estonia
Sweden	France
Switzerland	Germany
United Kingdom	Greece
United States	Hungary
	Italy
	Japan
	Latvia
	Lithuania
	Netherlands
	Norway
	Uruguay
	Poland
	Portugal
	Spain

Adapted from Huntington (1991, 14).

in the victorious democracies suffrage spread to incorporate women and the poor (Bessel 1997). In Ireland and Iceland, democratic governance ensued shortly after independence, with full universal suffrage emerging in 1922 and 1920 respectively. In the early 1930s, Chile and Spain also joined democracy's ranks (Huntington 1991). By the end of Huntington's first wave of democracy, 33 countries met at least the minimal threshold for national democratic institutions. As Table 1.1 indicates, only 11 would survive the subsequent wave of democratic reversal. In most cases, the newer democracies were the first to crumble. Of the 17 countries that adopted democratic institutions between 1910 and 1931, only four maintained these institutions throughout the 1920s and 1930s (Huntington 1991, 17).

Interwar democratic reversals (1922–39)

Given the catastrophic consequences of World War II (1939–45), much attention has been devoted to studying the demise of democracy in the interwar period. During this time, Wilsonian idealism proved no match for the realities of weak institutions and economic crisis. The economic toll of World War I, coupled with the global economic crisis of the Great Depression, strained the capacity of democratic institutions. In many countries, the economic meltdown was exacerbated by the disintegration of public order, as political violence and common crime escalated (Bermeo 2003). Bermeo notes that such violent disorder is particularly problematic for newer democracies, which tend to have fewer resources and less time "to develop more effective institutions facilitating civic order" (Bermeo 1997, 19). Since they are not well equipped to maintain order, it is easy for social unrest and violence to spiral beyond state capacity. In many cases political elites did little to address the twin challenges of economic crisis and social unrest, prioritizing political squabbling over effective governance. Democracy collapsed throughout Europe, giving rise to dictatorship and ultimately plunging the continent into war once again.

Mussolini initiated the antidemocratic movement with his march on Rome in 1922, and democracy's domestic foes unseated additional regimes in Poland (1926), Yugoslavia (1929), Portugal (1929), Germany (1933), Greece (1936) and Spain (1939).[5] These domestic reversals of democracy reverberated throughout Europe, as authoritarian successors waged war on the surviving democracies, toppling the regimes of Belgium, Denmark, France, the Netherlands, and Norway. Democratic reversal was not limited to Europe, however, as military coups ousted democrats in Brazil (1930), Argentina (1930), Uruguay (1933), and Japan (1936).

The second wave of democracy

In contrast to the first wave of democracy, Huntington characterizes the second wave as a much shorter one (1943–62). Rather than the slow adoption of democratic norms and practices characteristic of the Long Century, the second wave would witness a more rapid process of democratization. Two major events made rapid democratization a necessity: the defeat of the Axis powers in World War II, and decolonization. Both developments created political vacuums for democracy to fill. On the ruins of Germany, Japan, and Italy, the three western Allied powers (the United States, Great Britain, and France) sought to build democratic governments with capitalist economies.[6] The defeat of the Axis powers also liberated the territories they had held hostage. In cases like the Netherlands and Norway, prior democratic traditions were resuscitated following the defeat of the occupying army. In places like Libya and China, the political future was murkier. Allied victory vanquished foreign invaders, but domestic politicians did not have a stable political foundation upon which to build (much less a democratic foundation). Finally, although victorious, Great Britain and France were exhausted by the war, and their grip on colonial territories in Asia and Africa began to slip. Countries like India successfully grafted democratic governance onto the vestiges of colonial rule, but in cases like Pakistan, such efforts languished.

During this time, Latin America was largely untouched by war and colonialism, but political developments mirrored those of other global regions. Chile stayed true to its 1930s democratic foundations, at least for the time being. Costa Rica inaugurated a new democratic constitution in 1949, and banished the military to better preserve this constitution. Democratic governments emerged in Argentina, Brazil, Uruguay, Colombia, Peru, and Venezuela, but many of these initiatives quickly collapsed. Democracy in Colombia and Venezuela swiftly rebounded under negotiated elite power-sharing arrangements, however (Huntington 1991).

In the second wave, the term democracy corresponded more closely to today's meaning. At a minimum, in order to be called democratic countries needed universal adult suffrage, protection for civil liberties and political rights, and mechanisms to hold leaders accountable.[7] Of course, there were exceptions. Perhaps most glaringly was the United States, widely considered to be a democracy despite the practical limitations on black suffrage in the South.

Second wave democratic reversals

As Table 1.2 indicates, many of these democratic experiments flopped. Countries like India were able to overcome democratic setbacks, while in cases like Greece democracy continuously floundered in the face of military intervention. By the 1960s, democracy's position in the world was quite precarious. Authoritarian regimes of all different ideological stripes dominated Eastern Europe, parts of Southern Europe, Asia, and Africa. In Latin America, democracies fell like dominoes—even those with a long tradition like that of Chile. Many of these democratic reversals challenged conventional wisdom. Whereas economic crisis was the scapegoat for democracy's collapse in the 1930s, the 1970s collapse of Latin American democracies underscored the grim fact that economic growth was "no protection for democracy" (Markoff 1996, 6). Indeed, O'Donnell's (1973) seminal work

Table 1.2 Second wave democracies and reversals

Sustained democracies	Democracies with minor setbacks	Reversed democracies
Austria	Colombia	Argentina
Belgium	India	Bolivia
Botswana	Venezuela	Brazil
Costa Rica		Burma
Denmark		Chile
France		Czechoslovakia
Gambia		Ecuador
West Germany		Fiji
Italy		Ghana
Israel		Greece
Jamaica		Guyana
Japan		Hungary
Malaysia		Indonesia
Malta		Lebanon
Netherlands		Nigeria
Norway		Pakistan
Sri Lanka		Peru
Trinidad and Tobago		Philippines
		South Korea
		Turkey
		Uruguay

Adapted from Huntington (1991, 13–23)

pointed out that economic development had prompted the rise of antide-mocratic forces. By the mid-1970s, only three Latin American countries (Costa Rica, Colombia, and Venezuela) could be counted as democratic. Democratic prospects were bleak in other global regions as well. At the beginning of the second wave, roughly 50 countries could be considered democratic; by the 1960s approximately 30 had that title (Huntington 1991, 14).

Events in Southern Europe gave democrats reasons for optimism, however. Portugal, Spain, and Greece had sat out the second wave of democracy, but now seemed poised to join their Western European neighbors. Just as the military overthrew democratic governance in Chile, it was preparing to support democracy in Portugal. In Southern Europe, democratic practices were once again stirring, and would soon pave the way for the third, and largest, wave of democracy.

The third wave of democracy

Huntington's third wave describes a global trend of democratization that began with Portugal in 1974 and swept over much of Latin America, Eastern Europe, Africa, and Asia during the next 20 years. In Southern Europe, the military regimes of Greece and Spain followed Portugal's lead and ceded power. A few years later, South American militaries also began to return to the barracks, as military rule gave way to democratic elections in Ecuador, Peru, Bolivia, Argentina, Brazil, Uruguay, and eventually Chile. Given the notorious human rights violations of these military regimes, the transformation to civilian rule was striking. In the early 1980s many citizens of these countries faced arbitrary torture and murder in clandestine detention centers. At the end of the decade, they could freely vote in elections. By the end of the 1980s, Central American dictatorships had also weakened, and with the peace accords of the 1990s all the Central American countries were democratic. In places like Guatemala democratic institutions and practices were criticized as weak, but in contrast to the horrific violence of the 36-year civil war, the mere appearance of ballot boxes was remarkable.

Democratic milestones in Southern Europe and Latin America were mirrored in places like Turkey (1983), the Philippines (1986), South Korea (1987), and Taiwan (1988). The most dramatic events would occur in Eastern Europe, however. Throughout Eastern Europe communism had seemed impenetrable, particularly as the Soviets had demonstrated their power and resolve to quell dissent within their own borders as well as in their broader spheres of influence. Thus, the rapid demise of communist rule in 1988–1989 took the world by surprise. Soviet leader Mikhail Gorbachev liberalized the political environment of the Eastern Bloc, creating a modest space for political reform. Democratic activists took this space to launch their campaign for sweeping political, economic, and social change. Citizens throughout Eastern Europe took to the streets, and in the absence of Soviet tanks, successfully replaced communists with democrats in a remarkably short period of time.

Figure 1.1 provides an overview of these developments. While definitive classifications of countries into democratic and authoritarian camps is difficult, organizations like Freedom House provide rough estimates of national levels of political development.[8] Freedom House distinguishes between countries that are free (meaning they widely uphold democratic norms) and partly free (indicating they have at least a moderate commitment to some democratic norms). As Figure 1.1 highlights, from 1974 to 2009 the number of free countries has risen dramatically. The completion of decolonization processes and the implosion of the Soviet Union created many new countries during this time frame. The number of independent nations rose from

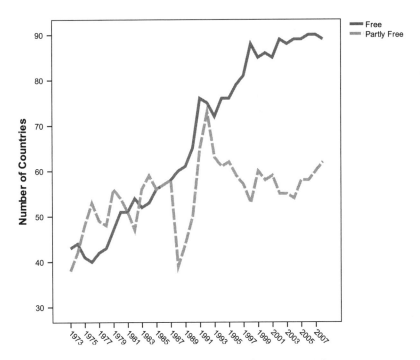

Figure 1.1 Number of democracies in the world (Freedom House 2009)

150 in 1972 to 193 in 2009, and many of these new nations joined the third wave of democracy (Freedom House 2009).

The milestones of these new democracies were widely celebrated, but problems quickly emerged. Third wave democracies, many of which were poor or middle income countries, seemed very different from those of previous waves. Scholars first noted this trend in the late 1990s, describing several third wave democracies as illiberal, "incomplete, partial, hollow, or shallow" (Smith and Ziegler 2009, 13). Indeed, some referred to third wave democracies as "democracies with adjectives." In many cases, free and fair elections became commonplace, but these elections proceeded while leaving behind other crucial components of democracy (like the rule of law). Citizens of third wave democracies were able to vote and live without fear of egregious human rights abuses; however, many continued to face limitations on their civil and political rights, and all too often watched angrily from the sidelines as officials abused power and engaged in wanton corruption.

Initially, many viewed this type of democracy as a temporary affair—democracy was hollow because it was in transition. The consensus held that democratic processes would gradually deepen and that competitive elections, political and civil rights, and institutional accountability would entrench themselves in the political landscape. Democracy was a process that did not happen overnight. There is truth to this view; however a decade into the twenty-first century it is clear that many third wave democracies are no longer on the road to something better. Democracy has been consolidated, but in most cases the type of democracy that has crystallized falls far short of expectations. In an examination of 19 Latin American countries from 1978–2004, Smith and Ziegler note that "illiberal democracy, combining free and fair elections with restrictions on citizen rights, was the most common of all [regime] types, appearing almost 40 percent of the time" (Smith and Ziegler 2009, 15). In a few cases illiberal democracy served as a stepping stone to full democracy but, more commonly, illiberal democracy tended to be an endpoint. In a longitudinal study, Foweraker and Krznaric measure the strength of eight core elements of liberal democracy, including competitive elections, civil and political rights, and accountability. In contrasting the strength of vertical accountability (through free and fair elections) and horizontal accountability (through institutional checks and balances), the authors note that "third wave democracies can and do survive without a fully effective rule of law" (Foweraker and Krznaric 2009, 67). In Latin America, a region at the forefront of the third wave of democracy, large numbers of citizens have stated that true democracy does not exist in their respective countries. According to the Latin American Public Opinion Project (LAPOP)—an organization that has gauged public attitudes toward democracy, governance, and political participation throughout the period of third wave democratization—most citizens do not think democratic practices are firmly rooted in their countries. In a 2008 survey of the region, only 17 percent of citizens in Latin America regarded their respective countries as very democratic, in contrast to the 76 percent who evaluated them as either not very democratic or only somewhat democratic.[9]

Third wave democratic reversals

In addition to problems with the quality of democratic governance, the third wave democracies have also been susceptible to reversal. Like their associates in earlier historic periods, the third wave democracies have watched many of their peers drop out of the democratic march. If we combine the number of free and partly free democracies in Figure 1.1, by 1992 this number was at an historical high of 148. Just five years later, this number

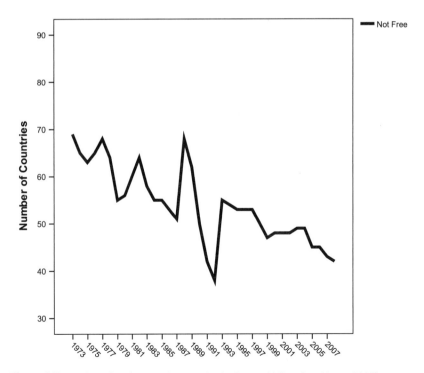

Figure 1.2 Number of undemocratic countries in the world (Freedom House 2009)

had dipped to 138. Of these countries, Russia perhaps features most prominently. According to Freedom House, Russia was partly free in 1991 as it geared up for its first competitive presidential election. Freedom House considered Russia partly free over the course of the next decade, even as it graded Russia's democratic performance with ever worsening marks. By 2005, democratic norms and practices had deteriorated so extensively that Freedom House considered it not free, a designation Russia retains to the present day.[10] Such notable examples aside, Figure 1.1 illustrates that democracy did rebound in many countries—by 2008 the number of free and partly free countries reached a high of 151. Indeed, Figure 1.2 confirms this trend, noting that while the number of not free countries rose precipitously in 1993, it has gradually tapered off.

Outline of the book

How can we explain these political developments? Why do some nations become democratic, while others remain mired in dictatorship? What drives democratization? What challenges, and even reverses, it? Can democratic theories originating to explain political development in the Long Century shed light on democratization in other time frames and regions? This book aims to answer these questions by examining the development of a very diverse group of democracies. The remaining chapters of Section 1 provide an overview of the various theoretical explanations of democratization, as well as critically examine democracy's potential benefits.

With this foundation, the emphasis of the book shifts to testing, with empirical evidence, theoretical explanations of democratization. Sections 2, 3, and 4 examine country case studies from the first, second, and third waves of democracy. The selected countries vary tremendously in terms of geography, economic development, and demographic diversity, providing the opportunity to examine theories of democratization in a very diverse group of successful democracies. Thus, this approach follows a most different systems design, in which successful democracies are examined to identify the factors they share in common. The goal is to pinpoint the factors that consistently explain democratization. One potential problem of this approach is that it focuses on "happy endings." "Is there nothing to be learned from instances of democratic failure?" critics might ask. This critique is a valid one, and to address it several of the cases (e.g., Germany and Chile) illustrate how democracy collapsed earlier in the country's history, and how later architects learned from these failings to rebuild democracy following the demise of authoritarianism.

Section 5 concludes this study of democratization in two ways. First, it assesses the potential for democracy in the Middle East, given what we have learned from previous successful cases of democratization. An additional chapter examines the potential for international democracy-promotion efforts to succeed in promoting democratic governance.

This book aims to answer questions currently at the heart of studies of comparative politics in a manner readily accessible to undergraduate students. To address contemporary trends in political development, scholars of comparative politics have strived to explain the current wave of democratization, its recent setbacks, and the future prospects for democratic governance. Such issues transcend mere scholarly concerns, as they also feature prominently in current policy debates. For example, the United States has touted the importance of promoting democracy in the developing world as a prescription for both peace and economic prosperity. The European Union insists that its member states respect at least some democratic principles. International organizations such as the World Bank and United Nations frequently tie development assistance to abidance to some democratic norms. Thus, the question of what leads countries to become democratic has a great deal of theoretical and practical import—for scholars, practitioners, politicians, and everyday people.

Notes

1 To further ensure the Assembly did not easily change or alter laws, other courts were set up to try cases against anyone introducing measures that were either in conflict with existing law or violated legal procedures. At times, especially the later part of the Peloponnesian conflict, these checks to ensure the rule of law did break down; overall, however, the rule of law protected the democracy from the arbitrary rule of one or even a few individuals.

2 Similar to the oligarchic Spartan assembly, the average soldier in this story is only allowed to listen and assent, but does not have the right to speak (Homer 1990, 2.210–80).

3 Athenian democracy generally is called "direct" or "radical" democracy because it did not elect representatives who voted on laws and policy; instead, each citizen theoretically had the right to participate directly in political decision making. In practice, those who lived far walking distances away from the city or had to work to make ends meet attended much less frequently than did wealthy city-dwellers.

4 France provides an excellent illustration of how democracy proceeds in ebbs and flows. As Tilly documents, "[B]etween 1789 and the present, France underwent at least four substantial periods of democratization, but also at least three substantial periods of de-democratization" (Tilly 2007, 34).

5 For a detailed discussion of democratic breakdown in interwar Europe, see Bermeo (1997, 2003).

6 In contrast, democratic movements in Eastern Europe were squelched by the Soviets. As Chapter 7 explains, the western Allies constructed democracy in their portion of occupied Germany, while the Soviets replicated their system of governance in their German zone.

7 These criteria conform to contemporary definitions of liberal democracy. Of the many efforts to identify democracy's characteristics, Dahl's (1989) procedural definition serves as a basis for most scholarship.

8 Chapter 2 discusses the difficulties in measuring democratic development in more detail, and introduces numerous sources of measures of democracy. This chapter relies upon the widely used Freedom House measure, available online http://www.freedomhouse.org/uploads/fiw09/CompHistData/CountryStatus&RatingsOverview1973–2009.pdf (accessed July 16, 2010). While this source is not without its flaws, it provides a very useful rough estimate of the prevalence of democratic practices.

9 In this survey, 7 percent of respondents replied that their countries were "not democratic at all." These percentages are based on survey data from the following countries: Mexico, Guatemala, El Salvador, Honduras, Nicaragua, Costa Rica, Panama, Colombia, Ecuador, Bolivia, Peru, Paraguay, Chile, Uruguay, Brazil, Venezuela, Argentina, Dominican Republic, and Haiti. We thank the Latin American Public Opinion Project (LAPOP), particularly director Prof. Mitchell Seligson, as well as LAPOP's major supporters (the United Stated Agency for International Development, the United Nations Development Program, the Inter-American Development Bank, and Vanderbilt University) for making the data widely available. For more information on the LAPOP surveys, see: http://www.vanderbilt.edu/lapop/.

10 For a thorough account of recent Russian political development, see McFaul, Petrov, and Ryabov (2004)

References

Aristotle. 1984. *Aristotle's Nichomachean Ethics*, HG Apostle, trans. Grinnell: Peripatetic Press.

Aristotle. 1985. *The Politics*, Carnes Lord, trans. Chicago: University of Chicago Press.

Bermeo, Nancy. 2003. *Ordinary People in Extraordinary Times: The Citizenry and the Breakdown of Democracy*. Princeton, NJ: Princeton University Press.

Bermeo, Nancy. 1997. "Getting Mad or Going Mad? Citizens, Scarcity and the Breakdown of Democracy in Interwar Europe." Center for the Study of Democracy, University of California, Irvine. Accessed June 3, 2009 from http://repositories.cdlib.org/csd/97–06/

Bessel, Richard. 1997. "The Crisis of Modern Democracy, 1919–39." In *Democratization*, edited by David Potter, David Goldblatt, Margaret Kiloh, and Paul Lewis, 71–94. Malden, MA: Blackwell Publishers, Inc.

Botsford, G. W. 1968. *The Roman Assemblies*. New York: Cooper Square Publishers.

Byock, Jesse. 2002. "The Icelandic Althing." In *Heritage and Identity*, edited by J. M Fladmark, Shaftesbury: Donhead Publishing, 1–18.

Coleman, Janet. 2000. *A History of Political Thought*. Malden, MA: Blackwell Publishing.

Dahl, Robert. 1989. *Democracy and Its Critics*. New Haven: Yale University Press.

Dunn, John. 2006. *Democracy: a History*. New York: Penguin Books.

Foweraker, Joe, and Roman Krznaric. 2009. "The Uneven Performance of Third Wave Democracies: Electoral Politics and the Imperfect Rule of Law in Latin America." In *Latin American Democratic Transformations: Institutions, Actors, and Processes*, edited by William Smith, 53–78. Malden, MA: Wiley-Blackwell.

Freedom House. 2009. "Freedom in the World Comparative and Historical Data." Accessed July 16, 2010 www.freedomhouse.org/template.cfm?page=439.

Goldblatt, David. 1997. "Democracy in the 'Long Nineteenth Century': 1760–1919." In *Democratization*, edited by David Potter, David Goldblatt, Margaret Kiloh, and Paul Lewis, 46–70. Malden, MA: Blackwell Publishers, Inc.

Hagopian, Frances, and Scott Mainwaring. 2005. *The Third Wave of Democratization in Latin America: Advances and Setbacks*. New York: Cambridge University Press.

Homer. 1990 *The Iliad*, Robert Fagles, trans. New York: Penguin.

Huntington, Samuel. 1991. *The Third Wave: Democratization in the Late Twentieth Century*. Norman: University of Oklahoma Press.

Johannesson, Jon. 1974. *A History of the Old Icelandic Commonwealth*, Haraldur Bessason, trans. Winnipeg: University of Manitoba Press.

Latin American Public Opinion Project (LAPOP). 2008. "The AmericasBarometer." Accessed August 20, 2010 www.LapopSurveys.org.

Manville, P. B. 1990. *The Origins of Citizenship in Ancient Athens*. Princeton: Princeton University Press.

Markoff, John. 1996. *Waves of Democracy: Social Movements and Political Change*. Thousand Oaks, CA: Pine Forge Press.

Marks, L. F. 1963. "Fourteenth-Century Democracy in Florence." *Past and Present* 25: 77–85.

McFaul, Michael, Nikolai Petrov, and Andrei Ryabov. 2004. *Between Dictatorship and Democracy: Russian Post-Communist Political Reform*. Washington, D.C: Carnegie Endowment for International Peace.

O'Donnell, Guillermo. 1973. *Modernization and Bureaucratic Authoritarianism: Studies in South American Politics*. Berkely, CA: Institute of International Studies.

Plato. 1968. *The Republic of Plato*, Allan Bloom, trans. New York: Basic Books.

Rokkan, Stein. 1999. *State Formation, Nation Building and Mass Politics in Europe*, edited by Peter Flora. Oxford: Oxford University Press.

Saxonhouse, Arlene. 2006. *Free Speech and Democracy in Ancient Athens*. Cambridge: Cambridge University Press.

Smith, William, and Melissa Ziegler. 2009. "Liberal and Illiberal Democracy in Latin America." In *Latin American Democratic Transformations: Institutions, Actors, and Processes*, edited by William Smith, 13–34. Malden, MA: Wiley-Blackwell.

Staveley, E. S. 1972. *Greek and Roman Voting and Election*. Ithaca, NY: Cornell University Press.

Thorley, John. 1996. *Athenian Democracy* 2nd ed. London: Routledge.

Thucydides. 2009. *The Peloponnesian War*, Martin Hammond, trans. Oxford: Oxford University Press.

Tilly, Charles. 2007. *Democracy*. New York: Cambridge University Press.

Tilly, Charles 2004. *Contention & Democracy in Europe*. Cambridge: Cambridge University Press.

Whitehead, Laurence. 2007. *Democracy*. Cambridge: Cambridge University Press.

Whitehead, Laurence. 2002. *Democratization: Theory and Experience*. New York: Oxford University Press.

Woodruff, Paul. 2005. *First Democracy*. Oxford: Oxford University Press.

In August of 2009, Afghans went to the polls to cast their votes in presidential and provincial council elections. The United States, together with allies in the international community, has promoted democracy in Afghanistan as part of its response to the global threat of terrorism. However, democracy in Afghanistan remains on shaky ground, as illustrated by widespread criticisms of the 2009 elections as corrupt and fraudulent.

Photo courtesy of UN/Eric Kanalstein

2

Why Democracy?

Alynna J. Lyon and Jonathan Hiskey

Chapter Outline

The end of the Cold War marked a watershed moment for democracy. The implosion of communism in the Soviet Union and throughout Eastern Europe left democracy without a serious ideological rival, and the Cold War victors used their foreign policies to promote democracy around the globe. For the past two decades, the international community has touted the many benefits of democracy, particularly throughout the developing world. Indeed, economic aid packages are frequently tied to democratic reforms, as many donors demand to see elections before writing checks. To justify the promotion of democracy, several scholars and practitioners have argued that democracy yields many benefits, such as protections for human rights, economic development, and international peace.

This chapter critically examines these arguments. As recovery from the global economic crisis of 2008–09 continues in fits and starts amidst a world arguably more democratic than at any time in history, the question of whether democracy offers any concrete benefits remains critical for understanding its prospects for survival around the world. At one level we have substantial evidence that democratic regimes do indeed deliver the goods, beyond giving citizens the right to throw the bums out. For example, the democratic peace literature tells us that democracies do not go to war with one another (Van Belle 1997). Sen notes that "there is hardly any case in which a famine has occurred in a country that is independent and democratic with an uncensored press" (as quoted in Zweifel and Navia 2000, 101). Shin (1994) sums up much of this research by stating quite simply that "citizens of democratic states experience a far better quality of life than those of non-democracies" (156).

Such unequivocal declarations should leave us with few doubts about how to answer the question, "Does democracy matter?" Indeed, there is widespread consensus that democracies boast the best track records in respecting human rights. Rummel (1995) is among numerous scholars identifying a significantly lower level of human rights abuses and repression among democracies. This does not, however, rule out the possibility that democracies can falter in this area on occasion. In notable cases democracies have failed to protect citizens' fundamental rights. For example, Chapter 5 highlights the pernicious effects of the Jim Crow laws in the American South. Still, overall human rights fare better in democracies than under dictatorships.

Democracy's relationship with both economic development and world peace is more contested, as critics have questioned the unilateral benefits of democracy in these areas. This chapter examines the theoretical and empirical nuances of democracy's impact on economic development and peace. If the international community touts democracy as the only game in town, it is crucial to examine the theoretical and empirical underpinnings for claims of democracy's superiority over authoritarian regimes.

Democracy and economic development

Democracy's ability to foster economic development has been hotly debated. Many scholars and government officials alike see authoritarian regimes as more conducive to rapid economic development. Such views were originally based upon evidence from the "Asian Tigers" (Hong Kong, Singapore, South Korea, and Taiwan), where authoritarian regimes were able to marshal the required resources (and quell dissent) to enact policies that facilitated rapid growth. China is the most recent and prominent case of a decidedly undemocratic political system fostering impressive economic development. Chinese growth is all the more striking as it occurred during a period when many democracies suffered through multiple economic crises. Former Singapore premier, Lee Kuan Yew, typifies the view that authoritarian regimes are far better equipped to implement the tough but beneficial policies seen as essential to economic growth, noting that "the exuberance of democracy leads to indiscipline and disorderly conduct which are inimical to development" (As quoted in Bhagwati 1995, 51). Bhagwati long ago characterized this tension between democracy and economic development as a "cruel choice" that developing countries face in deciding whether to strive for democracy or economic development, because they could not have both at the same time (Bhagwati 1966, 204). Three decades later, Sartori raised the same concern, noting that with all else being equal, "governments that are spared gridlock and popular pressures are in a better position to promote growth than governments encumbered by demo-demands and demo-distributions" (Sartori 1995, 107).

At the heart of these concerns lies the vulnerability of democratic regimes to redistributive pressures from society that theoretically will lead to policies undermining economic growth. For example, if workers use democratic liberties to organize and strike for higher wages, these higher wages could potentially make exports more costly and less competitive in global markets. It is this exact same feature of responsiveness, however, that others point to as the reason democracy will be more likely than authoritarian regimes to contribute to sustainable long-term development. Widespread demands for greater investment in public education will likely find a more receptive audience in democratic regimes, where public officials—if they wish to retain their jobs—depend on the electoral support of those making such demands. Such attention to education will then translate into greater, and more sustainable, economic development over the long term (Baum and Lake 2003).

The Baum and Lake study exemplifies recent research that challenges those earlier scholars and observers who viewed authoritarian regimes as far better equipped than democratic regimes to bring about economic development. As the authoritarian-filled decade of the 1970s made clear, for every dictatorship that successfully fostered economic growth, there were plenty of authoritarian regimes that brought economic ruin to their countries with misplaced economic policies, inattention to long-term investments in human capital, and corrupt and inefficient leadership. For example, authoritarian rule in contemporary China has ushered in an era of prosperity, but authoritarian rule in the 1960s brought famine to China's countryside. The question, then, of whether democratic political regimes have systematic effects on economic development patterns remains unresolved. In a frequently cited evaluation of this research, Przeworski and Limongi state simply that "we do not know whether democracy fosters or hinders economic growth," noting that "it does not seem to be democracy or authoritarianism per se that makes a difference but something else" (Przeworski and Limongi

1993, 64–65). To resolve this theoretical impasse, it is imperative to examine the theoretical mechanisms linking regime types to particular development outcomes.

Understanding the democracy-development nexus

To determine the impact of democracy on development, it is first important to engage in the difficult task of distinguishing between democratic and authoritarian regimes. Here, it is helpful to begin with the concept of "regime" itself. Regime is best understood as a term that refers to the underlying "philosophy of governance"[1] of a political system. In other words: What is the underlying philosophy that guides the game of politics? Is it the view that political power ultimately rests in the hands of the people, or the view that power should reside in the hands of the individual with the biggest gun? From this perspective, then, a political regime tells us how the game of politics is played, not what the outcome of that game will be. From a normative perspective, one certainly might hope for better development outcomes to occur in a democratic regime. To support such hopes, however, it is important to compare the critical differences between a generic democratic and generic authoritarian regime, and to generate a set of propositions related to *expected outcomes* for each regime type.

How are democratic and authoritarian regimes different? Philosophies of governance identify three important dimensions that separate democracies from dictatorships: access to power, transfer of power, and application of power. In an authoritarian regime, access to power is generally restricted to a small segment of the population, while in a democracy most adult citizens tend to have some means of gaining at least a small, or indirect, measure of power. The transfer of power in dictatorships is unpredictable, oftentimes violent, and almost inevitably destabilizing. Conversely, democracies tend to have procedural institutions in place that guide the transfer of power in very predictable, peaceful, and stable ways. Finally, dictatorships apply power in a largely arbitrary, exclusionary process, while power in democracies is procedurally institutionalized and predictable (at least in relative terms). Put another way, democracies are about contestation for power (Dahl 1971), inclusiveness in the application of power (Dahl 1971), and "institutionalized uncertainty" (Przeworski 1991) with respect to the transition of power. Authoritarian regimes are, in general, about the monopolization of power, society's exclusion from power, and absolute uncertainty about how, when, and to whom power will be transferred.

Table 2.1 Crucial Governance Differences in Democratic and Authoritarian Regimes

	Democratic Regimes	Authoritarian Regimes
Access to Power	most adult citizens have some means of gaining at least some power	restricted to a small segment of the population
Transfer of Power	predictable, peaceful, and stable	unpredictable and oftentimes violent and destabilizing
Application of Power	institutionalized and predictable	largely arbitrary and exclusionary

These differences are important for developing theoretical expectations for certain types of economic development outcomes under democracies and dictatorships. From these generic regime differences, we might posit that democracies will be more likely to offer better protection of civil, political, and human rights; engender a more active civil society; have greater government accountability and responsiveness to a larger segment of society; and experience more peaceful, stable, and predictable alternations in power. All these outcomes may then be linked to such development outcomes as better education and health standards, more transparent investment environments, stronger and more effective regulatory institutions and, thus, greater and more sustainable economic growth. Conversely, we should expect authoritarian regimes to invest more in internal security, respond to a much smaller segment of society, and experience sudden, violent transfers of power (Olson 1992).

These differences should correspond to less desirable development outcomes. Indeed, despite some theoretical concerns with the democracy–economic development connection, convincing empirical research points to democracy's positive impact in other areas of development. Democratic regimes tend to pay more attention to areas of social policy such as health care and education than do authoritarian regimes, particularly in times of economic crisis (Brown and Hunter 1999; Shin 1994). Democracies appear to be significantly superior to authoritarian regimes with respect to their track record in health outcomes (Zweifel and Navia 2000; 2003). Finally, echoing the findings of others, Baum and Lake (2003) identify an indirect effect of democracy on economic growth through its positive effects on health and education.

Still, there theoretically are equally plausible reasons to view democracies as problematic for both human and economic development outcomes. For example, the quest for reelection might lead some democratic officials to pursue shortsighted and/or self-serving policies that undermine longer-term development goals. Democracies also tend to be more vulnerable to interest group capture, opening the door to the possibility that development policies will run counter to the long-term development goals of the country. The common tendency of politicians (of all ideological stripes) in democracies to avoid making difficult, but necessary, fiscal policy decisions (e.g., raising taxes and/or cutting spending), often is the source of deficit issues that have the potential to undermine long-term growth, for example. Additionally, though in theory democracies allow for widespread participation, most tend to have a "participation bias" wherein certain segments of the population participate more than others, leading to unequal levels of access and influence over policy decisions across society (Huber et al. 1997). Finally, because of the many "veto points" typically involved in a democratic policymaking process, the status quo may tend to prevail more often than not, with governments being more reactive to existing economic and social problems rather than proactive in an effort to prevent them. Legislation in the United States, for example, before becoming law must survive multiple committee votes, House and Senate roll-call votes, and presidential approval. In an authoritarian regime, such veto points are minimal, allowing legislation to become law much more quickly and with far fewer modifications. All these potential problems should vary in severity depending on the quality of the democratic regime in question.

This relationship between regime type and economic development is complicated even further when scholars attempt to test these theories empirically. Especially problematic is the uneven nature of many contemporary democracies. Particularly in the developing world, many democratic regimes are decidedly "thin" and uneven in terms of their quality. As we will see below, the current global democratic landscape is marked by tremendous variance in terms of the quality of democratic regimes, both within and across nations.

Uneven democracies and development

The question of democracy's effect on economic development becomes even more difficult to answer when we consider the so-called third wave democracies that have emerged in the past 35 years. Huntington's oft-used metaphor describes a global trend of democratization that began with Portugal in the mid-1970s and swept over much of Latin America, Eastern Europe, Africa, and Asia during the next 20 years. By the mid-1990s, over 60 percent of countries around the world were considered democratic. Since that high-water mark, however, many observers of this spread of democracy began to question whether the third wave had begun to recede, both in quantity and quality (e.g., Diamond 1996).

Variations in democratic quality, internationally as well as within individual countries, make it more difficult to answer the question of whether democracy matters. Most research approaches this question from a cross-national analytical perspective, comparing the performance of democratic and non-democratic countries across time and space. For example, a researcher may turn to the World Bank's World Development Indicators (WDI) to obtain a measure of economic growth rates for all independent countries from 1945 to the present.[2] The researcher could then characterize these countries in terms of their regime types, using a well-known source like the Polity IV Project.[3] Comparisons among countries, or within one country over time, provide a ready means of determining whether democracies register higher levels of economic growth than dictatorships.

While advantageous in many ways, such large-N work suffers from well-documented conceptual and measurement problems (Linz and de Miguel 1966; Snyder 2001). Principal among these issues is the question of whether the oft-used measures of democracy can accurately capture the variations in the quality of newer democracies around the world. For example, researchers frequently rely upon measures of democracy available through well known organizations like Freedom House and Polity, which provide a numerical score to assess the quality of democratic governance cross-nationally over time.[4] Other scholars rely on categorical assessments of regimes as either democratic or authoritarian, with a "transitional" category occasionally making an appearance as well (Hagopian and Mainwaring 2005). Zweifel and Navia typify this approach, employing a dichotomous measure of regimes where democracies are simply those systems that "experience elections and alternations of power" (Zweifel and Navia 2003, 92).

In the context of the widespread democratization of much of the developing world over the past 40 years, this issue of measurement has become all the more important to consider when exploring the democracy–development connection. In some cases the division between democratic and authoritarian regimes is straightforward: Canada is a democracy, China is not. However, many of the third wave democracies defy such easy characterizations. For example, both Costa Rica and Guatemala experience elections and alternations of power, but does labeling both countries as democratic accurately capture their underlying philosophies of governance? Subnational variations within countries are also highly problematic. For example, Baum and Lake (2003) use the full Polity scale in their study of democracy's indirect effects on economic growth, but ultimately their measures of democracy do not account for internal variations within each country. Such work undoubtedly offers insights at the national level, but is still susceptible to the "whole-nation bias" that "neglect[s] highly significant variations" in political, economic, and social development levels within countries (Rokkan 1970). Linz and de Miguel (1966) highlight the analytical risks such a bias raises in their study of the "eight Spains" of Spain. They note: "The uneven economic and social development of a relatively industrial and advanced Spain and a rural Spain . . . contributed to make the social conflicts of the thirties so explosive" (Linz and de Miguel 1966, 278). Such social, economic, and political divides arguably run even deeper through many of the newly democratic countries of today, making it even more imperative that analysts incorporate these development divides into research on the impact of regimes on development.

To put it bluntly, many of these younger democracies are flawed in a variety of ways, both at the national and subnational levels, and the ability to adequately capture the full extent of these flaws in cross-national measures is understandably limited. Indeed, scholars have tried to employ a host of qualifiers to describe varying degrees of democracies, referring to hollow, illiberal, or incomplete democracies. This trend has resulted in a series of "democracies with adjectives" (Collier and Levitsky 1996; Diamond 2002; Elkins 2000; McFaul 2002). Table 2.2 offers a now standard picture of such attempts. Immediately clear from this table is the dearth of what Kekic refers to as "full democracies" and the predominance of countries falling in the "flawed democracy" category. While the categorization rules of this "Democracy Index" may differ from those of other democracy measures,

Table 2.2 Political regimes around the world (2006)

Region (number of countries)	Full democracies	Flawed democracies	Hybrid regimes	Authoritarian regimes
North America (2)	2	0	0	0
Western Europe (21)	18	2	1	0
Eastern Europe (28)	2	14	14	6
Latin America/Caribbean (24)	2	17	4	1
Asia/Australasia (28)	3	12	4	9
Middle East/North Africa (20)	0	2	2	16
Sub-Saharan Africa (44)	1	7	13	23
TOTAL (167)	**28**	**54**	**30**	**55**

Source: Kekic's Democracy Index (2007, 7)

the same general story emerges from all—the global political landscape of the first decade of the twenty-first century is best characterized as largely democratic in name, but highly uneven and varied in quality.

O'Donnell describes these uneven democracies as those where "by definition, fair and institutionalized elections [and] certain political rights exist. However, other important rights and guarantees are not effective" (O'Donnell 2001, 27). For example, elections might be the norm, but the judiciary might prove incapable of curbing government abuses of power or of applying the law evenly across the citizenry. Furthermore, O'Donnell pointed out that emerging Latin American democracies in the 1990s tended to have "[p]rovinces peripheral to the national center [that] create (or reinforce) systems of local power which tend to reach extremes of violent, personalistic rule open to all sorts of violent and arbitrary practices" (O'Donnell 1999, 138). Fox (1994) and Lawson (2000) identified these as authoritarian enclaves within the region's new democracies. Smith (2005) estimated that at the turn of the century, 93 percent of Latin Americans lived in electoral democracies where there was a significant restriction of civil liberties. In a similar vein, Heller's (2000) study of the subnational political regimes of India underscores the "degrees of democracy" existing within the country. Such a landscape makes an assessment of democracy's impact on development problematic, as many of the theoretical propositions relating democracy to development rest on the assumption that a country's "average" national-level democracy score adequately captures its subnational component parts. What has become increasingly clear over the past 30 years of democratic transitions is that there exist substantial subnational departures from these country-level means.

The curvilinear relationship between democracy and economic development

In addition to problems of measurement, the unevenness of third wave democracies poses further challenges for studies of democracy and economic development. Until recently, such studies generally operated within a linear theoretical (and analytical) framework, where democracy either had a positive or negative impact on some development outcome (or no impact at all). As a country became more democratic, the expected influence on the development outcome of interest would become more and more pronounced. For example, Baum and Lake's findings indicate that "among poor countries a maximum increase in democracy improves life expectancy by about 9.4 years" (Baum and Lake 2003, 342). According to this linear line of research, the more democratic a country is, the longer its citizens can expect to live.

In the past ten years, scholars have increasingly recognized the unevenness of democratic governance and aimed to model its effects accordingly. For example, Mousseau (2001) offers evidence of an inverted-U relationship between democratization and the probability of an outbreak of extreme political violence, particularly in heterogeneous ethnic societies. He finds "the process of democratization is associated with higher levels of political violence in ethnically heterogeneous societies" (Mousseau 2001, 561).[5] These findings suggest that as countries begin to democratize, the shifting sands of the political rules of the game can potentially reignite old conflicts and cause new ones as political actors seek advantage in the changing institutional environment. Assuming the fledgling democratic regime survives these initial outbursts of violence, the benefits of democracy with respect to providing competing factions a peaceful outlet for political competition may begin to emerge, producing a curvilinear effect of democracy on development.

The logic behind this research is important for understanding the democracy-economic development nexus. As a country democratizes, it begins with the introduction of elections as a mechanism for the selection of leaders. With such a fundamental shift in the political status quo, there is almost certain to be a power struggle between those who had enjoyed access to power under the previous set of political rules of the game and those denied it. More generally, democratization implies a challenge to the status quo. Those benefiting from the status quo typically will seek to preserve at least some of the old rules, or subvert the new rules to their advantage. Either course of action could produce lackluster economic development policies. While not the "cruel choice" described by Huntington and Nelson (1976), many of today's fledgling democracies may experience a democracy-development tradeoff, where democracy in the long term will contribute to sustainable growth, but at the expense of short-term development difficulties brought about by the initial destabilizing effects of democracy on government and society.[6]

This line of research indicates the missing piece to the puzzle of the democracy-development relationship may be found in a nonlinear specification of that relationship. It is not clear whether a regime's initial move from overtly authoritarian to nominally democratic practices will effect a positive change in development outcomes. Indeed, as regimes democratize, development outcomes could get worse before they get better. Collier explains how democracy has the potential to hurt development initially, analyzing the impact of perverse governance incentives that can emerge in what he refers to as "democracy in dangerous places" (Collier 2009, 1). The initial movement toward democracy in many of these countries, typically through the holding of internationally sanctioned national elections, is likely to contribute to a worsening of the development prospects of the country in the short term. In the absence, between elections, of effective accountability mechanisms, elections favor those politicians most adept at dirty, patronage-driven politics and drive out individuals inclined to play by the democratic rules of the game (Collier 2009; see also Collier 2007).

Work at the subnational level also sheds light on how exactly this non-linear relationship might work. Gibson and Calvo's (2000) work on the persistence of authoritarian enclaves in Argentina and Mexico highlights the need for a catalyzing, and typically destabilizing, event to break the grip of subnational authoritarian rulers, such as widespread protests that generate attention beyond the borders of the enclave itself.[7] Hiskey's (2005) work on economic recovery prospects in Mexico also found that state-level recovery from the country's 1995 economic crisis was in part a function of the country's uneven political landscape. One-party states and multi-party states enjoyed robust recovery rates, while the economies of those states in the midst of a democratic transition—characterized by destabilizing and violence-filled elections—experienced significantly lower levels of recovery from the crisis.

A case study of Oaxaca, Mexico, illustrates how this uneven relationship between democracy and development can unfold. In 2004, Oaxaca's hotly contested gubernatorial elections signaled the long-awaited arrival of real electoral competition after nearly 70 years of one-party dominance.[8] As Figure 2.1 reveals, the 2004 elections appeared to be the culmination of opposition efforts throughout the 1990s to chip away at the Institutional Revolutionary Party's (PRI) steel grip on state politics. In addition to winning all gubernatorial elections and the vast majority of other state-level offices throughout most of the twentieth century, the PRI's political machine reached all corners of the state's 570 municipalities. After suffering through multiple economic crises, and witnessing yet again the repressive hand of the state in the form of the 2002 massacre of 27 peasants, Oaxaca's main opposition parties finally put aside sharp ideological differences and presented a single candidate for governor. The opposition campaigned under the coalition label *Todo Somos Oaxaca* (We are all Oaxaca), and expected the PRI would finally be forced to loosen its control over the state government.

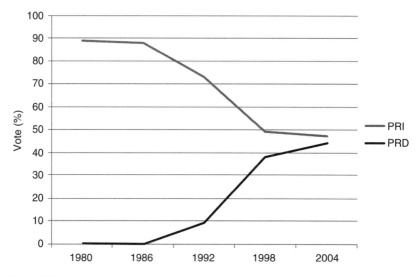

Figure 2.1 Gubernatorial Elections in Oaxaca, Mexico

Elections were held, hopes were high, but at the end of the day the PRI remained in power. Amid charges of electoral fraud, PRI candidate Ulises Ruiz declared victory and presided over one of the most tumultuous 6-year terms in the country's modern history. A *Washington Post* report captures the instability Ruiz brought to the job, describing his precarious, but tenacious, hold on power during widespread protests in the state in 2006:

> Ulises Ruiz, governor of the strike-scorched state of Oaxaca, is cornered. Mexico's Congress wants him to quit. Hordes of protesters want him to quit. His own party wants him to quit. But he won't budge." (Ruiz-Franzia 2006)

Rather than resign, Ruiz remained in power and undermined any development prospects Oaxaca, Mexico's second poorest state, may have had during the relatively prosperous years of 2004–08.[9]

Ruiz's reign in Oaxaca offers a clear example of how democracy in its early, flawed stages may directly contribute to inferior development outcomes. In a story reminiscent of Collier's account of electoral competition's pernicious development consequences in the fledgling democracies of Africa, we see the same process playing out in one of Latin America's most developed countries, where by most accounts national-level democracy is making great strides. Just as the lynchings and overt violation of political and civil rights continued in the American South well into that country's period of democratic consolidation, so too do authoritarian practices persist at the subnational level in many developing democracies. Even while democracy appears to flourish at the national level, undemocratic practices can prove tenacious in regions and municipalities.

The unevenness of the third wave democracies provides insight into why democracy does not always translate into positive economic development outcomes. The uneven democratization process experienced by many democracies in the developing world can potentially have a curvilinear impact on development. Governance and subsequent development outcomes may suffer from the system's initial steps toward democracy, but benefit as the quality of the democratic system improves. These posited countervailing effects of democratization on development are difficult to tease out empirically, however, as traditional measures of democracy and development struggle to capture these varied and dynamic processes. These difficulties stem largely from the fact that the effects being tested are ones that would occur over many years, while most data used offer only single-year snapshots.

Isolating the impact of regime change during the era of neoliberal reform

In addition to the challenges posed by uneven democratization, the third wave democracies bring an additional complication to the study of democracy and development. Throughout much of the developing world, democratization coincided with a paradigmatic shift in economic development strategy, from one guided by the state to one directed by the market. With Mexico's announcement to the world in August of 1982 that it would be unable to continue servicing its debt payments, the so-called lost decade began. In the 1980s, the debt crisis led country after country to the doorstep of the International Monetary Fund (IMF) in search of loans from the international community's "lender of last resort." In return for much-needed foreign exchange, countries submitted (in varying degrees) to a series of conditions, including painful reductions of government spending, the removal of policy barriers to trade and capital, strict budgetary constraints, and increased emphasis on joining regional and international free trade agreements. Instead of commanding the economy, the state was reduced to a laissez-faire role. As the United States was the most prominent advocate of these neoliberal reforms, this economic reform prescription was dubbed the "Washington Consensus." Thus, just as political systems in the developing world were opening to democracy and citizen influence, the range of economic policy options available to policymakers shrank. The policy constraints of the Washington Consensus have posed a fundamental democratic dilemma to those politicians truly interested in allowing societal input into the policymaking process.

The tension between these externally imposed policy constraints and political openings has contributed to the uneven and "thin" democratization process. As Weyland aptly states, "neoliberalism has strengthened the sustainability of democracy in Latin America, but limited its quality" (Weyland 2004, 135). The market-based policy reforms and integration with the global economy brought the region's countries under more international pressure to maintain the formal trappings of democracy, namely holding relatively free and fair elections and offering at least minimal protections of citizens' civil and political rights. Democracy as a regime type, therefore, has survived during difficult economic times when many observers thought it might succumb once again to the return of authoritarianism. The quality of the democracy that has survived, however, has been undermined by many of those same neoliberal forces that have aided democracy's survival in the region. Market-based policies allow policymakers to have far less latitude to respond to their constituents, and integration with the global economy has placed many traditionally domestic issues under the purview of international institutions, creating what many have referred to as a "democratic deficit" (e.g. Nye 2001). Thus, while democracies have survived the economic adjustments of the neoliberal age, they have not thrived (Weyland 2004).

The Latin American region perhaps illustrates most clearly the many features of these simultaneous economic and political transitions. For the past three decades, most Latin American countries made the dual transition to democratic forms of government and market economies, experiencing near-simultaneous watershed changes in their political and economic foundations. In the 1970s, led by the 1978 transition in Ecuador, Latin America transformed itself from a largely authoritarian landscape to an overwhelmingly democratic one in the present day. Though several countries have experienced setbacks, and many are decidedly less than perfect, the region's most recent democratic track record is historically unmatched.

Relying upon the World Bank's Governance Indicators, Figure 2.2 charts these trends in democratization.[10] Similar to the national level indicators of democratization discussed earlier, the Governance Indicators seek to

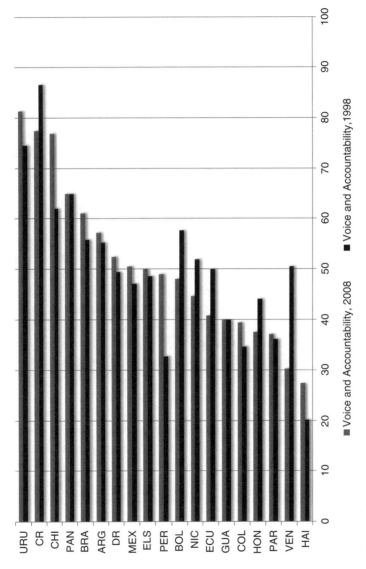

Figure 2.2 Latin America's Voice and Accountability Scores, 1998–2008

evaluate multiple dimensions of governance across countries and time. The "voice and accountability" dimension "measures the extent to which a country's citizens are able to participate in selecting their government as well as freedom of expression, freedom of association, and a free media."[11] For our purposes it simply provides a rough estimate of the ranking of democracies across Latin America and how they changed during the 2000s.[12] As discussed previously, all these measures are fairly blunt tools for capturing a complex concept, so those evaluating the rankings should proceed with caution and not make too much of the fact that Uruguay is ranked ahead of Costa Rica and Chile, for example. Rather, these rankings provide a rough overview of the quality of governance cross-nationally and within each country over time. In general, the same rank ordering in 1998 holds for 2008, with the notable exceptions of Venezuela, which became decidedly less democratic during this decade, and Peru, which became substantially more democratic.

To identify any patterns between these uneven democracies and economic development outcomes, it is helpful to compare the rankings in Figure 2.2 with some commonly used measures of economic development. Figure 2.3 lists the average GDP per capita growth rates, retaining the same "voice and accountability" order of Figure 2.2. Such superficial comparisons between national level governance rankings and economic indicators certainly cannot allow us to make definitive statements about the relationship between democracy and economic development, but they can highlight some important trends that merit closer scrutiny. What immediately jumps from Figure 2.3 is the poor economic performance of the three least democratic countries: Paraguay, Venezuela, and Haiti. Putting aside yet again any notion of assigning cause and effect, this association merely calls our attention to the potential recursive nature of flawed democracies and poor development outcomes. Not only do the three worst economic performers have flawed democracies, but four of the five countries with growth rates over 2 percent were among the top seven democratic countries, while only one country in the bottom 11 recorded an average growth rate over 2 percent. Though it is difficult to draw firm conclusions from these apparent patterns, these comparisons indicate there is at least some support for the idea that flawed democracies, poor development outcomes, and bad governance are intimately related to one another in mutually reinforcing ways. This lends support to the conceptualization of a nonlinear association between democracy and development. We have reason to suspect, then, that the long-running search for democracy's effect on development (and its equally long list of contradictory results), may in fact be the product of democracy's contradictory effects on development.

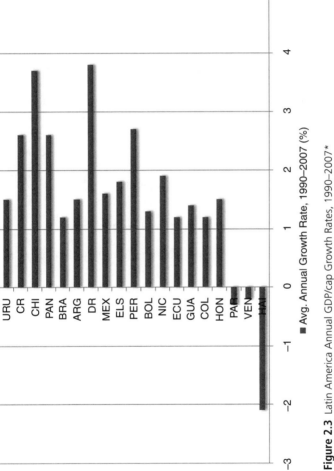

Figure 2.3 Latin America Annual GDP/cap Growth Rates, 1990–2007*

*Countries ranked by World Bank "Voice and Accountability" score for 2008. GDP/cap growth rates data from UNDP Human Development Report website (http://hdr.undp.org/en/)

Democratic peace theory

In addition to focusing on the impact of democracy inside a country, scholars and practitioners have also touted the value of democracy for international politics. The idea that representative liberal governments can diminish the occurrence of war is one of the most appealing, influential, and at the same time, controversial ideas of our time. For centuries, thinkers have proposed that a world of democratic countries would be a peaceful world. As early as 1795, Immanuel Kant wrote in his essay *Perpetual Peace* that democracies are less warlike. Within the United States, this suggestion holds particular sway. Presidents from Woodrow Wilson to George W. Bush have embraced this idea, advocating the creation of democracies to form a less belligerent world. Harry S. Truman once said, "Totalitarian regimes imposed on free peoples . . . undermine the foundation of international peace and hence security of the United States" (quoted in Rupert 2000, 27). This argument has evolved from basic theoretical assumptions to an entire research program, with numerous studies confirming a statistically significant relationship between democratic pairs and lack of war.[13]

Understanding the democracy-peace nexus

According to democratic peace theory, there are a variety of mechanisms by which democracy promotes peace. First, in democracies citizens can play a role in restraining elected leaders. Given the choice, citizens will be reluctant to bear the costs of war in terms of human life and finance. Indeed, empirical evidence indicates that democracies historically spend less on defense than so non-democracies and, therefore, there is a "demilitarizing effect" of democracy (Fordham and Walker 2005, 154). Belligerent leaders can also face steep electoral costs, as periodic leadership change encourages "a reversal of disastrous politics as electorates punish the party in power with electoral defeat" (Doyle 2005, 464). Overall, democracies provide distinct incentives for peace as they require supportive constituents who are susceptible to public costs of war (Reiter and Stam 2002).

Democratic political institutions also matter a great deal. Democracies are accustomed to using political institutions to settle their domestic disputes. Therefore, when conflict arises with another democracy, they will be more apt to use international institutions (e.g., the United Nations, International Court of Justice, G-8 summits) to resolve their international disagreements. Democratic institutions also provide checks and balances domestically. Thus, if a war-prone leader comes to power in a democracy, other institutions (e.g., Congress) will check bellicose acts and prevent an aggressive head of state from moving a country to war. Democratic institutions are thought to slow the march towards war and increase the likelihood of diplomatic engagement. The segmentation of decision-making capacity seems to slow the push for combat, and legal restraints on executives are effective at diminishing the use of force (Doyle 1986). Democratic institutions also foster political stability, which is positively associated with low rates of disputes (Moaz and Russett 1993).

Finally, democratic peace theory argues that democracies teach their citizens that violence is not the best means of conflict resolution, producing a political culture of negotiation and conciliation that is not conducive to war. Many advocates also believe people in democracies are more sympathetic and tolerant of people in other democracies (Weart 1998). Thus, whether it is common norms, institutional constraints, mutual respect, or popular will, there are many theoretical reasons to view democracy as a remedy for preventing war.

In the 1970s, scholars began using the tools of social science to explore democratic peace theory, producing a significant amount of empirical evidence to support these claims. Today, there are over a hundred authors who have published scholarly works on democratic peace theory. One study examined 416 country-to-country wars from 1816–1980 and found that only 12 were fought between democracies (Doyle 1996). Russett writes, "Established democracies fought no wars against one another during the entire twentieth century" (Russett 2001, 235). Another proponent found the probability of any two democracies engaging in war is less than half of 1 percent (Rummel 1997). This is not to say that democracies have not gone to war, but when considering pairs (or dyads) of democracies, there are almost no instances of war between two democracies. Four decades of research consistently find support for this position. Moreover, the correlations remain robust as the number of democracies in the world continues to grow. As Levy points out, democratic peace theory is "as close as anything we have to an empirical law in international relations" (Levy 1988, 88).

Critics

Does democracy really promote peace through the theoretical mechanisms outlined above? Can democracy curb war through common norms, institutional constraints, mutual respect, or popular will? Critics abound, and many scholars disagree on why exactly democracies are more peaceful. Current empirical research has come under heavy criticism, with scholars claiming that the evidence changes depending on how scholars define "democracy," "war," and "peace." Indeed, doubts can be found very early in American history. Alexander Hamilton rejected central tenets of democratic peace theory in Federalist No. 6, writing:

> Sparta, Athens, Rome, and Carthage were all republics; two of them, Athens and Carthage, of the commercial kind. Yet were they as often engaged in wars, offensive and defensive, as the neighboring monarchies of the same times. Sparta was little better than a well regulated camp; and Rome was never sated of carnage and conquest. (Hamilton 1787)

Skeptics like Hamilton question the assumption that democracies create peaceful peoples, doubting the idea that popular will can mitigate war, particularly since war seems rather popular in certain democracies (Rosato 2003). The United States presents an interesting example of this as public approval ratings of US presidents tend to skyrocket during war. For example, President George H.W. Bush saw his approval ratings rise to an unprecedented 89 percent during the 1991 Persian Gulf War, when Americans "rallied around the flag."

Additional critics argue that establishing correlation is relatively easy; however, establishing causation is more problematic. Many contend that the statistical relationship observed between democracy and peace is, in fact, spurious. That is, there is a correlation between democracy and peace, but that correlation is due to a third factor related to both, such as economic ties. For example, one rebuttal to democratic peace theory is dubbed the "Big Mac Peace Theory"; this cheeky modification points out that no two countries with a McDonald's have ever gone to war (Friedman 2000, 2005).[14] Such rebuttals claim that what scholars are actually measuring is economic development, not democracy (Rosecrance 1986). Here, some argue that a stable middle class (people who like their current financial status) will not support a war that may jeopardize their standard of living. Alternatively, the causal factors may be powerful economic elites who block any move toward aggression against a country where they hold financial ties, protecting their economic interests from risk. Thus, this line of research states it is economic development, global capitalism, and the interdependence of foreign trade that impedes war, not democracy (Weede 2004).

Others also point to the importance of economic development in a slightly different vein. Mousseau (2005) finds that democratic peace theory only holds true between two democracies that have reached high standards of economic development; poor democracies are more likely to fight each other.

Mansfield and Snyder (2005) point out that transitional states or "semi-democratic regimes" may be extremely dangerous and actually *more likely* to start wars. There is no guarantee that the introduction of democratic institutions will be smooth, permanent, or accepted by either the political elites or by the masses. Furthermore, Mansfield and Snyder (1995) contend democratic peace theory does not apply to new democracies, which tend to be unstable, easily reversible, and prone to border disputes. In transitional states it may take decades, or even generations, to establish embedded norms of tolerance and compromise and the value of power sharing. Once again, the importance of the quality of democratic regimes, particularly in the third wave democracies, emerges as very important.

Without necessarily discounting democracy's influence, some scholars have pointed to the importance of economic interactions in promoting peace. For example, some have argued that the economic interactions between democracies tend to favor more open trade relations and thus interdependence; here, the risks of economic loss within both states raise the cost of war (Russett, Oneal, and Berbaum 2003). In addition, as democracies create institutions within their borders, they also tend to create institutions outside their borders to manage foreign affairs and reduce transaction costs. These institutions then provide venues for conflict resolution (Oneal and Russett 1999). Doyle (2005) is quick to point out that no one particular aspect of democracies' engagement with other democracies is key, but that causality rests on the combination of several factors present in representative governments, such as institutional constraints, democratic norms, and economic interdependence.

The strongest opposition to democratic peace theory argues that "good science" is creating dangerous policy . There are those who fear this research provides justification for countries to go on "democracy crusades." Indeed, in some regions there is a backlash against democracy promotion efforts, as populations view the exportation of democracy as thinly veiled imperialism (Weiss 2007). In countries like the United States, democracy promotion has a long and checkered history. Early in American history, US foreign policy underscored the importance of bringing "civilization," "freedom" and "self-government" to the countries of the Western Hemisphere (Hunt 1987). Thomas Jefferson thought leadership by example would be contagious—the virtue, self-restraint, and rule of law practiced by Western and American governments would spark imitation. Jefferson proclaimed that, "A just and solid republican government maintained here will be a standing monument and example for . . . people of other countries" (Jefferson 1801). Others advocated a more active role in promoting democracy, and justified territorial and commercial expansion under the rationale that it was an American duty to democratize the continent (Smith 2000). Indeed, as early as 1829 Simón Bolívar noted the United States "seem destined by Providence to plague America with torments in the name of freedom."[15] Throughout the nineteenth and twentieth centuries many American leaders argued that active military intervention was necessary to promote democracy, but critics noted that the countries with the most US intervention (e.g., El Salvador, Guatemala, Haiti, Cuba, Dominican Republic, and Nicaragua) tended to have repressive authoritarian governments. Furthermore, critics pointed out that patterns of US intervention were not always conducive to democratization, but they did succeed in promoting US economic interests.

Despite critiques, recent American foreign policy has continued this emphasis on democracy promotion, embracing democratic peace theory as a foundation for foreign policy and a way to build world peace. In the 1994 State of the Union Address, President Bill Clinton proclaimed, "Ultimately, the best strategy to ensure our security and to build a durable peace is to support the advancement of democracy elsewhere. Democracies don't attack each other" (Clinton 1994). Ten years later, President George W. Bush stated, "And the reason why I'm so strong on democracy is democracies don't go to war with each other. . . . I've got great faith in democracies to promote peace. And that's why I'm such a strong believer that the way forward in the Middle East, the broader Middle East, is to promote democracy" (Bush 2004).

The idea that democracies do not go to war with other democracies is influential within several western European countries as well, and now serves as a point of consensus among the leaders of the Western world. Still, many are skeptical of these efforts, viewing them as attempts to spread geopolitical influence, homogenize the world, and/or reject local culture and institutions. Thus, rather than viewing themselves as liberated, people and their leaders in many non-democratic countries hear this policy mandate as smug rhetoric.

Conclusion

Democracy promoters have championed the ability of democracy to foster respect for human rights, economic development, and world peace. It is clear that democracies respect fundamental human rights better than do authoritarian regimes. However, the other benefits of democracy are not as clear-cut. The idea that democracy is a panacea for war has generated considerable excitement and promoted growing expectations by both policy makers and Western publics (Lyon and Dolan 2007). Still, while ample empirical evidence supports the notion that democracies do not go to war with each other, the causal mechanisms of this relationship remain unclear. Indeed, the evidence indicates that democracy's contribution to world peace is part of a package that includes economic development and robust international organizations (Russett and Oneal 1997). Thus, in order for the democratic peace theory to hold, democracy must be authentic, robust, stable, and accompanied by economic development.

The relationship between democracy and development is also nuanced, and evidence suggests the development effects of democracy run both ways. This might disappoint democracy's cheerleaders. However, it is important to keep in mind that this conclusion does not negate all the evidence we do have that supports Shin's contention that citizens enjoy a "better quality of life" in democracies. What the call for a nuanced understanding of democracy's impact on development merely serves to do is allow for a more realistic set of expectations to be attached to "the worst form of government except all of the others that have been tried."[16]

Notes

1 From an author discussion with Dr. Eduardo Gamarra in 1992.

2 The World Bank maintains a series of databases to measure economic and social indicators cross-nationally over time. The WDI is frequently used to gauge economic development outcomes like economic growth, GDP per capita, poverty levels, and inequality (http://data. worldbank.org/data-catalog/world-development-indicators). In addition to this data source, the United Nations also reports on economic and social indicators through its Millennium Development Goals Reports (www.un.org/millenniumgoals/reports.shtml) and Human Development Index (http://hdr.undp.org/en/statistics/).

3 Among other things, the Polity IV Project aims to measure the quality of democratic governance in all major independent countries from 1800–2008 (www.systemicpeace.org/polity/polity4.htm).

4 The Freedom House is another common source used to measure the quality of democracy cross-nationally over time, as it characterizes countries in terms of their respect for civil liberties and political rights each year, from 1973 to the present (www.freedomhouse.org/template. cfm?page=1, last accessed June 30, 2010).

5 Such findings recall Muller and Seligson's (1987) work on the inverted-U relationship between regime repressiveness and political violence, where the latter is found to peak in "semi-repressive" regimes.

6 This possibility offers a parallel to Kuznet's (1955) groundbreaking findings on economic development and inequality. Kuznet found a nonlinear relationship between income inequality and economic development, suggesting inequality will increase to a point as a country industrializes, only declining as it reaches higher levels of economic development.

7 Although they do not explicitly focus on the development consequences of such events, it does not require much of a leap to posit the deleterious effects of such events on development in the region.

8 At the national level, the PRI relinquished its monopolization of power definitively when it lost the 2000 presidential election to the opposition National Action Party (PAN).

9 A happy postscript to this story occurred in July of 2010 when Ruiz's party, the PRI, finally relinquished power to a coalition candidate supported by the state's two major opposition parties.

10 A lack of available data precluded the inclusion of Cuba.

11 Quote taken from the following page of the "Governance Matters" website: http://info. worldbank.org/governance/wgi/pdf/va.pdf, last accessed July 31, 2010.

12 The rank ordering of the countries displayed in Figure 2.2 is generally consistent with other more familiar measures of democracy, such as Polity and Freedom House.

13 The research generally defines democracy as close to universal suffrage, a representative government, and regular elections open to a majority of the population. A common definition of war is a militarized conflict between two states where 1,000 or more are killed. It is important to point out that there is significant debate how changing the definitions of war and democracy may change the positive correlation between democracy and peace (Brown et al. 1997).

14 Friedman has updated this to The Dell Theory, arguing that "no two countries that are both part of a major global supply chain, like Dell's, will ever fight a war against each other as long as they are both part of the same global supply chain" (Friedman 2005, 421).

15 Quoted in Holden and Zolov (2000, 18).

16 A quote famously attributed to Winston Churchill.

References

Baum, Matthew A., and David A. Lake. 2003. "The Political Economy of Growth: Democracy and Human Capital." *American Journal of Political Science* 47(2): 333–47.

Bhagwati, Jagdish. 1966. *The Economics of Underdeveloped Countries.* New York: McGraw Hill.

Bhagwati, Jagdish N. 1995. "The New Thinking on Development." *Journal of Democracy* 6 (4): 50–64

Brown, David S., and Wendy Hunter. 1999. "Democracy and Social Spending in Latin America, 1980–1992." *The American Political Science Review* 93(4): 779–90.

Bush, George W. 2004. "President and Prime Minister Blair Discussed Iraq, Middle East, the East Room." Accessed November 12, 2004, http://www.whitehouse.gov/news/releases/2004/11/20041112-5.html.

Clinton, William. 1994. State of the Union Address. January 25. Accessed July 17, 2010, http://www.washingtonpost.com/wpsrv/politics/special/states/docs/sou94.htm.

Collier, David, and Steven Levitsky. 1996. "Democracy 'With Adjectives': Conceptual Innovation in Comparative Research." Kellogg Institute Working Paper No. 230.

Collier, Paul. 2009. *Wars, Guns, and Votes: Democracy in Dangerous Places*. New York: HarperCollins.

Collier, Paul. 2007. *The Bottom Billion: Why the Poorest Countries Are Failing and What Can Be Done About It*. Oxford: Oxford University Press.

Dahl, Robert. 1971. *Polyarchy: Participation and Opposition*. New Haven: Yale University Press.

Diamond, Larry. 2002. "Thinking About Hybrid Regimes." *Journal of Democracy*, 13(2): 21–35.

Diamond, Larry. 1996. "Is the Third Wave Over?" *Journal of Democracy*, 7(3): 20–37.

Doyle, Michael. 2005. "Three Pillars of the Liberal Peace." *American Political Science Review* 99: 463–66

Doyle, Michael. 1996. "Kant, Liberal Legacies, and Foreign Affairs." In *Debating the Democratic Peace*, edited by Sean Lynn-Jones, Michael Brown, and Steven Miller, 3–57. Cambridge, MA: MIT Press.

Doyle, Michael. 1986. "Liberalism and World Politics." *American Political Science Review* 80: 1151–70.

Elkins, Zachary. 2000. "Gradations of Democracy? Empirical Tests of Alternative Conceptualizations." *American Journal of Political Science* 44(2): 293–300.

Gibson, Edward, and Ernesto Calvo. 2000. "Federalism and Low-Maintenance Constituencies: Territorial Dimensions of Economic Reform in Argentina." *Studies in Comparative International Development* 35(3): 32–55.

Fordham, Benjamin, and Thomas Walker. 2005. "Kantian Liberalism, Regime Type, and Military Resource Allocation: Do Democracies Spend Less?" *International Studies Quarterly* 49: 141–57.

Fox, Jonathan. 1994. "Latin America's Emerging Local Politics." *Journal of Democracy* 5(2): 105–16.

Friedman, Thomas. 2005. *The World is Flat*. New York: Farrar, Straus and Giroux.

Friedman, Thomas. 2000. *The Lexus and the Olive Tree*. New York: Anchor Books.

Hagopian, Francis, and Scott Mainwaring. 2005. *The Third Wave of Democratization in Latin America: Advances and Setbacks*. Cambridge: Cambridge University Press.

Hamilton, Alexander. 1787. *The Federalist No. 6*. Accessed July 17, 2010 http://www.law.emory.edu/cms/site/index.php?id=3138.

Heller, Patrick. 2000. "Degrees of Democracy: Some Comparative Lessons from India." *World Politics* 52: 484–519.

Hiskey, Jonathan T. 2005. "The Political Economy of Subnational Economic Recovery in Mexico." Latin American Research Review 40(1): 30–55.

Holden, Robert H., and Eric Zolov. 2000. *Latin America and the United States: A Documentary History*. New York: Oxford University Press.

Huber, Evelyne, Dietrich Rueschemeyer, and John D. Stephens. 1997. "The Paradoxes of Contemporary Democracy: Formal, Participatory, and Social Dimensions." *Comparative Politics* 29(3): 323–42.

Hunt, Michael H. 1987. *Ideology and US Foreign Policy*. New Haven: Yale University Press.

Huntington, Samuel P. 1991. *The Third Wave: Democratization in the Late Twentieth Century*. Norman: University of Oklahoma Press.

Huntington, Samuel, and Joan Nelson. 1976. *No Easy Choice: Political Participation in Development Countries*. Cambridge: Harvard University Press.

Thomas Jefferson to John Dickinson, 1801. ME 10:217. Accessed July 17, 2010 http://etext.virginia.edu/jefferson/quotations/jeff1750.htm

Kant, Immanuel. 1917. *Perpetual Peace: A Philosophical Essay. Translated by M. Campbell Smith*. London: George Allen and Unwin.

Kekic, Laza. 2007. "The Economist Intelligence Unit's Index of Democracy." In *The World in 2007*, published by *The Economist*.

Kuznets, Simon. 1955. "Economic Growth and Income Inequality." *American Economic Review* 45: 1–28.

Lawson, Chappell. 2000. "Mexico's Unfinished Transition: Democratization and Authoritarian Enclaves in Mexico." *Mexican Studies/Estudios Mexicanos*, 16(2): 267–87.

Levy, Jack S. 1988. "Domestic Politics and War." In *The Origin and Prevention of Major Wars*, edited by Robert I. Rotberg and Theodore K. Rabb. Cambridge: Cambridge University Press: 79–100.

Linz, Juan, and Amando de Miguel. 1966. "Within-Nation Differences and Comparisons: The Eight Spains." In *Comparing Nations: the Use of Quantitative Data in Cross-National Research*, edited by Richard Merritt and Stein Rokkan. New Haven: Yale University Press.

Lyon, Alynna, and Christopher Dolan. 2007. "American Humanitarian Intervention: Toward a Theory of Coevolution." *Foreign Policy Analysis* 3: 146–78.

Mansfield, Edward and Jack Snyder. 2005. *Electing to Fight: Why Emerging Democracies Go to War*. Cambridge, MA: MIT Press.

Mansfield, Edward D., and Jack Snyder. 1995. "Democratization and the Danger of War." *International Security* 20: 5–38.

Maoz, Zeev, and Bruce Russett. 1993. "Normative and Structural Causes of Democratic Peace, 1946–1986." *American Political Science Review* 87: 624–38.

McFaul, Michael. 2002. "The Fourth Wave of Democracy *and* Dictatorship: Noncooperative Transitions in the Postcommunist World." *World Politics*, 54(1): 212–44.

Mousseau, Michael. 2005. "Comparing New Theory with Prior Beliefs: Market Civilization and the Democratic Peace." *Conflict Management and Peace Science* 22: 63–77.

Mousseau, Demet Yakin. 2001. "Democratizing with Ethnic Divisions: A Source of Conflict?" *Journal of Peace Research*, 38(5): 547–67.

Navia, Patricio and Zweifel, Thomas D. 2003. "Democracy, Dictatorship, and Infant Mortality Revisited." Journal of Democracy 14 (3): 90–103.Nye, Joseph S., Jr. 2001. "Globalization's Democratic Deficit: How to Make International Institutions More Accountable." *Foreign Affairs*, 80(4): 2–6.

O'Donnell, Guillermo. 2001. "Democracy, Law and Comparative Politics." *Studies in Comparative International Development*, 36(1): 7–36.

O'Donnell, Guillermo. 1999. "On the State, Democratization, and Some Conceptual Problems: A Latin American View with Some Postcommunist Countries." In *Counterpoints*, edited by Guillermo O'Donnell, 133–57. South Bend: University of Notre Dame Press.

Oneal, John R., and Bruce Russett. 1999. "The Kantian Peace: The Pacific Benefits of Democracy, Interdependence, and International Organizations, 1885–1992." *World Politics* 52: 1–37.

Oneal, John R., Bruce Russett, and Michael L. Berbaum. 2003. "Causes of Peace: Democracy, Interdependence, and International Organizations, 1885–1992." *International Studies Quarterly* 47: 371–93.

Przeworski, Adam. 1991. *Democracy and the Market: Political and Economic Reforms in Eastern Europe and Latin America*. New York: Cambridge University Press.

Przeworski, Adam, and Fernando Limongi. 1993. "Political Regimes and Economic Growth." *The Journal of Economic Perspectives* 7(3): 51–69.

Reiter, Dan, and Allan C. Stam. 2002. *Democracies at War*. Princeton: Princeton University Press.

Rokkan, Stein. 1970. *Citizens, Elections, Parties: Approaches to the Comparative Study of the Process of Development*. New York: David McKay Company.

Rosato, Sebastian. 2003. "The Flawed Logic of Democratic Peace Theory." *American Political Science Review* 97: 585–602.

Rosecrance, Richard. 1986. *The Rise of the Trading State: Commerce and Conquest in the Modern World*. New York: Basic Books.

Ruiz-Franzia, Manuel. 2006. "Oaxaca's Embattled Governor Keeps a Tenuous Hold on Power." *Washington Post*, November 1. Accessed May 10, 2010 www.washingtonpost.com/wpdyn/content/article/2006/11/01/AR2006110100146.html.

Rummel, Rudolph J. 1997. *Power Kills: Democracy as a Method of Nonviolence*. New Brunswick, NJ: Transaction Publishers.

Rummel, R. J. 1995. "Democracy, Power, Genocide, and Mass Murder." *Journal of Conflict Resolution* 39(1): 3–26.

Rupert, Mark. 2000. *Ideologies of Globalization: Contending Visions of a New World Order*. London: Routledge.

Russett, Bruce. 2001. "How Democracy, Interdependence, and International Organizations Create a System for Peace." In *The Global Agenda (6th edition)*, edited by Charles W. Kegley, Jr., and Eugene Wittkopf. Boston: McGraw-Hill.

Russett, Bruce, and John Oneal. 1997. "The Classic Liberals Were Right: Democracy, Interdependence, and Conflict, 1950–1985." *International Studies Quarterly* 41: 267–93.

Russett, Bruce M., John Oneal, and Michael Berbaum. 2003. "Causes of Peace: Democracy, Interdependence, and International Organizations, 1885–1992." *International Studies Quarterly* 47: 371–93.

Sartori, Giovanni. 1995. "How Far Can Free Government Travel?" *Journal of Democracy* 6(3): 101–11.

Seligson, Mitchell A. 1987. "Development, Democratization, and Decay: Central America at the Crossroads." *Authoritarians and Democrats*, edited by James M. Malloy and Mitchell Seligson, 167–92. Pittsburgh: University of Pittsburgh Press.

Shin, Doh Chull. 2004. "On the Third Wave of Democracy: A Synthesis and Evaluation of Recent Theory and Research." *World Politics* 47: 135–70.

Smith, Peter. 1995. *Democracy in Latin America: Political Change in Comparative Perspective.* New York: Oxford University Press.

Smith, Peter H. 2000. *Talons of the Eagle: Dynamics of U.S.-Latin American Relations (2nd edition).* New York: Oxford University Press.

Snyder, Richard. 2001. "Scaling Down: Subnational Approaches to Comparative Politics." *Studies in Comparative International Development* 36(1): 93–110.

Van Belle, Douglas A. 1997. "Press Freedom and the Democratic Peace." *Journal of Peace Research* 34(4): 405–14.

Weart, Spencer R. 1998. *Never at War.* New Haven: Yale University Press.

Weede, Erich. 2004. "The Diffusion of Prosperity and Peace by Globalization." *The Independent Review* 9: 165–86.

Weiss, Thomas G. 2007. *Humanitarian Intervention.* Cambridge: Polity Press.

Weyland, Kurt. 2004. "Neoliberalism and Democracy in Latin America: A Mixed Record." *Latin American Politics and Society,* 46(1): 135–57.

Zweifel, Thomas and Patricio Navia. 2000. "Democracy, Dictatorship, and Infant Mortality." *Journal of Democracy* 11(2): 99–114.

To measure public attitudes towards democracy, the Latin American Public Opinion Project has gone door to door for almost four decades, conducting face-to-face interviews.

3

Explaining Democratization

Mary Fran T. Malone

> *What do we now know about the causes of democratization that we did not know nearly 50 years ago when Seymour Martin Lipset (1959) wrote his famous article linking development with democracy? The answer is: surprisingly little.*
>
> (*Geddes* 2009, 278)

In a recent article, leading scholar Barbara Geddes frankly assesses the field of comparative democracy, and points out that even after decades of research, political scientists have not conclusively identified the principal causes of democratization. The development of one grand theory to explain democratic development has proven elusive. As Geddes (2009) points out in a section aptly titled "Things We Used to Know but Now Aren't So Sure About," if anything, the large amount of scholarship produced has undermined traditional notions about democratization and its causes, but has not established a replacement. Why is this the case? Why do we know so little, after so much time and so many studies?

There are several reasons for this impasse. For example, a review of the democratization literature reveals that scholars have used different definitions and measurements of democracy. Furthermore, scholars have tested theories of democratization using different methodologies and cases. More importantly, beyond these issues of research design, the nature of democracy itself has changed dramatically over time. As the chapters in this edited volume explain, contemporary understandings of democratic governance differ dramatically from those of the past. When, for example, scholars examine the democratic trailblazers (e.g., the United States and Great Britain), they focus on explaining the emergence of a very limited type of democracy. Voting rights originally extended only to adult men, and frequently property restrictions also prevailed. In contrast, when we try to explain the emergence of the more recent third wave democracies, the term democracy includes, at a minimum, universal adult suffrage. Given the often violent contestation surrounding expansions of political franchise, it is arguably easier to establish a limited democracy of male property owners than it is to create a full democracy for the adult population as a whole, including men and women of all races, ethnicities, economic classes, and religions. Theories that explain the appearance of the very limited democracies of the 1800s might prove inadequate to explain the emergence of democracy with universal adult suffrage in the 1990s.

Geddes (2009) argues that the causes of democratization will also vary according to the characteristics of the old regime, as well as the features of the international political economy. More specifically, "democratization occurs through several different processes, depending on basic features of the economy from which the autocracy draws resources, international economic and political pressures that have varied over time, and characteristics of the old regime itself" (Geddes 2009, 293). In other words, there are several different paths to democracy, and in order to understand why some countries take one path as opposed to others, it is imperative to first identify some key characteristics of the old authoritarian government, as well as of the contemporary global economy. These different starting points can explain why theories of democratization explain some cases but not others.

This book does not offer a definitive answer to the long-standing question of what causes democracy. Instead, it provides students with the tools they need to engage in the debate and test the theories of democratization themselves. To help with this enterprise, this chapter begins by discussing definitions and measurements of democracy. It then provides an overview of the prominent theories of democracy and discusses how these theories have been empirically tested. The goal of this chapter is to provide a strong theoretical foundation to guide students' examination of the empirical evidence offered through the country case studies that follow.

Defining and measuring democracy

To begin, it is helpful to remind ourselves what exactly studies of democratization aim to demonstrate. Quite simply, "democratization" refers to "political changes moving in a democratic direction" (Potter 1997, 3). When scholars study democratization, they are typically trying to identify the factors that cause a democratic regime to emerge. Political scientists rely upon a specific terminology in these studies. They call democracy the *dependent variable*, or the outcome they are trying to explain. The factors they think might cause democracy to emerge are called the *independent variables*. Scholars then develop *hypotheses* to link specific independent variables to the dependent variable of democracy. For example, in an early seminal work, Lipset (1959) developed modernization theory, which linked (among other things) education to democracy (Lipset 1959). To test this theory, Lipset developed a hypothesis, testing whether "the better educated the population of a country, the better the chances for democracy" (Lipset 1959, 78). In addition to stating this hypothesis, Lipset also stipulated the *causal mechanism,* or the specific process by which education affects democracy. He argued that education increases the chances for democracy because it "broadens men's outlooks, enables them to understand the need for norms of tolerance, restrains them from adhering to extremist and monistic doctrines, and increases their capacity to make rational electoral choices" (Lipset, 1959, 79).

With just these few simple steps, some problems arise. First, are we interested in explaining why democracies emerge in the first place? Or how they become consolidated, or "the only game in town"? Linz and Stepan (1996) explain how these are two very different things. When democracies first emerge, they are said to be in transition. During this period of transition, political development is quite fluid, and initial democratic gains are subject to reversal. In contrast, when there is widespread consensus among elites and the mass public that democracy is the only legitimate form of governance, democracy is said to be consolidated. There is no real rival regime type. Democracy studies (and their subsequent results) will vary depending upon whether we want to know what causes democracy to appear in the first place, versus what causes democracy to be sustainable over the long haul. For example, Przeworski, Cheibub, and Limongi (2000) argue that economic development does not cause countries to become democratic in the first place; however, once democracy is established, higher levels of economic development make reversals to dictatorship less likely.

Scholars have also disagreed when defining their dependent variable, democracy. By democracy, do we mean just free and fair elections? Or should we take additional elements into account, like the standard of living of a democracy's citizens, or the degree of economic equality? Not only have definitions of democracy differed over time and place, scholars have difficulty agreeing on a definition for one time and place. Democratic theorists have engaged in heated discussions about these issues, with some preferring *minimum* definitions of democracy that center on elections, citizens' rights and liberties, and government accountability, while others prefer more *encompassing* definitions that incorporate more elements of equality.[1] In this debate, Dahl's work features prominently and forms a crucial part of the classical cannon of democratic theory. Among his many influential writings, Dahl's *Democracy and Its Critics* (1989) differentiates between the ideal of democracy, which is a theoretical utopia, and the practical reality of what typically passes as democratic governance. Dahl terms the latter a polyarchy, and identifies its crucial characteristics. Under Dahl's polyarchy, the government officials who control policy are chosen through free and fair elections based on inclusive suffrage. Citizens have the right to run for office, and there is widespread respect for freedom of expression, as well as access to alternative information and associational autonomy.

Reviewing this debate over the many conceptualizations of democracy, Sodaro identifies several fundamental principles that most democratic theorists agree "are absolutely essential for a system of government to be considered democratic" (Sodaro 2004, 165). These include:

- **The Rule of Law:** "the principle that the power of the state must be limited by law and that no one is above the law" (Sodaro 2004, 165).
- **Inclusion:** democratic rights (e.g., the right to vote) and freedoms (e.g., freedom of expression) are ubiquitous and are for everyone; they cannot be denied to "specifically targeted elements of the population, such as women or minority groups" (Sodaro 2004, 165).
- **Equality:** democratic rights and freedoms are accorded "to everyone on an equal basis. No group in society should have fewer democratic privileges than other groups" (Sodaro 2004, 167).

Sodaro focuses on the minimal elements a political system must have in order to wear the democratic label. To be sure, some theorists would argue that these elements are necessary, but not sufficient, for democratic governance. Hopefully students will join in these arguments, and think critically themselves about what is essential for democracy to exist. At the very least, these three elements establish a minimal threshold. A political system is not a true democracy if it systematically fails to uphold the rule of law, democratic rights and liberties, or equality.

If we rely upon Sodaro's concise definition of democracy, we now face the task of how to measure democracy. That is, based upon this definition, which countries (or subnational regions or cities) are democratic, and which ones are not? How can we use this definition to recognize democracy when we see it? For scholars who rely upon quantitative methodologies such as statistical analysis for their theory testing, these questions of measurement are crucial. There are many, many attempts to establish objective measures that indicate the degree to which a country upholds democracy. Not surprisingly, these attempts encounter numerous problems. These measurement problems do not mean we should dismiss such attempts automatically. In some cases this might be appropriate, but in others, we may be able to use the available data wisely and carefully once we understand its limitations.

Three commonly used measures of democracy are provided by the Freedom House Organization, the Polity IV Project, and the World Bank's Governance Indicators.[2] Freedom House, for example, provides both qualitative and quantitative measures of democracy in each country around the world, from 1972 to the present. Among other publications, Freedom House publishes an annual review of democracy around the world in its *Freedom in the World* reports. This annual publication includes country reports, which provide a qualitative overview of the quality of governance in each country, grounding current practices in historic trends. Relying upon multiple sources, Freedom House also grades each country with a numeric score, providing a quantitative indicator of governance based upon how well the country upholds democratic norms. Freedom House uses these quantitative scores to group countries into three categories: free, partly free, and not free. On one hand, it is very useful to have these empirical measures of democratic governance. On the other, these indicators sometimes demonstrate how difficult it is to measure democracy, and why such scores should be treated with caution.

An extreme case perhaps illustrates this point most clearly. In 1972, Freedom House struggled to classify the regime of South Africa. As Chapter 12 explains, during this time South Africa was ruled by a system of apartheid, wherein the black majority (comprising roughly 80 percent of the population) had no political rights and suffered under the hands of the white minority, which enjoyed full political rights and frequently participated in democratic elections. Freedom House gave South Africa two separate scores for this year, noting: "For 1972, South Africa was rated as "White"

(2,3 Free) and "Black" (5,6 Not Free)."[3] While we appreciate the difficulty Freedom House researchers faced in trying to characterize such a regime, if democratic rights were denied to 80 percent of the population, it is hard to think of such a country as a democracy at all. From 1973–93 Freedom House rated South Africa with only one designation, which was "partly free" for every year except 1982 (when it was designated "not free"). Again, it is hard to think of a regime that systematically repressed 80 percent of its citizens as even partially free or democratic, but it is clear that Freedom House was trying to account for the presence of some democratic rights and liberties extended to a small part of the population. This would distinguish South Africa from a dictatorship like the Soviet Union, where no segment of the population enjoyed democratic rights and liberties. This example aims to illustrate the challenges that emerge when scholars try to measure the level of democracy in a country. This does not mean the practice should be abandoned altogether, or that one organization in particular should be shunned. Rather, this example underscores the need to be very careful when grading the presence or absence of democracy, or using such measures in hypothesis-testing exercises.

Overview of democratic theory

Once scholars decide on a definition and measurement of the dependent variable, democracy, they must turn to specifying and defining their independent variables. To identify the variables that lead to democratic outcomes, scholars consult a large body of democratic theory. Indeed, efforts to determine what factors give rise to democratic governance date back to Aristotle. This section reviews the principal theoretical arguments of this large body of literature, providing an overview of the major theories of democracy. Students will test these theories with evidence from country case studies in the subsequent chapters. In testing these theories, it is important to remember that in social science, very rarely do our objects of inquiry have one cause. That is, it is next to impossible to say only one independent variable causes the dependent variable to occur. In reality, when we try to explain outcomes like democratization, these phenomena are always attributable to several factors. Oftentimes these factors, or independent variables, are also linked. For example, elites can interact with their respective political institutions to shape political development. Overly simplistic theories of democratization, relying on one causal factor, will not be helpful in trying to explain what is a complex political process.

Economic development

When Lipset published his now classic work, "Some Social Requisites of Democracy" in 1959, he set the stage for the contemporary study of comparative democratization. Lipset's work is the foundation for the modernization approach to democracy, which argues that democracy is strongly linked to a country's level of socioeconomic development. To explain the emergence and survival of democracy, Lipset focused on national levels of wealth, industrialization, urbanization, and education. Across these multiple indicators, Lipset found that, "In each case, the average wealth, degree of industrialization and urbanization, and level of education is much higher for the more democratic countries" (Lipset 1959, 75). Thus, there are social and economic prerequisites for successful democratic governance. To explain these correlations, Lipset identified the various mechanisms by which socioeconomic development can determine democratic development. For example, he pointed to the ways in which higher levels of wealth can shape the attitudes of social classes. For the poor and working classes, economic development means "increased income, greater economic security, and higher education," which in turn "permit those in this status to develop longer time perspectives and more complex and gradualist views of politics" (Lipset 1959, 83). If the lower classes are "relatively well-to-do" they will be more inclined to support moderate, reformist ideologies instead of extreme ones. They have some stake in the status quo. This higher standard of living for the lower classes, particularly higher levels of wealth and education, also promote democracy by integrating the lower classes into the national culture and exposing them to middle class values, instead of creating "an isolated lower class" culture (Lipset 1959, 83).

Lipset also pointed to the ways in which economic development fostered democracy by reducing inequality, noting that increased wealth changes "the shape of the stratification structure so that it shifts from an elongated pyramid, with a large lower-class base, to a diamond with a growing middle-class" (Lipset 1959, 83). High levels of inequality can deter democratic development in several ways. First, in poor countries the lower classes tend to have abysmal standards of living. This leads the upper classes to treat the poor as an inferior caste in order to justify the sharp difference in living standards. Sharp inequality conditions the attitudes of both the rich and poor:

> Consequently, the upper strata also tend to regard political rights for the lower strata, particularly the right to share in power, as essentially absurd

and immoral. The upper strata not only resist democracy themselves, but their often arrogant political behavior serves to intensify extremist reactions on the part of the lower classes. (Lipset 1959, 83–84)

According to Lipset, income inequality can also derail democracy by depriving it of a crucial advocate—the middle class. Lipset envisioned the middle class as a natural advocate of democracy, playing a "mitigating role in moderating conflict since it is able to reward moderate and democratic parties and penalize extremist groups" (Lipset 1959, 83).

The importance of the middle class was trumpeted by another famous democratic theorist, Barrington Moore, who argued quite famously that the middle class, or bourgeoisie, was the champion of democracy (Moore 1966). Pointing to the historic linkage between the growth of a middle class and the demand for greater representation, Moore succinctly stated, "No bourgeoisie, no democracy" (Moore 1966, 418). The bourgeoisie relies upon its own economic base, grounded in private enterprise, and chafes against the concentration of political power in the hands of the traditional upper class, the landed aristocracy. According to this line of reasoning, when the middle class is sufficiently large and strong enough, it will seek to protect its economic interests through the rule of law and accountable government. The bourgeoisie will "want a say in how the government deals with property rights, taxes, business regulations, and so on[; this] is what popular sovereignty is all about[;] democracy emerges as a mechanism for protecting property rights" (Sodaro 2004, 214). Furthermore, the middle class stake in private enterprise leads it to value economic freedoms as well as the corresponding political freedoms.

Thus, when examining the linkage between economic and democratic development, scholars have noted the importance of national wealth, income equality, a large middle class, and private enterprise. The theoretical arguments linking these factors to democracy are persuasive. However, decades of research and empirical evidence (particularly from developing countries) have challenged this conventional wisdom. As Huntington points out:

The relation between economic development, on the one hand, and democracy and democratization, on the other, is complex and probably varies in time and space. Economic factors have significant impact on democratization, but they are not determinative. An overall correlation exists between the level of economic development and democracy yet no level or pattern of economic development is in itself either necessary or sufficient to bring about democratization. (Huntington 1991, 59)

Scholars have observed that in developing countries, instead of promoting democracy, economic growth could actually *reverse* democratic gains. O'Donnell (1973) noted that in South America, the industrializing countries with higher levels of economic development were more susceptible to political instability and democratic breakdown. The very processes of economic development can raise citizens' expectations, stimulate demand for income redistribution, and consequently exacerbate socioeconomic divisions. The collapse of democracy in the Southern Cone in the 1970s, particularly in the democratic success story of Chile, lent a great deal of empirical weight to this view. During the third wave of democracy, once again Latin American regimes defied predictions of modernization theory, as democracies emerged and survived despite "widespread poverty, terrible inequalities, and (in most countries) bad economic performance" (Mainwaring and Hagopian 2005, 5).

In other global regions, scholars have worried that the type of economic development could undermine democratization. In countries that rely overwhelmingly on natural resources like oil for their economic development, elites can use riches not to foster prerequisites to democracy, but rather to buy off potential opponents and maintain an iron grip on power. Called *rentier state theory*, this line of reasoning has been widely used to explain the lack of democratic development in many Middle Eastern countries. As Geddes notes, however, "controversy continues about whether these are causal relationships or correlations explained by something else. Among those who believe relationships are causal, there are disagreements about the processes through which the causes produce the outcome" (Geddes 2009, 279).[4]

More recent scholarship has found the relationship between economic development and democracy varies depending upon the historic period. In a quantitative study of countries from 1850–1990, Boix and Stokes argue that "before 1925 development contributed powerfully to democratization," but after 1950 the effects of economic development dwindle (Boix and Stokes 2003, 531). For Geddes, this difference suggests "the causes of democratization might differ depending on levels of state ownership in the economy" (Geddes 2009, 288). During the "Long Century," many candidates for democratization also had market economies that protected private ownership and enterprise. In these cases, democratization "may have occurred through the kinds of processes identified by Lipset. . . . [A]s more citizens became educated, joined the middle class, and went to work in factories, they demanded the vote" (Geddes, 2009, 287). In contrast, later waves of democracy occurred against a backdrop of high levels of state intervention and/or ownership in the economy. In these latter cases, "educated, ambitious citizens who might have led the demand for democratization according to modernization theory were often accommodated by mid-twentieth century autocracies" (Geddes 2009, 288). Thus, in order to understand the connection between economic development and democracy, it is important to first establish the type of economy in place under authoritarian rule, and the incentives this economic order gave citizens and elites to either advocate or oppose democratic reforms.

In a different vein, another group of scholars has disputed the notion that the middle class is the democratic cheerleader. Rueschemeyer, Stephens, and Stephens (1992) highlight the historic role of the working classes in promoting democracy, particularly by advocating extensions of suffrage and associational autonomy (i.e., to join unions). This line of research underscores the importance of examining interactions among classes, arguing that "the position of any one class on democratization cannot be considered in isolation from others; various class alliances can occur in different countries which can be more or less favourable to democratization" (Potter 1997, 21). Thus, economic development can influence democratization because it changes class alignments, as well as the political incentives of these classes. This is not to say that capitalist private enterprise will necessarily promote democracy. As Sodaro notes, "Communist China today combines a vibrant private sector with unrelenting one-party dictatorship. It is still not entirely evident that the expansion of private enterprise in that country is stimulating pressures for democracy; to some extent it may actually be buttressing communist rule" (Sodaro 2004, 214). Sodaro's observation highlights the importance of examining how elites manage the processes of economic development, and the strategic choices elites face when deciding which paths of political reform to follow.

Elites

There is widespread agreement that elites are the principal actors during regime transitions. Scholars have emphasized the role of elites in different ways, however.[5] Some scholars have grounded their study of elites in the first wave of democracy, where they argue that interactions among a small group of elites eventually led to an elite culture that prioritized the norms of competitive politics, such as bargaining and compromise. Since these elites came from similar socioeconomic backgrounds, and often even had familial ties, severe conflict was constrained. In this setting, elites gradually developed norms of political interaction that were conducive to democracy, and these norms served as the basis for socializing newly franchised citizens as more people became eligible to participate politically.

Scholars focusing on later waves of democracy typically view the relationship between elites and democracy in a slightly different way. For example, in a seminal work on the third wave transitions, O'Donnell, Schmitter, and Whitehead (1986) analyzed the choices and strategic interactions of elites, and the ways in which these interactions were conducive to democracy, or not. Geddes (2009) expands this line of research, arguing that in order to understand motives for supporting or blocking democracy, it is important to examine the sources of elite power under authoritarianism. Is the authoritarian regime ruled by a military junta, for example? Or by a monarchy? The type of authoritarian regime will give elites different "backgrounds, support bases, and resources" and consequently create different incentives for democratization (Geddes 2009, 291). For example, O'Donnell, Schmitter, and Whitehead (1986) find military elites often initiate political reform. Negotiating a transition to democracy gives the military a good exit strategy, allowing them to return to the barracks before divisive infighting erodes their unified front. This facilitates the military's ability to negotiate favorable terms for itself under the new democratic regime (such as amnesty agreements), and return to their old jobs.

Elites whose power resides in hegemonic parties can also find reasons to democratize. Hegemonic party elites typically resist democratization as long as their power permits, but if they find themselves unable to fend off reform (i.e., economic crisis dries up patronage funds), democratization is a tolerable consolation prize. Hegemonic parties, such as Mexico's *Partido Revolucionario Institucional* (PRI), can still retain some political power by competing in subsequent democratic elections.

In contrast, Geddes (2009) argues that dictators who rely on cults of personality and tightly concentrated political power have virtually no incentives for pursuing democracy. Personalist dictators, like North Korea's Kim Jong-Il, have only one basis for their political and economic power—their complete personal control. A transition to democracy would typically destroy a dictator's base of economic and political power, making it an extremely costly venture with no reward. Indeed, oftentimes the former dictator does not have the political or economic clout to ward off prosecutions for human rights abuses and/or corruption.

When assessing elite commitment to democratic norms, as well as the strategic incentives elites have to democratize, it is helpful to group political elites into two groups—those who are willing to bargain and negotiate, and those who are not. This distinction is helpful when looking at both the

Table 3.1 Possible interactions between authoritarian and opposition elites

	Authoritarian regime	
Opposition	Moderates, Hardliners	Moderates, Softliners
	Radicals, Hardliners	Radicals, Softliners

authoritarian elites in power, as well as elites in opposition. The elites of the authoritarian regime who are willing to negotiate at least some political reform are known as "softliners," while elites holding fast to authoritarian rule and rejecting reform are called "hardliners." In the opposition camp, the elites who are willing to negotiate with the outgoing authoritarians are "moderates," as opposed to the "radicals" who demand major change and reject compromise. As Table 3.1 illustrates, the chances for democratization are stronger when softliners dominate the authoritarian government and moderates lead the opposition.

In sum, there are several ways in which to link elites to democratization. First, elites must be willing to adhere to democratic norms. If such democratic norms are not heartfelt, there must be some incentives pushing elites to the negotiating table. When making their strategic calculations about whether to democratize, authoritarian elites must find democracy to be at least a viable option for maintaining some remnants of their political and/or economic power. Second, elites have to find willing partners on the other side of the table. Even with incentives for authoritarians to democratize, reforms will fall flat if there is not a sympathetic ear in the opposition camp. Thus, the opposition's power and motivations are also important. Is the opposition powerful enough to govern alone? Or does it need to have some allies in the former authoritarian camp? Such allies need not be exclusively elites: the mass public and civil society can also be valuable partners.

Political culture and civil society

Theorists have long argued that there is a connection between the attitudes and actions of average citizens and the type of government these citizens have. In his famous tour of America, De Tocqueville (1835) focused squarely on American culture to understand why democracy thrived in the United States yet flopped in France. Since that time, several political scientists have argued that a country's regime type reflects fundamental characteristics of its citizens. These fundamental characteristics are referred to as political culture, or "a people's predominant beliefs, attitudes, values, ideals, sentiments, and evaluations about the political system of their country and the role of the self in that system" (Diamond 1999, 163). Given the important role reserved for citizen participation in democratic governance, it stands to reason that citizens' attitudes and behaviors can in some way influence the existence and quality of democratic governance.

In a groundbreaking study of political culture, Almond and Verba argued that a "stable and effective democratic government depends upon more than the structures of government and politics: it depends upon the orientations that people have to the political process—upon political culture" (Almond and Verba 1963, 366). To understand the relationship between political culture and democracy, Almond and Verba examined civic attitudes in five countries of varying levels of development: the United States, Great Britain, Italy, Germany, and Mexico. Almond and Verba's pioneering work has evolved into an expansive and multifaceted field of global public opinion research.[6] Global, regional, and national surveys help us understand political culture around the globe. For example, the World Values Surveys, Afrobarometer, Arab Barometer, Asian Barometer, and the Latin American Public Opinion Project (LAPOP) all gauge political culture through a series of survey questions about people's attitudes toward their government, fellow citizens, elected officials, democracy, and specific policies. Surveys also measure participation in political processes (e.g., voting, protest, campaigning) as well as participation in communities.

What attitudes are important? A democratic political culture has widespread support for democracy as a form of government but also values its norms of tolerance, compromise, and respect for the law. Support for gradual reform as opposed to violent and radical change is also important. Citizens should regard their government as legitimate and see at least some value and efficacy in political participation. A democratic political culture is one in which the people have at least a moderate amount of trust in political institutions, especially the nonpolitical institutions of the courts and police (Rothstein and Stolle 2008). Political culture hypotheses also stress the importance of citizens' interactions with each other. For example, do people trust their neighbors and members of broader society? Finally, a modicum of civic competence is needed. Citizens must have at least a rudimentary knowledge of how their government works so they can participate in politics, even at a minimum level. They should also be able to follow the platforms of candidates and parties.

Scholars emphasizing the importance of political culture do not discount other explanations for democratization. For example, Inglehart (1990) considers political culture to be an important link between development and democracy. While many theorists argue that political culture is important for democracy, contemporary mainstream scholarship avoids overly simplistic applications of political culture theory, whereby political culture is the primary causal determinant of political structures. Such explanations are generally not very helpful in understanding political development. First, political culture is not uniform throughout any country. For example, important variations exist among geographic regions, ethnic groups, and different institutional settings. Diamond notes: "It may even be argued that differences in basic culture biases are often greater within nations than between them" (Diamond 1999, 163–64). Second, the relationship between political culture and political development is reciprocal—causality runs in both directions. Political culture can influence political structures, but then political structures in turn shape political culture. Indeed, some parts of political culture, such as trust in political institutions, are quite malleable and respond to "regime performance, historical experience, and political socialization" (Diamond 1999, 164).

There are additional reasons why the connection between political culture and democracy is not straightforward. In a 1984 study of attitudes in authoritarian Mexico, Booth and Seligson (1984) found Mexicans were very supportive of democratic norms, in some cases on a par with their counterparts in democratic parts of the world, like New York City. However, the Mexican government proved adept at co-opting these values, channeling and misdirecting them through government-controlled organizations and corrupt elections.

Seligson and Booth (2009) provide a very useful analogy for understanding how political culture can shape a country's form of government. They describe the relationship between public opinion and regime type as being similar to weather forecasting: "Weather forecasters can tell very well whether the conditions are ripe for thunderstorms or tornadoes, but they cannot specify which towns or areas will get rain or suffer tornadic winds, or what hour the storms will come. Social scientists are in the same boat. . . ." (Seligson and Booth 2009, 1). Just as weather forecasters often cannot predict exactly when a storm will hit, studies of political culture typically cannot definitively predict whether a country will be democratic or not. Such studies can, however, identify whether a political culture is conducive to democracy. In a study of the 2009 military coup against the democratic government of Honduras, Seligson and Booth (2009) note that:

> Our public opinion data did not predict the Honduras democratic breakdown of 2009. They did, however identify Honduras as the single case in Latin America

with the highest level of triply dissatisfied citizens, with relatively low support for democracy and with high support for coups, confrontational political methods, and rebellion. Against this context of vulnerability—low consolidation of democratic norms and high dissatisfaction with government performance and institutions—local actors supplied the specific catalytic events that precipitated the breakdown. (Seligson and Booth 2009, 6)

Thus, the study of political culture can predict whether there is a greater or lesser likelihood of democratization. Political elites were the decisive actors in actively undermining democracy, but the political culture of Honduras facilitated such action, providing a fertile backdrop for undemocratic behavior.

Social capital theorists broaden the study of political culture to include citizens' participation in associations beyond the control of the state or civil society. Civil society organizations can range from bowling leagues to church groups, from interest groups to trade unions. De Tocqueville (1835) was an early social capital theorist, linking the success of American democracy to its vibrant network of civil society associations. In the more recent classic, *Making Democracy Work,* Putnam (1992) underscores the importance of civil society participation, linking civic engagement to successful democracy. When citizens participate in their communities, their civic engagement fosters interpersonal trust, norms of reciprocity, and the learning of organizational skills and social norms—all elements social capital theorists hypothesize can promote democracy. Thus, according to this theory, civil society participation creates "patterns of interaction that link society together at the grassroots level. . . . It is the social web that underlies democratic government, making it possible to limit the state's power and keeping it accountable to a self-organized citizenry" (Sodaro 2004, 217).

Education

In addition to public attitudes and behaviors, scholars have also highlighted the importance of citizens' education. Indeed, while modernization theory centered on economic development, it did acknowledge the significance of an important correlate, education. Lipset hypothesized that high levels of education and literacy create and sustain belief in democratic norms, as education broadens the outlooks of citizens and cultivates attitudes of tolerance. Lipset also argued that education restrains citizens "from adhering to extremist and monistic doctrines, and increases their capacity to make rational electoral choices" (Lipset, 1959, 79). The empirical evidence for the hypothesis linking education to democracy is quite strong. In addition to consistently robust correlations between national levels of education and democratic forms of government, survey data reliably report that, at the individual level, people with higher levels of education are more supportive of democracy and its norms.

Formal education also provides opportunities for socialization into political norms. Dewey (1916) was an early advocate for structuring education in a way to foster democracy. For example, he attributed the absence of democracy in Germany to its educational system, which he argued prioritized discipline and subordination to authorities over critical thinking. While Dewey's work has garnered much criticism, it does alert us to the importance of examining not just levels of education, but the nature of educational pedagogy and its accompanying socialization.

State institutions

Economic processes, and the reactions of elites and the public to these economic processes, provide the backbone of much of the research on democratization. However, all these forces operate within a defined institutional framework of governance. Political institutions set the rules of the game; they form the arena in which political players interact with one another. Thus, political institutions can shape democratic development in various ways. They can provide incentives for elite cooperation and the resolution of political disputes through democratic procedures and/or compromise. Alternatively, they can exacerbate political tensions by increasing the power of particular factions, creating too many political players, fostering instability, or failing to provide incentives for compromise and cooperation.

At the very basic level, to promote democracy political institutions must legitimately govern over a defined territory—this is a fundamental prerequisite of democracy. Linz and Stepan note that "Without a state . . . there can be no citizenship; without citizenship, there can be no democracy" (as quoted in Sodaro 2004, 208). Once political institutions establish their legitimate dominion over a territory, there are a variety of ways in which their design can facilitate or hinder democracy. In first wave democracies, some state institutions were amenable to democratic practices and evolved over time to provide a framework for modern democracy. For example, in Switzerland democratic practices in rural cantons were the building blocks for the eventual establishment of a democratic state. In many other democracies, particularly in the second and third waves, democratic institutions abruptly replaced authoritarian ones. In some cases authoritarian leaders felt pressured to acquiesce to opposition demands, negotiating *pacted* transitions to democracy. Under pacted transitions, authoritarians still retain some power, enabling them to leave their imprint on the new democratic system. In contrast, authoritarian toeholds are much weaker in other types of transitions, such as *revolutions from below*. In these cases, civil society provides the impetus for change, as broad-based mass movements shake "the foundations of authoritarian rule, confronting the discredited regime with pervasive—and potentially violent—unrest" (Sodaro 2004, 209). Sometimes reform-minded elites drive change, displacing their authoritarian counterparts and imposing *democratization from above*.

Some scholars hypothesize that the type of transition can determine the quality of new democratic institutions. In other words, the conditions under which countries become democratic can influence whether the new institutions are designed to uphold democracy and its norms or to preserve the power of one particular group. Of course, this invites the next question: What institutions are best capable of supporting democracy? For example: are presidential systems better than parliamentary ones? Are elections based on proportional representation better than winner-take-all? Should people vote for individual candidates or for political parties? Numerous debates have emerged concerning which institutional arrangements are best suited to promote democratic governance. In a classic work, Lijphart (1999) reviews the major institutions of democratic governance in 36 democracies, classifying them in terms of their consensus or majoritarian style. Lijphart finds that, overall, consensus democracies have the better track record, particularly when it comes to "the quality of democracy and democratic representation as well as with regard to . . . the kindness and gentleness of their public policy orientations" (Lijphart 1999, 301).[7] In a piece famous before it was even published, Linz (1990) argued that presidential democracies were far less stable than parliamentary ones. Linz's work sparked a series of debates throughout the field of comparative politics, a debate best showcased by three superb edited volumes that systematically compare the abilities of presidential and parliamentary governments to sustain democracy (Lijphart 1992, Linz and Valenzuela 1994, Mainwaring and Shugart 1997). Similar debates surround other institutions. For example, Diamond and Plattner's (2006) edited volume examines the connections between electoral systems and democracy from a variety of theoretical and empirical perspectives.

The lively debate surrounding which institutions are best reflects the importance scholars lend to institutional configurations. The diversity of opinions also underscores an important point: which institutions are "best" will hinge on national context. For example, what are the types of problems facing the country? What is the legacy of authoritarianism? What types of societal divisions define the country? Large countries with a great deal of geopolitical diversity might operate better under federal frameworks, for example. Countries with legacies of human rights violations typically need institutional remedies like strong judiciaries and expansive protections on individual rights and liberties. Furthermore, the government must be able to respond decisively to the needs of the population. In countries with severe problems, such as endemic poverty or soaring rates of violent crime, the government must be able to formulate effective policies to address the pressing needs of the country and its people. If institutions are susceptible to divided government or other types of gridlock, subsequent delays in formulating and implementing policy could lead to ineffective governance and a corresponding loss of legitimacy. Finally, institutional features need to be familiar to the population. That is, they should have some type of historical continuity or cultural tie to the people. For example, to foster a sense of legitimacy, contemporary democratization efforts in Afghanistan relied upon institutional frameworks like the *Jirga* to tie current political reforms to institutions of the past that are familiar to many Afghans.

National unity/social divisions

Scholars have also hypothesized that social divisions can reduce the chances for democracy's emergence and survival. Theorists like Rustow (1970) have argued that national unity is a precondition for democracy—if the people are to participate in governance, there must be consensus on who exactly "the people" are. This sense of national unity can be difficult to attain in countries that have polarizing divisions or cleavages. For example, many observers of contemporary efforts to promote democracy in Afghanistan have pointed to the problems posed by ethnic divisions, as some Afghans prioritize regional or ethnic identities over a national one. These polarizing divisions tend to be particularly problematic when there are overlapping cleavages—for example, when ethnic divides overlap with economic ones. To complicate matters further, some social divisions are more or less important at different historical periods. The political salience of racial, ethnic, religious, and economic divides rises and falls over time. Political elites frequently play an important role in these trends, using rhetoric and/or public policy to ameliorate or exacerbate social divides.

Some argue that social divisions can undermine democratization, an argument buttressed by several contemporary examples (like that of Afghanistan).

Still, the evidence is equivocal. Some countries find ways to make democracy work despite social divisions. For example, Lijphart (1968) used the case of the Netherlands to illustrate how elites were able to overcome possibly polarizing divisions in the first half of the twentieth century. To mitigate the effects of societal cleavages, elites devised a series of compromises to divvy up political power relatively equally among societal groups, an arrangement Lijphart called *consociational democracy*.

International context

Theories of democratization do not, however, focus solely on domestic factors. Particularly in third wave democracies, scholars have extensively assessed the role that international context plays in fostering or thwarting democratization. As Whitehead notes, almost "two-thirds of the democracies existing in 1990 owed their origins, at least in part, to deliberate acts of imposition or intervention from without" (Whitehead 2001, 9).[8]

There are several ways in which the international context can shape domestic democratization. First, there are major global events that can either facilitate or thwart democracy. The Cold War was one such event. During the Cold War, many countries found the quest for autonomous political development trapped in the crosshairs of the two superpowers. The Soviet Union brutally crushed pro-democracy movements throughout Eastern Europe. In places like Chile, democracy also fell casualty to the Cold War, as the United States labeled the economic policies of Chile's democratic government a communist threat, and supported a military coup. As the Cold War drew to a close, a very different international climate emerged. The implosion of the Soviet Union freed its many satellite countries to democratize, and new democracies sprouted all over Eastern Europe and in many republics of the Soviet Union itself. In the developing world, the United States relaxed its engagement in many cases, creating space for democratic reformers. Indeed, as Chapter 14 explains, the United States provided substantial aid to many of these democracy advocates.

The international context may shape domestic political development in additional ways. For example, some scholars have pointed to the diffusion effects of "living in a good neighborhood," as countries with many democratic neighbors are more prone to be democratic themselves. Pevehouse (2002) hypothesized that regional organizations (e.g., Organization of American States) may also facilitate democracy, as membership in regional organizations increases the likelihood of democratization, as long as most of the members are democratic.

The international economy also affects prospects for democracy. For example, Weyland (2009) argues that today's international consensus surrounding neoliberal reforms has facilitated democratization in the developing world. The global acceptance of free market principles has reassured economic elites that their capital will not be subject to nationalization, or even to high rates of taxation. The virtual elimination of rival economic models decreases political polarization, reassuring economic and military elites that democratic governments do not pose much threat to the status quo. Since elites do not have to fear government encroachments on their property, they are willing to sign off on democracy. Indeed, the need for foreign capital drastically constrains the viable choices available to elected officials, leading even leftist leaders to continue to strengthen market reforms. Thus, the consensus around free market reforms enhances the stability of democratic regimes.[9]

Conclusion

This book does not provide a clear and definitive answer to the question of what causes democracy. Instead, as illustrated by Table 3.2, this book outlines the major theories of democratization, and provides students with the tools to test these theories themselves.

Now that this chapter has introduced the major debates in the field of comparative democracy, we turn to examining specific cases. When we look

Table 3.2 Theories of democratization

Variables
Economic development
• National wealth
• Private enterprise
• Middle class
• Inequality
Elites
Political culture/civil society
Education
State institutions
Social divisions/national unity
International context

at a diverse group of successful democracies, what does the evidence tell us? It is important to remember that such hypothesis-testing exercises are not mechanical. One does not check independent variables (like middle class, GDP per capita, and international context) off a list. Rather, students need to explore the causal mechanisms that link the various independent variables to the dependent variable democracy. For example, "how" exactly did a middle class lead to a democracy? This emphasis on "how," rather than just on "what" reminds us these relationships are dynamic. It is not enough to observe that an independent variable and a dependent variable move in tandem. Instead, one must demonstrate that one variable in fact *causes* the other to occur. Causality goes beyond correlation. Strong causal arguments are sure to identify the causal mechanisms—"how" exactly does the independent variable affect the dependent variable of democracy? What are the mechanisms by which this relationship takes place? This focus on causal mechanisms is not just good social science, it is also important for contemporary policy making. For example, when appraising contemporary democracy-promotion efforts, politicians and pundits sometimes parrot phrases like "a middle class is essential for democracy" without understanding the dynamics of this relationship, and whether these same dynamics exist in all cases and time periods.

On a different note, it is also important to think about the way in which these theories of democratization are tested. For example, should we study the political development of a small number of cases in great depth? Or, should we use statistical analysis to examine many cases? This book relies upon a most different systems approach, selecting a group of very diverse cases that nonetheless are similar on the dependent variable—they have established and sustained successful democracies. This approach allows us to observe the historical processes of democratization in successful cases, and to identify what commonalities they share. It is important to remember, however, that this is just one approach among many. As discussed in the afterword of this book, there are a variety of other approaches to test these theories. These additional methodological approaches provide ways for us to "double check" our results and make sure that findings derived from one methodology can be replicated with others.

Notes

1 For a remarkably concise yet comprehensive overview of the many definitions of democracy, see Grugel (2002, 1–30)

2 These sources all make data readily accessible through their respective websites: Freedom House www.freedomhouse.org/template.cfm?page=15, Polity IV www.systemicpeace.org/polity/polity4.htm, Governance Indicators http://info.worldbank.org/governance/wgi/index.asp (all accessed September 10, 2010).

3 As stated on the Freedom in the World Comparative and Historical Data spreadsheet, www.freedomhouse.org/template.cfm?page=439 (accessed September 10, 2010).

4 In this volume, Chapter 13 assesses the utility of rentier state theory in explaining patterns of political development in the Middle East.

5 Diamond (1999, 172–74) provides a succinct overview of the evolution of the study of elites and democracy, as well as a critique of the different theoretical perspectives of elite actors.

6 For a thorough overview of the field, see Norris (2009).

7 Such policy orientations include social welfare expenditures, energy efficiency, incarceration rates, and foreign aid.

8 Whitehead (2001) identifies three possible ways in which international forces can influence democratic development: contagion (countries "catch" the democracy bug from their democratic neighbors); control (outside powers impose democratic institutions); and consent (willingness of domestic actors to accept democratic initiatives).

9 Still, Weyland emphasizes there are steep costs to this stability, as neoliberal reforms have simultaneously weakened popular sector organizations, contributing to declining rates of political participation and popular legitimacy. The result is a painful trade-off: 'market reform has bolstered the survival of democracy' while abridging the quality of it (Weyland 2009, 47).

References

Almond and Verba. 1963. *A Civic Culture: Political Attitudes in Five Western Democracies*. Princeton, NJ: Princeton University Press.

Boix, Carles, and Susan Stokes. 2003. "Endogenous Democratization." *World Politics* 55(4): 517–49.

Booth, John, and Mitchell Seligson. 1984. "The Political Culture of Authoritarianism in Mexico: A Reexamination." *Latin American Research Review* 19(l): 106–24.

Dahl, Robert. 1989. *Democracy and Its Critics*. New Haven: Yale University Press.

de Tocqueville, Alexis. 1835 [2004]. *Democracy in America*. New York: Bantam Dell.

Dewey, John. 1916. *Democracy and Education*. New York: The Free Press.

Diamond, Larry. 1999. *Developing Democracy: toward Consolidation*. Baltimore: The Johns Hopkins University Press.

Diamond, Larry, and Marc Plattner. 2006. *Electoral Systems and Democracy*. Baltimore: The Johns Hopkins University Press.

Geddes, Barbara. 2009. "Changes in the Causes of Democratization through Time." In *The SAGE Handbook of Comparative Politics*, edited by Todd Landman and Neil Robinson. Thousand Oaks, CA: SAGE Publications Ltd.

Grugel, Jean. 2002. *Democratization: a Critical Introduction*. New York: Palgrave.

Huntington, Samuel. 1991. *The Third Wave: Democratization in the Late Twentieth Century*. Norman: University of Oklahoma Press.

Inglehart, Ronald. 1990. *Culture Shift in Advanced Industrial Society*. Princeton, NJ: Princeton University Press.

Lijphart, Arend. 1999. *Patterns of Democracy: Governance Forms and Performance in Thirty-Six Countries*. New Haven: Yale University Press.

Lijphart, Arend. 1992. *Parliamentary Versus Presidential Government: Oxford Readings in Politics and Government*. New York: Oxford University Press.

Lijphart, Arend. 1968. *Politics of Accommodation: Pluralism and Democracy in the Netherlands*. Berkeley: University of California Press.

Linz, Juan. 1990. "The Perils of Presidentialism." *Journal of Democracy* 1(1): 51–69.

Linz, Juan, and Alfred Stepan. 1996. *Problems of Democratic Transition and Consolidation: Southern Europe, South America, and Post-Communist Europe*. Baltimore: Johns Hopkins University Press.

Linz, Juan, and Arturo Valenzuela. 1994. *The Failure of Presidential Democracy*. Baltimore: The Johns Hopkins University Press.

Lipset, Seymour M. 1959. "Some Social Requisites of Democracy: Economic Development and Political Legitimacy." *American Political Science Review* 53(1): 69–105.

Mainwaring, Scott, and Frances Hagopian. 2005. "Introduction: The Third Wave of Democratization in Latin America." In *The Third Wave of Democratization in Latin America: Advances and Setbacks*, edited by Frances Hagopian and Scott Mainwaring, 1–13. New York: Cambridge University Press.

Mainwaring, Scott, and Matthew Shugart. 1997. *Presidentialism and Democracy in Latin America: Cambridge Studies in Comparative Politics*. New York: Cambridge University Press.

Moore, Barrington. 1966. *Social Origins of Dictatorship and Democracy: Lord and Peasant in the Making of the Modern World*. Boston: Beacon Press.

Norris, Pippa. 2009. "The Globalization of Comparative Public Opinion Research." In *The SAGE Handbook of Comparative Politics*, edited by Todd Landman and Neil Robinson. Thousand Oaks, CA: SAGE Publications Ltd.

O'Donnell, Guillermo. 1973. *Modernization and Bureaucratic-Authoritarianism: Studies in South American Politics*. Berkeley: Institute of International Studies.

O'Donnell, Guillermo, Philippe C. Schmitter, and Laurence Whitehead. 1986. *Transitions from Authoritarian Rule: Latin America*. Baltimore: The Johns Hopkins University Press.

Pevehouse, Jon. 2002. "Democracy from the Outside-In? International Organizations and Democratization." *International Organization* 56(3): 515–49.

Potter, David. 1997. "Explaining Democratization." In *Democratization*, edited by David Potter, David Goldblatt, Margaret Kiloh and Paul Lewis, 1–40. Malden, MA: Blackwell Publishers, Inc.

Przeworski, Adam and M Alvarez, Jose Cheibub, and F. Limongi. 2000. *Democracy and Development: Political Institutions and Well-Being in the World 1950–1990*. Princeton, NJ: Princeton University Press.

Putnam, Robert, with Robert Leonardi and Raffaella Nanetti. 1992. *Making Democracy Work: Civic Traditions in Modern Italy*. Princeton, NJ: Princeton University Press.

Rothstein, Bo and Dietlind Stolle. 2008. "The State and Social Capital: An Institutional Theory of Generalized Trust." *Comparative Politics* 40(4): 441–59.

Rueschemeyer, Dietrich, Evelyne Huber Stephens, and John D. Stephens. 1992. *Capitalist Development and Democracy*. Oxford, UK: Polity Press.

Rustow, 1970. "Transitions to Democracy: toward a Dynamic Model." *Comparative Politics* 3: 337–63.

Seligson, Mitchell, and John Booth. 2009. "Predicting Coups? Democratic Vulnerabilities, the AmericasBarometer and the 2009 Honduran Crisis." AmericasBarometer Insights Series, 2009 Special Report on Honduras: 1–6. www.AmericasBarometer.org (accessed September 10, 2010).

Sodaro, Michael. 2004. *Comparative Politics: A Global Introduction (second edition)*. Boston: McGraw Hill.

Weyland, Kurt. 2009. "Neoliberalism and Democracy in Latin America: A Mixed Record." In *Latin American Democratic Transformations: Institutions, Actors, and Processes*, edited by William Smith. Malden, MA: Wiley-Blackwell.

Whitehead, Laurence. 2001. "Three International Dimensions of Democratization." In *The International Dimensions of Democratization: Europe and the Americas, Expanded Edition*. New York: Oxford University Press.

Section 2
First Wave of Democracy

4

The Development and Growth of British Democracy

Nicoletta F. Gullace

"No one allows a slave to share in happiness any more than in the life of a citizen"

—Aristotle[1]

"Rule Britannia! Britannia Rule the Waves. Britons never, never, never shall be slaves"

—Rule Britannia

Britain is heralded as one of the oldest and best-functioning democracies on the planet, yet its history of political democratization has often taken place against a backdrop of highly illiberal limits on popular participation. The Magna Carta (Great Charter), which the British regard as the foundation of

English liberties, was signed in 1215, making it one of Western Europe's oldest documents protecting civil rights. Yet the baronial councils (which foreshadowed the establishment of Parliament in the later Middle Ages) were in no way democratic in the popular sense (Prestwitch 1990). If the liberties enshrined in the Magna Carta theoretically applied to all Englishmen, in reality they protected the baronial class from royal encroachments. Even when the idea of popular sovereignty became a powerful intellectual force in the eighteenth century, few imagined it would extend to the empire, encompass the poorest men, or grant women the right to vote. Indeed, during the apex of empire in the early twentieth century, Britain enjoyed a degree of manhood suffrage at home, but gave little thought to extending democracy to nonwhite colonial subjects, many of whom were becoming increasingly restive for some form of popular self-government (Levine 2007).

For most of Britain's long history of democratization, elites protected their own liberties from centralized authority while doing little to extend participatory rights to the lower classes. In the case of Britain, it is therefore important to distinguish between "democratization" as a process of extending positive rights and liberties (such as taxation by consent, freedom of speech, right to fair trials, protection of private property, religious toleration, rule of law, and economic liberty) from "democratization" as a process of extending direct political participation in the form of universal suffrage to a broad spectrum of the population. As this chapter explains, democratization in Britain was an elite-led process that slowly and incrementally expanded suffrage under increased popular pressure, which intensified during the age of democratic revolutions. Significant electoral expansion began only with the Great Reform Bill of 1832. It did not conclude until 1948, with the end of plural voting for university graduates, which finally based British democracy on the principal of one person, one vote.

Economic expansion, particularly during the Industrial Revolution, greatly accelerated the process of democratization by creating new middle class elites eager to participate in self-government. During this period, Britain often used piecemeal democratization to avoid the perils of violent revolution. Reform bills extending the franchise were passed in the 1830s, 1860s, 1880s, during World War I, and in the 1920s, along with other significant legislation (offered to ameliorate the welfare of workers) passed at various times from the 1840s to the postwar period (Machin 2001). These bills coincided roughly with periods of turbulence at home and on the Continent, showing how the British deftly used parliamentary concessions to appease restive groups while avoiding the type of social upheaval experienced in other countries, such as France. Because from the 1830s onwards the British franchise was based largely on property qualifications, the British could extend the franchise incrementally by modifying these qualifications. The gradual nature of British enfranchisement prevented a radical shift in the democratic electorate at any one time, and the use of government to radically realign wealth did not take place until after World War II (Fraser 1973).

Because British democracy grew out of a concern for protecting aristocratic privilege, it had a libertarian cast, committed to principals of rule of law as well as freedom of speech and press. A commitment to freedom of religion took longer to establish, largely because of vitriolic anti-Catholicism, which grew out of the English Reformation, and a bureaucratic imperative to subordinate Irish Catholics to Protestant rule (Hind 1992). Beginning in 1828, however, Parliament began to extend religious freedoms, passing Catholic emancipation in 1829 and removing remaining discriminatory rules against dissenters and, eventually, Jews (McCord and Perdue 2007).

Britain's commitment to democracy was perhaps most vividly displayed during World War II, when the country stood alone against Hitler's Germany in a Europe where one democracy after another had succumbed to the pressures and allures of fascism. Following the war, Britain's colonial empire rapidly crumbled, and India, the "jewel in the crown" of the Victorian empire, established one of the most successful parliamentary democracies in the developing world—based on a British parliamentary model and made workable by the establishment, during the colonial era, of English as a common bureaucratic language (Dartford 1978). In 1948, the new postwar Labour government passed sweeping legislation acknowledging the citizenship rights of colonial British subjects and granting them open immigration to Britain. Massive influx from the Caribbean, India, and other Commonwealth countries gave rise to a conservative backlash as nativists tried to erode the entitlement of former colonial subjects to settle in the mother country. Responding to popular uproar during the 1960s, Parliament curbed the rights of nonwhite subjects to immigrate freely to Great Britain, creating a deeply fraught system of nationality, based implicitly on race (Paul 1997). As a result of having rights extended and revoked, many nonwhite Britons are skeptical about the universality of Britain's democratic claims.

Today, Britain remains a strong bastion of liberal democracy, despite the establishment of a postwar welfare state, the nationalization of several key industries, and the ascendancy of the Labour Party in the postwar era. Indeed, it is a testament to the persistence of the libertarian tradition that New Labour has moved away from its socialist roots toward a more centrist political agenda, while the Conservative Party of Margaret Thatcher (1979–90) successfully paraded "Victorian values" of low taxes, self-help, and small government (Reitan 2003). Significantly, the current Conservative government of David Cameron holds its parliamentary majority only through an alliance with the Liberal Democrats. Yet, despite the homage of every major political party to some form of classical Liberalism, Britain remains a monarchy. While Parliament's political agenda is prepared by the elected party in office and bears no relation to the will of the monarch, the retention of a crowned head of state shows that Britain's liberal democracy retains a sentimental homage to its feudal past.

Early origins of British democracy

The British constitutional system was built up incrementally for over a thousand years and remains largely unwritten. While documents such as the Magna Carta and the Bill of Rights make up an important part of the British Constitution, it also reflects a seemingly infinite number of legal judgments, customs, common laws and conventions that were inherited or grew up out of necessity over the last millennium (Dartford 1978).[2]

During the early Middle Ages, the executive, legislative, and judicial branches of government were all united in the person of the king. Democratization began with the slow process by which these powers were gradually delegated to others, and the king himself was forced to concede some authority to other noble lords (Prestwitch 1990). After the Norman Conquest of 1066, Anglo-Saxon England was tied into the feudal system. During this time under William the Conqueror, leading feudal lords and bishops made up part of the Great Council, which advised the king on important matters of policy (Dartford 1978; Prestwitch 1990).

With the Great Council, the king aimed to consolidate his power over the nobility and clergy and, through them, over the localities of his realm. Yet a concilliar body made up of powerful magnates always ran the risk of curbing the king's power as much as enhancing it. Under King John (1199–1216), humiliating military defeats and brutal domestic rule led to a baronial uprising, which resulted in John's being forced in 1215 to approve the Magna Carta, widely regarded as "the foundation stone of English liberties" (Dartford 1978, 4). The Magna Carta established that the king was not above the law, that no taxation should be levied without the consent of the Great Council, that every man had a right to trial, and that the Church should be independent. The Magna Carta also showed concern for the prosperity of the realm by calling for the establishment of fixed weights and measures and by maintaining privileges for London and other commercial centers. While the Magna Carta is heralded for its attention to individual rights, its provisions concerning feudal rights applied only to the tiny class of great barons. "It was their rights rather than those of the people at large which the charter was to protect" (Dartford 1978, 5). Baronial councils were in no broad sense democratic, but they were crucial linchpins in the process of dispersing political power and establishing the primacy of the rule of law (Keen 2000). Such councils also set the framework for the subsequent establishment of Parliament in the later Middle Ages.

The Tudor Revolution in government

If the British trace their democratic tradition back to the Magna Carta and the beginning of parliamentary ascendancy in the Middle Ages, democratization was abruptly halted with the charismatic and authoritarian rule of the Tudor dynasty. While "the king in England was often referred to as the Sovereign Lord[,] . . . in practice the power of the Medieval kings was always limited by law, by custom, and by geographical conditions" (Dartford 1978, 10). Throughout the Middle Ages, monarchs competed with strong regional lords as well as the Catholic Church, but under the Tudors the monarchy began to gain a decisive upper hand.

Royal power grew when Henry VII (1485–1509) ascended to the throne after winning the War of the Roses. To consolidate his power, Henry dealt firmly with the feudal lords, governing through a Privy Council composed of men beholden to him for their positions. He raised money without parliamentary consent and ruthlessly subdued his enemies. By the time his son Henry VIII (1509–47) succeeded to the throne, the crown was increasingly wealthy and stable. Henry VIII strengthened the crown's power by exerting royal authority over the independent nobility, uniting England with Wales, and definitively breaking with the Catholic Church during the English Reformation (vastly enriching the monarchy through the dissolution of the Catholic monasteries). To further consolidate his power, Henry granted monastic lands to his supporters, creating a class of lords entirely beholden to the king. Through such measures, Henry was able to exert far more power over Parliament than his Medieval forbearers, and to gain legal assent for many acts of royal centralization. His daughter, Elizabeth I (1558–1603), maintained Parliament's passivity, largely because of her military successes and popularity with the commoners. At her death in 1603, the British monarchy was at the apex of its power, and the democratic traditions of the previous age seemed a thing of the past (Edwards 2001).

Parliamentary ascendancy

Succeeding Elizabeth, James VI of Scotland became James I of England (r.1603–25), establishing the Stuart dynasty. James believed in the divine right of kings, but had none of the charisma, popularity, or authority of his beloved cousin, Elizabeth. Against this backdrop, Parliament began again to reassert its ancient rights. An unpopular king wedded to principals of a divine-right monarchy was anathema to a Parliament with increasing Puritan representation. Indeed, James had an almost impossible time persuading Parliament to grant him money, and he searched for ever more despotic ways to raise revenue. Continually dissolving Parliament in the hope of eventually getting a more compliant one, James tried to avoid calling Parliament altogether, but was never able to consolidate his own authority without it (Jones 2000).

Under James's son, Charles I (r.1625–49), the already tense relations between the monarch and Parliament worsened still further. A cash-strapped Charles summoned Parliament in 1628, only to have his request for money refused unless he conceded to the Petition of Right, which reasserted two of the most important clauses of the Magna Carta: no new taxes were to be raised without Parliament's assent, and no one was to be imprisoned merely by the order of the king. While Charles conceded to the Petition of Right, he soon went back on his word, refusing to convoke Parliament at all between 1629 and 1640 (Dartford 1978).

This impasse came to an end when the Scots rebelled in 1639 over religious reforms Charles had imposed on the largely Presbyterian country. A Scottish invasion forced the king to convene Parliament in 1640 to raise money for war. Parliament refused to grant funds without a series of concessions, establishing more frequent meetings of Parliament, more parliamentary control over fiscal matters, and the abolition of Star Chambers and other special courts. As parliamentary demands grew more radical, however, elites in Parliament divided. Puritans pushed for the curtailment of royal prerogative and the abolition of bishops, while more moderate Protestants sided with the king in favor of royal authority and the Church of England. This split eventually erupted into the English Civil War, when, in 1642, the king waged war against the radical faction of Parliament (Edwards 2001).

Parliament's war against the sovereign was unprecedented and caused severe anxiety among men who, despite their radical beliefs, had not shed completely their awe of royal authority. As one parliamentarian cautioned, "If we defeat the king ninety-nine times, yet still he is king. But if he defeats us once we will all be hanged as traitors." Kishlansky notes that, "Parliamentarians believed they were fighting to defend their religion, their liberties, and the rule of law. Royalists believed they were fighting to defend their monarch, their church, and social stability" (Kishlansky 1995, 497–8).

After three years of inconclusive fighting, Parliament won a decisive victory and captured the king, who was finally tried and executed in 1649. The victors abolished the monarchy and the House of Lords, declaring England a commonwealth with a republican form of government. The military, however, did not relinquish power. Oliver Cromwell led a military coup and Parliament found itself once again subordinated to the rule of a single despot backed by an army. Ironically, the republic collapsed into chaos after Cromwell's death, forcing the army to restore the Stuart monarchy in 1660. Despite turning full circle, the revolution had a significant impact on English democratic tradition. As Kishlansky notes:

> Parliament became a permanent part of civil government and now had to be managed rather than ignored. Royal power over taxation and religion was curtailed. . . . Absolute monarchy had become constitutional monarchy, with the threat of revolution behind the power of Parliament and the threat of anarchy behind the power of the crown. (Kishlansky 1995, 502)

During this period, plebeians and radical members of the army also voiced sweeping democratic arguments. Radical Levelers deeply penetrated the army and, during the Putney debates of 1647, Colonel Thomas Rainsborough famously declared that, "the poorest he that is in England hath a life to live as the greatest he[, and] every man that is to live under a government ought first by his own consent to put himself under that government" (Edwards 2001, 352–3). Rainsborough and the Levelers seemed to espouse universal manhood suffrage, a shockingly radical idea at the time, which would not be put into practice in Europe until the French Revolution nearly 150 years later. The idea of government by consent of the people would, however, gain force during the Enlightenment, and during the eighteenth century democratic ideas would be debated in the elegant salons of Europe and in radical working men's clubs.

The Restoration and the Glorious Revolution

The Restoration of the Stuart monarchy in 1660 returned constitutional order to Britain and set the foundation for the future institutional framework of British democracy. The king would no longer bid for absolute power but, rather, would function as head of the executive branch of government. Still, wrangling between Charles II and Parliament continued during the Restoration, eventually giving rise to political parties—the Tories (those who supported the king) and the Whigs (those in opposition). Charles was disgruntled with parliamentary attempts to curb royal power, and conspired with Louis XIV to secure the succession of his Catholic brother James, terrifying the now staunchly Protestant parliamentary majority and threatening another rebellion. When James II succeeded to the throne in 1685, only his lack of a son and the memory of the English Civil War prevented another conflict; meanwhile, Britons awaited James's death and the ascent to the throne of his Protestant daughter, Mary, the wife of William of Orange (Wilcox and Arnstein, 1996).

When, James's Queen unexpectedly gave birth to an heir, parliamentary Whigs rebelled. They invited William of Orange to assume the throne, guaranteeing a Protestant succession and protecting the liberties of Britain's Protestant subjects. In 1688, William of Orange landed in Devonshire, and the country largely abandoned James, accomplishing England's "Glorious Revolution" without significant bloodshed. Parliament offered the throne jointly to William and Mary, and drew up the Declaration of Right, which reasserted long-held constitutional principles regarding the raising of money and the distribution of powers between the monarchs and Parliament. The Declaration of Right was put into statute as the Bill of Rights (Wilcox and Arnstein 1996).

The Glorious Revolution ended any pretense of the divine right of kings, since William and Mary obviously owed their throne to Parliament. In 1701, the Act of Settlement assured the succession would go to the closest Protestant heir, further strengthening the conditional nature of royal succession by disqualifying Catholic heirs. After the Glorious Revolution, the British monarchy was definitively subject to the authority of Parliament (which now met regularly), to the rule of law, and to Protestant succession. British subjects also enjoyed protection from the monarch's arbitrary fiscal and legal whims, receiving guarantees of legal protection and taxation through Parliament. Acts protected religious toleration for Dissenters (though not for Catholics), and also freedom of the press through the ending of censorship.

William's reign also witnessed the first steps toward an independent judiciary (Dartford 1978). While Protestants in the colonies generally accepted the new monarchs, Irish Catholics fought a bloody struggle against the imposition of ultra-Protestant rule, suffering a crushing defeat by Protestant forces at the Battle of the Boyne in 1690. Scotland was formally joined to England in 1707, uniting their parliaments and furthering the consolidation of parliamentary authority over various parts of what was now called the United Kingdom of Great Britain (Wilcox and Arnstein 1996).

Despite the constitutional importance of the Glorious Revolution, Britain was not yet a democratic country in the popular sense. Though the power of the king was embedded in the authority of Parliament and the rule of law, few at this time regarded the lower classes as entitled to political participation. When the term "the people" was used, it referred to the narrow class of men who sat in Parliament and those men of wealth and stature who put them there. The popular classes were often regarded as "the mob," and while they could make their opinions felt through rioting, protests, or petitions, they were not deemed part of the "political nation." Political participation resided with those who had a "stake in the nation"—in other words property that invested them in the well-being of the state. Parliament represented the commoners by representing the land on which they lived, but individuals without property were thought to have no "stake in the nation" and were generally barred from taking part in the selection of those men who would represent them in Parliament (Namier 1929, 1930).

During this period, the House of Lords became secondary to the House of Commons, yet the latter was still full of the younger sons of aristocratic families and the associates of powerful magnates. The leader of the majority party in Parliament began to act as a prime minister, beholden to party as well as to the monarch. The importance of party grew under the weak leadership of Queen Anne (1702–14). Under her rule, the monarchical veto fell out of use. Her Tory ministers tried to subvert the Act of Settlement by conspiring with Jacobites, but this ultimately backfired and ushered in an era of Whig Party dominance for the next 50 years. The Tory failure to restore the Stuart monarchy led to the succession of George I of Hanover in 1714, since this minor German princeling was the closest Protestant heir to the throne. George (1714–27) spoke no English, a deficiency that allowed his cabinet ministers to assume greater importance. In 1721, Sir Robert Walpole, the First Lord of the Treasury, was recognized as the first de-facto prime minister as he took over control of cabinet meetings the king no longer attended (Brewer 1981).

Radical reform and the revolutionary era

When George III (1760–1820), the first Hanoverian king born in Great Britain, assumed the throne, tensions once again erupted between Crown and Parliament, particularly over budgetary authority (Brewer 1981). Such tensions were exacerbated by radical calls for expanded democratic participation—calls articulated with new force and respectability (Rose 1898). In 1770, Edmund Burke published his *Thoughts on the Present Discontents*, wherein he complained that the House of Commons was "beginning to exercise control *upon* the people," whereas it was designed "as a control *for* the people." Protesting the oligarchy that concentrated undue power in the hands of the king and his ministers, Burke called upon statesmen to attend to public opinion so the House of Commons might again reflect the will of the people (Rose 1898, 11).

Burke's insights reflected growing discontent among radical reformers such as John Wilkes, Major John Cartwright, Horne Tooke, and Charles James Fox, who began to form societies, publish pamphlets, and launch political campaigns to urge a thorough reform of Parliament. During the 1780s, the great Whig orator, Charles James Fox, outlined a radical program calling for annual parliaments, universal suffrage, equal voting districts, abolition of property qualifications for members of parliament, payment of members, and vote by ballot at parliamentary elections (Brewer 1981; Thompson 1963). Such radical ideas gained powerful momentum among reformers sympathetic to the libertarian demands of the American and French revolutions.

During this revolutionary era, the international environment shaped political developments in Britain. Both the American Revolution (1776–83) and the French Revolution (1789–99) initially fomented radical demands among those sympathetic to the call for more representative and democratic government. The case for democratic transformation was a transatlantic phenomenon, growing out of the Enlightenment, and igniting the enthusiasm of so-called Friends of Liberty worldwide (Gould 2002). Indeed, there was considerable sympathy among radicals in Britain for the case of the colonists in America, even before Cornwallis's 1781 surrender at Yorktown finally forced George III make peace. The French Revolution of 1789 once again reinvigorated the movement for radical reform in Britain, but that momentum proved temporary. The excesses of the Reign of Terror and the rise of Napoleon, which thrust Britain into war with France, fueled a conservative backlash and diverted popular energy from radical to patriotic concerns (Colley 1992; Rose 1898).

During the Napoleonic Wars (1803–15), anxiety over national security resulted in the passage of a number of harsh and antidemocratic measures. In 1801, in exchange for a promise of Catholic Emancipation, the de facto Prime Minister, William Pitt (1783–1801, 1804–06) dissolved Ireland's parliament and formalized an Act of Union. As Dartford notes, the king rejected this proposition as a violation of his oath to uphold the Protestant religion, stating the union with Ireland, "founded upon broken faith," would be one of the most disastrous relationships in British history (Dartford 1978, 32). After nearly 20 years of war, Britain and her allies finally defeated Napoleon at Waterloo in 1815. The alleviation of this military and imperial threat made it possible, once again, to discuss constitutional amendments with more democratic provisions. As Prime Minister,the Duke of Wellington (1828–30, 1834) adamantly opposed any reform measures and kept them at bay during the 1820s. Ultimately, however, he would witness one of the most far-reaching series of reforms ever imagined, including the first significant expansion of the franchise (Colley 1992).

The Industrial Revolution and the Age of Democratic Reform

By the 1830s, conditions in Britain had changed radically as a result of the Industrial Revolution. During the reign of George III (1760–1820), the population of England and Wales increased dramatically and many relocated to new urban industrial areas. "Along with this increase in population came the growth in the numbers and wealth of the middle class, now reinforced by many families who had made fortunes in industry. This class was no longer content to leave control of government to the landowning aristocracy that had dominated it since the Revolution of 1688–9" (Dartford 1978, 33). Discontent also grew among the working classes, who had been ready to take up arms in the Napoleonic Wars, but had little or no say in the government of the realm (Colley 1992; Thompson 1963).

Despite industrialization, economic expansion, and demographic change, the constitutional system of government had altered little since the Glorious Revolution. Parliament itself was selected under an electoral system that had remained virtually unchanged for 400 years. Many boroughs and counties, which returned two members each to Parliament, had experienced radical loss of population, as populations shifted toward industrial areas. The industrial areas swelled, but under the old unreformed system they had virtually no political representation (Machin 2001; O'Gorman 1989). Consequently, a quasi-Medieval form of government represented a modernizing nation, where representation and population had no relation to one another. Despite calls for reform during the eighteenth century, the radicalism of the French Revolution and the need to wage war against Napoleon had strengthened conservative forces and tarred any reform efforts as being revolutionary (Pugh 1999).

In addition to these ideological fears, many elites had practical interest in safeguarding the status quo, as the unreformed Parliament held enormous benefits for those sitting in both houses. With the depletion of population in many counties, the process of electing representatives fell to the powerful magnates who owned the land. These so-called pocket boroughs were literally in the pocket of the local aristocrat who possessed the vote or a decisive influence over the few remaining voters in the constituency. Similarly, "rotten boroughs" were equally corrupt; they had no remaining population, but still returned two members to Parliament. Thus, Parliament was full of stakeholders in the old system. Those powerful Lords who controlled rotten and pocket boroughs had no desire to see their own influence wane. The Members of Parliament (MPs) who owed their seats to such uncontested elections were also reluctant to see them abolished. Finally, the House of Lords, which represented the landed interests, adamantly opposed changes to a system that allowed many of its members virtually to appoint representatives for their constituencies in the House of Commons. The House of Lords itself was unelected and based on hereditary peerage or high ecclesiastical office. For these men, popular elections looked like a dangerous subversion of the age-old constitutional system that preserved their power and privilege (Arnstein 1996; Machin 2001).

If the representation of both the rural counties and the urban boroughs was anything but rational or equitable, the selection of the electorate was even more bizarre. No two boroughs had the same qualifications for the vote, and while the county electorate was limited to 40-shilling freeholders (those who owned land yielding at least 40 shillings a year in rent), many wealthy renters and other types of freeholders were left out of the electoral process. The boroughs were even more complex. While some had as few as a single elector, others were so democratic that elections became drunken festivals, with candidates treating voters to alcoholic beverages, in the hope of securing votes. There is even some evidence that women, barred from the vote by custom rather than statute, may have occasionally cast a ballot. Since balloting was open, magnates, employers, clergy, and other influential individuals exerted enormous influence over the votes (Dartford 1978; Seymour 1970).

Criticism of this system came from a number of directions. Powerful, reform-minded elites, especially within the Whig Party, recognized the inefficiency and irrationality of the unreformed system and wanted to see a more equitable distribution of seats and a more standardized set of electoral requirements. Many of them argued that to avoid the type of violent revolution experienced on the Continent, Parliament would need to take the necessary steps to reform itself. Middle-class industrialists who had made fortunes in industry and trade also resented the weighting of the franchise toward landed wealth and the lack of representation for industrial districts. They put their wealth and considerable political organization behind the reform campaign. Finally, radicals (many from the working class) found inspiration in the ideals of the American and French revolutions, and clamored for a more democratic and representative Parliament. During the summers of 1831 and 1832, when the question of reform was the most contentious political issue of the day, the lower classes agitated relentlessly for change.

The Great Reform Bill

The passage of the Great Reform Bill of 1832 required complex political brinkmanship. It involved the election and disillusion of several ministries, popular rioting, a vitriolic press campaign and, finally, a threat by the king (made under duress) to add 50 Whig peers to the House of Lords to pass the bill, should opposition persist. In June 1832, the House of Lords, faced with the prospect of radical dilution by newly minted Whig peers, allowed the bill to pass by exercising mass abstentions and absences. To a modern audience, what is most remarkable about these reforms is that they were undertaken by a parliament that had everything to lose by them (Arnstein 1996).

In addition to the redistribution of seats, reforms expanded and standardized voting rights. In the boroughs, reforms extended the vote to urban householders who either owned or rented a house worth at least ten pounds. In the counties, both leaseholders and freeholders could qualify to vote. While the most democratic boroughs lost voters, the total electorate increased by nearly 50 percent, allowing one in five Englishmen to vote. This tremendous expansion of the franchise created a political space for the middle classes but ignored the working class radicals, who had been so vociferous and important in giving momentum to the bill. Women, for the first time, were explicitly excluded from the franchise. And landlords and magnates still held disproportionate influence, since all voting was tallied through public declaration, rather than by secret ballot. Despite these limitations, the Great Reform Bill of 1832 was a significant step toward democracy and would lead to the further reorganization of municipal government as well as to broader franchise reform later in the century (Arnstein 1996).

The expansion of popular democracy

As many opponents of reform realized, the Great Reform Bill was by no means final. "The Revolution is made," declared the Duke of Wellington sadly in 1833, "that is to say, power is transferred from one class of society, the gentlemen of England professing the faith of the Church of England, to another class of society, the shopkeepers being dissenters from the church, many of them being [Unitarians] and other atheists" (Arnstein 1996, 15). Once the principle of democracy was conceded, subsequent reform bills incrementally expanded the electorate, and further legislation would insure the autonomy of the voter and the independence of members of Parliament. Additional reform bills passed in 1867, 1884, 1918, and 1928. In 1872 the Ballot Act consolidated popular democracy by allowing votes to be cast in secret, thereby reducing the influence of magnates, landlords, and employers over dependent voters.

Popular pressure from those groups that had been excluded from the Great Reform Bill was key to further expansion of the franchise. This agitation, however, succeeded only when backed by powerful political elites. The 1840s witnessed the rise of the Chartist movement, a working-class rejuvenation of the eighteenth-century radical tradition (Stedman Jones, 1983). The Chartists prioritized the economic welfare of the working class, but their People's Charter included male suffrage as one of its primary platforms. Chartism reflected growing working class discontent with political exclusion, rendering it a democracy movement as much as a labor movement. Democratization, the Chartists contended, was the key to securing the economic well-being of the working classes (Brown 1998).

The People's Charter was adopted at an enormous meeting in Birmingham in 1838, initiating a popular campaign to bring the demands of the Chartists before Parliament. A petition with 1.28 million signatures was presented in June 1839, only to be promptly rejected by a vote of 235 to 46, precipitating rioting, arrests, and continued unrest. Similar mammoth petitions were rejected in 1842 and 1848, revealing the hostility of many liberal Englishmen to further democratization. As Thomas Babington Macaulay, the Whig historian and MP put it in 1842, "universal suffrage was 'utterly incompatible with civilization.' "[3] Educated Britons feared an ill-educated electorate would fall prey to demagogy, causing the mass confiscation of property and impoverishing the nation to the detriment of rich and poor alike (Arnstein 1996).[4]

While the Chartist platform was heavily political, many rank-and-file Chartists understood political rights in economic terms. As one Chartist orator declared to his listeners, "If a man ask what I mean by universal suffrage, I mean to say that every working man in the land has a right to a good coat on his back, a good hat on his head, a good roof for the shelter of his household."[5] In the 1840s, parliamentary elites stole the thunder of the Chartist movement, passing a series of measures to ameliorate the condition of the working class without granting them further political rights. First, the government of Sir Robert Peel abolished the Corn Laws (tariffs that kept the price of food high), spurred by working class agitation, free-trade sentiment, and the disastrous food shortage and famine in Ireland. At the local level, a series of factory and town acts did much to improve the condition of workers in various industries and to improve the health and hygiene of urban dwellers. While the condition of the working class remained far from desirable or comfortable, the improvements in material circumstances prevented serious protest over democratic rights until the 1860s (Brown 1998).

Many hoped and believed the Great Reform Bill of 1832 had achieved a near-perfect constitutional settlement. The mid-Victorian period was one of prosperity, "equipoise," and a vast expansion in liberal policy, particularly in areas of taxation and trade. The power of the monarch became increasingly symbolic and the Lords lost much of their weight vis-a-vis the Commons. According to the great constitutional theorist Walter Bagehot, "a republic had insinuated itself beneath the folds of a Monarchy."[6] Nevertheless, while many British elites were committed liberals, few were enthusiastic democrats. Liberal elites favored open discussion and a high degree of freedom of speech, press, and enterprise, but "few . . . looked forward to an age of universal manhood or adult suffrage" (Arnstein 1996, 118).

During the 1860s, economic downturn and a revival of radical ideas gave momentum to calls for further expansion of the franchise. Liberal and Conservative elites, eager to reap the gratitude of newly enfranchised voters, alarmed rank and file party members by proposing another reform bill. Ironically, it would not be the Liberal Party of William Gladstone, but the Tory Party of his archrival, Benjamin Disraeli , that would pass a surprisingly radical reform bill in 1867. Disraeli (1868, 1874–80) proposed to extend the franchise to all urban rate-payers, drastically reducing the property qualifications for the vote. In order to reconcile his Tory party to this move, he proposed to give additional votes to all university graduates, owners of savings accounts of 50 pounds or more, and to members of learned professions. These "fancy franchises" were meant to insure the educated electorate would not be swamped by the ill-educated. The 1867 Reform Bill was far more democratic that any of its architects had initially imagined, nearly doubling the electorate (Bentley 1984). Yet, the enfranchisement of working men, clerks, and shopkeepers did not radically change the makeup of Parliament, since the new voters continued to support established parties. While the Tories had brought about the bill, working men, with their long radical affiliations, gravitated toward the Liberals, securing the election of Gladstone's Liberal Party in 1868.

William Gladstone's first ministry (1868–74) was one of the most reform-minded in British history. Religious disestablishment in Ireland, the abolition of the purchase of military commissions, education reform, and judicial reform were just some of the issues it addressed. The Ballot Act of 1872 introduced, for the first time, the secret ballot, finally guaranteeing every voter the liberty to cast his ballot without fear of reprisals from his employer, clergyman, or landlord (Arnstein 1996).

Britain's Great Depression of 1873–96, however, posed formidable challenges for the Liberal Party, undercutting its creed of laissez-faire economic policy as more and more people looked to government intervention to remedy the decline in prosperity. During this period, the price of newspapers fell, giving the lower classes more access to print culture. Both political parties further strengthened their party apparatus in order to cultivate new working class voters. During the 1870s, this worked to the advantage of the Conservatives, especially as Benjamin Disraeli began to showcase empire as the antidote to Britain's ills. Disraeli launched his New Conservatism in his famous Crystal Palace Speech of 1872, outlining a platform of paternalistic social reform, reverence for monarchy, and building the British Empire. Disraeli advocated a series of bread-and-butter concessions to the working class, like public health and better housing. During Disraeli's second ministry (1874–80), Parliament passed the Trade Union Act, allowing peaceful picketing; the Artisan's Dwellings Act, sanctioning the destruction and reconstruction of slums by local authorities; the Food and Drug Act, meant to prevent the tainting of food with harmful fillers; and the Public Health Act, that allowed municipalities to impose proper water, sewage, and drainage facilities. Finally, Britain's prisons were nationalized in 1878, making the government, rather than localities or families, liable for their upkeep (Arnstein 1996).

Despite this spate of social legislation, Disraeli's conservatism showed through in his aggressive imperialist policies. In a symbolic gesture, Disraeli passed the Royal Titles Act, which gave Queen Victoria (1837–1901) the title "Empress of India," and won him the eternal affection of the Queen. More tangibly, in 1875 he bought controlling shares in the Suez Canal from the bankrupt khedive of Egypt, sent troops to fight the Zulus in South Africa, and orchestrated a fatal showdown with the Russians in Afghanistan, where Afghan mutineers in Kabul massacred the new British minister and his entire entourage (Arnstein 1996). The cost of these campaigns began to wear on the public, however. In 1880, Gladstone challenged these aggressive policies, pioneering modern electioneering with a series of whistle-stop speeches and open-air meetings, in what came to be known as the Midlothian Campaign.

Gladstone won by a landslide and used his new majority to expand the electorate once again. While the Reform Bill of 1867 had extended the franchise to rate-payers living in towns, the 1884 act extended these provisions to the counties, encompassing hundreds of thousands of rural residents who had been excluded under the previous bill. The bill increased the electorate from 3.15 million to 5.7 million and tripled the number of voters in the counties. Yet, even the 1884 bill did not institute full manhood suffrage. Men who did not have a stable residence, especially itinerant workers, soldiers, and paupers, bachelors who lived with their parents, and servants who lived with their masters were all excluded. Perhaps what is most significant about this act is that it did not excite much opposition (Arnstein 1996, 151).

Despite these domestic victories, foreign policy remained an intractable problem for Gladstone. The Midlothian Campaign had centered on foreign policy, as he appealed to the masses by opposing Britain's international unilateralism and its often ill-fated consequences. Difficulties in South Africa, Afghanistan, and Egypt, however, pushed Gladstone to make difficult and unpopular decisions. The final straw occurred during a crisis in the Sudan, which brought down Gladstone's second ministry after a fundamentalist army massacred a British general at Khartoum. Among the British public only Gladstone's attempts (all unsuccessful) to grant Home Rule to Ireland would prove to be more unpopular than his government's military endeavors.

Democracy and imperialism

The growth of British democracy at home coincided with vastly expanding colonization abroad. Just as ordinary Britons enjoyed more liberties and voice in government than ever before, more and more inhabitants of the globe, from Ireland to India, found themselves unwillingly subject to British rule. During the final 30 years of the nineteenth century Britain acquired colonies and protectorates that spanned 750,000 square miles, with 20 million people, in Asia and the South Pacific. Additionally, it gained approximately 4.4 million square miles, with a population of 60 million, in Africa (Arnstein 1996, 169). Empire-building became a national obsession, with adventurers acquiring territory that had no value whatsoever, simply to fly the British flag over it. In terms of popular culture and entertainment, empire took on a life of its own (MacKenzie 1984).

A number of factors contributed to the rise in imperialism, but none was more significant than its appeal among the newly enfranchised masses. The high tide of imperialism coincided with the rise of the popular press, and the daily papers enthusiastically followed imperial developments, lauding its heroes and glorying in every British victory. Unlike the earlier mainly white-settler colonies, which exercised a measure of self-government and autonomy, the conquest of nonwhites involved stripping indigenous peoples of self-rule and imposing British authority, either directly, or through local potentates who had been co-opted by the new rulers. The British justified this despotism by claiming to bring civilization to "savage" peoples. As Rudyard Kipling wrote in the *White Man's Burden* (1899):

> Take up the White Man's Burden
> Send forth the best ye breed
> Go bind your sons to exile
> To serve your captive's need;
> To wait in heavy harness,
> On fluttered folk and wild—
> Your new-caught, sullen peoples,
> Half-devil and half-child.[7]

Such portrayals of the benevolent and civilizing role of British imperialism aimed to reconcile a policy of conquest with the liberal belief in democracy and progress.

The popularity of imperialism crushed Gladstone's efforts to grant home rule to Ireland. Once Britain revived its taste for empire, a moderate proposition like granting Ireland its own parliament to oversee domestic affairs seemed tantamount to treason. The proposal to grant an Irish parliament stimulated such heated opposition that Sir Edward Carson and radical Conservatives threatened to back rebellion in Ulster if home rule were granted.

Despite Britain's certainty of its superior right to rule abroad, by the 1880s independence movements had formed among the intelligentsia of the non-white colonies.

The Indian National Congress, for example, began to meet and plan, advocating home rule and an independent India, just as the Irish had done. The wars of the twentieth century, however, would weaken the mother country sufficiently to make dreams of independence a reality.

World War I and women's suffrage

One group of adults was consistently excluded from all the franchise reform bills: women. In the debates over the 1867 Reform Bill, John Stuart Mill, then a Liberal Member of Parliament, proposed an amendment to strike the word "male" from the proposed reform bill, thereby creating an equal franchise. The amendment was soundly defeated. Mill was ridiculed in the press and shunned by his constituents. His book, *The Subjection of Women*, became a Bible of sorts for Millicent Garrett Fawcett, Elizabeth Cady Stanton and other pioneers of the Women's Suffrage Movement. From 1867 onward what had been a relatively small and quiet feminist movement became more vocal and public.

While women made little headway in their campaign for voting rights before the World War I, they did gain other civil rights. The Married Women's Property Acts of 1870 and 1882 gave women the right to their own property and earnings, which previously under coverture had been the property of their husbands. A local-government act gave female property holders the right to vote in local (as opposed to parliamentary) elections. Education reform, new women's colleges, and an alliance with the Labour Party all turned women's rights into one of the central issues of the latter half of the nineteenth century. Parliamentary rejection of women's suffrage amendments frustrated the mostly middle class feminists who worked for the vote. In 1903, Emmeline Pankhurst founded the Women's Social and Political Union and subsequently launched a militant suffrage campaign modeled on the activities of the Russian anarchists. While Mrs. Pankhurst cautioned her followers to stop short of taking human life, the suffragettes heckled MPs, sabotaged mailboxes, burned churches, slashed paintings, stormed Parliament, and staged hunger strikes in an escalating series of theatrical acts that brought the suffragettes considerable publicity between 1903 and 1914 (Smith 1998).

World War I ushered in a crucial change in attitudes toward women's suffrage. During the war, a shortage of manpower led unprecedented numbers of women to enter war industries. In 1915, Mrs. Pankhurst led a huge procession to demand, not the right to vote, but the right to work for the war effort. The patriotic response of suffragettes, along with the tremendous efforts of women workers, doctors, ambulance drives, and ordinary women carrying on at home while husbands, sons, and brothers went to war, won women the admiration of the nation. When a new franchise bill was proposed during the war (to re-enfranchise soldiers who had lost their votes as a result of moving out of their rateable dwellings into temporary military housing), women demanded to be included on the register, too. After much debate, women were included in the Representation of the People Bill of 1918 (Gullace 2002). Ironically, however, while the bill eliminated property and residential requirements for men, only women householders over 30 were enfranchised. If the heroic women workers who served nobly in war industry provided the pretext for granting women the vote, they would be precisely the group cut out of exercise of the franchise. The rationale given for this unequal franchise was that enfranchising women on equal terms with men would have given the register a preponderance of women, due to war casualties. Furthermore, many worried about the consequences of bestowing the vote on flighty young working class women and simply could not imagine an electorate that included young women. Indeed the opposition to this group exercising the vote can be seen in the furor over the so-called flapper vote, a measure that in 1928 finally succeeded in giving women the vote on the same terms as men (Gullace 2002).

In the meantime, women slowly accrued the right to take civil service exams, the right to stand at the bar, the right to practice medicine, and the right to earn university degrees, and they were gradually overcoming the legal barriers that stood in the way to civil equality. Women nevertheless continued to experience severe discrimination in the job market and in educational institutions. Following the "Great War," as World War I was termed, many women were summarily thrown out of jobs so returning soldiers could be employed. Marriage law made women subject to the nationality of their husbands, and it would be many years before women successfully won the right to keep their own nationality upon marriage to a foreigner (Higonnet 1987; Baldwin 2001).

The Great War also advanced the cause of laboring men. Working class men had enjoyed gradual enfranchisement through the reform bills of 1867 and 1884, but significant numbers of them remained ineligible to vote because they were itinerant workers or too poor to pay rates. The Representation of the People Bill of 1918 enfranchised these men, along with middle class women over 30, and made it possible for common soldiers to vote for the first time (Gullace 2002).

The political voice of the working class was also amplified in the years leading up to World War I. In 1909, Chancellor of the Exchequer Lloyd

George proposed a "People's Budget" that would have offered a measure of social welfare to the working classes, including pensions for the indigent elderly. The House of Lords roundly defeated the bill. In response, the subsequent Parliament Act of 1911 permanently reduced the power of the House of Lords, rendering it unable to do more than delay the passage of legislation that had the support of the House of Commons. The reduction of the power of the Lords once again shifted power toward the elected House of Commons. The Labour Party, the first political party meant to address directly the needs of British workers, gained momentum at this time. While the party began as a small endeavor in 1900 under the leadership of James Kier Hardie, who wore his cloth cap to Parliament, coordination with the Trade Union Congress, the largest amalgamated labor union in Britain, turned the Labour Party into a significant force after World War I. The great historian George Dangerfield attempted to describe the prewar factors that resulted in the "strange death" of liberalism after World War I and its hallmark: replacement by the party of organized labor. Indeed, the 1920s would see the first Labour government, under the leadership of Ramsay MacDonald (1929–31). Though short-lived, it would presage the triumph of Labour in the post–World War II era (Dangerfield, 1935).

"People's War" and the rise of the welfare state: Expanding the scope of democracy

World War II posed perhaps the greatest threat to British democracy, but ultimately marked its greatest triumph. As Chapter 1 explains, the interwar period was a time marked by democratic reversal, as one European nation after another fell to fascism. While Britain's prime minister, Neville Chamberlain (1937–40), initially attempted to appease German leader, Adolf Hitler, once the Nazis invaded Poland in September 1939 both Britain and France declared war on Germany. With the collapse and surrender of France in the summer of 1940, Britain stood alone against the forces of fascism. Winston Churchill (1940–45, 1951–55), the new prime minister, emphasized the democratic values of Great Britain in stirring radio addresses, wherein he rallied the people to show fortitude.

To facilitate his conquest of Europe, Hitler planned to knock Britain out of the war by destroying the morale of its people. After his failure to gain air superiority over the English Channel during the "Battle of Britain," Hitler began to target civilian sites, bombing London every night for two months. The royal family did not quit Buckingham Palace during the "Blitz," as the air assault was called, and instead stood firm, enduring damage to the palace and joining the prime minister for daily visits to areas destroyed by German bombs the night before. Londoners, huddled together in underground tunnels, enjoyed a new type of democratic spirit as rich and poor alike shared in the terror of nightly bombing. The British thus remember World War II, and the blitz in particular, as a democratic moment when the entire country pulled together to face a hostile enemy—an enemy with values antithetical to British liberalism and democracy. For this reason, World War II is remembered as "The Peoples War"—a time where both duchesses and milkmen were subject to food rationing, and no one was exempt from suffering and loss (Rose 2003).

Not surprisingly, the greatest transformation of British democracy took place directly after World War II. In the first election after peace had returned to Europe, Winston Churchill, the Conservative prime minister who had guided the United Kingdom through the war, was turned out of office in favor of Clement Atlee (1945–51), the Labour Party leader. On the surface, this leadership change appears odd: Why would the British turn out a great wartime leader on the heels of victory? The explanation lies in British postwar expectations. Britons wished to turn the People's War into a People's Peace. To realize this vision, the Atlee government instituted some of the most sweeping welfare reforms ever seen. A national health care system, unemployment insurance, free education, and milk money for all children (regardless of need) were just some of the sweeping provisions provided in the new welfare state. To finance social welfare, the government levied high taxes on wealth and property and nationalized key industries. The influx of Marshal Plan aid from the United States helped finance reconstruction, making the ambitious social agenda of the Labour government feasible (Fraser 1973).

The basic guarantee of a decent standard of living, as well as health care and education for every citizen, undercut many of the old Liberal principals of small government and self-reliance. This change proved quite popular, however, since social entitlements were offered to all, making the middle classes stakeholders in the welfare system. The welfare state resulted in soaring standards of living, following a difficult readjustment from the war economy during the 1950s. Britons, for the first time in their long history, enjoyed adequate nutrition and health care. Every baby in Britain was entitled to untainted and plentiful milk. The old would not die destitute, and a capable working class student could obtain, free of charge, a university degree at one of the ancient universities.

The welfare state came at a hefty price, however. Budget deficits slowed the economy in the 1970s. Nationalized industries often proved inefficient, providing little incentive to workers, who were guaranteed an income even if they did not work. Growing recognition of the price of the welfare state led to a backlash, ushering in the "Thatcher Revolution" (1979–90) and ultimately a more fiscally cautious New Labour Party, under Tony Blair (1997–2007). Today the question of Britain's ties to the European Union is one of the main issues dividing the political parties. Having declined to join the euro, the British must decide how far they wish to go in endorsing and submitting to the open immigration and technocratic left-wing norms of the EU (Reitan 2003). In many ways the so-called Euro-skeptics adhere to an older model of laissez-faire liberalism and are deeply reluctant to relinquish national sovereignty over fiscal, domestic, or foreign policy.[8]

End of empire and multi-cultural Britain

On the international front, World War II ushered in the rapid disintegration of the British Empire. Reluctantly bowing to democratic sentiment in India and to its own financial limitations, Britain conceded the transition to independence in 1947. To placate Muslim fears of a Hindu state, the British partitioned India into a Hindu south and the Muslim state of Pakistan. This partition was accomplished with unimaginable amounts of bloodshed, but as Chapter 9 details, the resulting parliamentary democracy in India is a model to other developing nations (Levine 2007).

Most British colonies in Africa, Asia, and the Middle East followed India's lead during the 1950s and 1960s. Ireland, however, remained a problem fraught with emotion and difficulty. Ireland had gained its independence from Britain in 1922, but Northern Ireland remained part of the British Empire, governed as a noncontiguous part of the United Kingdom itself. This settlement reflected the wishes of the Protestant majority in Northern Ireland, but it deeply offended Irish Catholics who dreamed of a unified Ireland free of British rule. As a result, terrorist violence erupted in the 1970s, starkly highlighting the "Irish Question" as one that would not disappear until peace accords in 1998 established an uneasy truce (Coohill 2002).

As a bankrupt Britain watched its empire collapse after World War II, it turned to the idea of a commonwealth of former colonies, which would remain part of a sterling economic area and retain nominal allegiance to the Crown. In order to make this gesture meaningful, the postwar Labour government granted the full rights of British citizenship to all members of the Commonwealth of Nations. Additionally, the government invited white European "guest workers" to find work rebuilding a war-ravaged Britain. Waves of immigrants promptly began to arrive from the Caribbean, India, and Pakistan, as well as Eastern Europe, creating enclaves in British cities and diversifying Britain beyond recognition to many of its subjects. The postwar flood of nonwhite immigrants, many of whom provided essential labor in rebuilding decimated cities, caused a racially charged backlash. Hostility to immigration ended full citizenship rights to former colonial subjects and set immigration quotas to reduce the number of strangers in the land (Paul 1997). Britain, however, was already irrevocably transformed. Despite new restrictions on immigration passed in the 1960s, Britain was now a multicultural society.

Today, women's rights, gay rights, and minority rights (particularly the rights of Muslim citizens to abide by Islamic law) have been debated in Parliament and in the press. The greatest challenge facing British democracy may be gauging the degree to which the Western liberal tradition can accommodate cultural diversity among citizens who do not share that tradition. Would allowing Muslims to practice *sharia* be a democratic concession to Muslim minorities living in Britain? Or does it violate the civil rights protections afforded all subjects, including females, under British law? Such controversies mark current debate over the meaning of democracy in a modern multicultural society (Jamieson 2009).

Additional resources

The emergence of democratic practices in Great Britain is succinctly captured in Simon Schama's BBC documentary *History of Britain*. For a firsthand account of the fight for women's suffrage, see Emmeline Pankhurst's autobiography, *My Own Story*. Winston Churchill provides a riveting account of British solidarity during "The Peoples War" in *The Second World War, Volume 2: Their Finest Hour*.

Notes

1 Aristotle, *Nic. Ethics* bk. x. ch. 6, quoted in Rose (1898).

2 Some constitutional provisions are contained in those acts of Parliament concerned with the governance of the realm, while others are based on traditional interpretations of political liberty. As Dartford remarks, "The constitutional rights of the individual citizens, which in America are defined in the first ten amendments to the Constitution (commonly called the Bill of Rights), are in Britain basically protected by the common law of the land, that body of customary law defined by precedents established by the decisions of judges" (Dartford 1978, ix).

3 Quoted in Arnstein (1996, 36).

4 Literacy rates in Britain rose with the Education Act of 1870, which established mandatory primary education. Marital registers suggest that in the 1840s, half of the brides and 65 percent of the grooms could write their names. <www.bl.uk/collections/early/victorian/pr_intro.html> (Accessed 8/18/2010)

5 Quoted in Arnstein (1996, 36–7).

6 Quoted in Arnstein (1996, 118).

7 Rudyard Kipling, *White Man's Burden* (1899). Kipling wrote this poem to the United States upon the acquisition of the Philippines in the Spanish-American War.

8 To these skeptics, the European Union appears to be yet another European autocracy threatening Britain's hard won and vigorously defended liberties. The debate itself suggests that the meaning of "Liberalism" has become increasingly contested in Britain, with older Victorian notions vying against the vision of a community run by an educated technocratic elite.

References

Arnstein, Walter. 1996. *Britain Yesterday and Today: 1830 to the Present*. New York: DC Heath.

Baldwin, M. Page. 2001. "Subject to Empire: Married Women and the British Nationality and Status of Aliens Act." *Journal of British Studies* 40(4): 522–66.

Bentley, Michael. 1984. *Politics without Democracy, 1815–1914*. London: Fontana.

Brewer, John. 1981. *Party Ideology and Popular Politics in the Age of George III*. Cambridge: Cambridge University Press.

Brown, Richard. 1998. *Chartism*. Cambridge: Cambridge University Press.

Colley, Linda. 1992. *Britons: The Forging of the Nation*. New Haven: Yale University Press.

Coohill, Joseph. 2002. *Ireland: A Short History*. Oxford: Oneworld.

Dangerfield, George. 1961 [1935]. *The Strange Death of Liberal England*. New York: Capricorn.

Dartford, Gerald P. 1978. *The British Constitution: A Study of Parliamentary Democracy*. Wellesley Hills: IPS Press.

Edwards, Philip. 2001. *The Making of the Modern English State, 1460–1660*. New York: Palgrave.

Fraser, Derek. 1973. *The Evolution of the British Welfare State: A History of Social Policy since the Industrial Revolution*. New York: Barnes & Noble.

Gould, Eliga H. 2002. "Revolution and Counter-Revolution," in *The British Atlantic World, 1500–1800*, edited by David Armitage and Michael J. Braddick, pp. 196–213. Basingstoke: Palgrave.

Gullace, Nicoletta F. 2002. *"The Blood of Our Sons:" Men, Women, and the Renegotiation of British Citizenship during the Great War*. New York: Palgrave.

Higonnet, Margaret. 1987. *Behind the Lines: Gender and the Two World Wars*, edited by Jane Jenson, Sonya Michel, and Margaret Collins Weitz. New Haven: Yale University Press.

Hind, Wendy. 1992. *Catholic Emancipation: A Shake to Men's Minds*. Cambridge: Blackwell.

Jamieson, Alastair. 2009. "'Muslims want Sharia Law in Britain' Claim," *Telegraph Online*. October 15, 2009, www.telegraph.co.uk/news/newstopics/politics/lawandorder/6334091/Muslims-want-sharia-law-in-Britain-claim.html

Jones, Whitney R. D. 2000. *The Tree of Commonwealth, 1460–1793*. London: AUP.

Keen, Maurice. 2000. *England in the Later Middle Ages, 2nd edition*. London: Routledge.

Kelly, James. 2010. "'Era of Liberty': The Politics of Civil and Political Rights in Eighteenth-Century Ireland." In *Exclusionary Empire: English Liberty Overseas, 1600–1900*, edited by Jack P. Greene, 77–111. Cambridge: Cambridge University Press.

Kipling, Rudyard. 1899. *White Man's Burden*. McClure Magazine.

Kishlansky, Mark, Patrick Geary, and Patricia O'Brien. 1995. *Civilization in the West*. New York: Harper Collins.

Levine, Philippa. 2007. *The British Empire: Sunrise to Sunset*. Harlow: Pearson.

Machin, Ian. 2001. *The Rise of Democracy in Britain, 1830–1918*. Basingstoke: Macmillan.

MacKenzie, John. 1984. *Propaganda and Empire: The Manipulation of British Public Opinion 1880–1930*. Manchester: Manchester University Press.

McCord, Norman, and Bill Perdue. 2007. *British History 1815–1914*. Oxford: Oxford University Press.

Namier, Sir Lewis. 1930. *England in the Age of the American Revolution*. London: Macmillan.

Namier, Sir Lewis. 1929. *The Structure of Politics at the Accession of George III*. London: Palgrave Macmillan.

O'Gorman, F. 1989. *Voters, Patrons and Parties: The Unreformed Electoral System in Hanoverian England, 1734–1832*. Oxford: Oxford University Press.

Paul, Kathleen. 1997. *Whitewashing Britain: Race and Citizenship in the Postwar Era*. Ithaca: Cornell.

Prestwich, Michael. 1990. *English Politics in the Thirteenth Century*. New York: St. Martin's Press.

Pugh, Martin. 1999. *Britain Since 1789: A Concise History*. New York: St. Martin's Press.

Reitan, Earl A. 2003. *The Thatcher Revolution: Margaret Thatcher, John Major, Tony Blair, and the Transformation of Modern Britain, 1979–2001*. Lanham, MD: Rowan & Littlefield.

Rose, J. Holland. 1898. *The Rise and Growth of Democracy in Great Britain*. Chicago and New York: Herbert S. Stone & Co.

Rose, Sonya O. 2003. *Which People's War? National Identity and Citizenship in Wartime Britain 1939–1945*. Oxford: Oxford University Press.

Seymour, C. 1970 [1915]. *Electoral Reform in England and Wales: the Development and Operation of Parliamentary Franchise, 1832–1885*. London: Newton Abbot.

Shoenberg, Shira. "The Virtual Jewish History Tour of England" (Jewish Virtual Library) accessed March 21, 2010 <http://www.jewishvirtuallibrary.org/jsource/vjw/England.html#Emancipation>

Smith, Harold L. 1998. *The British Women's Suffrage Campaign, 1866–1928*. London: Longmans.

Stedman Jones, Gareth. 1983. "Rethinking Chartism." In *Languages of Class: Studies in English Working Class History, 1832–1982*, 90–178. Cambridge: Cambridge University Press.

Thompson, E. P. 1963. *Making of the English Working Class*. New York: Vintage.

Wilcox, William B., and Walter L. Arnstein. 1996. *The Age of Aristocracy 1688–1830*. Lexington: DC Heath.

The racial divide in the United States has long been an emotionally charged fault line in American democracy. To end the segregation of schools, President Eisenhower dispatched soldiers from the 101st Airborne Division to escort black children past angry protestors in Little Rock, Arkansas, on September 25, 1957. The children have since been known as "the Little Rock Nine."

Photo courtesy of the US National Archives

5

The American Road to Democracy: An Early Start, but Late Finish

Marvin P. King, Jr. and Stephanie McLean

Chapter Outline

Founded in 1776 in the throes of separation from Britain, the United States is one of the oldest, most stable democracies in the world. The US Constitution and its institutions of government have weathered centuries of political and economic change, a Civil War that threatened to tear the nation apart, slavery and its abolition, the humbling Great Depression of the 1930s, and the social turmoil of the 1960s civil rights movements. In 2009, the first black American president assumed office, arguably a testament to the progress made by the American people in overcoming a long and ugly history of racism. While American democracy still faces challenges, such as the disproportionate influence of powerful special interests, crucial democratic norms like freedom of speech and of association and the right to vote have become and remain fundamental rights that all Americans hold dear.

This chapter traces the development of American democracy, examining its unique founding as well as its struggle to deliver on promises of true equality to all citizens. This examination addresses the central paradox of American democracy—why did one of the world's first democracies stubbornly cling to undemocratic practices for so long? In 1787, the US Constitution granted a small group of Americans the right to vote, yet did not fully extend this right to all citizens until 1965. This chapter explains both the founding and gradual extension of American democracy, highlighting the ways in which economic forces motivated elites to wrest power from Great Britain, and how these elites in turn founded a republic with a strong institutional framework for accountable and representative government. As both economic power and education spread among the populace, the pool of American voters grew larger. Still, some elites were able to manipulate institutions to isolate many black Americans from democratic processes, maintaining the historical racial divide in America. A large portion of civil society vehemently contested this systematic exclusion and launched a protest movement that succeeded in expanding American democracy to include all citizens.

Historical overview: The founding of the United States

The United States was born out of dispute over representation. Could a people have true representation without directly electing their representatives? Emissaries of the Crown, unsurprisingly, claimed Parliament virtually represented the colonists. The colonists most vehemently disagreed, arguing that by taxing the colonists without representation the British Empire unfairly profited off their labor. The most notable example was the Stamp Act of 1765, requiring a stamp for many public documents. After a brief rebellion, the British Parliament rescinded the Stamp Act. However, Parliament then passed the Declaratory Act, requiring that all laws passed by Parliament be binding on the American colonies.

To determine the best way to respond, each colony sent representatives to the Second Continental Congress in Philadelphia. Colonists were concerned with two intertwined issues—representation and economic liberty. The infamous Boston Tea Party was an aspect of the quintessential debate over both the power of taxation and who would then control those tax dollars. Colonists disagreed with Parliament's views on representation but did not, by any means, advocate universal suffrage. Rather, it would be more accurate to say that economic elites thought their economic power should translate into political power.

Thomas Jefferson penned these concerns in loftier terms and led the drafting of the Declaration of Independence, adopted by representatives on July 4, 1776. This document remains one of the world's great examples of the power of democracy. First, it introduced the notion of accountability, as citizens of the colonies enumerated over two dozen specific allegations of crime and ill treatment the king had levied against his subjects. Second, the document unequivocally declared that all humans have "certain unalienable Rights, that among these are Life, Liberty, and the pursuit of Happiness."[1] Just as importantly, it declared that government only receives its powers and can only act "from the consent of the governed."[2] After declaring independence, the Congress moved on to questions of governance, addressing the need to create a governing structure that could coordinate the thirteen colonies and begin the process of establishing an independent nation. In an attempt to compromise among the needs of large and small states, the Congress avoided creating a strong national government that might compete with state governments (a tension that has had longevity in American democracy). The Congress adopted the Articles of Confederation, which permitted it to act as the legitimate government until it was replaced by the Constitution.[3]

The signing of the Declaration of Independence meant war between the American colonies and Britain. After the colonies' surprising military success in the Revolutionary War, the arduous task of constructing a government began. Colonists quickly realized that revolutionary rallying cries, such as "No taxation without representation," were little help in unifying states in any cause deeper than repelling the British. Other than a shared dislike for the British Crown, there was little comity among the states.

The short-lived Articles of Confederation best exemplify the complexities of creating a document that could actually govern the diverse group of states. The Articles of Confederation governed the American states from 1781–89, but left much to be desired. The weak, ineffectual central government scarcely provided any semblance of security, a fact that became abundantly clear during Shays's Rebellion of 1786–87, when mobs of farmers essentially held the Massachusetts government hostage. The absence of an executive made other policy areas unmanageable as well. Typically, a legislature develops laws and the executive branch enforces them, but without an executive, the federal government under the Articles needed the states to enforce the laws. This seldom happened because states often saw each other as competitors; they developed their own currencies and taxed each other's goods. In short, the Articles exacerbated already sharp differences among the states, doing little to bring them together as one country.

Constitutional framework for individual rights and democratic institutions

It was clear the Articles could not govern the thirteen states, yet exactly how to reform the Articles was less clear. People soon divided into two camps. On one side were the Federalists, who advocated for a much stronger central government with a powerful executive. Members of the opposition were appropriately labeled the Anti-Federalists. This side reasoned that a strong central government would eventually usurp the powers of the states, become distant from the people, override court decisions, and consequently limit liberty (Coleman, Goldstein, and Howell 2010).

Both sides hashed out their differences at the 1787 Constitutional Convention in Philadelphia. That summer, delegates from twelve states (Rhode Island chose not to participate), decided to scrap the Articles and write a new constitution. This document would create a new government: an executive branch with "vested" power and a Congress with powers enumerated. States had certain restrictions placed on them, such as the prohibition of entering into treaties with other countries separate from the other states. Additionally, the Constitution established an independent judiciary that eventually would have the power to pass judicial review over the actions and laws of the executive and legislative branches, and even over state laws.

The federalists and the anti-federalists

The 1787 Constitutional Convention hammered out many differences among the elites, but the Constitution was not yet law. Stipulations required nine of the thirteen states to ratify the Constitution before it could take effect. As it happened, this process took nearly a year. To sway wayward citizens to place their trust in the new Constitution, Federalists countered with the aptly titled *Federalist Papers*, 85 essays penned under the pseudonym Publius. In truth, Alexander Hamilton, James Madison, and John Jay authored the essays. Each essay laid out in painstaking detail why Americans should wholly scrap the Articles and replace them with the new Constitution. These papers incorporated foundational democratic principles that went on to guide political and legal institutions of the United States for centuries thereafter. For example, they stressed the importance of curbing government power through the separation of powers and a system of checks and balances. The Federalist papers also underscored the need to restrain the "tyranny of the majority," arguing that the United States should be a republic instead of a pure majority-rule democracy. In "Federalist number 10," James Madison explicitly addressed this issue, arguing that in a pure democracy factions would inevitably develop in the course of political decision making, as interested parties banded together to enhance their own stations at the expense of the public good. Thus, the "conflicts of rival parties" would be resolved not by a rational process of determining the best solution for all the people, but by a simple question of numbers. In a pure democracy, in which all individuals are permitted to participate directly in decision making, the will of the majority will invariably override the concerns of the minority, "in other words, the most powerful faction must be expected to prevail" (Rossiter 1961, 46).

To prevent this likely outcome, Madison advocated the creation of a republican system of government, in which the powers of the many are devolved to a few representatives. According to Madison, this would be the most effective way of ensuring that all interests were represented to the best extent possible. Although "enlightened statesmen will not always be at the helm," vesting power in a smaller number of individuals delegated by the people was expected to diminish the possibility that the individuals running the government would fall into chaos. In practice, this led to the democratically representative republican system that characterizes the US government to this day, with a legislative branch comprised of elected delegates to advocate on behalf of the people in the political decision-making process.

In the *Federalist Papers*, a critical group of elites clearly articulated their reasons for a strong centralized federal government, where three separate branches of government would check each other's power. Furthermore, the Federalists explained how their form of democracy would avoid popular pitfalls, such as the trampling of minority rights. Given the centrality of the *Federalist Papers* to the establishment of American democracy, these documents have also served as a guiding force in the evolution and interpretation of the Constitution.

The Anti-Federalists were not to be outdone, however. Led by revolutionary heroes like Patrick Henry, Anti-Federalists rejected the original Constitution because it lacked guarantees for the individual. Many state constitutions included a bill of rights, but Anti-Federalists deemed this insufficient, and they were not alone. They feared the strong national government under consideration would dwarf the rights of individuals. To win support for the proposed Constitution, elites forged a compromise in the form of the Bill of Rights. Shortly after the Constitution's ratification, delegates to the first US Congress agreed to the necessity of an enumerated Bill of Rights. Collectively, the first ten amendments of the Constitution, ratified by three-fourths the states in 1791, became the Bill of Rights.

The Bill of Rights

To protect citizens from the excesses of government power, particularly that wielded by a strong centralized state, the Bill of Rights enshrines individual rights and civil liberties (freedoms protecting citizens from the state). A brief sampling of the Bill of Rights includes a prohibition on Congress from establishing a religion, and from abridging freedom of speech, the press, or the right of people to peaceably assemble. People are to be secure in their persons, houses, papers, and effects against unreasonable searches and seizures. The government cannot require excessive bail, nor inflict cruel and unusual punishment. No person shall be compelled to be a witness against himself and the accused shall enjoy the right to a speedy trial.

Given the primacy of concerns over economic rights during the American Revolution, not surprisingly when the Framers put pen to parchment, they set out to design a system that would protect the individual's right to participate freely in the marketplace. The one portion of the market most cherished by the Founders to be beyond government reproach was private property. Prohibitions on government seizures of private property without "just compensation" guaranteed that the former colonists could use their property how they best saw fit, as well as leverage their property for economic gain.[4] As such, the protection of property was included in the Fifth Amendment of the Constitution, "No person shall be . . . deprived of life, liberty, or property . . . nor shall private property be taken for public use, without just compensation."

In addition to these protections on physical private property, the Framers also aimed to found a republic wherein individuals would have full freedom in how they interacted with the market. As Moore (1966) argues, the commercial middle classes pushed for greater political power to further their own interests, and in doing so laid the foundations for liberal democratic institutions. It is important to remember that at this point in history, both wealth and land ownership were more equally distributed among the population than in most other countries (with the glaring exception of slavery, of course). The size of the propertied class was, thus, much larger than was the norm, particularly when compared to countries with historically powerful aristocracies. Furthermore, from the very beginning of the colonization movement, earning a living was much more democratic in the New World than in Europe at that time. In America, families were free to engage in whatever labor their talent allowed. There were limited preconceived notions of birth permanently consigning one to a particular vocation. Economic development, itself, was democratic. Against this backdrop, to promote their own economic interests, the middle classes sought to carve a place for themselves in the state. Their emphasis on unencumbered economic freedom was highly conducive to similar views on political freedoms, making them natural advocates for democratic practices. That is, the "bourgeoisie's economic circumstances generated a set of economic and political beliefs that were conducive to democratization" (Goldblatt 1997, 55). While initially political participation was limited to this small bourgeoisie class, as education and economic empowerment expanded, the pool of eligible voters enlarged as well. Most importantly, the institutions designed in 1787 proved quite malleable and able to incorporate these new participants quite readily.

Designing accountable institutions: The principle of the separation of powers

In addition to offering strong protections for individual rights and liberties, the Framers also sought to check government power through institutional design, particularly through the separation of powers. This division of power facilitated a system of checks and balances across the three branches of government. It also aimed to safeguard against the possibility that one individual or faction could monopolize power (a safeguard made all the stronger by federalism's further dispersal of power between national and state governments). The Founders devised this system to ensure none of the three branches of government could dominate the others. The legislative, executive, and judicial branches each have particular responsibilities but, in theory, none is more important than the others. However, many scholars assert that because the Framers discuss the legislative branch first in the Constitution—and more has been written about it in comparison to the other two branches—they intended the legislative branch to be first among equals. Perhaps that was once the case, but over time the executive branch has gained more power vis-à-vis the legislative branch, with the judicial branch maintaining its role as resolver of disputes.

The legislative branch

The United States Congress is the legislative branch of American government. It is a bicameral institution comprised of the Senate (upper house) and the House of Representatives (lower house). Article I, Section 8 of the Constitution enumerates many of Congress's powers, specifically entitling it to declare war, borrow money, lay and collect taxes, coin money, develop a uniform rule of naturalization, establish post offices, and regulate commerce with foreign nations. Among other privileges, these powers belong exclusively to Congress.

Congress was designed according to the Burkean idea of legislatures comprised of "trustees" (the Senate) and "delegates" (the House). As such, the Senate follows a model in which constituents elect trustees who have autonomy to deliberate and act in the national public interest, rather than restrict themselves to the narrow interests of their own constituents. The 6-year length of a Senate term is intended to relieve these members from constant electioneering, and each state receives equal representation in the form of two senators. By contrast, Burke's delegate model, embodied in the House of Representatives, aimed to foster close ties between representatives and constituents. Delegates to the House are elected every two years, and as such, cannot abandon the direct interests of their constituents if they want the opportunity to return. Members of the House are also elected on a proportional basis, each state sending representatives to the House according to the size of its population, for a total of 435.

Given these roles, Congress is arguably the branch of government most directly related to real democracy. Its core responsibilities are to pass and oversee legislation and to represent constituents in the decision-making process (Clem 1989). The Founders envisioned Congress as the policy-making engine of the United States, giving it broad legislative powers, perhaps most importantly the "power of the purse," or the power to lay and collect taxes, and use the money to pay debts and "provide for the common defense and general welfare of the United States."

The executive branch

The Framers feared the possibility of a tyrant rising to power and therefore sought to curtail the executive branch. However, the dismal failure of the

Articles of Confederation made clear that a stronger executive branch was sorely needed to provide guidance and leadership to Congress. Without this leadership, Congress struggled to fulfill its role due to its limited ability to enforce compliance with its edicts. In this context, the Constitution, ratified in 1788, incorporated under Article II a separate executive branch of government, headed by the president of the United States. The executive discharges the duties of a commander in chief, nominates cabinet officers and members of the judiciary, negotiates treaties, and perhaps most importantly, sees "that the laws be faithfully executed." These powers render the president of the United States the highest political office in the land. The president serves as head of state and of government and as leader of the executive branch.

The president and vice president are the only two nationally elected federal officers. They are elected indirectly by the people via the Electoral College, an archaic feature of the electoral system designed to dilute the impulses of the masses, but which is now often viewed as outdated and unnecessary for the original purpose.[5] The president's term of office lasts four years and, as of 1951, each individual may serve only two terms. Among other powers, the president is commander in chief of the armed forces, and has the ability to direct foreign policy and military strategy. Congress constrains these powers, however, as it retains the power to declare war and to raise armies.

The Constitution also empowers the president to "faithfully execute" federal law via the employees of the federal executive branch, to nominate executive and judicial officers with the advice and consent of the Senate, and to grant pardons. Perhaps most importantly for the legislative process, the president has the power to veto legislation passed by Congress; to overturn the veto requires a two-thirds majority in both houses of Congress. This provides a powerful check on the legislative abilities of Congress, particularly in periods of "divided government" whereby different factions (i.e., political parties) control the legislative and executive branches.

The judicial branch

Article III of the Constitution created the judiciary. The pinnacle of the American judiciary system, the US Supreme Court, is the highest federal court in the United States. Congress has the power to determine its size and, currently, the Supreme Court consists of one chief justice and eight associate justices. The president, with congressional approval, appoints members to the Supreme Court for life—they may only be removed by impeachment, death, or resignation. The Supreme Court decides cases by majority vote, and its decisions are final. For much of American history, the Supreme Court has worked largely in collaboration with the other two branches of government, but on occasion, has placed itself in opposition to them (Baum 2007).

The Supreme Court also holds the power of judicial review, whereby it may review the actions of other branches of government as well as state governments, and assess whether or not they violate state or federal constitutions. Interestingly enough, the US Constitution did not clearly spell out the concept of judicial review. It was not until *Marbury v. Madison* (1803) that the Supreme Court established itself as the final arbiter on the constitutionality of federal and state laws.

Theoretically, the decisions of the Supreme Court were intended to be ideologically neutral. Justices were expected to account only for the facts of the case, legal precedent, and the text of the Constitution. However, much research has indicated that, in fact, the vast majority of a justice's opinions on a given case can be attributed to political ideology and individual political and legal philosophy (George and Epstein 1992, Rohde and Spaeth 1976). The written word can be interpreted in many ways, and as Emanuel Celler famously said in Congress:

> When one group of lawyers and judges upholds the constitutionality of desirable laws and another group declares such laws to be unconstitutional it is perfectly plain that, in the language of Chief Justice Hughes, "the Constitution is what the judges say it is." (Clayton and Gillman 1999)[6]

The ideological tenor of the Supreme Court depends heavily upon the presiding individuals (Clayton and Gillman 1999). For example, in the 1950s and 1960s the court was marked by relative liberalism under Chief Justice Earl Warren. This stance contrasts sharply with the comparative conservatism of the current court under Chief Justice John Roberts. Democratic and civil rights have expanded and contracted along with the shift in ideological currents, as the Supreme Court has interpreted and reinterpreted the Constitution and the Bill of Rights.

While the Supreme Court can have a powerful role in governance, it is important to remember that it has no way of enforcing compliance with its decisions. As such, the court is reliant on the other branches of government and on the bureaucracy to enforce its decisions. When the costs of compliance are considered to be high compared to the costs of noncompliance, federal agencies will often simply ignore a Supreme Court ruling (Spriggs

1997); they may outright defy the decision, evade compliance, or comply narrowly, rather than fully.

Despite these limitations, the judicial branch has played a pivotal role in the expansion of American democracy, particularly as civil society has used the court as a venue for challenging undemocratic practices. The most dramatic examples of this interaction occurred under the leadership of the Warren Court (1953–69), named after Chief Justice Warren. During this time, the court issued a series of historically significant decisions that fundamentally reshaped American democracy. The Warren Court expanded the definition of democratic rights related to desegregation,[7] voting and redistricting,[8] criminal procedure,[9] free speech,[10] the establishment[11] and free exercise of religion,[12] the right to privacy and reproductive rights,[13] and cruel and unusual punishment.[14] Each of these rulings expanded the rights of Americans under the court's interpretation of the Constitution, many overturning decades-old rulings restricting the degree to which rights and liberties exist under the law.

American federalism

In addition to checks and balances among federal institutions, the United States employs a method of federalism to divide power between the national government and the fifty states. In essence, federalism is a power-sharing arrangement whereby the national government retains some powers, the states retain others, and some powers belong concurrently to both levels. The actual practice of federalism in the United States is an ever-evolving mix of give-and-take between the national and state governments. How one interprets the proper role of the different governments is the root cause of partisan and ideological divisions. Needless to say, many policymaking debates, constitutional questions arising for judicial review, and even the Civil War have invoked federalism.

In sum, the Framers designed the institutions of American government to maintain the stability of republican democracy via the separation of powers and checks and balances. The three branches of government complement and constrain each other as "separated institutions sharing powers" (Neustadt 1960). The Constitution enumerates the functions of each branch of government, and few amendments have altered their capacity and key structure over the centuries. In addition, federalism ensures power is further divided between national and state governments. Although the powers of these various institutional actors have waxed and waned with variations in the political climate at home and abroad, the flexibility of the design and each institution's ability to maintain and protect its powers have been essentially untouched since their inception. This system has long been considered a key mechanism by which American democracy weathers economic and international storms and protects the democratic rights and liberties of the people from incursion by various governmental institutions.

Expanding democracy

Institutions set the stage for American democracy, but elites have interacted with these institutions to shape American political development. Since the time of independence, elites have played a crucial role in molding American governance. Indeed, the foundation of American democracy was an elite-led process. Two groups of elites, the Federalists and Anti-Federalists, engaged in heated debate about the best form of governance and aimed to sway public opinion through oral debates or published editorials. Most importantly, early American elites did not rely on military might to enforce their ideals, as transpired in other newly independent countries.

Still, for quite some time elites were leery of popular participation in governance, impeding the spread of democracy in the truest sense of the word. Most states limited suffrage to property-owning white males. Protecting and encouraging electoral participation among citizens is a fundamental criterion for truly democratic states. Even the most minimal definition of a democratic state stipulates electoral accountability of political representatives (Held 1996). However, universal suffrage for all American adults, regardless of gender and race, is relatively new. For more than a century after the founding of the republic, the right to vote was denied to women and slaves, and in practice, to all African-Americans and many others. The extension of suffrage was a long, and often violent, process. To understand this expansion of American democracy, it is important to examine the interactions of both elites and civil society with political institutions.

For the first fifty years the US Constitution was the law of the land, voting was largely restricted to property owners. While property qualifications for voting were low compared to the rest of the world, these stipulations barred the majority of the population from voting. Not until the Jacksonian era (1829–37), with its accompanying wave of populism, did reforms loosen requirements so that all white males could vote. Under Jackson, 80 percent of white men became eligible voters. While not democratic by today's standards, American governance "by no stretch of the imagination could any longer be described as elite" (Maidment 1997, 123). Instead of fearing the tyranny of the majority, political leaders increasingly sought to connect with the mass public, at least in public discourse. Elites needed the masses to win elections. Jackson in particular sought to heighten public participation in politics and governance. For example, he advocated replacing appointed judges with elected ones, and assigning the "common man" to civil service positions under a system of patronage.

Economic factors played a large role in the expansion of white male suffrage. Following Jackson's widespread removal of Native Americans from many of their lands, the greater availability of land for white settlers created a larger propertied class than in other parts of the world. In addition, the growing industrialization of the economy in the North changed the status quo, as the "rapid expansion of commerce and industry provided new sources of economic power, [which] required and demanded political representation" (Maidment 1997, 123).

Advances in education also propelled expansions of suffrage. In his famous journey across America, De Tocqueville (1945 [1835, 1840]) observed that access to education created a far more literate population in America than in Europe. Helping education flourish was the absence of a landed aristocracy that in other countries separated and restricted education for elites. Relative to many other Western countries, America had a head start in educating its population. By the end of the nineteenth century, well over half the states had compulsory state education laws. Besides producing youngsters clever enough to use their wits to make a living and not rely solely on manual labor for employment, these laws created a population with knowledge enough to challenge the very government providing that education. In other words, producing sharp citizens requires the state to stay sharp itself. A more educated population has greater economic mobility and demands greater political participation for itself and for others.

Such demands are often contested, however, as the Civil War (1861–65) painfully demonstrated. The relatively easy spread of suffrage throughout the white male population stands in stark contrast to the violent resistance its expansion to other groups provoked. The large-scale granting of rights to nonwhite men started in the immediate aftermath of the Civil War. The Thirteenth, Fourteenth, and Fifteenth Amendments, known together as the Civil War amendments, freed the slaves, defined citizenship, and extended suffrage to black males respectively. In the wake of the Civil War and the passage of the Fifteenth Amendment to the Constitution in 1870, the victorious North, initially through military might, enforced black men's right to vote. With military enforcement, the Fifteenth Amendment was a success, leading to the election of two black senators in Mississippi and twenty black southern representatives to the House of Representatives during the period of Reconstruction.[15] In addition, hundreds of former slaves served in Southern state legislatures.

America was, for one brief period, the only large nation in which former slaves enjoyed a genuine measure of political power after emancipation. This lasted just over a decade, however, as a tremendous wave of violence transformed these revolutionary gains into the Jim Crow perversion of democracy that dominated the South in the early twentieth century (Alexander 2004). Elites led the charge against the extension of suffrage. South Carolina's Senator "Pitchfork" Ben Tillman, who spearheaded one of the bloodiest campaigns against black enfranchisement, expressed most clearly what happened after Reconstruction: "We have done our level best. We have scratched our heads to find out how we could eliminate every last one of them. We stuffed ballot boxes. We shot them. We are not ashamed of it (Logan 1965, 91)." All over the South, African-Americans, and those perceived to support black political equality, met with violent repression when they attempted to vote or run for office.[16]

Ultimately, the federal government met this violence by abandoning Reconstruction. In 1877, Southern Democrats struck a deal with the Republican presidential candidate, Rutherford B. Hayes, to help him prevail in the contested election of 1876.[17] In exchange for Hayes's win, the military force that had protected the burgeoning political gains of African-Americans in the South was withdrawn. By supporting Hayes, Southern Democrats were able to regain control of the region, and shortly thereafter introduced the notorious Black Codes and the discriminatory laws of the Jim Crow era. The Black Codes were laws enacted to regulate black labor, essentially perpetuating the chattel-like treatment of black Americans that predated the Civil War. "Jim Crow" generally refers to state and local laws passed both in the North and the South in the period 1876–1965. These laws rested on the "separate but equal" doctrine and mandated segregation in all public facilities. The process of disenfranchisement that followed in every Southern state dominated political life in the region, as states called constitutional conventions and passed amendments. The Southern white political elites used violence, intimidation, and corruption to regain power (Logan 1965).

Legal barriers, including poll taxes and outrageously difficult literary tests, were employed in a discriminatory fashion to ensure African-Americans could not contest power in any meaningful way. "Grandfather clauses" were enacted to enable white illiterates whose grandfathers had voted to bypass these obstacles. By the middle of the twentieth century, much of the violence and intimidation that prevented black Americans from voting actually took place long before election day. Just registering to vote was the most danger-ous step, so intimidation at the polls was not as important as it became in later decades. Most African-Americans simply never got as far as the poll-ing booths. Without the right to vote, they could not serve on juries and could not hold office. Disenfranchisement had far-reaching democratic consequences.

Black men won the constitutional right to vote in 1870, but most could not effectively practice this right until the 1960s. In contrast, white women were denied suffrage at the national level until passage of the Nineteenth Amendment in 1920, but they were able to exercise their newly won rights immediately after their right was enshrined in the Constitution. The Nineteenth Amendment represented the culmination of a long struggle. Elizabeth Cady Stanton led early efforts to secure the right to vote, pre-senting the Declaration of Sentiments in 1848, which historians credit with kick-starting the women's suffrage movement. Many suffragettes ardently supported the abolitionist movement, and were dismayed to find the Fifteenth Amendment prohibited voting restrictions based on race, color, or previous condition of servitude, but not on gender. As World War I ground to a close in 1918, women activists watched from across the Atlantic as women won suffrage in a wave of European countries. Finally, in 1920, Tennessee became the 36th state to ratify the Nineteenth Amendment, and women's suffrage became a reality. Following this accomplishment, women became active participants in a full range of electoral activities, and featured particularly prominently in the Civil Rights Movement of the 1960s, when conflict over racial equality consumed the nation.

The Civil Rights Movement aimed to restore the rights stripped from African-Americans for nearly a century. Throughout the first half of the nineteenth century, attempts to extend real equality to black Americans had been stymied. Southern congressional Democrats proved particularly adept at using institutional rules to block efforts at extending political rights and civil liberties. The institutional checks designed as safeguards against the tyranny of the majority meant that change often came slowly to the American political system. In the legislature, numerically small groups could block the passage of controversial legislation through mechanisms like the filibuster, which requires a "super majority" to end debate in the Senate. Unless a super majority voted to end debate, Southern Democrats could discuss any topic for as long as they wished on the Senate floor. These long discussions, sometimes completely unrelated to the topic of civil rights or even to politics more broadly, were employed to delay a Senate vote on civil rights.

Civil society was not deterred by such tactics. Given Congressional impediments, civil society turned to the courts to press for full equality. Several court victories paved the way for the landmark case of *Brown v. Board of Education* (1954), in which the Supreme Court unanimously declared that in public school education separate but equal could not possibly be equal, and therefore was unconstitutional. This decision set off a decade of marches, sit-ins and demonstrations as African-Americans and their white allies impatiently tried to end Jim Crow rule throughout the South.[18] Black churches supplied crucial organizational resources, and figures like Dr. Martin Luther King, Jr., provided inspirational leadership (Calhoun-Brown 1996). Civil society mobilized to protest the denial of rights through momentous events like the 1955 Montgomery, Alabama, bus boycott (inspired by Rosa Parks) and the 1961 Freedom Rides (led by an interracial group of college students trying to call attention to the lack of voting rights for Southern blacks). This wave of civil action was violently contested. For example, during the 1964 Freedom Summer in Mississippi, racial bigots murdered three civil rights workers who were trying to register blacks to vote.

Perseverance paid off in the form of the Civil Rights Act of 1964. This act abolished much of the *de jure* segregation of the races in daily life across the South. No longer could Southern laws make blacks drink from separate water fountains, sit in the back of the bus, or watch a movie from the balcony—among dozens of other daily humiliations. The *coup de grace*, perhaps, was the Voting Rights Act of 1965 (VRA). This act, which ended Jim Crow voting restrictions, was the linchpin of racial equality in the political process. A monumental legislative achievement of modern democracy, the VRA—accompanied by intense and sustained federal involvement and enforcement—at last made it possible to secure meaningful and lasting voting rights for African-Americans.

The 1965 VRA built on legislation passed in 1957, 1960, and 1964, strengthening the ability to bring legal challenges to court and adding other enforcement mechanisms, including federal registrars and observers as well as requirements for areas with poor voting rights records. The VRA outlawed literacy tests as qualifications for voting and provided for federal registration of voters in areas in which less than fifty percent of the population was registered to vote (Howard 1999).

Even with these positive changes, however, enforcing the law was a struggle against what, in many areas, was by then a deeply ingrained system of racism and repression. After the initial focus on the VRA faded, new ways to curtail minority political power evolved. In 1968, the United States

Commission on Civil Rights (USCCR) published a report evaluating the effect of the VRA on African-Americans in ten Southern states (USCCR 1968). This report noted the great upsurge in voter registration, voting, and other forms of political participation by black Americans in the South, but it identified the emergence of many new barriers to political participation. For example, to prevent African-Americans from becoming candidates or winning office, some elites simply abolished or changed the name of a particular office, or extended the term of a white incumbent. States kept black Americans off voting lists, failed to give them proper instructions at the polls, disqualified ballots incorrectly, or failed to provide sufficient voting facilities. Finally, fraudulently boosting the vote for opposing candidates, and simple physical and economic intimidation (for example, threatening to fire a politically active African-American) have been noted over the years following the passage of the VRA (USCCR 1981).

Do such problems persist in the twenty-first century? It has been alleged that a strong current of racial antipathy drove many of the conflicts that tainted the 2000 and 2004 presidential elections. Following the 2000 Florida debacle, the USCCR held hearings in Miami and Tallahassee with over one hundred witnesses, including Florida Governor Jeb Bush, Florida Secretary of State Katherine Harris, and a number of election workers and voters who had firsthand knowledge of election day problems. Having uncovered extensive evidence of voter fraud and intimidation, the commission issued a report on a range of racially related issues relevant to the 2000 election (USCCR 2001). The report concluded that the Voting Rights Act had been violated in the administration of the 2000 election.[19] In particular, the dramatic undercount of votes that resulted from erroneous registration challenges that year produced widespread disenfranchisement that fell most heavily on the shoulders of minority voters (Fessenden 2004). After months of postelection debate, Congress passed the *Help America Vote Act* (HAVA) in 2002, a comprehensive piece of legislation representing the first federal involvement in elections administration since the Voting Rights Act of 1965. Millions of federal dollars were budgeted to assist states in meeting election reform mandates, with deadlines set for 2004 and 2006.

In 2004, racially motivated voter intimidation tactics were reported all over the country, but particularly in the battleground states of Florida, Ohio, and Pennsylvania. The NAACP also documented a wide variety of other intimidation and suppression tactics throughout the nation, apparently aimed directly at minority voters, and often limited to predominantly black geographic locations. Signs were found posted at polling places warning of penalties for "voter fraud" or "noncitizen" voting, or illegally urging support for a particular candidate. Poll workers were seen illegally "helping" voters fill out their ballots, and instructing them on how to vote. Criminal tampering with voter registration rolls and records was discovered in some places. Fliers and radio advertisements containing false information about where, when, and how to vote; voter eligibility; and bogus threats of penalties blanketed some African-American communities. Finally, internal memos from party officials were discovered in which the explicit goal of suppressing black voter turnout was outlined (NAACP 2004).[20] However, perhaps the most positive thing that could be said about the 2004 election was that by sheer good luck, the winning side "exceeded the margin of litigation" (Election Reform Information Project 2004). In other words, had the results of these elections been as close as in 2000, the many serious problems that continued to riddle the system would have provided ample grounds for challenge, and further undermined confidence in American democracy. While the dramatic postelection drama of 2000 was narrowly avoided in 2004, by 2008 the presidential election went off without a hitch. Thus, while recent elections have not completely escaped the problems of racial inequality, Congress has continued to address these inequalities through subsequent legislation, and has succeeded in improving political equality in practice.

These lingering problems notwithstanding, the civil rights movement showcases how civil society extended American democracy despite the ways in which some elites manipulated institutions to maintain social divisions that undermined democracy. Elites may have created American democracy, but civil society was instrumental in extending and strengthening it through the push for universal adult suffrage. Racial divides have historically threatened to undermine and weaken American democracy, but the civil rights movement and subsequent legislation demonstrates how civil society has successfully challenged this status quo, and in the process strengthened and deepened American democracy.

Political culture

Racial divisions and inequality are the most glaring exceptions to a political culture that is widely considered to be supportive of democracy. De Tocqueville was one of the first to note the pervasiveness of equality in American political culture and to link American political culture to the success of democracy. Indeed, as early as the 1830s he viewed the destruction of slavery as imminent, as it was completely incompatible with the ubiquitous nature of equality in American life. While American political culture has long been thought to support democracy, this political culture does take distinct regional forms. Historically, American political culture has tended to be individualistic, almost libertarian, egalitarian, and is arguably derived from Calvinist underpinnings that stipulate, in effect, that most people get what they deserve. The founding principles of American political culture can be found in the Constitution and the Bill of Rights, along with historical documents such as the Federalist Papers and the Declaration of Independence. In addition to the norms described in these papers, researchers have described a clear typology for different variants of American political culture. These are grounded in historical, demographic, and attitudinal shifts (Elazar 1984).

Briefly, the *moralistic* subculture developed from the norms and values of early Puritan colonists, whose influence spread over New England and the upper northern states, and over to the West, including the entire West Coast. The political system of the moralist state looks like a commonwealth, and is perhaps the most likely to induce political efficacy among the citizenry: legislation tends to be based on communitarian principles of good government, and citizens are expected to participate fully in the democratic process. The bureaucracy is supposed to be isolated from political influence, and there is little tolerance for corruption (Elazar 1984).

In contrast, the *individualistic* subculture follows a more libertarian definition of democracy. This type was founded by immigrants searching for economic opportunity, who colonized the mid-Atlantic states and later settled much of the Midwest and parts of the Southwest. This culture is reminiscent of a political market: the passage of legislation is contingent on public demand, and politics is treated as a much more specialized business than in moralistic states. Rather than encouraging full participation by all citizens, the individualistic culture requires more qualifications from those who would involve themselves in politics. Electoral competition in these states is highly partisan, and the bureaucracy is expected to be responsive to elected officials (Elazar 1984).

The third type of political subculture is the *traditionalistic,* found primarily in the South. The protection of the existing sociopolitical status quo is perceived as the function of government. Politics in traditionalistic states tends to be hierarchical and paternalistic, with less mass participation. Bureaucracies in these states are less powerful (Elazar 1984).

Although the political culture of the United States clearly varies in important ways from region to region, and commitment to ensuring full democratic rights for all members of the population also varies from region to region, the founding principles of American democracy are shared across the nation. Americans tend to enthusiastically support their system of democratic governance, even while disparaging specific elites, political parties, or institutions.

International context

The international context shaped the inception of American democracy. Colonists broke free from the British yoke of monarchy to establish their republic in 1776. Taxation without representation and the quartering of troops had sufficiently angered enough colonists that they were willing to abandon the British Empire. Throughout the Revolutionary War, France provided aid and assistance to the nascent democracy. French political ideals also inspired colonists seeking to shape their own republic. Once the United States succeeded in separating from Britain, however, its isolated geographical location and subsequent super-power status made the international context less important for the extension of democracy than did domestic factors. To be sure, international events often encouraged domestic developments. For example, when black soldiers fought for democracy in World War II, they returned home less willing to accept a status quo that denied them equal democratic rights. In this sense, international context did have some impact on the extension of democracy; however, domestic factors tended to have more of an influence over American political development.

Conclusion

To explain the emergence of one of the world's oldest democracies, economic factors are very important. The early American bourgeoisie pushed for political reform as a means of protecting their private property and promoting private enterprise. These entrepreneurs and landholders transformed themselves into political elites and established strong institutions to protect their economic interests and preserve their voices in politics. As education and economic mobility spread throughout the population, political rights and participation in governance also spread, at least among the white male population. Unfortunately for those seeking the voting franchise, however, social divisions impeded democracy until relatively recently. Elites in particular used institutional loopholes to preserve the status quo of inequality. Civil society successfully challenged systematic political exclusion, although problems still remain in the twenty-first century.

Race has historically been the dividing factor in American democracy; however, other divisions have emerged in more recent times. Recent research indicates that a tremendously important cleavage has arisen and currently shapes partisan identification. This new cleavage places evangelical Protestants and religious conservatives from other faiths on the Republican side of the two-party equation. By contrast, Democrats have come to represent the secularists and religious liberals from various faith traditions (Layman 2001). This divide began to emerge in the early 1980s, as evangelicals from around America began to mobilize politically for the first time since the debacle of the Scopes "Monkey Trial" of the 1930s.

While American democracy is a story of success, nonetheless, challenges to democratic rights and freedoms are found on both sides of the political aisle to this day. Powerful special interests lobby successfully to influence legislation. The tremendous expense of a successful political campaign prevents the vast majority of Americans from contemplating this kind of democratic participation. The criminal justice system disproportionately targets some demographic groups, particularly African-Americans, and the ramifications of this reality influence the rights and freedoms of all black Americans. Finally, as was dramatically in evidence in the 2000 presidential election, the hodgepodge of state and local voting systems, and the occasional disastrous effects of outdated or faulty voting technology, can seriously undermine the reality of "one person, one vote" in US elections. These challenges illustrate that even once established, democratic governance requires vigilance and constant care to remain successful.

Additional resources

For an overview of the initial expansion of democracy in the United States, Alexis de Tocqueville's classic *Democracy in America* offers insights that inform both historical and contemporary debates on American political culture. A PBS documentary also provides an overview of Andrew Jackson's presidency and Jacksonian democracy: www.pbs.org/kcet/andrewjackson/ (accessed September 10, 2010). For more recent times, there are several excellent firsthand accounts of the struggle to extend democracy to all American citizens. Carlotta Walls Lanier's autobiography, *A Mighty Long Way: My Journey to Justice at Little Rock Central High School*, provides a riveting account of the desegregation of schools in the South from the perspective of the black students. Martin Luther King, Jr.'s *Stride toward Freedom: the Montgomery Story* powerfully narrates the work of the civil rights movement. Two documentaries complement these readings, Peter Gilbert's *With All Deliberate Speed* (2004) and Orlando Bagwell and Noland Walker's *Citizen King*.

Notes

1 As quoted in Vile (1997, 255). Ellis writes that the other delegates regarded these words as a "mere rhetorical flourish" but that in fact, "With these words, Jefferson had smuggled the revolutionary agenda into the founding document, casually and almost inadvertently planting the seeds that would grow into the expanding mandate for individual rights that eventually ended slavery, made women's suffrage inevitable, and sanctioned the civil rights of all minorities" (Ellis, 2007, 56).

2 As cited in Vile (1997, 255).

3 Debate over the Articles of Confederation involved questions of the representation of states of varying sizes, methods of representation, territorial debate regarding undeveloped land to the west, and issues of funding the new government. Ultimately, it was settled that Congress would operate on the principle of one state, one vote, with a unicameral legislature and no executive or judiciary branch. States were asked to continue funding Congress not by taxation, but with requisition requests (Rakove, 1979).

4 For a deeper understanding of how this process economically benefited America and the West, see De Soto's (2003) *Mystery of Capital.*

5 Rather than vote directly for president and vice president, citizens in the United States vote for Electoral College representatives. These representatives are not technically bound by anything but convention to vote for the individual they pledge to support. However, "faithless electors"—those who do not vote for the pledged candidate—are very rare, and have never altered the outcome of an election. In terms of American democracy, the Electoral College can have deleterious effects: for instance, it has been argued that presidential campaigns tend to focus obsessively on the outcomes in large swing states, ignoring states with small populations or predictable outcomes. In the aftermath of the 2000 president election, critics sharply assailed this feature of the electoral system, as the Electoral College winner (George W. Bush) did not win the popular vote.

6 He made this statement in reference to President Franklin Roosevelt's court-packing plan.

7 *Brown v. Board of Education*, overturning the "separate but equal" ruling of *Plessy v. Ferguson*, and *Loving v. Virginia*, declaring anti-miscegenation laws to be unconstitutional.

8 *Reynolds v. Sims*, ruling that state legislatures must be roughly equal in size, in proportion to the population, and *Baker v. Carr*, declaring that reapportionment of political districts contained justiciable questions, and could not be left to the political jurisdiction alone.

9 Including *Miranda v. Arizona*, which ensured that statements made prior to informing an individual of the right to an attorney were inadmissible; and *Katz v. United States*, which protected individuals in a telephone booth from wiretaps without a warrant.

10 *Yates v. United States*, protecting radical and revolutionary speech unless it posed a "clear and present danger" and *Tinker v. Des Moines Independent Community School District*, protecting free speech at schools.

11 *Engel v. Vitale*, preventing state officials from composing and requiring the recitation of an official school prayer in public schools, and Abington *School District v. Schempp*, declaring school-sponsored Bible reading in public schools to be unconstitutional.

12 *Sherbert v. Verner*, imposing strict standards on the government in denying unemployment compensation to people fired because their job conflicted with their religion.

13 *Griswold v. Connecticut*, which overturned a Connecticut ban on contraception.

14 *Trop v. Dulles*, which prevented the state from canceling citizenship as punishment.

15 The Reconstruction era refers generally to the post-Civil War period in the United States, and more specifically to the postwar period in the South, during which substantial political, economic, and social change took place, driven in part by policies imposed by the federal government and intended to support the economic redevelopment of the South as well as bring it into compliance with federal law (Valelly 2004).

16 One particularly brutal episode, the Colfax Massacre, took place following a disputed election in Louisiana's Red River Valley. Whites armed with rifles and a cannon attacked a courthouse being held by black freedmen and black state militia. Most of the freedmen were killed following their surrender, and many others were killed after having been held for several hours. Although estimates vary, the total deaths may have included as many as 150 black men and three white men (Keith 2007).

17 Having lost the popular vote to his opponent, Samuel Tilden, by approximately 250,000 votes, Hayes's victory was eventually determined by a Congressional commission. Three states whose votes were in dispute—Florida, Louisiana, and South Carolina—were in the South. In order to win the election, Republicans gave assurances to Southern Democrats that the military occupation of the South would end, and troops would be withdrawn.

18 Northern elites felt particularly pressured by these tactics, as many of their newer constituents were black Americans who had migrated from the South to the North to take advantage of employment opportunities in industrial sectors.

19 It should be noted that the VRA does not merely apply to *intent* to discriminate—rather, violations can be "established by evidence that the action or inaction of responsible officials and other evidence constitute a 'totality of the circumstances' that denied citizens their right to vote." In other words, differences in voting technology and procedures that advantage whites and disadvantage minority voters can still be condemned as discriminatory violations of the VRA, absent clear intent or conspiracy to discriminate.

20 In one instance, Michigan State Representative John Pappageorge was quoted as having said "If we do not suppress the Detroit vote, we're going to have a tough time in this election." Detroit's population at the time was 83 percent African-American.

References

Alexander, Danielle. 2004. "Forty Acres and a Mule: The Ruined Hope of Reconstruction." In *Humanities,* January/February, vol. 25, no. 1.

Baum, Lawrence. 2007. *The Supreme Court.* Washington D.C.: CQ Press.

Bernard, Bailyn, ed. 1993a. *The Debate on the Constitution: Federalist and Antifederalist Speeches, Articles, and Letters during the Struggle for Ratification. Part 1: September 1781–February 1788.* New York: Library of America.

Calhoun-Brown, Allison. 1996. "African American Churches and Political Mobilization: The Psychological Impact of Organizational Resources." *The Journal of Politics,* 58, 4:935–53.

Clem, Alan L. 1989. *Congress: Powers, Processes and Politics.* CA: Pacific Grove, CA: Brooks and Cole Publishers.

Clayton, Cornell W., and Howard Gillman, eds. 1999. *Supreme Court Decision-Making: New Institutionalist Approaches.* Chicago and London: University of Chicago Press.

Coleman, John, Kenneth Goldstein, and William Howell. 2010. *Understanding American Politics and Government.* New York: Longman.

De Soto, Hernando. 2003. *The Mystery of Capital: Why Capitalism Triumphs in the West and Fails Everywhere Else.* New York: Basic Books.

De Tocqueville, Alexis. 2004 [1835–40]. *Democracy in America.* New York: Bantam Classic.

Elazar, Daniel J. 1984. *American Federalism: A View from the States.* New York: Thomas Y. Crowell.

Election Reform Information Project. 2004. *Briefing: The 2004 Election.* Washington, D.C.: The University of Richmond and Electionline.org. Accessed January, 2005. www.electionline.org.

Ellis, Joseph J. 2007. *American Creation.* New York: Random House.

Fessenden, Ford. 2004. "Florida List for Purge of Voters Proves Flawed." *The New York Times,* July 10.

George, Tracey E., and Lee Epstein. 1992. "On the Nature of Supreme Court Decision Making." *American Political Science Review,* 86:323–37.

Goldblatt, David. 1997. Democracy in the "long nineteenth century": 1760–1919. In *Democratization*, David Potter, David Goldblatt, Margaret Kiloh and Paul Lewis, eds, 46–70. Malden, MA: Blackwell Publishers, Inc.

Held, David. *Models of Democracy.* 1996. Stanford: Stanford University Press.

Howard, John R. 1999. *The Shifting Wind: The Supreme Court and Civil Rights from Reconstruction to Brown.* New York: State University of New York Press.

Keith, LeeAnna. 2007. *The Colfax Massacre: The Untold Story of Black Power, White Terror, and the Death of Reconstruction.* New York: Oxford University Press.

Layman, Geoffrey. 2001. *The Great Divide: Religious and Cultural Conflict in American Party Politics.* New York: Columbia University Press.

Logan, Rayford W. 1965. *The Betrayal of the Negro, from Rutherford B. Hayes to Woodrow Wilson.* New York: Da Capo Press.

Maidment, Richard. 1997. "Democracy in the USA since 1945." In *Democratization*, David Potter, David Goldblatt, Margaret Kiloh and Paul Lewis, 118–39. Malden, MA: Blackwell Publishers, Inc.

Moore, Barrington. 1966. *Social Origins of Dictatorship and Democracy: Lord and Peasant in the Making of the Modern World.* Boston: Beacon Press.

National Association for the Advancement of Colored People. 2004. *The Long Shadow of Jim Crow: Voter Intimidation and Suppression in America Today.* People for the American Way Foundation and the National Association for the Advancement of Colored People. August 25. Accessed April 2005 at www.pfaw.org.

Neustadt, Richard E. 1960. *Presidential Power: The Politics of Leadership.* New York: Wiley.

Rakove, Jack. 1979. *The Beginnings of National Politics: An Interpretive History of the Continental Congress.* New York: Knopf.

Rohde, David W., and Harold J. Spaeth. 1976. *Supreme Court Decision Making.* San Francisco: W. H. Freeman & Company.

Rossiter, Clinton, ed. *The Federalist Papers.* 1961. New York: New American Library.

Spriggs, James F. II. 1997. "Explaining Federal Bureaucratic Compliance with Supreme Court Opinions." *Political Research Quarterly,* 50(3):567–93.

United States Commission on Civil Rights. 2001. *Voting Irregularities in Florida during the 2000 Presidential Election.*

Valelly, Richard M. 2004. *The Two Reconstructions: The Struggle for Black Enfranchisement.* Chicago: University of Chicago Press.

Vile, John R. 1997. *A Companion to the United States Constitution and Its Amendment, second edition.* Westport, CT: Praeger.

6

The Emergence and Evolution of Democracy in Switzerland

Paolo Dardanelli[1]

In the modern period, democracy has been crucial to the Swiss state and its people to an extent probably unmatched elsewhere. Not only was the acquisition of democracy one of the forces driving the creation of the Swiss federal state, but democratic ideals have formed an important part of Swiss national identity and even provided justification for the existence of the country itself. Switzerland's historic path to democratization and the nature of its contemporary democratic government are also rather distinctive, making the country an interesting test case for democratization theories.

Perhaps most interesting is the way in which diversity did not impede early democracy. Despite its small size, Switzerland has long housed a very diverse population, ranging from the urban belt stretching from Southwest to Northeast (including the cities of Geneva and Zurich) to the mostly Alpine and sparsely populated areas in the South and Southeast. Geographic diversity is coupled with linguistic diversity, with about 70 percent of the population speaking German, 20 percent speaking French, 5 percent speaking Italian and less than 1 percent speaking Romansh, all of which have official status. Religious divides also abound, particularly between a traditionally dominant Protestant community and a large Catholic minority, as well as minorities of more recent formation, such as the Muslim population.

This chapter explores the emergence and evolution of democracy in Switzerland. The first section provides a concise historical overview of the development of the Swiss political system and outlines its emergence by the mid-nineteenth century as a democratic federal state. The second section traces the development of Swiss democracy since the formation of the federal state, devoting particular attention to Switzerland's distinctive system of semi-direct and consensual democracy. This section also analyzes an intriguing paradox: Switzerland was one of the first countries to democratize, but did not extend suffrage to women at the federal level until 1971. The third section turns to examine Swiss democracy today. The conclusion identifies both the similarities and differences between Switzerland's political development and that of other countries, pointing to insights the Swiss case offers for the comparative study of democratization and democracy.

The establishment of limited democracy

The old confederation

The origins of the Swiss political system are traditionally traced to a series of complex treaty systems dating back to the late thirteenth century. One of the most famous of these treaties emerged in 1291, when an oath of mutual support and defense between representatives of the three valley communities of Uri, Schwyz, and Unterwalden (*de jure* subject to the German emperor but *de facto* enjoying virtual autonomy) reaffirmed the desire to preserve their freedom from imperial encroachment. After the battle of Morgarten in 1315, when the "confederates" defeated the Habsburg army, the initial alliance attracted other members and slowly acquired a more permanent character. By the mid-fourteenth century, five other *Orte,* or localities (Lucerne, Zurich, Glarus, Zug, and Berne) joined the alliance. The arrival of powerful cities such as Berne and Zurich greatly strengthened the nascent confederation and at the same time introduced a cleavage between rural and urban areas that would be an enduring feature of Swiss politics.

In the subsequent century or so, the *Orte* embarked on aggressive territorial expansion and consolidated their de facto independence within the empire, acquired at the end of the Swabian War in 1499. By 1515, five other members had joined (Fribourg, Solothurn, Basle, Schaffausen, and

Appenzell) bringing the number of confederated units to thirteen. In the same year, the defeat at Marignano marked the end of the phase of military conquest and set the stage for the eventual adoption of a policy of neutrality. By this time, the confederation was widely seen as a "distinct political unit within the German Empire" (Sablonier, quoted in Zimmer 2003, 21) and had acquired relative stability both internally and externally. However, the Reformation, which was adopted in a patchwork fashion, introduced a second deep cleavage, that between Protestants and Catholics, which would be a source of recurrent conflicts down to the end of the nineteenth century. In fact, while the confederates stuck to their neutrality and kept out of the Thirty Years' War, they could not avoid a series of internecine religious wars. With the Treaty of Westphalia, the independence of the Swiss *Orte* from the Holy Roman Empire received official recognition. The neutrality of the *Orte* was also confirmed. Over the following one hundred years, the confederation enjoyed a period of renewed stability, facilitating the consolidation of government.

The institutional structure of the system was a form of confederation based on a complicated set of alliances among the thirteen *Orte* (of which the oldest eight had some privileges), nine allied states, and some subject territories. The system was based on a series of treaties and governed by a confederal Diet, made up of two representatives per *Ort*. Some of the allied states, such as St. Gallen, had the right of representation in the Diet while others, such as Geneva, did not (de Capitani 1983, 130–31). The territories conquered during the expansion of the fifteenth century had the status of subject territories, governed individually or collectively by the *Orte* with no right of representation in the Diet but a substantial degree of local self-government (Hughes 1975, 90–92; de Capitani 1983, 137). The full members of the confederation were all German-speaking, with the partial exception of Fribourg. German was the sole official language in use, but allied states and subject territories comprised large French- and Italian-speaking populations.

Among the thirteen *Orte*, seven went on to develop an oligarchic form of government, while six had a rudimentary form of democracy. The oligarchic cantons, of which Berne was the most prominent, were governed by a small executive council and a larger assembly, both dominated by wealthy and often aristocratic families who perpetuated their power largely by co-optation. In some of them, notably Zurich and Basle, the social basis of members of the ruling institutions was wider—especially due to the power of guilds—but government was still fundamentally oligarchic.

In contrast, the mountain cantons of central and southeastern Switzerland, notably the three original "forest cantons" (Uri, Schwyz, and Unterwalden) and what is now the Grisons were governed through forms of democratic participation by free and equal citizens. Integral to democracy in these mountain cantons was the *Landsgemeinde*, an annual popular assembly of all (male) citizens, in which key decisions were taken and the main offices filled by election. In some cases, practices of the *Landsgemeinde* have survived to the present day. The first still-existing records of a *Landsgemeinde* date back to the thirteenth century, and by the early fourteenth century it was a traditional feature of the central cantons of the confederation. This early form of democracy stood in sharp contrast to most of Europe, where feudalism or absolutism reigned. To explain Swiss exceptionalism, scholars have focused on the small population size of the mountain cantons, their geographical isolation from one another, and the nature of their economies, in which the exploitation of communal land took center stage (Kobach 1994, 99–100; Barber 1974).

These very different governance styles did not coexist peacefully together. Indeed, the institutional asymmetry existing at the level of the confederation was to a large extent replicated within the *Orte* themselves, particularly between city dwellers, who enjoyed political rights, and the inhabitants of the countryside, who were largely excluded. A number of revolts and disturbances directed in general against these forms of subordination and oligarchic government took place throughout the eighteenth century across the confederation (de Capitani 1983, 131–40).

The impact of the French Revolution

Many democratic practices emerged in the 1790s, when internal developments coupled with the impact of the French Revolution brought about the end of the old regime and a process of transformation, leading to the establishment in 1848 of a democratic federal state. The revolution had the greatest impact in one of the subject territories, the Vaud, where it fueled demands for emancipation vis-à-vis Berne and Fribourg. The radicalization of such demands led to revolutionary movements in some parts of western Switzerland and offered a pretext for the French invasion of 1798 (Bonjour et al. 1952, esp. 211). With the cooperation of a number of Swiss pro-revolution sympathizers, France imposed a radically new political system named the Helvetic Republic. Modeled on the French constitution of 1795, this unitary republic espoused liberal-democratic principles of national citizenship, representative democracy, equality of rights, official status for the French and Italian languages, uniform and secular education, and freedom of settlement. The old *Orte* were stripped of their independence and became—on a reorganized basis—mere administrative districts (Zimmer 2003, 85).

Although a fair number of Swiss had initially welcomed the French Revolution and supported the principles of the Helvetic Republic, the new regime never acquired sufficient legitimacy, and in three years suffered four coups (Lerner 2004, 74–75; Bonjour et al. 1952, 224). Opposition to the republic was particularly strong in central Switzerland, where the new liberal-democratic principles clashed with the traditional ideals of corporate peasant democracy, Catholic principles, and the material interests of those communities. The introduction of freedom of settlement best exemplifies this conflict. Under freedom of settlement, Helvetic citizens became free to settle and carry out economic activities in any municipality of the country. While this was a core principle of the new regime, it ultimately undermined local autonomy and deprived municipalities of their most important sources of revenue (Zimmer 2003, 102–10). The chronic instability of the Helvetic Republic led to a partial return to the cantonal system, through personal intervention by Napoleon, under a regime known as the Mediation. This change involved an important innovation to the previous cantonal system, as the former associated or subject territories of Argovia, Grisons, St. Gallen, Ticino, and the Vaud were added to the old thirteen cantons with full cantonal status.[2]

Although the Helvetic Republic failed as a regime, it did have a lasting influence on the evolution of the Swiss political system and marked an important phase in the process of democratization, as well as fostering a sense of Swiss nationality. Most immediately, the republic's propagation of new liberal-democratic ideas fatally undermined the old system of oligarchies and privileges. It firmly established the principle of equality, be it in terms of individuals, territories, or languages. From a long-term perspective, it also introduced two institutional elements that, as discussed more widely below, would become defining features of the Swiss democratic system: direct democracy and a collegial executive.

The international context played a decisive role in this period. New democratic ideas imported from France and the latter's direct intervention in Swiss politics marked a crucial phase in Swiss evolution toward democratic practices. Still, domestic elites were also important actors in linking foreign ideas and actions with the development of democratic and national beliefs in Switzerland. Initial elite acceptance of liberal democratic ideals, as well as subsequent domestic opposition to French influence, ultimately drove political development.

Restoration, regeneration, and radicalism

After the fall of Napoleon, the cantons—now including Geneva, Neuchâtel, and the Valais—regained their sovereignty and reestablished a confederation under the terms of the Federal Treaty signed in 1815. This "new" confederation was an explicit attempt to restore the pre-1798 order,[3] although it did introduce some institutional innovations and retain principles adopted under French hegemony. The Diet returned as the main decision-making body, but Zurich, Berne, and Lucerne were given the role of "managing canton" on a rotating biennial basis and entrusted with the general administration of the confederation. The fundamental principle governing the confederation was explicitly cantonal "freedom" as opposed to individual freedom. Cantons' representatives to the Diet were delegates of their respective governments and voted according to the latter's instructions. Cantons were all on equal footing, with one vote each in the Diet regardless of population size. Decisions were normally taken by simple majority, with the exception of very important ones—such as military matters –which required a three-quarters supermajority. Citizens had political rights only within their own canton and were considered foreigners in all other cantons. The long-standing variety of weights, measures and currencies remained unaffected and cross-cantonal trade still had to pay tariffs and duties.

It is against this background that the process of democratization began in earnest. Paralleling the 1830 revolution in France, a broad reform movement called "Regeneration" gathered momentum. The Regeneration Movement (1830–48) demanded constitutional change at the cantonal level, bringing about citizen equality, universal male suffrage, clearer limits on government, and formal citizen approval. The "regenerated" cantons adopted new constitutions and submitted them to a popular referendum (Aubert 1974, 20). If, in some cases, these reforms were achieved more or less peacefully, in others it was not so. In some extreme cases the confrontation between liberal and conservative forces led to bloodshed; in canton Basle it even led to secession of the countryside to form a new half-canton in 1833.[4]

Elites played a crucial role in this reform movement. Local elites drove the process of regeneration in their respective cantons, and united under the liberal-radical movement as a national elite demanding unification and democratization. According to Tilly (2004), these elites were primarily the product of the incipient Industrial Revolution, which had transformed the economic and social patterns in a number of cantons. The growing importance of commercial and industrial activities vis-à-vis landholding created a deepening mismatch between economic and social importance on the one hand and political power on the other, as the landowning class still controlled public affairs and excluded the rising middle class. Tilly points out how this mismatch helped create pressure for democratization as "it was precisely against partial exclusion from public politics and against the domination of landed elites that merchants, professionals, and industrial bourgeoisie banded together in favor of political reform" (Tilly 2004, 185).

The role of lower classes, however, should not be overlooked. The Industrial Revolution also created a rapidly expanding working class in the industrializing urban centers. The economic and political interests of this new proletariat were, of course, much more closely linked to those of the industrial bourgeoisie than to those of traditional elites. In several cases, this relative convergence of interests led the bourgeoisie to ally with industrial workers to demand radical political reforms to wrest power away from the old oligarchic classes. This alliance should be understood as the price the middle classes were prepared to pay to strengthen their hand in the struggle against the old elites (Andrey 1983, 175–203, 250–57; Tilly 2004, 184–87).

Most of the regenerated cantons in turn became increasingly vocal in pushing for more government responsibilities to be exercised at the central level—especially defense and economic affairs—and for a stronger institutional infrastructure to carry them out. The radical wing of the movement demanded no less than the creation of a central government and a central parliament in what would have amounted to a transition from a confederation of states to a federal state (Zimmer 2003, 120–22; Aubert 1974, esp. 20; Bonjour et al. 1952, 249–58). The movement was thus seeking a profound transformation of the system at all levels in a liberal-democratic and national, as well as anti-Catholic, direction.

The building up of pressures for the creation of a democratic Swiss state, and the deepening divide on religious matters, alarmed several conservative Catholic cantons to the point where seven of them signed a secret defensive pact known as the *Sonderbund* (Bonjour et al. 1952, 262).[5] In the 1840s, the radical wing of the movement became dominant, and several cantons—notably Berne—were taken over by Radical forces. The change of camp by the leading canton in the confederation decisively tilted the balance of forces in the Diet and consolidated the Radical ascendancy, which by now also enjoyed mass support.[6] The clash between the opposing sides came to a head in 1847 when a dispute nominally concerning religious orders, but clearly rooted in constitutional issues,[7] triggered a short civil war in which the radical forces prevailed (Remak 1993).

Although the elites driving this process were predominantly Protestant and German-speaking, both French and Italian speakers and liberal Catholics were fully represented (Zimmer 2003, esp. 152). More generally, and somewhat surprisingly from a contemporary perspective, the linguistic cleavage did not play a significant role in the process of establishing a new constitutional order because it cut across other cleavages and remained largely depoliticized. The religious cleavage, in contrast, was clearly prominent, not least because it largely overlapped with the urban-rural cleavage and, especially, the economic one. The economically advanced, city-dominated, Protestant cantons were at the forefront of the democratization and federalization drive, which was bitterly opposed by the economically backward, rural and Catholic cantons.

Economic motives were at the forefront of the drive toward federation and eventual democratization. Bourgeois reformers in the rapidly industrializing cantons came to see the country's economic fragmentation as one of the greatest obstacles to the nation's progress. They pushed for greater centralization as the best way to bring about a unified economic space, the essential precondition for economic growth (Humair 2009). What we now call civil society also played a prominent role, as the proliferation of national societies and festivals in the first half of the century (Bonjour et al. 1952, 237–39; Andrey 1983, 21–23) was an essential phase in the process of building a Swiss national identity and thus of laying the foundation for a constitutional transition from confederation to federation. A remarkable expansion of the press, which led to Switzerland having one of the highest newspaper densities in the world, played a key role in facilitating the circulation of ideas and the formation of a national public sphere (Zimmer 2003, 126). Although its role should not be overestimated,[8] it is likely the more egalitarian political tradition of Switzerland and the absence of a monarchical and feudal past made elite opinion more receptive to democratic ideas and ensured that, once the question of the country's constitutional order had been settled, democracy would be stable and unchallenged.

The international environment was again influential, although less so than in the period of the Helvetic Republic. The process of democratization elsewhere in Europe had a significant demonstration effect, and the thousands of activists who took refuge in Switzerland played a prominent role in the latter's struggles for democracy. Indirectly, but importantly, growing economic competition among national economies in Europe provided a powerful economic rationale for federalization, a rationale the liberal-radical movement did not hesitate to exploit.

The formation of a democratic federal state

The victorious Radicals set up a constitutional commission charged with reforming the 1815 treaty, in which most of the defeated cantons were also represented. The commission ultimately decided to replace the treaty-based confederation with a constitution-based federal state, thus accepting the core demand of the Radicals. Yet centralization was kept to a minimum and a number of concessions to the former *Sonderbund* cantons were made. In June 1848 the new constitution was endorsed by the Diet, with 13 votes in favor and nine against, or abstaining. It was then ratified by the cantons with 15½ in favor and 6½ against, in all cases bar one through a popular referendum (Aubert 1974, 27–28). In September, the last Diet gathered to promulgate the new constitution and establish the new federal state although, strictly speaking, the procedures by which the new constitution was being adopted were illegal under the terms of the existing Federal Treaty. The cantons defeated in the civil war voted against the new constitution, both at the Diet and in the ratification process, but ultimately accepted the outcome and participated in the subsequent election for the new federal parliament.[9] This parliament gathered for the first time in November 1848 in Berne—which was made the permanent capital. The 1848 constitution established a liberal-democratic federal state and marked a decisive turning point in Swiss history and in the process of democratization.

The institutional architecture of the Swiss federal state

The new Switzerland was a federation of 22 cantons, each having equal status and retaining a great deal of autonomy, but now subordinate to federal sovereignty. The constitution established a bicameral parliament inspired by the US model. The lower house, the National Council, represented the Swiss people on the principle of citizen equality. The upper house, the Council of States, represented the cantons on the principle of cantonal equality. Members of the lower house would be directly elected every three years, whereas members of the upper house would be elected by cantonal assemblies following canton-specific procedures.[10] The two houses were given equal powers, thus establishing a system of perfect bicameralism. The cantons were allocated a number of seats in the lower house proportional to their population and two seats each in the upper house. The so-called half-cantons, the results of splits in previously whole cantons at different points in history, had full cantonal status save for having only one seat in the upper house and half a vote in the calculation of cantonal majorities in referendum votes, as explained below.

The executive—the Federal Council—was a collegial body of seven ministers, each of them assuming the role of president on an annual rotating basis.[11] The seven ministers would be elected individually every three years by the two houses of parliament sitting jointly about two months after the parliamentary elections. Once elected, the ministers would not be politically responsible before parliament and could not be dismissed either individually or collectively by the latter until the next election. The absence of parliamentary confidence thus created a form of semi-presidentialism, intermediate between the classic parliamentary and presidential systems. Written and unwritten rules stipulated that not more than one federal councilor could come from the same canton and at least two out of seven should be non-German speakers.

The 1848 constitution also established a Federal Tribunal but did not entrust it with strong powers, leaving virtually the whole judicial system under the cantons' control. The constitution established uniform Swiss citizenship, giving citizens the ability to exercise their rights throughout the federation regardless of their canton of residence, although such citizenship remained dependent on cantonal citizenship.[12] Political rights were given to all adult male citizens, thus making Switzerland the first European country to grant near universal male suffrage on a stable basis, although Jews were still excluded until 1866 (Tilly 2004, 178, 214). Following in the footsteps of the Helvetic Republic, German, French, and Italian were all given official status at the federal level, but no attempt was made to introduce multilingualism in the cantons (where it did not already exist). Most cantons remained monolingual. Finally, to protect cantonal autonomy, granting new policy-making competences to the federal level would only be possible on the basis of a constitutional revision. Constitutional revision was no easy process, entailing endorsement in a referendum by a double majority, of the people *and* of the cantons.

The development of democracy

Despite two full constitutional revisions (in 1874 and 1999), the institutional structure of 1848 has remained remarkably stable. Still, several important aspects of the practice of democracy in Switzerland have changed significantly since the establishment of the Swiss federal state. Three developments in particular deserve our attention: direct democracy, consensual power-sharing, and the late granting of the right to vote to women at the federal level.

Direct democracy

Perhaps more so than any other feature of its political system, direct democracy has come to symbolize Swiss-style democracy. The origins of direct democracy can be traced back to two roots. On one hand, the modern form of direct democracy was a French import, as the first countrywide referendum took place in 1802 in the context of the adoption of the second constitution of the Helvetic Republic (Kobach 1994, 100). On the other hand, the tradition of the *Landsgemeinde* loomed large in Swiss political culture and its myths, lending historical legitimacy to the introduction of modern forms of direct democracy.

Swiss direct democracy developed through the introduction of a range of instruments at seven points in time: 1848, 1874, 1891, 1921, 1949, 1977, and 2003 (Kriesi and Trechsel 2008, 50–55). The first constitution introduced the mandatory constitutional referendum, whereby each change in the constitution—from a single amendment to a total revision—must always pass a referendum of a majority of the people *and* a majority of the cantons.

The first extension of direct democracy came with the 1874 constitution, which introduced the legislative referendum, allowing 30,000 (increased to 50,000 in 1977) citizens or eight cantons to call for a vote to strike down any law or decree passed by parliament (based on a simple majority of votes cast).[13] In 1891, a further instrument appeared when the initiative for a partial revision of the constitution was adopted. Under this initiative, 50,000 (increased to 100,000 in 1977)[14] signatories can ask for a proposal to amend the constitution to be put to a vote, subject to the double majority of voters and cantons. In 1921, direct democracy extended to foreign affairs with the introduction of an optional referendum on some international treaties. This instrument was extended in 1977 to include other types of treaties; that same year a mandatory referendum subject to a double majority was introduced for proposals to join international organizations deemed to have constitutional significance (e.g., the European Union). In the meantime, mandatory and optional referenda were introduced in 1949 to approve urgent parliamentary decrees (Kriesi and Trechsel 2008, 189–90). Lastly, the so-called general initiative was adopted in 2003. This instrument allowed 100,000 citizens to put forward a proposal formulated in general terms and required parliament either to turn it into a bill or into a constitutional amendment. This would then be put to a vote governed respectively by a simple or double majority (Kriesi and Trechsel 2008, 50–51). The general initiative, however, proved unviable, and in 2009 its withdrawal was approved in a referendum. Over the past century and a half, the use of direct democracy has also grown considerably at the cantonal level (notably in the German-speaking part of the country), and to a lesser extent at the local level, so that all levels of government of the Swiss political system have come to be profoundly marked by direct decision-making by the people.

Direct democracy has thus expanded extensively over time, both in terms of the range of instruments available[15] and the intensity of their use, to a degree unmatched anywhere in the world (Kobach 1994, 98). Direct democracy's impact on the political system can be conceptualized as either a "brake" or a "spur." Referenda, both mandatory and optional, tend to act as brakes in that they constitute a potential popular veto at the end of a process of representative decision making. Initiatives, in contrast, tend to act as spurs as they empower citizens to push public policy beyond where representative institutions are willing to go. Out of all popular votes held in the period 1848–2003, 70 percent were referendums and 30 percent initiatives (Trechsel 2004, 507). On the whole, then, direct democracy in Switzerland has acted much more as a brake on the system than as a spur. Two examples are emblematic of this. The delayed granting of the vote to women—discussed below—provides one of the clearest examples of this braking effect. The arena of international relations offers an equally eloquent example, with the rejection of membership in the European Economic Area (EEA), widely seen as a precursor to European Union membership, in 1992. While Austria, Finland, and Sweden, which negotiated the EEA agreement at the same time, have been EU members since 1995, Switzerland is still a nonmember and is linked to the EU by an increasingly complex set of bilateral treaties.

How can we account for the extraordinary development of direct democracy in Switzerland? The initial adoption of the constitutional referendum in 1848 is best explained as part of the Radicals' drive to democratize the Swiss political system. During the Regeneration period, the constitutional referendum emerged as a key element in the cantonal reforms demanded by liberal and radical forces. As constitutional transformation at the confederation/federal level was intimately linked to constitutional reform at the cantonal level, the adoption of federation-wide instruments of direct democracy likely appeared as a natural step to the framers of the first federal constitution.

The introduction of the legislative referendum and the initiative for constitutional amendments (the two key instruments of Swiss direct democracy) was, however, a product of the democratic movement's desire to go further than the "liberal parliamentarianism" espoused by the Radicals. Indeed, the Radicals were seen as an increasingly self-serving regime (Bonjour et al. 1952, 299–301, quotation on 301). This movement triumphed at cantonal level first, notably in Zurich and Berne, and put pressure on the radical elite for adoption at the federal level, too, with support from the French-speaking and the Catholic-conservative minorities. These two instruments put an end to the full control of the political system hitherto enjoyed by the elites dominating the representative institutions and ushered in the system of semi-direct democracy as we know it today (Linder 2004, 103).

The further expansion of direct democracy in the twentieth century is the product of three factors—one that is common to all the new instruments introduced, and two that are more specific. The common element was that by then the people had the ability—by using the instruments already acquired—to expand direct democracy virtually without limits, save for those placed by the people themselves. More specifically, the extension of direct democracy to foreign affairs was an inevitable corollary of the rise of international cooperation and integration and of its growing impact on the Swiss polity. It was thus seen as a natural complement to the popular rights in the domestic sphere. On the other hand, the extension of the referendum to cover urgent decrees was a reaction to the wide use of such devices in the 1930s and 1940s, which many saw as an abuse of parliament's prerogatives (Jost 1983, 98–99; Trechsel and Kriesi 1996, 189–90).

Consensual democracy

Switzerland has long been considered a classic example of consensual, if not outright consociational, democracy. In his classic comparative study of consensual and majoritarian democracies, Lijphart (1999, 33–41) uses Switzerland to illustrate the consensual model. If the degree to which Switzerland was ever consociational is debatable (Church 1989; Steiner 2002), there is no doubt the country is governed in a more consensual way than most other democracies. However, this was by no means always so. As already seen, politics was deeply contentious in the 1830–48 period and, even after the creation of the federal state, relations between the Radical majority and the minorities, notably the Catholic-conservatives, were far from amicable. Although often internally divided, Radicals dominated the federal parliament and monopolized the federal executives; no power-sharing arrangement was in place. The contemporary form of consensual democracy has thus taken shape over a fairly long period of time as a result of a series of distinct, but connected, developments.

Things started to change after the 1874 constitutional revision and the adoption of the legislative referendum. Several governmental defeats at the hands of informal coalitions of minorities—a frequent coalition was that between French speakers and Catholic-conservatives—signaled the days of the all-powerful Radicals were drawing to a close. A degree of negotiation and power-sharing with the other political forces was necessary. In 1891, this realization led to the first step in the emergence of one of the most characteristic aspects of Swiss consensual democracy: power-sharing in the executive. In that year, the first Catholic-conservative was elected to the Federal Council, even though the Radicals still had full control of parliament. Following this initial step, the other main parties—notably, the socialists—gradually gained access to the executive. From 1959 through the beginning of the twenty-first century, the principle of representation, in the executive, of the main parties in rough proportion to their parliamentary strength—the so-called magic formula—was a cornerstone of the Swiss political system. While this is often seen abroad as a grand coalition, it is important to appreciate that it is merely an arrangement to share executive seats and does not involve any programmatic agreement among the governmental parties.

The natural consensual complement to power-sharing in the executive was the change of the electoral system for the National Council, away from a majoritarian system and toward proportional representation (PR). Even more so than representation in the executive, however, the shift to PR took a long time to see the light. PR was one of the key planks of the democratic movement of the 1870s and, in the time-honored Swiss fashion, led to change at the cantonal level first. Two initiatives, launched in 1899 and 1909 by socialist and Catholic forces, were rejected in the subsequent popular votes, and only at the third attempt was PR finally approved in 1918 (Ruffieux 1983, 66). The introduction of PR, with cantons as electoral constituencies, has contributed to making the Swiss party system one of the most fragmented in Europe (Kriesi and Trechsel 2008, 84).[16] Given the architecture of the Swiss political system, however, such a fragmentation has not had the negative consequences on governability that other national systems have experienced. This is because the semi-presidential and collegial nature of the executive insulates it to a significant extent from parliamentary politics, and because direct democracy provides a channel through which controversial questions can be settled without the possibility to "appeal," at least in the short term.

The third main consensual aspect of Swiss democracy is the system of pre-parliamentary consultations, whereby proposals for new legislation are extensively scrutinized and debated prior to parliamentary consideration. These consultations involve the federal civil service, on one side, and a wide range of institutional and societal actors (e.g., parties, cantons, and interest groups) on the other side. The consultations aim to ensure all interests likely to be affected by the proposed legislation—notably all actors "capable of making a credible referendum threat" (Kriesi and Trechsel 2008, 115)—are given an opportunity to have a say in its formulation. The phase of pre-parliamentary consultation is a distinctive trait of the Swiss political system and is the main element accounting for the length of the federal decision-making process, which is considerably longer than in most other European democracies (Kriesi and Trechsel 2008, 115–19; Becker and Saalfeld 2004, 58). Somewhat surprisingly, though, pre-parliamentary consultations do not appear to reduce significantly the degree of conflict in the parliamentary phase of legislation, so their role as a conflict-reducing mechanism should not be overestimated (Kriesi and Trechsel 2008, 119).

Female suffrage

The last but, of course, not the least notable feature of Swiss democratic development is the extremely late hour of female suffrage. The contrast between male and female suffrage could not be greater. Switzerland was the first European state to grant near universal suffrage to adult men in 1848, yet it was the last to extend this right to women at the federal level, despite pressures going back to the beginning of the twentieth century.[17] In a similar way to the introduction of PR, female suffrage also failed several times to be accepted—including in a popular vote in 1959—before finally gaining approval in 1971. The immediate cause for this delay is clearly found in the direct democracy requirements for constitutional change, whereby female suffrage had to be approved in a popular vote by an all-male electorate. Once again, direct democracy acted as a crucial "veto player" in the system. The deeper cause, though, was arguably the generally conservative stance of Swiss voters, which has manifested itself in many ways throughout the history of the Swiss federal state (Linder 1998, 69–71). While female turnout in both federal elections and federal referendums still trails that of males, the gap has progressively narrowed and is likely to disappear soon.[18] On average, approximately 25 percent of members of parliament tend to be women, a percentage that is relatively high compared to other Western democracies. Women have expanded even more dramatically their representation in the Federal Council. Following elections in 2007 and 2010, four of the seven seats - as well as the post of Federal Chancellor, the top position in the federal civil service - are currently held by women.

Assessing the development of Swiss democracy

Whereas the initial phase of democratization in Switzerland did not deviate significantly from the trajectory followed by most other Western states, the development of democratic practices outlined in this section appears to have followed a more peculiarly Swiss path. Essentially, this is due to the role played by direct democracy. As seen above, the effects of direct democracy loomed large both in the Swiss polity's acquisition of increasingly consensual features and in the late granting of the right to vote to women. The prominent influence of direct democracy, especially from the 1870s onwards, also implies that elites played a less important role in this process than in the earlier phase. By the end of the nineteenth century, elites had effectively lost their full control of the Swiss system and had to accept severe constraints, as well as initiatives, originating in civil society and exercised through direct democracy. Political culture arguably played a crucial role in that the role of democratic ideals—and of direct democracy in particular - in the discourse on Swiss identity provided crucial legitimacy to the expansion of direct democratic rights and led to its acceptance by the elites. Although over the course of the same period Switzerland also became one of the wealthiest countries in the world, economic factors do not appear to have played a decisive role in the expansion of Swiss democracy throughout the late nineteenth and twentieth centuries. Remarkably, the presence of deep societal cleavages—linguistic, religious, territorial, and social—did not prevent the full democratization of the country and the extraordinary development of direct democracy. This should be attributed, among other factors, to the cross-cutting nature of such cleavages and especially to the fact that the linguistic cleavage never developed into an ethnonational one. The Swiss language communities retained their loyalty to the Swiss multilingual nation and did not develop separate ethnolinguistic national identities (Dardanelli 2011). Thus, Swiss society never experienced the degree of polarization many other countries did in the course of the twentieth century.

Given the extraordinary development of direct democracy, the Swiss people have the ability to control decision-making processes and shape public policy to a degree unmatched anywhere else in the world. Kriesi's

(2005, esp. 227–39) magisterial analysis of direct democracy in Switzerland has shown that many criticisms laid against this form of democracy are not inevitable, and in many respects the inclusion of direct democracy instruments does strengthen democracy as a whole. On that basis, it is justifiable to argue that Switzerland is by some distance the most democratic state in today's world. Swiss citizens themselves share this appreciation of direct democracy by showing a very high degree of esteem for, and attachment to, it. A 2001 survey found 90 percent were "very" or "quite" proud of direct democracy, and 94 percent considered it "very" or "quite" important for the country's future (Kriesi and Trechsel 2008, 66). The very expansion of direct democracy has also, however, led it to clash with other fundamental principles of the Swiss constitutional state.

Two recent developments illustrate this problem. In 2003 the practice by some municipalities of deciding on naturalizations through direct democracy instruments was ruled contrary to the human rights provisions of the constitution by the Federal Tribunal.[19] This ruling was mainly on the grounds that rejected applicants have a right to know why their application was rejected, which, of course, is impossible if the decision is taken by ordinary citizens through secret ballots. The Swiss People's Party, a populist and right-wing conservative party, reacted to this ruling by launching a popular initiative to write into the constitution the right of citizens to vote on naturalizations. The initiative collected the required number of signatures and went to a vote in 2008, but was rejected by 64 percent of voters. Even more recently, the success in November 2009 of an initiative to ban the construction of minarets has been judged by some to be against fundamental human rights enshrined in the Swiss constitution and in the European Convention on Human Rights, of which Switzerland is a signatory state. Several lawsuits have been lodged with the European Court of Human Rights, and there is a distinct possibility of the court ruling that this new clause of the Swiss constitution is incompatible with the principles of the Convention. Were this to happen, Switzerland would find itself in an extremely delicate and unprecedented situation. It would face a daunting choice between either not implementing the constitutional change—which would itself be unconstitutional—or finding itself in breach of the Convention and potentially having to denounce it, a humiliating prospect for a country that has always prided itself on championing human rights. This example highlights how direct democracy can sometimes pit the constitutional rights of Swiss citizens against their country's international commitments.

Both these examples highlight two additional tensions in contemporary Swiss democracy: challenges to consensual democracy (brought about by the Swiss People's Party) and the impact of migration. The transformation of the Swiss People's Party (SVP in its German abbreviation) and its rapid growth over the last twenty years have placed serious strains on the fabric of Swiss politics. Formerly a centrist, Protestant, and agrarian party, the SVP has turned into a right-wing, populist, and nationalist party under the leadership of the charismatic Christoph Blocher, a controversial former businessman. The party has built a professional campaigning machine to great success and exploited its key themes of zero-tolerance law and order, hostility to immigration, radical "Euroscepticism," and a general nationalist conservatism. From an average of 10 percent support throughout the post-war period, the SVP has now become the largest party in Switzerland, in 2007 winning the highest ever number of seats in the PR era. Its disregard for the traditional consensual practices of Swiss democracy, which culminated in the decision to withdraw into opposition from 2007–09 (Church and Vatter 2009), and its over-exploitation of direct democracy present a significant challenge to the system and may lead to profound changes. For example, the party has launched an initiative for the direct election of the Federal Council, an initiative which, if approved, would introduce a "collective presidential" system and may have serious consequences for the delicate balance among the multiple cleavages of the Swiss political system.

Increasing migration within the country, as well as from without, has already diluted the original ethnic and religious homogeneity of the cantons and is likely to continue doing so in the future. This also means the populations of the small, rural, Catholic cantons are no longer the only minorities in the country, let alone the most significant. Since many features of Swiss federalism were explicitly designed to protect the interests of those cantons, it follows that the institutional framework of Swiss federal democracy is increasingly ill-adapted to the realities of Swiss society. Moreover, given that the new minorities are not geographically concentrated, as the old ones were, one could go even further and argue that federalism is not an appropriate institutional mechanism to ensure them effective democratic representation. In other words, the rising heterogeneity of the cantonal populations and the concomitant erosion of differences between cantons place the institutional design of Swiss federalism increasingly at odds with democratic principles.[20]

While these are important points, it would be difficult to assess contemporary Swiss democracy in anything but highly positive terms. Switzerland has always been a model of democracy to the rest of the world, and it is still true to this role today. All indications are that beliefs in democratic principles and support for democratic institutions will remain extremely solid in the foreseeable future, thus guaranteeing a bright future for democracy in Switzerland.

Conclusions

Switzerland's democratization experience has been both fairly standard and exceptional. Despite the peculiar historical trajectory of the Swiss political system, its early process of democratization did not deviate dramatically from the paths followed by its fellow early democratization states. For example, in the first half of the nineteenth century its protagonists were broadly the same type of socioeconomic actors who drove similar processes in the United States and Great Britain. Like elsewhere, democratization was achieved through a period of very contentious politics, including widespread use of violence, revolutionary episodes, and even a brief civil war. The cleavages that structured the struggle for democracy in other countries—notably the church–state, urban–rural, and economic ones—also featured prominently in the Swiss case. Even the fact that the linguistic cleavage failed to play a significant role does not make Switzerland a significant outlier, as the same was true in that phase of other countries, such as Belgium, Canada, and Spain, all of which would later be deeply affected by ethnolinguistic divisions. Only in the timing of the process does Switzerland stand out significantly from its peers, for it achieved stable democratic institutions and universal male suffrage earlier than the other European states.

In contrast, the subsequent phase of democratization—that marked by the extension of the franchise and the development of direct democracy—shows a very distinctive and contrasted trajectory. On the one hand, Switzerland was very late in achieving full democracy, as Swiss women had to wait until 1971 to gain the right to vote at the federal level—almost 70 years after Finnish women did so. From 1848 to 1971, Swiss democracy was thus Janus-faced: highly stable and developed as far as men were concerned, but still excluding half the population. The extraordinary development of direct democracy sets Switzerland even more sharply apart from the other democratic states. Nowhere else has direct democracy expanded so much and come to play such a central role in the workings of the political system. Last, but not least, the fact that the linguistic cleavage is still by and large the "dog that hasn't barked" in Swiss politics also contrasts with the experience of a number of other multilingual states, where such a cleavage has divided the country into a majority nationality and one or more minority nationalities and negatively affected the practice of democracy.

As a result of these historical trajectories, Switzerland is now at the same time a fairly ordinary Western European democracy and a *Sonderfall*, or special case, as many Swiss are often keen to remark. These characteristics make it an important case for the comparative analysis of the paths through which democracy can be achieved and how democracy can be practiced in the contemporary world.

Additional resources[21]

The Centre for Research on Direct Democracy (c2d) offers an extensive database on direct democracy votes in Switzerland and the rest of the world, available at www.c2d.ch/index.php. In addition, the Portal of the Federal Authorities houses a wealth of official documents and information, a large portion of which is also available in English, available at www.admin.ch/. To see direct democracy in action, as well as listen to the debates on the reintroduction of the *Landsgemeinde* in a canton, see the following online video: www.swissinfo.ch/eng/multimedia/video/Back_to_the_past.html?cid=9035930.

For contemporary news coverage of Switzerland, see *SwissInfo*, an English-language news website run by the Swiss television and radio companies, available at www.swissinfo.ch/. Other quality news sources include the leading German-language daily newspaper, *Neue Zürcher Zeitung* (www.nzz.ch/) and the leading French-language daily newspaper *Le Temps* (www.letemps.ch/).

Notes

1 I wish to thank Clive Church for alerting me to this project and Mary Malone for inviting me to participate in it (as well as for her expert editorial guidance). Both offered very helpful comments on previous drafts of this chapter, for which I am very grateful.

2 By then the old *Orte* were commonly referred to as cantons (Germann and Klöti 2004, 318). Geneva, the Valais, what is now the Jura canton, and Neuchâtel had in the meantime been annexed by France and remained in French hands until 1814.

3 Revealingly, the treaty had no amendment clause, thus barring reform through legal means (Bonjour et al. 1952, 245).

4 The new half-canton was called Basle-Country (Church 1983, 57–69). Schwyz, Glarus, and the Valais also suffered temporary splits but eventually managed to preserve their territorial integrity (Andrey 1983, 252).

5 The seven include the three original forest cantons of Uri, Schwyz, and Unterwalden plus Lucerne, Zug, Fribourg, and the Valais.

6 Berne was the largest canton and the strongest military force and had been the leader of the conservative reaction in 1815 (Kohn 1956, 68).

7 See Bonjour et al. (1952, 263) and Kohn (1956, 106).

8 As Tilly (2004, 168–205) reminds us, the period leading up to the establishment of a democratic federal state was marked by severe contention and political violence culminating in a brief civil war.

9 Three tried to challenge the legality of the new constitution, but their challenge failed (Friedman Goldstein 2001, 99–140).

10 In 1931 a constitutional amendment extended the term to four years.

11 The collegial form of the Council was inspired by the executive of the Helvetic Republic, itself modeled on France's *Directoire* government of the period 1795–97 (Kriesi and Trechsel 2008, 75).

12 In its French version, art. 42 stated: "Tout citoyen d'un canton est citoyen suisse" (Everyone who is a citizen of a canton is a Swiss citizen).

13 The signatures have to be collected within 100 days (90 until 1996).

14 A time limit of eighteen months to collect such signatures was also introduced in 1977.

15 Although several other extensions of direct democracy were rejected by the citizens themselves; see Kriesi and Trechsel (2008, 55).

16 In addition, the PR system has buttressed the power-sharing arrangement for the executive, thus playing the role of the second main "pillar" of consensual democracy.

17 Some cantons did introduce female suffrage earlier. Indeed, in cantonal elections, there was considerable temporal variation in achieving female suffrage.

18 See Wernli (2004, 462) for the elections and Trechsel (2004, 484–85) for the referendum votes.

19 Under federal and cantonal law, Swiss citizenship depends on cantonal citizenship, which in turn generally depends on citizenship of a municipality. In most cantons municipalities are thus the bodies that grant naturalization in Switzerland.

20 On a related note, given the difficulties of the naturalization process, many migrants do not have Swiss citizenship and lack political rights. Approximately 20 percent of the population does not have Swiss citizenship.

21 All listed websites were accessed on September 7, 2010.

References

Andrey, Georges. 1983. La quête d'un Etat national—1798–1848. In *Nouvelle histoire de la Suisse et des Suisses, tome II,* Jean-Claude Favez, ed. 171–272. Lausanne: Payot.

Aubert, Jean-François. 1974. *Petite histoire constitutionelle de la Suisse.* Berne: Francke.

Barber, Benjamin. 1974. *The Death of Communal Liberty—History of Freedom in a Swiss Mountain Canton.* Princeton, NJ: Princeton University Press.

Becker, Rolf, and Thomas Saalfeld. 2004. "The Life and Times of Bills." In *Patterns of Parliamentary Behavior*, Herbert Döring and Mark Hallerberg, eds, 57–90. Aldershot: Ashgate.

Bonjour, Edgar, H. S. Offler, and G. R. Potter. 1952. *A Short History of Switzerland*. Oxford: Clarendon Press.

Church, Clive. 1989. "Behind the Consociational Screen: Politics in Contemporary Switzerland." *West European Politics* 12/1: 35–54.

Church, Clive. 1983. *Europe in 1830*. London: George Allen & Unwin.

Church, Clive, and Adrian Vatter. 2009. "Opposition in Consensual Switzerland: a Short but Significant Experiment." *Government and Opposition* 44/4: 412–37.

Dardanelli, Paolo. 2011. *Multi-lingual but Mono-national—Exploring and Explaining Switzerland's Exceptionalism*. In *Federalism and Plurinationality - Theory and Case Analyses*, Miquel Caminal and Ferran Requejo, eds, in press. London: Routledge.

de Capitani, François. 1983. "Vie et mort de l'Ancien Régime—1648–1815." In *Nouvelle histoire de la Suisse et des Suisses, tome II*, Jean-Claude Favez, ed., 97–170. Lausanne: Payot.

Friedman Goldstein, Leslie. 2001. *Constituting Federal Sovereignty*. Baltimore: Johns Hopkins University Press.

Germann, Raimund, and Ulrich Klöti. 2004. "The Swiss Cantons: Equality and Difference." In *Handbook of Swiss Politics*, Ulrich Klöti, Peter Knoepfel, Hanspeter Kriesi, Wolf Linder, Yannis Papadopoulos, and Pascal Sciarini, eds, 317–48. Zurich: Neue Zürcher Zeitung Publishing.

Hughes, Christopher. 1975. *Switzerland*. London: Ernest Benn.

Humair, Cédric. 2009. *1848: Naissance de la Suisse Moderne*. Lausanne: Antipodes.

Jost, Hans-Ulrich. 1983. "Menace et repliement—1914–1945." In *Nouvelle histoire de la Suisse et des Suisses, tome III*, Jean-Claude Favez, ed., 91–178. Lausanne: Payot.

Kobach, Kris. 1994. Switzerland. In *Referendums Around the World—The Growing Use of Direct Democracy*, David Butler and Austin Ranney, eds, 98–153. Washington, D.C.: AEI Press.

Kohn, Hans. 1956. *Nationalism and Liberty: the Swiss Example*. London: Allen and Unwin.

Kriesi, Hanspeter. 2005. *Direct Democratic Choice—The Swiss Experience*. Lanham, MD: Lexington Books.

Kriesi, Hanspeter, and Alexander Trechsel. 2008. *The Politics of Switzerland*. Cambridge: Cambridge University Press.

Lerner, Marc. 2004. "The Helvetic Republic: an Ambivalent Reception of French Revolutionary Liberty." *French History*. 18/1: 50–75.

Lijphart, Arend. 1999. *Patterns of Democracy*. New Haven: Yale University Press.

Linder, Wolf. 2004. "Direct Democracy." In *Handbook of Swiss Politics*, Ulrich Klöti, Peter Knoepfel, Hanspeter Kriesi, Wolf Linder, Yannis Papadopoulos, and Pascal Sciarini, eds, 101–20. Zurich: Neue Zürcher Zeitung Publishing.

Linder, Wolf. 1998. *Swiss Democracy—Possible Solutions to Conflict in Multicultural Societies*. 2nd ed. Basingstoke: Macmillan.

Lutz,Georg, and Peter Selb. 2007. "The National Elections in Switzerland." In *Handbook of Swiss Politics*, Ulrich Klöti, Peter Knoepfel, Hanspeter Kriesi, Wolf Linder, Yannis Papadopoulos, and Pascal Sciarini, eds, 405–33. Zurich: Neue Zürcher Zeitung Publishing.

Remak, Joachim. 1993. *A Very Civil War: the Swiss Sonderbund War of 1847*. Boulder, CO: Westview Press.

Rhinow, René. 2006. "Le fédéralisme suisse: l'approche juridique." In *Le fédéralisme suisse—La réforme engagée. Ce qui reste à faire*, René Frey, Georg Kreis, Gian-Reto Plattner, and René Rhinow, eds, 61–87. Lausanne: Presses polytechniques et universitaires romandes.

Ruffieux, Roland. 1983. "La Suisse des radicaux—1848–1914." In *Nouvelle histoire de la Suisse et des Suisses, tome III*, Jean-Claude Favez, ed., 7–90. Lausanne: Payot.

Sciarini, Pascal. 2005. "Les cantons, tiraillés entre la volonté de coopération intercantonale et la tentation de faire cavalier seul." *Le Temps*, February16.

Steiner, Jürg. 2002. "Consociational Theory and Switzerland—Revisited." *Acta Politica* 37/1–2: 104–20.

Tilly, Charles. 2004. *Contention and Democracy in Europe, 1650-2000*. Cambridge: Cambridge University Press.

Trechsel, Alexander. 2004. "Popular Votes." In *Handbook of Swiss Politics*, Ulrich Klöti, Peter Knoepfel, Hanspeter Kriesi, Wolf Linder, Yannis Papadopoulos, and Pascal Sciarini, eds, 479–507. Zurich: Neue Zürcher Zeitung Publishing.

Trechsel, Alexander, and Hanspeter Kriesi. 1996. "Switzerland: the Referendum and Initiative as a Centrepiece of the Political System." In *The Referendum Experience in Europe*, Michael Gallagher and Pier Vincenzo Uleri, eds, 185–208. London: Macmillan.

Vatter, Adrian. 2004. "Federalism." In *Handbook of Swiss Politics*, Ulrich Klöti, Peter Knoepfel, Hanspeter Kriesi, Wolf Linder, Yannis Papadopoulos, and Pascal Sciarini, eds, 71–99. Zurich: Neue Zürcher Zeitung Publishing.

Wernli, Boris. 2004. "The Federal Elections in Switzerland." In *Handbook of Swiss Politics*, Ulrich Klöti, Peter Knoepfel, Hanspeter Kriesi, Wolf Linder, Yannis Papadopoulos, Pascal Sciarini, eds, 431–78. Zurich: Neue Zürcher Zeitung Publishing.

Zimmer, Oliver. 2003. *A Contested Nation: History, Memory and Nationalism in Switzerland*. Cambridge: Cambridge University Press.

Hypothesis testing exercise and discussion questions for Section 2

Using the guide below, assess how well the classical theories of democratization explain democratization in Great Britain, the United States, and Switzerland. Be sure to specify the causal mechanisms, or processes by which each independent variable determined the dependent variable. Also, differentiate between the independent variables that caused the emergence of democracy from those that caused its eventual consolidation. Given the long historical trajectory of democratization in these cases, also identify the factors that facilitated the expansion of suffrage in each case, as well as the variables that impeded it.

Hypothesis testing exercise

Independent Variables	Evidence from Great Britain	Evidence from United States	Evidence from Switzerland
Economic development • National wealth • Private enterprise • Middle class • Inequality			
Elites			
Political culture/civil society			
Education			
State institutions			
Social divisions/national unity			
International context			

Section 2: Discussion questions

1 Why are some cleavages divisive, derailing or delaying democratization, while others are not? Why are cleavages divisive in some countries but not others?

Even within one individual case, like Switzerland, why were some cleavages (i.e., linguistic ones) not divisive, while others (religious, urban v. rural) were? What factors politicize cleavages?

2 In designing institutions for democratic governance, many countries emphasize the importance of safeguarding minority rights. By designing institutions with many brakes, or veto players, institutions can curb the will of the majority. This was a principal concern of the Federalists, for example. In Switzerland and the United States, however, these institutional safeguards ultimately delayed the full extension of democracy to all members of society. How exactly did institutions block democracy, instead of safeguarding minority rights? Should these institutional checks and balances be replicated in newer democracies? Why or why not? Is there a trade-off between respecting minority rights and increasing the power of veto players?

3 At what historical point could each country claim the democratic label? Was democratic development an incremental, linear process in each case? Or did democratization experience setbacks?

Section 3
Second Wave of Democracy

7

From Defeat and Division to Democracy in Germany

Paul Fritz

Studies of democracy gravitate to the case of Germany. The devastating consequences of Germany's democratic breakdown in the 1930s have led to exhaustive scrutiny of Germany's first attempt at democracy under the Weimar Republic. If the Weimar Republic illustrates pitfalls to avoid, the Federal Republic of Germany has become an example to emulate. The Federal Republic of Germany, commonly referred to as West Germany during the Cold War, emerged in 1949 with a solid liberal democratic foundation.[1] By the 1960s, the institutions of West German democracy garnered a great deal of legitimacy from the West German public and elites.

Many factors contributed to the success of West German democracy: elite consensus, economic success and stability, strong institutions, and the emergence of a democratic political culture. Above all, however, West Germany's postwar democratic development highlights the critical role outside powers can play in promoting democracy. As this chapter explains, the United States, Britain, and France imposed a democratic system on their erstwhile enemy. While many West Germans played a critical role in creating a solidly liberal domestic order, the Western Allies essentially jumpstarted democracy through a process of coercive socialization. Taking advantage of the physical and ideational devastation the war brought to Germany, the United States and its allies were able to plant democratic practices and norms in the defeated country. The victorious powers co-opted or promoted Western-oriented political elites, exerted control over the creation of democratic institutions, and implemented reforms in the West German media. Once the victors set this course, the institutions, practices, and norms of democracy were legitimated over time by a variety of processes, providing a foundation for a stable democracy. Indeed, these foundations proved strong enough to serve as the basis for a reunified country, as East Germany adopted West German institutions and norms on October 3, 1990, uniting Germany after four decades of division.

The collapse of the first German democracy

Germany's first experiment with democracy also arose from the ashes of war. In 1919, the short-lived Weimar Republic emerged amidst domestic revolution and German defeat in World War I. The Weimar constitution was one of the most progressive in the world, guaranteeing universal suffrage for all citizens over 21, as well as extensive political, economic, and social rights. The constitution set lofty goals, but the political system proved unable to meet these high expectations. Indeed, plagued by economic crisis and massive social upheaval, the Weimar Republic faced steep challenges. War reparations siphoned off monies to rebuild infrastructure and provide services to veterans. Printing money to cover costs led to hyperinflation and further eroded living standards. The Great Depression of 1929 only intensified economic misery.

Institutional weaknesses crippled Weimar's ability to address these economic and social crises. The semi-presidential system concentrated extraordinary emergency powers in the popularly elected president, enabling the last president of Weimar to rule essentially by decree. Elections to the lower house of parliament, the *Reichstag*, relied upon strict proportional representation. Reflecting the fractured nature of Weimar politics, small parties all over the ideological spectrum were able to gain representation in the *Reichstag* fairly easily. This often made coalition building and sustaining governing coalitions exceedingly difficult. Indeed, political elites proved unable to forge coalitions to govern the country; in fourteen years, the Weimar Republic had 22 governments (Sodaro 2004). Small, polarized parties prioritized ideological purity over pragmatic compromise, and ultimately failed to address Germany's multiple crises. Amidst economic ruin, social chaos, and elite squabbling, Hitler assumed the Chancellorship in 1933.[2] Because of the atrocities the Nazi regime committed after it subverted democracy—prosecuting an aggressive war and the horrors of the Holocaust in particular—the creators of Germany's second democracy were mindful to avoid the many weaknesses of the Weimar Republic.

Germany under occupation (1945–49)

After Germany's unconditional surrender, the victors of World War II ultimately decided Germany's future. The Soviets sought to replicate their economic and political system in the East, while the remaining Allies shaped political and economic development in the West. Thus, it is imperative to examine the occupation policies of the Western victors to understand the foundation and eventual character of German democracy. This is not, however, to claim Germans themselves had nothing to do with building democracy in their own state. Though small in number, some committed democrats did survive the war. The United States and its allies actively courted these democrats, promoting them above others. However, due to the devastation Germany brought upon itself with its aggressive war, and the Allied policy of unconditional surrender, in the immediate postwar era there were no Germans in positions of power to dictate the course of political development independently.

At the time of its defeat, Germany was on the brink of total physical destruction. Most of the ideas of the past, especially the recent past, were completely discredited. In this sense, there was a void in German politics. In each of their occupation zones, the United States, Britain, and France immediately began using their overwhelming power advantages to fill this void with their occupation policies, which included democratization. As the strongest of the Western victors, the United States eventually took the lead in the occupation of western Germany. As such, its policy had the largest impact on postwar political development. During the initial period of the occupation (1945–47), Joint Chiefs of Staff Directive 1067 (JCS 1067) largely guided US policy.[3] Under this directive, the United States first focused on destroying the vestiges of German power. This included the complete destruction of the remnants of the German military. Industrial capacity was limited and could only be used for contributing to the operation of occupation forces or maintaining a standard of living just high enough to prevent starvation, widespread disease, or civil unrest. The goal of these economic controls was not to make Germany an entirely agricultural nation without any industrial capacity, but rather, to ensure that Germany would be able to support itself without threatening others.[4]

While these policies aimed to destroy German power, ultimately the Western Allies decided to create a viable democratic government. In August of 1945, American President Harry Truman declared the Western Allies would "do what we can to make Germany over into a decent nation" (Quoted in Beschloss 2002, 269). The creation of this decent nation involved controlling German education, reorganizing the government, and encouraging free speech, free press, freedom of religion, and the right of labor to organize.

Before any of this could take place, however, the remnants of the old regime had to be purged. De-Nazification polices outlawed all vestiges of Nazism in Germany, and individual Nazis were punished for their crimes. At the time, however, many Germans viewed de-Nazification policies as hypocritical and illegitimate, as often only lower-level Nazis were punished and some of the "big fish" got away (Olick 2005). This was not the case with the Nuremberg Trials. Held from November 20, 1945, until October 1, 1946, these trials saw the prosecution of individual German political and military leaders for waging aggressive war, violations of the rules of warfare, and crimes against humanity. Stemming from the atrocities of the Holocaust, the charge of crimes against humanity "made clear the Allies' attempt to respond not only to Germany's culpability for the outbreak of the war and the brutality of its conduct but also to the previously unimaginable quality of the crimes against noncombatants." (Jarausch 2006, 8) In the end, three individuals were found not guilty while the rest of the defendants received sentences that ranged from short prison terms to life sentences and even death. While the trials were not uncontroversial, as they could be portrayed as "victors' justice," they played a key role in exposing the crimes of the Nazi state to German citizens and the world. Moreover, the precedent set at the Nuremberg trials played a pivotal role in the post-World War II evolution of international human rights law.

Nazism had also corrupted the education system, so the entire system was shut down. Before reopening, all textbooks were purged of Nazi propaganda, and all teachers with Nazi backgrounds were dismissed (Bark and

Gress 1993). The goal was to institute a system of control over German education and a program of reorientation designed to "eliminate Nazi and militaristic doctrines and to encourage the development of democratic ideals" (JCS 1067, 22). Still, practical problems abounded with these purges, including student–teacher ratios as high as 80:1 because of shortages of acceptable teachers (Dorn 2005, 273). When acceptable pre-Nazi textbooks were finally located on microform, paper shortages and diminished publishing capacities limited their widespread dissemination.

In addition to education, the democratic Allies also tightly controlled political participation. Germans had opportunities to participate in democracy at the local level, but with restrictions. Political parties, both newly formed and those with roots in the Weimar Republic, were subject to licensing. Only parties that met with the approval of occupation authorities were allowed to operate. Moreover, the Western Allies prohibited these parties from engaging in issues outside their own regions. In confining political activity to the state-level, or *Land*, occupation authorities aimed to break the power of the centralized German state by forcing political parties to develop strong regional-level platforms. Beyond this promotion of decentralization, Allied officials immediately selected anti-Nazi mayors for each occupied village, and appointed anti-Nazi *Land* officials.

In light of the media's critical role under democracy, the United States exerted direct censorship until September of 1945. After this, the United States instituted a licensing program that constrained the media by revoking the license of outlets that regularly criticized the occupation or occupation authorities. The United States also funded new media outlets, including *Die Neue Zeitung* ("The New Newspaper"). The first issue of *Die Neue Zeitung* included a statement from US Chief of Staff, General Dwight D. Eisenhower, that the paper was one way to reeducate and democratize German citizens and eliminate militarism in Germany (Olick 2005). All these steps set the stage for reforming Germany along democratic lines and in 1946 paved the way for the first real (albeit heavily constrained) elections in the US occupational zone.

As tensions mounted between the United States and the Soviet Union, American policy toward Germany shifted. The looming Cold War pushed the United States to solidify its commitment to democratize Germany. In 1947, JCS 1779 replaced JCS 1067, introducing a new occupation directive that stressed more clearly the basic objective of US policy was to "lay the economic and educational bases of a sound Germany, encouraging bona fide efforts and of prohibiting those activities which would jeopardize genuinely democratic developments" (JCS 1779, 124).[5] The United States started to encourage West Germans to develop democratic political institutions and promoted market-based economic activity.

The United States also increased the authority granted to the legislatures representing each *Land* (*Landerat*), hoping that empowered *Länder* would eliminate the possibility of a strong central government. However, the United States retained ultimate veto power over any German legislation in local and regional political bodies. The United States renewed its emphasis on economic rebuilding, but maintained restrictions limiting economic activity to the non-military realm. While the United States continued its direct and indirect control over German education, media, and general political development, it placed new emphasis on the "good" parts of German history and culture (those not associated with the Nazi regime) as a way to channel German efforts into building a new kind of state. At the same time, some Germans were starting to do the same (Olick 2005).

In general, by 1947 Germans were given more leeway in constructing new political and economic institutions. However, the United States and its allies closely supervised all these efforts, prohibiting Germans from choosing any alternative path to the principles of democracy as understood by the victors. Even the formation of a new formal democratic system in West Germany was not left to the Germans themselves.

Building democracy in the Federal Republic of Germany

By early 1948, the United States, Britain, and France had forged a consensus on the foundations for a democratic West Germany. But, never assuming they "would themselves define the terms of their own constitution," West Germans were largely excluded from the discussions (Spevack 2002, 113). The victors conveyed their ideas in the 1948 Frankfurt Documents, which provided vague guidelines on the construction of the new government. A constitutional assembly, composed of *Länder* officials and vetted by the allies, aimed to make these vague guidelines concrete in the form of a new constitution. Every aspect of the constitutional assembly's work was subject to British, French, and US approval.

Decentralization was one hallmark of the Frankfurt Documents. The United States, Britain, and France aimed to create a weak central government to check West Germany's ability to mobilize resources for the purposes of war (Clay 1984). The victors placed strong limits on the central government, denying it power over education, culture, churches, local administration, and public health. The central government's power over public welfare and policy, as well as taxation, was limited. A decentralized federal organization of government disbursed power over local, state, and federal entities, but the victors sought to divide power even further over the three branches of government. A highly independent judiciary would adjudicate conflict between federal and *Länder* governments, as well as protect individual rights against the state. The legislature would convene in a bicameral parliament, with sufficient power reserved for the chamber representing the *Länder*.

The Frankfurt Documents also outlined the residual rights of the three Allied powers, including continued control of foreign trade and industry, monitoring the implementation of the new constitution, and representing West Germany in foreign affairs. Furthermore, the victors reserved the right to subject any amendments to the West German constitution or any law passed by the West German parliament to Allied approval. Even more sweepingly, Allied forces could seize total control of the state if democracy or the occupation forces were threatened (Spevack 2002). Thus, the victorious states, especially the United States, tightly controlled the process of West German democratization. Some Germans chafed under this control, comparing the Allied demands to the reviled Treaty of Versailles (Hitchcock 1997). Ultimately, however, they had no choice in the matter.

Formed in September of 1948, the Parliamentary Council worked under the supervision of occupation authorities until the spring of 1949. To ensure the final product met with Allied approval, occupation authorities relied upon some overt interventions to forcefully guide the Germans, as well as informal contacts with the members of the Council. By May of 1949, a document emerged that met with Allied approval. To stress the impermanence of the division of Germany, the Parliamentary Council purposely avoided the term "constitution," calling the final document the Basic Law (*Grundgesetz*) (Spevack 2002). The Basic Law paved the way for the first national elections on August 14, 1949, whereby Konrad Adenauer of the Christian Democratic Union (CDU) became the Federal Republic's first Chancellor.

The victors threatened, cajoled, and co-opted West Germans to create a state bound to and constrained by democratic and federal principles. The Western Allies (particularly the United States) exported their views on basic individual rights, federalism, and judicial review to create a liberal, democratic basis for the state (Krüger 1999). Still, the Basic Law was not really an imposed constitution. It contained indigenous German elements taken from the best parts of the Weimar constitution and other German traditions, such as aspects of judicial control of constitutionality and reliance on a professional bureaucracy (Kommers 1989; Jarausch 2006).

While the Basic Law created the Federal Republic of Germany, the new state was far from sovereign, as the victors had wide latitude for intervention. Between 1949 and 1954, however, the heating up of the Cold War drove a movement toward the normalization of West Germany. Western Allies (particularly the United States) recognized the importance of West German power to contain and curb the Soviets. Rather than merely restraining West German power, the victors shifted to allow West Germany more latitude to conduct its own affairs, while still ensuring the democratic system remained intact and on the correct trajectory.

State institutions

Despite the temporary nature originally envisioned by the Parliamentary Council, the institutions enshrined in the Basic Law have over the long term proven remarkably stable, as well as adaptable. In part this is due to the fact that the framers of the Basic Law, directed and monitored by the US and its Allies, crafted a constitution that avoided some of the aspects of the Weimar Republic that had made it so unstable. The framework was not a guarantee of democratic success, but the safeguards the Basic Law provided and the way it addressed the critical weaknesses of the Weimar constitution gave the new democracy a chance at stability (Fulbrook 1992).

One critical institutional change was that the Basic Law greatly reduced the power of the president. Under the Weimar Republic, the popularly elected president had tremendous powers, creating what some referred as a "substitute Emperor." Among others, the Weimar president had the power to appoint and dismiss chancellors, dissolve parliament and call for new elections, and authorize the chancellor to rule by presidential decree. These powers are in large part what, in 1933, allowed Hitler to assume the chancellorship through completely constitutional means, and then to proceed with a systematic destruction of Weimar democracy. This tragic failure of Weimar—where much depended upon the character of the person holding the office of president—cannot be repeated under the Basic Law (Fulbrook 1992). The president of the Federal Republic, elected indirectly through the Federal Convention rather than by popular vote, is little more than a figurehead.

In addition to weakening the presidency, the Basic Law also addressed the many deficiencies of Weimar's electoral system and legislature. Parliament consists of two chambers—the *Bundestag*, or national parliament, and the

Bundesrat, representing the *Länder*. The *Bundestag* elects the chancellor, the head of the executive branch of government. To avoid the parliamentary polarization and fragmentation of the Weimar era, the new electoral system established a hurdle of 5 percent of the popular vote for political parties to gain representation in the legislature. The electoral system also sought to balance party discipline and voter accountability. Through a system of personalized proportional representation, West Germans vote for both a party and a candidate in *Bundestag* elections.[6]

The Basic Law further addressed the instability of the Weimar Republic with limitations on the dissolution of parliament. Instituting a constructive vote of no confidence, a chancellor can only be ousted if the majority in the *Bundestag* agrees on a replacement. The 5 percent barrier and the constructive vote of no confidence, combined with the strong position of the chancellor vis-à-vis other ministers, have helped make the *Bundestag* remarkably stable.

The other chamber of parliament, the *Bundesrat,* reflects federal principles. Essentially, the *Bundesrat* is a "forum of *Länder* governments embedded in the federal legislative process" (Jeffery 2005, 78). The members of the *Bundesrat* are selected by the *Landtag,* and members of *Länder* governments can hold positions in the *Bundesrat* concurrently. The *Bundesrat* holds veto power on issues that directly concern the *Länder,* and can delay and amend *Bundestag* legislation. Combined with the significance of local elections within the Federal Republic and the rights over cultural and educational policy, the *Länder* thus retain a large amount of influence against the central government. This federal structure represents an institutional innovation that creates relatively empowered *Länder* to safeguard against the centralization of power that Hitler used to destroy the first German democracy. As an additional protection, Article 79 of the Basic Law prohibits the amending of the principle of federalism.

The judiciary has also played a vital role in protecting democracy. The Federal Constitutional Court is the final arbiter of constitutionality and adjudicates between levels of government. The judiciary is also empowered to eliminate potential threats to democracy. Article 21 authorizes it to declare unconstitutional any political party that seeks to "impair or abolish the free democratic order" of the Federal Republic (Kommers 1989, 139). Over time, the court has gained an unprecedented reputation as a strong, independent and legitimate judicial element of democracy (Krüger 1999).

The Basic Law also clearly enshrines the ideals of liberal democracy with strong protections for individual rights. It classifies individual rights as "preconstitutional," meaning they originate not in the state but rather emanate from a higher law. To address the systemic and horrific abuses of human rights under the Nazi regime, the new democracy explicitly acknowledged the inviolability of individual rights and prohibited any amending of these rights (Kommers 1989). These staunch protections of individual rights, combined with other protections, such as the Federal Constitutional Court's ability to declare illegal antidemocratic parties, construct a so-called militant democracy (Spevack 2002).

Additional mechanisms have also served to protect this militant democracy. Article 87, section 1, allowed for the creation of the Office for the Protection of the Constitution. Essentially an intelligence service, this office monitored extremist groups and other threats to democracy. During the early years of the Federal Republic, the Western victors also played a role in protecting nascent institutions. For example, until West Germany regained sovereignty in 1954, the Allies retained the right to scrutinize all *Bundestag*-passed laws to ensure they were consistent with democratic principles (Spevack 2002).

These institutional innovations acted as safeguards for democracy, designed to shield the system "against being overwhelmed by the excesses of popular democracy," something the Weimar system could not do (Kommers 1989, 139). In this regard, institutional design has been critical to the Federal Republic's democratic success. It is important to note that the "crucial push from the outside" played a pivotal role in giving the small number of committed German democrats a chance to create such a stable system (Jarausch 2006, 138). However, it is equally important to recognize that once this critical push was made, West Germans made the democratic system their own. Indeed, between 1949 and 1983, 34 different laws were passed to change the Basic Law, effecting 47 existing articles and creating 73 new ones (Fulbrook 1992). Thus, while the democratic institutions in the Federal Republic have proven remarkably strong and stable, they also have been flexible enough to adapt to changing times and issues.

With a strong democratic foundation in place, the Western Allies appraised political development in largely positive terms, and restored formal sovereignty to the western German state in 1954. But this was done as West Germany was integrated into the North Atlantic Treaty Organization (NATO). This meant West Germany was permitted to construct a new military, but it also brought some restrictions that made West Germany unlike other NATO members. These included limitations on the size of the military, a renouncement of biological, chemical, and nuclear weapons, and prohibitions against West Germany unilaterally unifying the German nation. In addition, NATO allies retained troop-stationing rights and emergency powers within West Germany, meaning the Western Allies could claim supreme authority "if the democratic regime in Germany were threatened."[7] With these developments, the victors solidified their influence over West German domestic institutions and designed a web of international institutions to restrain as well as protect the young democracy.

Elites

The Basic Law explicitly addressed the institutional weaknesses of the Weimar Republic and ensured the new democracy did not begin with these flaws. This solid institutional basis presented an opportunity for democratic stability, but the success of German democracy would also depend greatly on the ways in which elites interacted with this new system. Under the Weimar Republic elites actively exploited loopholes in the constitution to undermine democracy instead of uphold it. By 1949, however, nearly all West German elites were committed to democratic principles. The Federal Republic ultimately secured "the support, the allegiance, or at least the acquiescence of the key elite groups, and avoid[ed] the development of powerful anti-system opposition of the sort that helped to bring about the collapse of the Weimar Republic" (Fulbrook 1992). This was due in part to Germany's unconditional surrender and discrediting of the former Nazi elite. Furthermore, the occupation policies of the Western victors promoted certain elites over others and authorized only democratically committed political parties to contest for power, effectively truncating the political spectrum in West Germany. Fear of Soviet expansionism also made Western democracy much more appealing (Turner 1992). What emerged in West German politics was a group of political elites with a strong commitment to democratic principles willing to work within the system.

Center-right political elites dominated West German politics during these early formative years. In fact, all political and economic development milestones occurred on the 14-year watch of Konrad Adenauer. Adenauer had been a local politician until the Nazi takeover led to his early retirement. Untainted from association with the Nazi Party, the democratization of Germany brought him back into politics. Leading the Christian Democratic Union (CDU), Adenauer was a prominent member of the Parliamentary Council that constructed the Basic Law. A committed democrat with a clear Western orientation, in 1949 he led his party to winning 31 percent of the vote in the first national election. Forming a coalition government with the Free Democratic Party (FDP), Adenauer became the Federal Republic's first chancellor and remained in that office until 1963.

Though his legacy is contested, Adenauer's leadership was incredibly important for the eventual solidification of West German democracy.[8] All critical junctures in early democratic development occurred under his watch. For example, Adenauer's clear commitment to the West led the United States to trust the democratic nature of the Federal Republic enough to return sovereignty to the state by bringing it into the NATO system (Craig 1995). Moreover, Adenauer's finance minister, Ludwig Erhard, engineered the economic miracle of the 1950s, which significantly improved the material conditions of West German citizens. In 1957, running largely on the same platform that led to astounding economic growth earlier in the decade, the CDU and the Christian Social Union of Bavaria (CSU) gained over 50 percent of the vote, achieving for the first time an absolute majority in the *Bundestag* (Fulbrook 1992). Though Adenauer stepped down from the chancellorship in 1963, the CDU remained one of the two dominant political parties for the duration of the Cold War and beyond.

The early success of the CDU precluded the governing of center-left political elites until the 1960s. However, the Social Democratic Party (SPD) did counter the dominance of the CDU while still working within and supporting the nascent democratic system. Kurt Schumacher, a passionate democrat and leader of the SPD, best exemplified this. Imprisoned during the war, Schumacher was also untainted by association with the Nazi regime. He differed with the CDU on many important policies, including German national unification and the exact constitution of the social market economy, but he ultimately led the SPD to act as a responsible opposition to the CDU-led government. After Schumacher's death in 1952 and a series of electoral defeats, the SPD reshaped its political image in 1959 under the *Bad Godesberg* program. In light of the growing alarm at the establishment of communism in East Germany, this move eliminated the electorally damaging Marxist language from its platform and allowed the SPD to reinvented itself as a catch-all people's party focused on increasing equality within the market-oriented democratic system. This change brought the SPD much closer to the ideological position of the CDU. From this point on, the differences between the SPD and CDU were more differences in method than principle (Fulbrook 1992).

Still, there were concerns about the ability of elites to uphold democratic norms. While Adenauer was firmly committed to democracy, critics called his leadership style authoritarian and questioned the precedent set by his long tenure in office. Critics also questioned whether West German democracy could survive any sort of true test. In 1963 the transition from Adenauer to Erhard as chancellor provided the first such test (Jarausch 2006). Although no more than a change in leadership within the CDU, the transition was greeted with great relief. In contrast to the incredibly unstable previous German democratic experiment, the *Frankfurter Allgemeine Zeitung* (Frankfurt General Newspaper) claimed "the strongest proof of democracy that anyone could present during these days was the refusal to return to the parliamentarianism of the Weimar Republic." This first transition in government leadership occurred "in a way that corresponded to the best conventions of democracy" (Quoted in Jarausch 2006, 148).

Other tests of the democratic system soon followed. After a period of inept political maneuvers, the Erhard government fell when the FDP withdrew from the coalition in 1965. In November 1966, the CDU/CSU and the SPD formed a grand coalition to govern with the CDU's Kurt Kiesinger as chancellor and the SPD's Willy Brandt as foreign minister.[9] The participation of the SPD in the government marked a new era in West German political development, showing the party that had been in opposition during most of the postwar period was capable of contributing to governing within the democratic system (Fulbrook 1992).

The SPD's fortunes rose throughout the 1960s. In September of 1969, the CDU/CSU gained the largest number of seats, though still shy of the majority needed to form a government on its own. The SPD finished a close second, and capitalized on the FDP's drift to the left in the late 1960s to form a governing coalition (Fulbrook 1992). When the SPD's Willy Brandt assumed the chancellorship in October 1969, West Germany experienced its first transfer of government responsibility to the opposition party. In part because of these elites working within the system, the young democratic state successfully managed several power transitions in the 1960s.

With this shared commitment to core principles, the major groups of political elites settled into a pattern of two-party dominance within the West German government, alternating power by forming coalitions with smaller parties such as the FDP and later the Green Party. Policymaking took on a consensus style, as all relevant actors participated in negotiations, often even before legislation or policies were made public. Included in this inter-elite process were the "latent political elites," or business, labor, and farming interests (Fulbrook 1992). In the end, the contrast between the Federal Republic and Weimar could hardly be starker: instead of undermining democracy, all sectors of the elite class acted in ways to support the democratic system.[10]

Economic development

The institutions of the Federal Republic of Germany did not face the same dire economic challenges as those of the Weimar Republic. By the late 1950s, the West German economy had grown tremendously, ushering in high standards of living and citizen contentment. In the immediate aftermath of World War II, however, this outcome had been far from clear. In 1945, major industrial centers lay in ruins, and goods—including food and other necessities of life—were scarce (Botting 1985). The Allies' initial economic restrictions exacerbated the economic devastation, making it difficult to see how the vanquished state could rebound economically.

By 1948, however, the economy changed course, and high rates of growth played a large, albeit somewhat indirect, role in legitimizing the new democratic system. Indeed, the early 1950s were a time of great optimism. Industrial production and overall economic activity registered strong growth by the late 1940s. The outbreak of the Korean War in 1950 created additional opportunities, as the United States and its allies turned to West Germany for material for the war effort. These dynamics led to the phenomenal growth of the 1950s, dubbed the "economic miracle." Importantly, this economic boom translated into material benefits for average Germans.

Table 7.1 documents this remarkable economic growth from 1949 through 1960, averaging 9.8 percent a year. Other indicators of economic recovery during this time are equally astounding. West German average disposable income grew four hundred percent from 1950 through the 1960s (Fulbrook 1992). Between 1948 and 1953, industrial production tripled and unemployment was halved (Jarausch 2006). As West Germans began to feel this recovery directly, the boom lent tremendous credibility to the economic policies of the Federal Republic. Indeed, the success of the market economy, combined with the protections of large social safety nets, essentially vanquished the widespread sentiment in the immediate postwar years that socialism was the best route to economic recovery and stability (Bark and Gress 1993).

Table 7.1 GDP Growth 1949–60

%	1949	1950	1951	1952	1953	1954	1955	1956	1957	1958	1959	1960
GDP Growth	16.5	19.4	9.8	9.2	8.8	7.7	12.0	7.6	5.9	4.4	7.8	8.7

Source: Maddison (1995)

The social market economy's long-term performance contributed greatly to feelings of good will, or reserves of diffuse support, toward the West German institutions responsible for guiding the economy (Conradt 1989). Because these institutions were the very same ones that defined politics within the state, over time the democratic system started to enjoy greater legitimacy in the eyes of West German citizens. For example, in 1959, after the economic miracle and several years of increasing prosperity, 33 percent of West Germans pointed to the economic system as a source of pride. By 1978, this number increased to 40 percent. In the same time span, West German pride in governmental and political institutions jumped from seven percent to 31 percent (Conradt 1989).

In addition to this remarkable recovery, the West German economy was also integrated more fully into the Western European system. In 1950, the Schuman Plan launched this process of integration, leading to the construction of the European Coal and Steel Community (ECSC) in 1951. In addition to stimulating further economic recovery, economic integration also tied West Germany to the rest of Western Europe, making war "not simply unthinkable, but materially impossible."[11]

The economic success of West Germany greatly facilitated the consolidation of the democratic system. Becoming the second richest country in the world by 1959 and having an increasingly stable middle class, the economic success of the Federal Republic cultivated an enduring attachment to the democratic political system, allowing it to retain high levels of support even during times of economic downturn, such as the 1974–76 recession. Under Weimar the economy posed an insurmountable challenge to the political system; in the 1950s and 1960s, the economy helped legitimize it.

Political culture

Given the legacy of Nazism, in the 1940s and 1950s many feared German political culture would impede democratic development. Several public opinion polls supported this fear. In November of 1945, 53 percent of Germans in the American zone of occupation and in two sectors of Berlin stated they thought Nazism was a good idea that was badly carried out (Merritt and Merritt 1970). This support faded fairly quickly, but was not successfully replaced with anything else. West Germans disengaged from politics as a whole throughout the 1950s (Merritt 1995). When West Germany gained formal sovereignty in 1954, many doubted democracy had actually taken root in the state. In *The Civic Culture*, a groundbreaking work on political attitudes and democracy, political scientists Gabriel Almond and Sidney Verba found average West Germans had no real connection to the democratic system (1963). Any attachment they had to the institutions of West Germany was purely pragmatic, based upon the economic success of the country in the 1950s. Such findings suggested democratic reforms were reversible if the performance of the system waned.

While this sentiment may have existed among West Germans in the 1950s, there was no real threat that West Germany could embark on a non-democratic path. The continued influence of the victors' and elites' commitment to parliamentary democracy closed the door to alternate forms of political development. Despite the initially small number of West Germans committed to democracy, the democratic protection of the Basic Law and the external support of the Allies played critical roles in sustaining the system, even in the absence of a real democratic political culture. Still, to strengthen and sustain the foundations of West German democracy, it was essential to foster a political culture tied to democratic ideals. In some ways, there was a unique opportunity to do this. Many Germans saw the end of the war as zero-hour (*Stunde Null*), or a critical point at which the history of Germany was wiped clean. This, combined with the overwhelming power of the victors and the discrediting of Nazi ideology and German militarism, meant German political culture was in many ways "profoundly up for grabs" (Olick 2005, 141). The United States and its allies aimed to fill this void with democratic ideals. The occupation policies of the United States and its Allies included important elements to mold a democratic political culture, including de-Nazification, reeducation, and media reforms.

By the 1960s, several indicators point to the mass public's rallying behind the new democratic state. Instead of simply feeling a pragmatic attachment to a system providing material benefits, by the 1960s more and more West Germans began to value the ideals of democracy as well as the institutions that represented those democratic ideals (Conradt 1989). For example, the public greeted the Basic Law with ambivalence at best in 1949, but by the 1960s (and even more so in the 1970s), the founding text of the Federal Republic became a critical and valued part of West German political culture (Spevack 2002). Furthermore, by the 1970s 90 percent of West Germans claimed democracy to be the best form of government, and very few identified any other period of German history as a time when the country was better off (Conradt 1989).

The democratic political culture in West Germany can also be seen in the responses to challenges to democracy. During the occupation, and through the 1950s, parties inconsistent with democratic principles enjoyed much greater support than in the 1960s and 1970s (Merritt 1995). Other sorts of challenges, such as the terrorist wave of the 1970s, were met with mostly measured responses that preserved democratic ideals due to high expectations from the increasingly democratically oriented public (Orlow 1999).

The growth, and indeed strengthening, of the democratic political culture in the Federal Republic is quite remarkable given the nature of political beliefs in 1945. The generations of West Germans exposed only to a liberal democratic framework, who also witnessed its track record of good performance, exhibit the most robust support of liberal democratic ideals (Conradt 1989). Such a dynamic shows the important role institutions can play in shaping preferences, identity, and even culture (Steinmo, Thelen, and Longstreth 1992). What is so interesting about the West German case is that many features of the institutions that played such a fundamental role in shaping the democratic political culture have roots in external sources, yet all these institutions and the democratic political culture they have helped to shape have been indigenized.

Social divisions/national unity

The issue of national unity holds special significance for the Federal Republic. German nationalism, after all, played a key role in leading to the horrors of World War II. Moreover, the victorious states of World War II divided the German nation in two. For quite some time into the postwar era, most Germans hoped for quick reunification. Even in 1965, over 70 percent of West Germans considered reunification the most pressing foreign policy issue. But by 1973, only 23 percent felt the same way (Conradt 1989), as West Germany started to take on its own unique identity separate from the German nation as a whole (Maier 1999). Still, the notion of the "German Question," or what it meant to be German in the Federal Republic, lingered throughout the entire postwar era.

The division of Germany between East and West may also have played a critical role in effectively eliminating some societal cleavages that had long plagued democratic development in Germany, and had a significant role in weakening the Weimar democracy. In important ways, the division between East and West left the Federal Republic with the most modern part of Germany in terms of industrialization and social structure. Moreover, it isolated West Germany from the "bedrock of authoritarianism" in the East, namely the aristocratic, agrarian, and militaristic elites, called the *Junkers*, that since unification in 1871 had inordinate influence on German politics (Bernhard 2001). While societal cleavages remained within West Germany, the division of the German nation thus eliminated at least this one important polarizing cleavage. What was left was a relatively simple pattern of social cleavages based on class, religion, and region, and articulated via a small number of political parties (Jeffery 2005). However, immigration issues have proven difficult for German democracy and have somewhat divided the nation. This is particularly true of Turkish "guest workers" who became the target of right-wing anger starting in the 1970s, a problem that continues to this day. Immigration from East Germany after 1989 has also proved a divisive issue, as the Federal Republic struggled to absorb all those abandoning the former Democratic Republic.[12]

Even though there are problems with societal cleavages, and to some extent the "German Question" persists to this day, the absence of the polarizing pluralism of Weimar and the existence of a relatively stable party system to express the social cleavages that are present have helped democratic consolidation in the Federal Republic.

Education

The German educational system has long been a source of pride, boasting very high literacy rates and a strong system of higher education, both before and after World War II. Still, the Nazi's corruption of the educational system led the Western Allies to worry that the system would not foster democratic ideals. With the 1946 Educational Mission to Germany, the United States in particular sought to revamp the German educational system to eradicate the last vestiges of Nazi influence and establish in its place respect for democratic norms. The *Länder*, which maintained control over the educational system under the decentralized political system, agreed to the process of de-Nazification, including the widespread dismissal of teachers and creation of new textbooks, but adamantly opposed any alterations to the traditional German three-tier educational system. Because of this resistance, the United States ultimately gave up its massive efforts to totally reform the structure of the education system (Dorn 2005).

Despite concerns the three-tiered educational system would preserve authoritarian values, contemporary evidence indicates this has not been the case. The cumulative effect of reform and reeducation efforts became evident only after a generation of Germans experienced it firsthand, and it is clear that generations growing up only under the Federal Republic and its educational system have internalized democratic values (Tent 1982).

International context

This chapter has highlighted how the international context was critical to the success of West German democratization. In the early postwar era, the United States, Britain, and France decisively directed democratization efforts. The victors molded the institutions that would govern the state and imbued West Germans with democratic ideals by allowing only democratically committed political parties, reforming education, and shaping a supportive media. Committed German democrats also worked to push the state into a new trajectory, but they were only able to do this after being vetted by the United States and within the confines of occupation policies. By using their coercive capabilities to do all these things and more, the groundwork for a process of socialization to democratic norms had clearly been laid during the occupation period and through the late 1950s. The fruits of these efforts by the victors and West Germans alike were readily apparent by the 1960s.

Two forces in particular drove the victors: the threat of Germany once again rampaging through Europe, and the escalating Cold War between the United States and the Soviet Union. Initially, security concerns pushed occupation directives on democratization. Knowing German power would eventually rebound, the victors aimed to ensure that Germany would not be a source of postwar instability (McAllister 2002). Wedding Germany to liberal principles seemed the most viable means to guarantee this. The imposition of democracy, supported by the web of international institutions tying the state to the rest of Western Europe, were thus victor-constructed constraints on West German power (Banchoff 1999).

While the impetus for democratization in Germany existed independently, the cold war heightened the urgency of such efforts. As US fear of Soviet expansion mounted, Germany became the linchpin of the European front of the Cold War. To contain the Soviets, the United States aimed to cultivate allies and harness the tremendous potential of West Germany. These goals drove US decisions to ease economic restrictions and accelerate democratization plans. To ensure West German economic and political development would serve US interests, however, America and its allies carefully directed and controlled the construction of democracy.

The international context, therefore, is critical to the story of West German democracy and makes clear how, under certain conditions, outside actors can help shape democracy. The United States and its Allies, taking advantage of the overwhelming devastation in Germany in 1945, clearly set out to craft a new, democratic state in their erstwhile enemy. Exploiting its power advantages in the immediate postwar era, the United States was able to promote the ideas, people, and institutions to set the stage for democratic ideals eventually being internalized by West Germans, and thereby provide the basis for a strong, stable democracy. This process of coercive socialization, then, can be an important dynamic in imposing democracy from the outside.

Conclusions

Though German democracy has its roots in the ashes of World War II, it has emerged as a remarkably strong system. The strength of the system comes from a number of components thought to be critical for democratic development. Specifically, the Federal Republic saw early and sustained economic success, the elites' willingness to work within the system, the emergence of a strong democratic political culture, and institutions designed to protect against the worst democratic excesses. Moreover, the international context proved extremely conducive to creating and sustaining democracy within West Germany.

Indeed, the foundations of democracy in the Federal Republic were solid enough to provide a basis for the reunification of the divided German nation. With the end of the Cold War and the collapse of the communist systems of Eastern Europe, on October 3, 1990, the Federal Republic essentially absorbed what was the German Democratic Republic. There was a commission charged with exploring the construction of a new German constitution, but this fell into inactivity, and the Basic Law went untouched as the East was incorporated into the Federal Republic. As such, the temporary constitution of 1949 took on a new sense of permanence (Merritt 1995). While reunification has posed many challenges—including coping with the financial costs of modernizing the East and some renewed national identity questions—the fundamental character of democracy in the Federal Republic has remained unchanged.

Additional resources

For a good general history of Germany from the end of World War I through reunification, see Mary Fulbrook (1992). Konrad H. Jarausch (2006) traces the fundamental changes in both West and East Germany in the postwar era as well as issues lingering since reunification. Dennis L. Bark and David R. Gress's two-volume *A History of West Germany, Second Edition*

(1993) provides enormous detail on nearly every aspect of West German political development. *The Postwar Transformation of Germany: Democracy, Prosperity, and Nationhood* (1999), edited by John S. Brady, Beverly Crawford, and Sarah Elise Wiliarty, is an excellent critical examination of the way Germany evolved in the postwar era. Marc Trachtenberg's *A Constructed Peace: The Making of the European Settlement 1945–1963* (1999) puts the German Question into the context of the Cold War struggle between the United States and the Soviet Union.

Memoirs and biographies that paint vivid pictures of the birth of West German democracy include: Konrad Adenauer's *Memoirs, 1945–1953* (translated by Beate Ruhm von Oppen: Chicago: Henry Regnery, 1966); Gen. Lucius D. Clay's *Decision in Germany* (Garden City, NY: Doubleday, 1950); Thomas Alan Schwartz's *America's Germany: John J. McCloy and the Federal Republic of Germany* (Cambridge: Harvard University Press, 1991). The novel *The Tin Drum* by Günter Grass (New York: Pantheon Books, 1963) paints a picture of German society during the rise of the Nazis through the immediate postwar period, showing some of the changes in the postwar era. For contemporary coverage of German politics and society, *Spiegel International*, the online English version of *Der Spiegel*, provides excellent coverage (available at: www.spiegel.de/international).

Notes

1 After World War II, the Soviets occupied the eastern portion of Germany, eventually establishing a communist state, the German Democratic Republic (GDR), or East Germany. Despite its name, the GDR was decidedly not democratic.

2 See Weitz (2007) for a thorough overview of the political and social conditions that led to the construction and eventual demise of the Weimar Republic.

3 The text of the revised JCS 1067 (JCS 1067/8 date May 10, 1945) is reprinted in US Department of State *Documents on Germany 1944–1985*, 15–32 (hereafter referred to as JCS 1067).

4 The economic provisions of JCS 1067 lay between Treasury Secretary Henry Morgenthau's plan for pastoralization and President Roosevelt's desire to maintain German industrial capacity to "the fullest extent necessary to maintain the Germans so that we don't have the burden of taking care of them" (stated in March of 1945, quoted in Eisenberg 1996).

5 JCS 1779 replaced JCS 1067 and all its amendments as the US occupation directive on July 11, 1947. JCS 1779 is reprinted in US Department of State *Documents on Germany 1944–1985*, 124–35 (hereafter referred to as JCS 1779)

6 For an excellent introductory overview of the German electoral system, see Sodaro (2004: 457–61).

7 Trachtenberg (1999, 126). This formidable power was held until 1968, when the *Bundestag* finally passed an emergency powers law.

8 Left-leaning critics have charged that Adenauer's legacy includes prohibiting West Germany from atoning for its World War II sins and embarking on a truly democratic path (Carter 2001).

9 The Christian Social Union of Bavaria (CSU) is linked to the CDU. Although the two parties retain separate identities, these Christian conservative parties work together in federal elections. The CDU does not run candidates in Bavaria and the CSU does not run candidates outside Bavaria.

10 This is especially true of the reconstituted West German military, which understood it could not play any sort of independent political role in the state (Fulbrook 1992). This fits well with another aspect of democracy in the Federal Republic: a postwar culture of antimilitarism among the vast majority of the population; see Berger (1998).

11 Schuman's May 9, 1950, declaration (quoted in Hitchcock 1997, 603).

12 See Jarausch (2006, 239–66) for the complexity of the immigration issues and the manner in which the Federal Republic has responded.

References

Almond, Gabriel A., and Sidney Verba. 1963. *The Civic Culture: Political Attitudes and Democracy in Five Nations*. Princeton: Princeton University Press.

Banchoff, Thomas. 1999. "The Enduring Transformation of Postwar German Foreign Policy." In *The Postwar Transformation of Germany: Democracy, Prosperity, and Nationhood*, edited by John S. Brady, Beverly Crawford, and Sarah Elise Wiliarty. Ann Arbor: The University of Michigan Press.

Bark, Dennis L., and David R. Gress. 1993. *A History of West Germany, Second Edition*. Cambridge: Blackwell Publishers.

Berger, Thomas U. 1998. *Cultures of Antimilitarism: National Security in Germany and Japan*. Baltimore: Johns Hopkins University Press.

Bernhard, Michael. 2001. "Democratization in Germany: A Reappraisal." *Comparative Politics* 33(4): 379–400.

Beschloss, Michael. 2002. *The Conquerors: Roosevelt, Truman, and the Destruction of Hitler's Germany 1941–1945*. New York: Simon & Schuster.

Botting, Douglas. 1985. *From the Ruins of the Reich: Germany, 1945–1949*. New York: Crown.

Brady, John S., Beverly Crawford, and Sarah Elise Wiliarty, eds. 1999. *The Postwar Transformation of Germany: Democracy, Prosperity, and Nationhood*. Ann Arbor: The University of Michigan Press.

Carter, Erica. 2001. "Culture, History, and National Identity in the Two Germanies, 1945–1999." In *Twentieth Century Germany: Culture and Society 1918–1990*, edited by Mary Fulbrook. London: Arnold.

Clay, Lucius D. 1984. "Proconsul of a People, by Another People, for Both Peoples." In *Americans as Proconsuls: United State Military Government in Germany and Japan, 1944–1952*, edited by Robert Wolfe. Carbondale: Southern Illinois University Press.

Conradt, David P. 1989. "Changing German Political Culture." In *The Civic Culture Revisited*, edited by Gabriel Almond and Sidney Verba. Newbury Park: Sage Publications.

Craig, Gordon A. 1995. "Konrad Adenauer and the United States." In *The American Impact on Postwar Germany*, edited by Reiner Pommerin. Providence: Berghahn Books.

Dorn, Charles. 2005. "Evaluating Democracy: The 1946 U.S. Education Mission to Germany." *American Journal of Evaluation* 26(2): 267–77.

Eisenberg, Carolyn. 1996. *Drawing the Line: The American Decision to Divide Germany, 1944–1949*. Cambridge: Cambridge University Press.

Fulbrook, Mary. 1992. *The Divided Nation: A History of Germany 1918–1990*. New York: Oxford University Press.

Hitchcock, William I. 1997. "France, the Western Alliance, and the Origins of the Schuman Plan, 1948–1950." *Diplomatic History* 21(4): 603–30.

Jarausch, Konrad H. 2006. *After Hitler: Recivilizing Germans, 1945–1995*. New York: Oxford University Press.

Jeffery, Charlie. 2005. "Federalism: The New Territorialism." In *Governance in Contemporary Germany: The Semisovereign State Revisited*, edited by Simon Green and William E. Patterson, 78–93. Cambridge: Cambridge University Press.

Kommers, Donald P. 1989. "The Basic Law of the Federal Republic of Germany: An Assessment after Forty Years." In *The Federal Republic of Germany at Forty*, edited by Peter H. Merkyl, 133–59. New York: New York University Press.

Krüger, Peter. 1999. "The Federal Republic as a Nation-state." In *The Postwar Transformation of Germany: Democracy, Prosperity, and Nationhood*, edited by John S. Brady, Beverly Crawford, and Sarah Elise Wiliarty. Ann Arbor: The University of Michigan Press.

Maddison, Angus. 1995. *Monitoring the World Economy 1820–1992*. Paris: OECD.

Maier, Charles S. 1999. "The End of Longing? (Notes toward a History of Postwar German National Longing)." In *The Postwar Transformation of Germany: Democracy, Prosperity, and Nationhood*, edited by John S. Brady, Beverly Crawford, and Sarah Elise Wiliarty. Ann Arbor: The University of Michigan Press.

McAllister, James. 2002. *No Exit: America and the German Problem, 1943–1954*. Ithaca and London: Cornell University Press.

Merritt, Anna J., and Richard L. Merritt, eds. 1970. *Public Opinion in Occupied Germany: The OMGUS Surveys, 1945–49*. Urbana: University of Illinois Press.

Merritt, Richard L. 1995. *Democracy Imposed: U.S. Occupation Policy and the German Public, 1945–49*. New Haven: Yale University Press.

Olick, Jeffrey K. 2005. *In the House of the Hangman: The Agonies of German Defeat, 1943–1949*. Chicago: University of Chicago Press.

Orlow, Dietrich. 1999. *A History of Modern Germany, 1871 to Present*. Upper Saddle River: Prentice Hall.

Sodaro, Michael J. 2004. *Comparative Politics: A Global Introduction (2nd edition).* Boston: McGraw Hill.

Spevack, Edmund. 2002. *Allied Control and German Freedom: American Political and Ideological Influences on the Framing of the West German Basic Law (Grundgesetz).* Münster and London: Lit Verlag.

Steinmo, Sven, Kathleen Thelen, and Frank Longstreth, eds. 1992. *Structuring Politics: Historical Institutionalism in Comparative Analysis.* Cambridge: Cambridge University Press.

Tent, James E. 1982. "Mission on the Rhine: American Education Policy in Postwar Germany, 1945–1949." *History of Education Quarterly* 22(3): 255–76.

Trachtenberg, Marc. 1999. *A Constructed Peace: The Making of the European Settlement 1945–1963.* Princeton: Princeton University Press.

Turner, Henry A. 1992. *Germany from Partition to Reunification.* New Haven: Yale University Press.

United States Department of State. 1985. *Documents on Germany 1944–1985.* Washington D.C.: Department of State Publication.

Weitz, Eric D. 2007. *Weimar Germany: Promise and Tragedy.* Princeton: Princeton University Press.

Photo by author of Hiromi Nagano in front of her rice paddy. Ms. Nagano is one of Japan's new generation of political leaders. She is a member of the Nishinoomote City Council. In her political and social activism, Nagano represents a blend of new (female politician and NPO activist, with international education and work experience) and old (she returned to her rural hometown to care for her aging parents, continues to cultivate rice, and lives in a traditional farm house) characteristics.

8

The Transformation of Japanese Democracy

Mary Alice Haddad

Chapter Outline

Japan was one of the first non-Western countries to democratize, and its political transformation teaches us a great deal about the nature of democracy, the process of democratic transition, and the varieties of democracy found around the world today. The Japanese case illustrates that identifying the "most" important factor facilitating democratization is far less important than discovering the ways different forces interact with one another to shape a country's path to democracy, and the ways they continue to influence political development long after democracy's establishment.

Japan's early experience with democracy

When Commodore Perry arrived in Edo Bay (now called Tokyo Bay) on July 8, 1853, he ushered in the beginning of the end for Japan's largely peaceful 200-plus years of feudal rule under the *Bakufu* lords. His arrival was a crucial catalyst for the dramatic political, economic, and social changes now dubbed the Meiji Restoration. The Meiji Period (1868–1912) transformed Japan from an isolationist, feudal state to a global power, as extensive reforms touched all aspects of Japanese life. Among other things, reforms introduced land reform, a social welfare system, and a national education system (elementary education was made compulsory in 1872), while also creating a national police force and a modern financial system. Reformers matched these economic and social transformations with political developments, experimenting for the first time with democracy. Political elites and grassroots leaders sought the best form of government to shield Japan from seemingly imminent colonization by Western powers, while also positioning it well for the modern age. The Japanese studied examples from abroad, and found elements to admire in Prussian, British, French, and US models of government. Heated debates quickly ensued on the models that would best fit Japan, as well as on the pace of reform efforts.

The 1889 Meiji Constitution embodied both traditional and more liberal democratic political values. Reflecting the values of the old feudal system, the constitution itself was a gift, which the benevolent Emperor bestowed upon the people of Japan. The constitution referred to the Japanese people as subjects rather than citizens. Reflecting the interests of liberal democrats, the constitution also established a bicameral national assembly and guaranteed a wide range of individual rights, including the freedoms of assembly, speech, due process, and protection against unlawful search and seizure.

At the turn of the twentieth century, Japan's ambitious and wide-reaching reforms at home coincided with diplomatic and military campaigns for territorial expansion. Japan's 1894–95 war with China led to Japan's occupation of Manchuria and Korea. In 1905 Japan became the first modern Asian country to defeat a European power when it ousted Russia from Port Arthur and solidified Japanese control of northern Manchuria.

The year 1912 marked the end of an extraordinary chapter in Japanese political history with the passing of the Meiji emperor and the enthronement of Crown Prince Yoshihito, who adopted the name Taishō for his reign, and ushered in what has come to be called the period of "Taishō Democracy." The chronically ill Taishō emperor did not inherit his father's political adeptness, creating an opening for a new generation of politicians to wrest power from the aging oligarchs. The opposition Kenseikai party began to call for universal manhood suffrage.

Many viewed this first push for universal male suffrage as conforming to international trends. Authoritarian governments in Europe had fallen either through their defeat in war (World War I) or by collapse from within (Tsarist Russia). Although the measure failed in this first attempt, it succeeded five years later when the Kenseikai Party took control of the cabinet. The General Election Law passed the Diet in 1925, granting all Japanese men over the age of 25 the right to vote.[1] Reformers were cautious, however. To mitigate the possibility that widespread unrest could accompany such a dramatic increase of the franchise, and to appease wary conservatives, reformers enacted the Peace Preservation Law. This law aimed to enforce loyalty to the emperor and the state and enhance the power of the police to suppress political opposition.

Democratic breakdown and the rise of militarism

The breakdown of Japan's nascent democracy and the rise of fascism in the 1930s resembled the experience of interwar Germany. When the Great Depression hit Japan in 1930, the economic, political, and military expansions of the 1920's were already taking their toll. By 1932 Japan supported colonies in Taiwan and Korea and a puppet state in Manchuria, stretching the military and government budgets. By the late 1930s, the military became more aggressive, jealously guarding and even expanding its rights to select cabinet officials and influence policy, circumventing established political channels in favor of direct consultations with the emperor. In 1936, following several smaller coup attempts, several young officers commanding 1,400 soldiers occupied the government section of Tokyo and assassinated several cabinet ministers. Together with an increasingly invasive use of the Peace Preservation Law, these actions intimidated more liberal politicians into acquiescing to the military's demands (Kato 1974, 232–33). By the following year Japan had launched a full-scale invasion of China.

Wartime Japan saw a nearly complete eradication of liberal and leftist elements in government and civil society, and the rise of "ultranationalism." The military regime mobilized and controlled the population through mandatory membership in neighborhood associations and other groups. The state used this highly mobilized and militarized society to wreak havoc on its neighbors, resulting in catastrophic devastation for the entire region and the world.

On August 6, 1945, the United States dropped a nuclear bomb on the city of Hiroshima. When an unconditional surrender was not immediately forthcoming, it dropped another on Nagasaki three days later. On September 2, 1945, the Japanese government signed the formal Instrument of surrender on board the USS *Missouri*. On January 1, 1946, the Emperor Shōwa issued an Imperial Rescript in which he denied the divinity of the Japanese emperor and the superiority of the Japanese race. This declaration marked the end of another era, one far more decisive and dramatic (and with much greater cost in human life) than Commodore Perry's arrival nearly a century prior.

Building democracy from outside and above: The Allied occupation 1945–52

Just as society had changed dramatically nearly a century earlier under the Meiji Restoration, the reforms implemented by the Allied occupation of Japan left few aspects of Japanese life untouched. Douglas MacArthur, the Supreme Commander of Allied Powers (SCAP), and his staff transformed many key institutions of Japanese life. Land reform swept away the last of the feudal relationships in the countryside. Education reform retired all the old textbooks and started fresh. Finance reform broke up the *zaibatsu* business conglomerates and reorganized the banking system. Electoral reform enfranchised women and instituted elections for local and prefectural leaders. Police functions were disentangled from firefighting, and both were returned to local control. The Allied occupation banned many local associations and abolished mandatory membership in favor of voluntary participation in community groups.

One of the first tasks of the new Japanese government was to draft a new constitution. After several months of careful study and consultations, the constitutional committee appointed by the Diet created two drafts, both essentially slightly revised versions of the Meiji Constitution. SCAP General Headquarters (GHQ) deemed them both far too conservative. In a frantic bid to design an alternative, SCAP staff designed their own draft in one week's time and presented it to the Japanese government on February 13, 1946. After significant back and forth between GHQ and the Japanese, the final document was voted into law and went into effect on May 3, 1947. It has remained in force, without amendment, ever since.

Very early on, cultural and administrative difficulties led the SCAP to decide that the occupation of Japan would differ from that of Germany. In lieu of a direct military government, SCAP opted for indirect rule that relied heavily on the existing civilian bureaucracy to carry out SCAP initiatives. Major reorganizations (such as the dissolution of the Home Ministry and the return of policing functions to local control) and purges of unwanted officials certainly disrupted the old bureaucratic structure. Still, in large part the personnel, practices, and institutions of the national bureaucracy remained largely consistent with their prewar counterparts. Since SCAP held the real policy making power, Japanese politicians exercised their power in large part as a mediating influence rather than as policy innovators. The GHQ crafted significant legislation, reshaped by the relevant ministry bureaucrats, and introduced to the Diet by the cabinet. This pattern of the cabinet rather than members of parliament introducing most legislation intensified in the years following the occupation and has only recently been reversed (Pekkanen and Krauss, 2010).

By the end of the occupation, SCAP's influence on Japan's democracy was mixed. On the one hand, it left a number of pro-democratic legacies, including the 1947 constitution, decentralization of the police, comprehensive educational reform, land reform, and secularization of the government. However, while SCAP had initially encouraged labor organization and other left-leaning political activities, rising Cold War ideological tensions and the Korean War caused SCAP to reverse course. SCAP shifted its policy focus from "democratization" to "development." It cracked down on labor unrest, purged the government of "troublemakers," and helped reinforce and strengthen Japan's centralized bureaucracy as well as its conservative political parties. Thus, by the end of the occupation, Japan had many of the necessary institutions for democratic governance, but also retained a number of political values and practices inconsistent with democracy.

Re-building democracy from the bottom: 1952–90

When SCAP officials left Japan in 1952, most Japanese were still suffering from serious privation. The government and people redoubled their efforts to promote Japan's economic recovery and growth, with impressive results. As Japan rose from the devastation of war to become one of the largest economies in the world, its economic rebound earned the illustrious title of an "economic miracle." Whether carefully planned or the result of lucky and prescient business and political decision making, Japan's industrial policy was wildly successful.[2] Its companies became globally competitive, its population richer, and its government and society more powerful.

The 1960s and 1970s were politically tumultuous for Japan. Although the Liberal Democratic Party (LDP) remained the dominant party in national politics, left and progressive parties made significant gains in local elections, benefiting from rising discontent. Urban workers felt they were working hard and earning more, but higher standards of living remained elusive. Peace activists objected to the government's support of the US war in Vietnam, and environmentalists protested the government's willingness to turn a blind eye to industrial polluters. Students shut down universities, protesters occupied airports and construction sites, and lawyers sued negligent corporations for pollution damages.

Protest calmed by the mid 1970s, and by the 1980s Japan had become so wealthy that books with titles such as *Japan as Number One* (by Ezra Vogel) had become popular. Japan's economic success created tensions with the US. Friction arose over various trade disputes, and high profile purchases of American landmarks such as Rockefeller Center lent symbolic weight to Japan's economic power. However, the era of high speed growth ground to a halt by the end of the decade when the housing bubble burst, bringing the rest of the economy with it. Although for the next two decades Japan was able to retain its number two status in terms of total economic size, its economic growth remained largely stagnant.

Japan's stagnant economy did not lead to stagnant politics, however. Japanese politics changed dramatically during the period of slow growth. Most strikingly, in 2009 the liberal Democratic Party of Japan (DPJ) ascended to replace the dominant conservative LDP. From the time of its formation in 1955 the LDP had remained largely unchallenged, ruling Japan for almost 60 years. The ever growing postwar economy granted it the resources to pay off any "losers" in its growth-first policies (such as rural farmers). The economic slowdown changed the rules of the game, and by 2009 electoral losses forced it into opposition status.

Japan's twenty-first century democratic renewal

Economic downturn and subsequent partisan realignment have ushered in a new era of reform in Japanese politics. Historically, Japan's democratization has been a very long process with several reversals en route. While it achieved all the institutional requirements of a democracy by the end of the occupation in 1952 (e.g., written constitution, free press, and free and fair elections), it has taken considerably longer for Japan's everyday practices to democratize (e.g., the methods for selecting community leaders, acceptance of anti-government political protests, gender equality in the workplace). While it has certainly been a "full" and "robust" democracy for many years, there is still considerable room for Japan (indeed, for any country) to become "more" democratic, and recent changes in its political landscape have further deepened Japanese democracy.

Institutions

Japan's core democratic institutions were established during the occupation period; these include both formal institutions and more informal practices. Several of the formal, as well as the informal, institutions have been reshaped recently, with profound effects for Japanese democracy. This section will focus on two institutions that have been particularly important in shaping Japan's postwar democracy: the electoral system and the central bureaucracy.

The constitution of 1947 established the legal framework for Japan's postwar democracy. Based on the British parliamentary system, the legislature (Diet) is bicameral, with a larger, more powerful lower house (House of Representatives) and a smaller, less powerful upper house (House of Councilors). Executive power is vested in the cabinet, and the prime minister is elected by members of the House of Representatives. The judiciary is independent and the constitution guarantees the Supreme Court the power of judicial review.

Japan's 1947 constitution shared commonalities with many other democracies, establishing the organs of government and respect for basic freedoms. Two aspects of Japan's constitution were (and are) quite unusual, however: the renunciation of war and the extent of guaranteed human rights. Article 9 states, "the Japanese people forever renounce war as a sovereign right of the nation and the threat or use of force as means of settling international disputes." This renunciation of war has profoundly affected Japan's dealings with the outside world. A second unusual aspect of its constitution is the broad scope of guaranteed freedoms, including academic freedom (Art. 23), freedom of movement (Art. 22), equal education according to ability (Art. 26), and the right to "minimum standards of wholesome and cultured living" (Art. 25). This combination of war renunciation and far-reaching respect for individual rights renders the Japanese constitution one of the most radical constitutions in the world.

Electoral system

Reflecting its cobbled-together origins, Japan's postwar electoral system was highly unusual. In elections a citizen casts a single, nontransferable vote in multimember medium-sized electoral districts. Individual voters cast ballots for multiple candidates at one time, and multiple candidates from the same party can win seats in the same district. For example, a district may have five seats available, and parties would run up to five candidates in the district with the hope they would win all the seats.

In practice, this often meant the largest party (LDP) would win most, but not all, the seats, with the smaller parties gaining a seat or two. To continue the example given above, the LDP might win three seats with two smaller parties each gaining one. Over time, this led to the development of one, dominant, catch-all party—the LDP—and numerous, smaller, niche parties (e.g., Socialist, Communist, nationalist, etc.). This configuration of parties and the nature of the electoral system encouraged significant electoral competition *within* parties (especially the LDP), but relatively low levels of competition *between* parties.[3]

The LDP has generally been characterized as a conservative, catch-all party. Its political base lay with big business, farmers, and rural communities. During the high-growth years, it was able to please all its core supporters while contributing to the rising incomes of most citizens. To big business it gave generous protection from foreign competition and facilitated the expansion of manufacturing through its industrial policy. To farmers it granted hefty agricultural subsidies (especially for rice). This arrangement worked fairly well through the bubble years of the 1980s, faltering only with the economic stagnation of the 1990s.[4] By then, urban Japanese began to question the LDP's governing strategy, which seemed to benefit large corporations and the small number of rural farmers at the expense of the majority of Japanese working in small and medium-sized companies in the cities. This line of questioning continues to the present day, redefining the political landscape. Further discredited by a series of financial scandals, the LDP incurred a serious electoral defeat in 1993 when it lost its outright majority in the Diet and was unable to form a ruling coalition.[5]

The following year, the election law was changed, fundamentally altering the institutional structure in which parties operated, thereby transforming the party system.

The new electoral system is a "mixed proportional representation system" where most (300 of 480) House of Representative members are elected by a winner-take-all rule from small electoral districts, while the remainder are elected by proportional representation. Thus, an individual voter casts two votes, one for a single candidate in his district and one for a party, which has a list of candidates for each (larger) district. The House of Councillors also has mixed elections wherein some seats (146) are filled by votes cast directly for candidates (in multimember districts) and some seats (96) are filled by party lists according to the proportion of voters supporting various parties.

The introduction of small districts and winner-take-all elections in the House of Representatives has dramatically changed the nature of electoral competition in Japan. Winner-take-all electoral systems encourage two-party competition rather than multiparty competition because voters cannot vote for multiple people in a single election.

In Japan's case, it took more than a decade after the enactment of these electoral reforms for a sizable opposition party to form and offer the LDP serious competition in elections. In 2007 the DPJ took control of the House of Councilors, and in 2009 the DPJ defeated the LDP in a landslide victory in the House of Representatives. Electoral reforms have had numerous, far ranging effects on Japanese democracy, such as increasing interparty electoral competition, accountability, and raising public interest and awareness in policy issues. Still, many of the effects of electoral reform are only now becoming visible with Japan's first real alternation in power since the end of World War II.[6]

The bureaucracy

The strong institutional power of the bureaucracy is perhaps the best known feature of Japan's political structure. Although Japan's bureaucracy is small compared to bureaucracies of other advanced democracies, it has far reaching influence in government and society. The bureaucracy has received credit for facilitating Japan's "economic miracle" even as it is often blamed for causing the more recent "economic stagnation."[7]

The Japanese bureaucracy first emerged as a powerful force during the political centralization efforts of the Meiji period. In line with classical Confucian political philosophy at the time, reformers viewed bureaucrats as the actors with the expertise necessary to guide the country wisely into an uncertain and dangerous future. Elites and the public thought politicians favored the parochial interests of their constituents while central government bureaucrats looked after the interests of the country as a whole.

Even after the destruction of World War II and the promulgation of the democratic constitution, a number of formal and informal institutions helped reinforce the power of the central bureaucracy in Japanese politics. Before, during, and after the war, employment in the Japanese civil service was a highly prestigious career. To enter government service one had to pass a highly competitive civil service examination and a new civil servant's first several years of employment included extensive on-the-job training.

During the war as well as the occupation, central bureaucrats crafted policy, which the cabinet then introduced to the bicameral Diet. The asymmetric allocation of resources has further reinforced this informal practice. For example, Diet members have very few staff to assist in researching policy—only 180 staff for the Legislative Bureau, resulting in four to five Diet members sharing a single staffer. In contrast, the Congressional Research Service (the equivalent institution in the US), has 700 staff, providing each member of Congress with an average of 1.3 staff).[8] This lack of resources has made it virtually impossible for Diet members to develop policy themselves.

Informal institutions reinforce these formal asymmetries in power. For example, before the system was decried by the DPJ in 2009, it had long been common practice for retiring bureaucrats to become politicians (usually LDP) or to join the private sector through the practice of *amakudari* (descent from heaven). This practice facilitated a reliance on informal channels of communication, or "administrative guidance," whereby bureaucrats can communicate directly with local governments and key business leaders in the development and enactment of government policy, essentially bypassing politicians in the policy process.[9]

In many ways the strong role of the bureaucracy in policymaking can be viewed as an undemocratic element in the Japanese political system since bureaucrats are not subject to voter accountability in the form of regular elections in the way politicians are.[10] Certainly, when the military co-opted and directed the bureaucracy during the 1930s it operated in a highly undemocratic manner. However, Japan's bureaucratic structure today is not antidemocratic. Indeed, in many ways its close connections to the private sector and civil society (discussed in greater detail below) give citizens additional, direct, and effective channels into policy making that are much less available to citizens in democracies with a more constrained or isolated bureaucracy. Although not directly accountable to voters, formal and informal institutions are increasingly enabling citizens to hold public servants accountable (Haddad 2007b; 2010; Tsai 2007).

Additionally, a number of recent reforms have significantly enhanced the accountability of the bureaucracy and of the government as a whole. Three in particular have been highly influential. First, decentralization efforts have increased the autonomy of local governments. Second, the spread of freedom of information laws and practices have enhanced government transparency. Finally, the development of internet-based technologies have expanded citizen access to information and created greater opportunities for civic participation.

The first institutional reform to enhance the power of local authorities significantly was the Decentralization Promotion Act of 1995, later supplemented by additional legislation such as the Omnibus Decentralization Act of 1999 and the Decentralization Reform Promotion Act of 2006. These acts have aimed to reduce central government liabilities for local governments and increase local autonomy. These acts gave local government units greater responsibility for paying for municipal services while also granting them enhanced capacity to tax their residents.

As one would expect, these reforms have been a boon for cities with large populations and many businesses, and a potential death knell for sparsely populated rural communities, many of which decided to merge.[11] Scholars and policymakers may debate the economic and even political benefits of these reforms, but there have been some identifiable prodemocratic effects in terms of local autonomy (Mabuchi 1991; Takaharu (2007). When the central government can no longer coax compliance with extra yen, prefectural governors and city mayors have less incentive to cooperate with policies made in Tokyo that do not serve local interests. One of the most common ways local politicians are resisting central government policy is to refuse nationally planned but locally unpopular public works projects such as dams, landfills, and nuclear power plants.[12]

A second notable prodemocratic reform is the expansion of freedom of information laws and the attendant proliferation of citizen ombudsman groups and taxpayer lawsuits. What began as a disparate set of local initiatives culminated in 1999 with passage of the Law Concerning Access to Information Held by Administrative Organs (often abbreviated as the FOI Law).[13] This legislation, which went into force in 2001, has enabled citizens and a wide array of citizen groups to use their claims to the new right to information (or, to phrase it differently, their claims that government officials fulfill their duties to the public) to demand government officials provide an accounting of the monies they use.

This legislation was catalyzed when Miyagi governor, Shirō Asano, chose not to appeal a negative ruling of the district court in an information disclosure case in his prefecture. Additionally, he took the bold move of allowing public access to police records to make government more transparent, and declared that no government money could be used to entertain public officials. This policy has become standard across Japan. Other governors and mayors followed Asano's example, campaigning (and winning) on "clean government" platforms (Kerr 2002).

Finally, the spread of internet technology, and government's greater reliance on that technology, have also contributed to more transparent and accessible government. Internet usage has skyrocketed in the last decade, from just over 2,000 users in 1999 to more than 88 million by 2007. This latter figure represents nearly three quarters of the entire Japanese population older than six, with a 90 percent usage rate for people between ten and 50 years old.[14] These technological developments have enabled governments to post policies, disseminate information, and engage with citizens in policy-related chat-rooms, dramatically enhancing both the transparency of the Japanese government as well as ability of citizens and citizen groups to engage in advocacy (Ducke 2007; Takao 2007).

Elites

Historically, elites have played pivotal roles in the creation and evolution of Japanese democracy. Elites drove reform throughout crucial historic junctures: the Meiji constitution, the Taishō era's adoption of universal male suffrage, the creation of the postwar constitution, and the more recent demand for freedom of information laws. Elites initiated nearly every major democratic step in Japan's political history. It is not the case, however, that "regular" citizens are apathetic or uninvolved; Japanese are among the most civically active peoples in the world. However, elite actors have long dominated Japanese politics. Indeed, its democratization process has often been described as a "top-down" democracy, and its politics as "elite politics," in contrast to the people-power movements of other East Asian countries, or the mass uprisings of Eastern Europe or Latin America (Curtis 1988; Johnson 1995; Pempel 1982; Yamamoto 1999).

The elite nature of Japanese politics has not changed much over the past several centuries, but the composition and size of the elite class has changed dramatically. In particular, Japanese politics has become much more open to new and different actors than in the past. Rather than being the exclusive purview of men, politics is increasingly the domain of women too. Younger people, too, are becoming more active, challenging the accepted wisdom that politics is limited only to citizens in their fifties and sixties with extensive life experience. In the past, central government bureaucrats monopolized policymaking power; now politicians and NGO activists are increasingly involved. Elite actors still dominate Japanese politics, but they are fewer in number and much less homogeneous than they have been in the past. As the previous section explains, power has spread outward from a small group of central government bureaucrats to politicians and even nongovernmental actors, while also extending down to prefectural and local governments as well as to citizens. Thus, while central government bureaucrats are still very powerful, they are sharing power with more actors than ever before.

Political culture and civil society

For scholars of comparative politics, one of the most fascinating aspects of Japan is how this non-Western country has incorporated democratic values, institutions, and practices into its political culture. One of the places this merger has been most evident is in civil society. Japanese civil society has experienced a dramatic transformation in the last 20 years. On one hand, civil society has retained and even enhanced traditional cultural values and practices, many of which are rooted in Confucian political philosophy and predate democratization. On the other hand, it has also embraced democratic values and expanded prodemocratic institutions and practices. Thus, Japan's contemporary political culture demonstrates that a country can retain core traditional values, even those values that may seem highly antithetical to democracy, and still fully democratize. A transition to democracy does not require a country to give up its culture and conform to some Western ideal, although in most cases it will require significant adjustment of traditional political culture to accommodate democracy.

Japanese citizens are civically involved in a wide array of organizations. They join and support advocacy organizations that lobby the government for certain policies, international nongovernmental organizations that engage in foreign development projects, local and national parent–teacher associations, alumni associations, religious organizations, and sports clubs, as well as less desirable groups such as street gangs, mafia (called *yakuza*), and religious cults (Haddad 2007b; Maclachlan 2002; Osborne 2003; Schwartz and Pharr 2003; Yamamoto 1999). There has been an extraordinary growth in civic organizations since the outpouring of an estimated 1.2 million volunteers to assist in the rescue and reconstruction effort in the Kansai region after a devastating earthquake in 1995 killed more than 6,000 people. Indeed, since the 1998 creation of a law that eased restrictions on the incorporation of nonprofit organizations (NPOs), nearly 40,000 NPOs have been incorporated.[15] The evolution of neighborhood associations, the largest and oldest civic organization in Japan, illustrates the dramatic transformation of Japan's civil society and the challenges of adjusting traditional values and practices to accommodate new democratic values and practices.

Japan's neighborhood associations are by far the largest civic organization in the country. An estimated 90 percent of all Japanese are at least nominal members of their local neighborhood association.[16] These groups function primarily as mutual aid organizations for neighborhoods, and they work closely with local governments to solve local problems (e.g., public safety, sanitation, care for elderly and youth). They meet regularly with local government officials to consult on policy, and also act as umbrella organizations for more informal community groups such as hiking or *ikebana* (flower arranging) clubs. They are primarily funded through the individual contributions of members.

Neighborhood associations trace their roots to the Tokugawa era (1603–1868). The military regime of the World War II era fully incorporated these associations into the imperial regime, where they helped the government with military recruitment, frugality and health campaigns, tax collection, and other services related to the war effort. While their military purpose ended with the war, and they were officially banned during the Allied occupation, these associations continued to serve important mutual aid purposes as citizens struggled with the poverty and privation of the postwar years. Their political culture remained largely consistent with their wartime predecessor organization. Membership was socially, although no longer legally, mandatory. A male member represented each household, leadership passed from father to son, and younger members deferred to older members. Meetings convened in the leader's house or in a building owned by the leader.[17]

How did such an undemocratic organization democratize? Slowly. In tandem with the rest of Japanese political culture, these groups have gradually incorporated democratic values, institutions, and practices into their organizations. Gradually, Japanese educated in a democratic educational system started to fill the ranks of the organization and, eventually, its leadership positions. Democratic values gained currency in the broader culture, and demographic and social changes forced these organizations to adapt to the changing world around them or they would lose members and die. In the words of one city-level neighborhood association chief, "In the post war period [the neighborhood association chief] was really a revered position—kind of like a boss. But now, it is much more like a servant of the people."[18]

These neighborhood associations have reconfigured power relations within their group to become more democratic and have also realigned their relationship to local government. According to one neighborhood association chief, there has been a complete reversal of power. "It used to be that the city would ask us to do things, to cooperate with them on projects, and now we decide things to do ourselves. . . . We decide what our problems are and then try to solve them, asking help from the city when necessary."[19]

These groups have retained, and in some ways even enhanced, traditional cultural values and practices. They are still the primary organizers of community rituals such as New Year's Day celebrations and summer festivals. They continue to be responsible for maintaining many public spaces such as town greens, river banks, and community roads and sidewalks. Their members and leaders serve as vital examples of "good citizens" who look after their families and neighbors and help socialize new community members and young adults to the benefits and obligations of community membership (Garon 1997; Takao 2007; Haddad 2007a). Experience in these civic groups provides future political leaders with important civic skills and knowledge of managing organizations, persuading and negotiating with others to find solutions to common problems, and working with (and sometimes against) government.

A retired city council chairman interviewed in 2006 offers a very typical example. When asked whether he had belonged to any civic organizations in the city, his expression indicated, "Which ones haven't I been part of." He then held up both hands to count off the organizations on his fingers: Young Men's Association, 20-plus years; PTA, 16 years; volunteer fire department, 20-plus years; neighborhood association, as division leader or chief for 16 years. When asked which was the most useful in preparing him to serve in politics, after thinking a while he responded: "The neighborhood association leader sees all of the problems in the community. He has to bring them to the legislators. You get to understand the city and other problems in a broader way." Japan's neighborhood associations, transformed from an institutionalized component of a fascist state to (arguably) the most important civic organization in the country, offer millions of Japanese everyday experience with democratic politics, even as they reinforce and inculcate traditional values of community responsibility.[20]

National unity

Comparatively speaking, Japan is a highly homogeneous country; less than 2 percent of the people living in Japan are of foreign descent.[21] Indeed, there remains considerable pride and interest in what is believed to be a unique Japanese ethnicity and culture. Most Japanese universities continue to have units, or even entire departments, that study "Japaneseness" (*nihonjinron*). The Meiji government originally promoted this preoccupation with ethnic identity and unique culture as a means to help unify a fragmented country. The fascist wartime regime exploited this nationalism to justify imperial expansion and domination of Asian neighbors. Echoes of these themes can still be heard today in contemporary right-wing groups and nationalist organizations.

More recently, however, identity movements have arisen among minority groups, such as Japanese of Korean descent, the native Ainu and Okinawan peoples, and the Burakumin. The emergence of these identity groups reflects the realities of labor shortages as well as the success of inculcating democratic values of equality and diversity throughout the population. As multiethnic Japanese such as Crystal Kay and Tsuchiya Anna become national (and international) pop stars, with the election of an "ex-foreigner" to the Japanese Diet,[22] and active discussions about granting local voting rights for permanent residents, Japan is increasingly emerging as a multiethnic, multiracial, multicultural country (Weiner 1997; Chung 2010; Lie 2001; Shipper 2008).

Economic development

Japan boasts the third largest economy in the world, and its people are among the richest on the planet. Japanese economic growth has had a complex relationship with democratization. As discussed in the beginning of this chapter, Japan's first period of high-speed growth, during the Meiji period, led to the rise of liberal democratic values during the Taishō era. Rapid urbanization accompanied rapid industrialization, and the spread of labor unions accompanied the spread of companies. During the early part of the twentieth century, the Japanese watched authoritarian regimes fall across Eurasia, and many leaders advocated similar reforms in Japan. However, during this era of economic growth corporate interest in developing new markets and accessing new sources of raw materials became transformed into imperial campaigns to conquer foreign territories. Powerful business conglomerates (*zaibatsu*) consolidated their wealth and began to exercise undue influence over politicians, parties, and politics. They began to use the power of the state to throw labor activists in jail, intimidate political opponents, and quash voices of dissent. While economic growth was partly responsible for the rise of liberal democratic values and the spread of democratic institutions, it was also partly the cause of the backlash against those same democratic trends and of the rise of militarism that followed.

The rapid economic growth of the postwar period had, on balance, much more positive outcomes for democratic development, but it also contained some drawbacks. On the positive side, rising incomes moved nearly all Japanese into the middle class, promoting democratic values of equality, and providing sufficient education and leisure to engage in politics. With the diversification of society and the increasing demands of citizens to enhance government services, the government expanded its reliance on civic organizations to identify and express citizen needs and provide social welfare goods. All these trends empowered civil society.

The extraordinary revenues gained from the booming economy also empowered the state. Leaders in the early postwar period worked hard to forge a national consensus prioritizing economic growth. Their producer-oriented, growth-first policies enabled politicians to satisfy businesses, and hefty subsidies to farmers brought rural communities on board as well. Despite the struggles to keep up with citizen demands, the economic boom years provided the government sufficient revenues to expand public works projects and extend the social welfare net. These trends expanded the reach of the state and continued an imbalance in state power vis-à-vis civil society.

When the economic bubble collapsed at the end of the 1980s and remained stagnant for nearly two decades, the government found itself without the resources to buy civil society cooperation. Rather than complying with central government requests to assist in the implementation of their programs, civil society organizations, empowered and emboldened by their new generation of democratically educated leaders, began to demand greater governmental accountability and a greater influence over policy making. Unable to buy compliance, the government was forced to negotiate, and is increasingly allowing nongovernmental voices into the policymaking process (Haddad, 2010b).[23]

Thus, economic growth has had complex, and sometimes paradoxical, effects on Japan's democratization. Economic growth has spurred the development of a large middle class and empowered a strong civil society, but it has also led to the empowerment of business and government, which have sometimes colluded to obstruct democratic development. Ironically, it has been in a context of stagnant economic growth that Japanese civil society has seen its greatest expansion and, not coincidentally, a dramatic proliferation of prodemocratic reforms.

Education

Although Japanese is a difficult language, requiring the memorization of more than 3,000 characters and versatility in three alphabets to achieve basic literacy, for more than a century Japan has enjoyed very high literacy rates. The Meiji period introduced universal elementary education, and now more than half of Japanese young people continue on for post-secondary education.[24] Most Japanese read a newspaper daily, and the world's top five newspapers (by circulation) are Japanese.[25]

Support for education is one of the areas in which traditional Confucian political values reinforce newer democratic ones. Confucianism places high value on the "investigation of things" and bestows very high levels of respect toward intellectuals. American philosopher and educational reformer John Dewey heavily influenced early Japanese democratic thinkers, particularly with his emphasis on education's ability to create good citizens and his philosophy of "learning by doing." Dewey visited Japan in 1919 and made several trips during the 1920s, meeting with and inspiring Taishō progressives during each visit (Nolte 1984).

The US occupation also prioritized sweeping educational reform. The occupation expanded compulsory education from six to nine years, but the true emphasis of reforms was less about the quantity of education and more about the quality and content. Postwar reforms focused on instilling educational practices with democratic values, such as equality, and teaching skills, such as compromise and consensus-building. Japanese education continues to emphasize student self-reliance. For example, Japanese schools generally do not employ janitors, and students are responsible for keeping their own schools clean. Collaborative learning also features prominently. The importance of education in the spread of democratic values and practices is inestimable. Indeed, many of the recent prodemocratic reforms have been initiated by that first cohort of Japanese who experienced their entire education in a democratic educational system.

International context

Foreign influence has shaped Japanese democracy at crucial historic junctures. Initially, Commodore Perry's arrival precipitated the dissolution of the Tokugawan shogunate and the start of the Meiji modernization effort, which included a number of democratic reforms. International influence returned more powerfully with the postwar occupation, which established most of the important institutional foundations for Japan's contemporary democracy, even as it reinforced patterns that supported conservative elite politics. Additionally, during the Cold War Japan's strategic position encouraged the US to keep its markets open to Japanese goods, enabling an export-oriented development policy that fueled Japan's high levels of postwar economic growth.

Many of the prodemocratic reforms that have been passed and/or are being actively debated today are adjustments to exactly those institutions established by occupation officials more than 60 years ago. In the words of one journalist, "In Japan, democracy isn't something Japanese made ourselves. So, we need to fix it so it is something we made ourselves."[26] International actors can help a country establish democratic institutions, but as Japan's experience demonstrates, in order for those institutions to endure and for democracy to take root, they need to be remade and renewed by the local people in ways that accommodate local culture, even as the local culture is modified and adapted to accommodate democracy.

Conclusions

Japan's democratization experience offers many insights into the nature of democracy and democratic transition. It highlights the important roles all of the theorized factors have on democratization. It also draws attention to the interplay of those factors. For example, economic growth can enrich and empower civil society organizations, and over time a democratic educational system can transform both political culture and the behavior of elites.

Perhaps the most important lesson to learn from Japan's democratization experience is that, while foreign actors can promote the establishment of democratic institutions, democracy cannot endure if it is not indigenized. In order for democracy to take root and become real to the citizens, it must be adapted to local political culture. Traditional institutions and political values must accommodate democratic ways of thinking and doing, even as they modify democratic ideas and practices to retain and reinforce some of the most important traditional values and institutions. This process of accommodation and transformation means that democracy itself will take many different forms across the globe.

In contemporary Japan, political power has shifted in ways that are more democratic. Political power has been redistributed away from the center, out to local governments, and even from governmental to non-governmental actors. Japanese politics remains elitist, but the number of elites has grown, their backgrounds and interests have diversified, and their accountability to ordinary citizens has increased. Consistent with traditional political values and practices, most civil society actors tend to work with the government, rather than against, and decisions are reached through consensus.

Additional resources

Novelist Haruki Murakami examines the legacy of postwar Japan in *The Wind-Up Bird Chronicle*. In a different vein, Ichiro Ozawa's *Blueprint for a New Japan* offers an insider's account on Japanese reform and contemporary politics. Several documentaries also provide important insights into the processes of constructing Japanese democracy. For example, "The Pacific Century," video series examines important eras of Japanese political development, and Chapter 5, in particular, does an excellent job covering the war and the occupation.[27] To examine contemporary democracy, *Campaign* by director Kazuhiro Soda offers a firsthand look at a contemporary political campaign from the perspective of a young, first-time candidate for local election.

Most major Japanese newspapers have English editions that are available online. The leading English-language Japanese newspaper is *Japan Times*: www.japantimes.co.jp/. The most popular English version of a Japanese paper is arguably the *Daily Yomiuri*: www.yomiuri.co.jp/dy/, and a very close competitor is the *Mainichi Daily News*: http://mdn.mainichi.jp/.

Notes

1 In 1925 there were some limited property qualifications that were lifted three years later.

2 Several scholars give different actors credit, but all agree it was a miracle in economic growth (Johnson 1982; Okimoto 1989; Ramseyer and McCall Rosenbluth 1993; Sakakibara 1993).

3 There is an extensive literature on Japan's electoral system. Some of the best works include Cox and Thies (1998), Cox (2000), Curtis (1988), and more recently Scheiner (2006), and Pekkanen and Krauss (2010).

4 This succeeded in keeping power at the national level. It did not work so well at the local level, however. By the mid 1970s many important local governments were governed by non-LDP mayors and governors, including the cities of Tokyo, Osaka, and Kyoto (Steiner, Krauss, and Flanagan 1980).

5 For more details about the LDP's decline, see Pempel (1998), Curtis (2000), and Pekkanen and Krauss (2010).

6 For more details on the effects of the electoral reform see Martin and Steel (2008).

7 See Johnson (1982) for the miracle perspective and Katz (1998) for the stagnation.

8 For the staff supporting the Japanese Diet see www.shugiin.go.jp/index.nsf/html/index_e_guide.htm (accessed January 15, 2010). For the Congressional Research Service see www.loc.gov/crsinfo/aboutcrs.html#staff (accessed January 15, 2010).

9 For more details on the workings of the administrative guidance system see Samuels (1983, 1987).

10 This was the accusation of the incoming DPJ, and many of their new policy initiatives in 2009 were designed to reduce the power of central bureaucrats.

11 Between 1995 and 2007, the number of city/town/village units shrank from 3,232 to 1,820. For more on the municipal consolidation, see Takaharu (2007) and Mabuchi (World Bank, 1991).

12 See Kerr (2002) for an account of some upstart governors, and Aldrich (2008) for accounts of battles over the siting of public works projects.

13 For a good overview of the origins of information disclosure laws, see Kingston (2004). A similar pattern has occurred with genetically modified food (GMO) regulations (Tiberghien 2006).

14 The 1999 figure is from Historical Statistics of Japan www.stat.go.jp/data/chouki/zuhyou/11-05.xls (accessed May 6, 2009), and the 2007 figure is from Statistical Handbook of Japan 2008, available www.stat.go.jp/english/data/handbook/c08cont.htm (accessed May 6, 2009).

15 NPO Hiroba www.npo-hiroba.or.jp/ (Japanese, accessed February 10, 2010).

16 Keizai Kikakusho 2004, chart 3–1-7: www5.cao.go.jp/seikatsu/whitepaper/h16/01_zu/zu301070.html (Japanese, accessed March 25, 2007).

17 For accounts of prewar, wartime, and early postwar neighborhood associations, see Garon (1997), Hastings (1995).

18 Author interview with block-level chief in large city, 2006.

19 Author interview with city-level neighborhood association chief from a medium-sized city, 2006.

20 For more details about contemporary neighborhood associations, see Bestor (1989), Haddad (2010a2010b).

21 www.moj.go.jp/ENGLISH/IB/ib-01.html (accessed February 10, 2010).

22 Marutei Tsurunen was born in Finland, was naturalized as a Japanese citizen in 1979, and elected to the Diet in 2002.

23 In addition, for an excellent account of how this process has worked in foreign policy, see Hirata (2002).

24 Historical Statistics of Japan, Chart 25–12 Enrollment Rate and Advancement Rate www.stat. go.jp/data/chouki/zuhyou/25–12.xls (accessed February 10, 2010).

25 The world's largest newspaper is *Yomiuri Shimbun* with a circulation of 14 million, followed by the *Asahi Shimbun* with 12 million; the top non-Japanese newspaper is Germany's *Bild*, with a circulation of 4 million. www.wan-press.org/article2825.html (accessed February 11, 2010).

26 Author interview, 2006.

27 Information on this series is available at: www.pacificcentury.org/page/page/4030356.htm (accessed September 7, 2010).

References

Aldrich, Daniel P. 2008. *Site Fights: Divisive Facilities and Civil Society in Japan and the West*. Ithaca, NY: Cornell University Press.

Bestor, Theodore, C. 1989. *Neighborhood Tokyo*. Stanford: Stanford University Press.

Bix, Herbert. 2000. *Hirohito and the Making of Modern Japan*. New York: HarperCollins.

Calder, Kent E. 1988. *Crisis and Compensation: Public Policy and Political Stability in Japan, 1949–1986*. Princeton: Princeton University Press.

Chung, Erin Aeran. 2010. *Immigration and Citizenship in Japan*. New York: Cambridge University Press.

Cox, Gary. 2000. "On the Effects of Legislative Rules." *Legislative Studies Quarterly* 25: 169–92.

Cox, Gary and Michael F. Thies. 1998. "The Cost of Intraparty Competition: The Single, Nontransferable Vote and Money Politics in Japan." *Comparative Political Studies* 31: 267–91.

Curtis, Gerald L. 2000. *The Logic of Japanese Politics: Leaders, Institutions, and the Limits of Change*. New York: Columbia University Press.

Curtis, Gerald L. 1988. *The Japanese Way of Politics*. New York: Columbia University Press.

Dower, John W. 1999. *Embracing Defeat: Japan in the Wake of World War II*. New York: W. W. Norton & Company.

Ducke, Isa. 2007. *Civil Society and the Internet in Japan*. New York: Routledge.

Garon, Sheldon. 1997. *Molding Japanese Minds: The State in Everyday Life*. Princeton,: Princeton University Press.

Haddad, Mary Alice. 2010a. "The State-in-Society Approach to the Study of Democratization with Examples from Japan." *Democratization* 17(5): 997–1023.

Haddad, Mary Alice. 2010b. "From Undemocratic to Democratic Civil Society: Japan's Volunteer Fire Departments." *Journal of Asian Studies* 69(1): 33–56.

Haddad, Mary Alice. 2007a. *Politics and Volunteering in Japan: A Global Perspective*. New York: Cambridge University Press.

Haddad, Mary Alice. 2007b. "Transformation of Japan's Civil Society Landscape." *Journal of East Asian Studies* 7(3): 413–37.

Hastings, Sally Ann. 1995. *Neighborhood and Nation in Tokyo, 1905–1937*. Pittsburgh: Pittsburgh University Press.

Hirata, Keiko. 2002. *Civil Society in Japan: The Growing Role of NGOs in Tokyo's Aid and Development Policy*. New York: Palgrave.

Johnson, Chalmers. 1995. *Japan: Who Governs? The Rise of the Developmental State*. New York: W. W. Norton & Company.

Johnson, Chalmers. 1982. *Miti and the Japanese Miracle: The Growth of Industrial Policy 1925–1975*. Palo Alto, CA: Stanford University Press.

Kato, Shuichi. 1974. *The Japan–China Phenomenon: Conflict or Compatibility?* Translated from the Japanese by David Chibbett. London: Paul Norbury Publications.

Katz, Richard. 1998. *Japan, the System That Soured: The Rise and Fall of the Japanese Economic Miracle*. Armonk, NY: M. E. Sharpe.

Kerr, Alex. 2002. "People Power." *Time Asia*. September 16, 2002, 19.

Kingston, Jeff. 2004. *Japan's Quiet Transformation: Social Change and Civil Society in the Twenty-First Century*. New York: RoutledgeCurzon.

Lie, John. 2001. *Multiethnic Japan*. Cambridge, MA: Harvard University Press.

Mabuchi, Masaru. 1991. "Municipal Amalgamation in Japan." World Bank Report. Washington, D.C.: World Bank Institute. http://siteresources.worldbank.org/WBI/Resources/wbi37175.pdf (accessed September 7, 2010).

Maclachlan, Patricia L. 2002. "Japanese Civil Society in the Age of Deregulation: The Case of Consumers." *Japanese Journal of Political Science* 3 (2): 217–42.

Martin, Sherry, and Gill Steel, eds. 2008. *Democratic Reform in Japan: Assessing the Impact*. Boulder: Lynne Rienner.

Nolte, Sharon. 1984. "Industrial Democracy for Japan: Tanaka Ōdō and John Dewey." *Journal of the History of Ideas* 45(2): 277–94.

Okimoto, Daniel I. 1989. *Between Miti and the Market: Japanese Industrial Policy for High Technology*. Stanford: Stanford University Press.

Osborne, Stephen, ed. 2003. *The Voluntary and Non-Profit Sector in Japan*, Nissan Institute/ Routledgecurzon Japanese Studies Series. New York: RoutledgeCurzon.

Pekkanen, Robert. 2006. *Japan's Dual Civil Society: Members without Advocates*. Stanford: Stanford University Press.

Pekkanen, Robert, and Ellis Krauss. 2010. *The Rise and Fall of Japan's LDP: Political Party Organizations and Historical Institutions*. Ithaca, NY: Cornell University Press.

Pempel, T. J. 1998. *Regime Shift: Comparative Dynamics of the Japanese Political Economy*. Ithaca, NY: Cornell University Press.

Pempel, T. J. 1982. *Policy & Politics Japan: Creative Conservatism*. Philadelphia: Temple University Press.

Pempel, T. J. 1974. "The Bureaucratization of Policymaking in Postwar Japan." *American Journal of Political Science* 18 (4): 647–64.

Ramseyer, J. Mark, and Frances McCall Rosenbluth. 1993. *Japan's Political Marketplace*. Cambridge, MA: Harvard University Press.

Sakakibara, Eisuke. 1993. *Beyond Capitalism: The Japanese Model of Market Economics*. New York: University Press of America.

Samuels, Richard. 1987. *The Business of the Japanese State: Energy Markets in Comparative and Historical Perspective*. Ithaca, NY: Cornell University Press.

Samuels, Richard. 1983. *The Politics of Regional Policy in Japan: Localities Incorporated?* Princeton: Princeton University Press.

Scheiner, Ethan. 2006. *Democracy without Competition in Japan: Opposition Failure in a One-Party Dominant State*. New York: Cambridge University Press.

Schwartz, Frank, and Susan Pharr, eds. 2003. *The State of Civil Society in Japan*. New York: Cambridge University Press.

Shipper, Apichai. 2008. *Fighting for Foreigners: Immigration and Its Impact on Japanese Democracy*. Ithaca, NY: Cornell University Press.

Steiner, Kurt, Ellis Krauss, and Scott Flanagan, eds. 1980. *Political Opposition and Local Politics in Japan*. Princeton: Princeton University Press.

Takaharu, Kohara. 2007. "The Great Heisei Consolidation: A Critical Review." *Social Science Japan* 37: 7–11.

Takao, Yasuo. 2007. *Reinventing Japan: From Merchant Nation to Civic Nation*. New York: Palgrave Macmillan.

Tiberghien, Yves. 2006. "The Battle for the Global Governance of Genetically Modified Organisms: The Roles of the European Union, Japan, Korea, and China in a Comparative Context." *Les Etudes du CERI* (124): 1–49.

Tsai, Lily. 2007. *Accountability without Democracy: How Solidary Groups Provide Public Goods in Rural China*. New York: Cambridge University Press.

Weiner, Michael. 1997. *Japan's Minorities: The Illusion of Homogeneity*. New York: Routledge.

Yamamoto, Tadashi, ed. 1999. *Deciding the Public Good: Governance and Civil Society in Japan*. New York: Japan Center for International Exchange.

9

India's Democracy:
Success against the Odds

Laura Dudley Jenkins and Harita Patel

Chapter Outline

How has democracy in India survived? The world's largest democracy confounds the expectations of many democratic theorists by persisting without several factors assumed to be conducive to, or even prerequisites for, democracy. Indian democracy has not been deterred by a low literacy rate, a huge population, a developing economy, a history of colonial exploitation, and sporadic tensions and violence between different religious and cultural groups. Despite a major setback in 1975–77, Indian democracy has thrived since independence from Great Britain in 1947.

India adopted the parliamentary system of its former colonizer, but with important variations from the British model, including the Supreme Court with the power of judicial review. In contrast to the limited right to vote introduced in the late colonial era, India's founders instituted universal suffrage. Elections, a massive undertaking, are held regularly and result in high participation rates and increasing competition. Far-reaching policies to accommodate religious and cultural communities, as well as to uplift disadvantaged citizens, contribute to the country's commitment to democratic unity in diversity. As countries like Iraq and Afghanistan struggle to accommodate religious and ethnic diversity and balance majority and minority interests to achieve democratic stability, India's long and innovative experience with democracy can provide potential models and revealing lessons.

Replacing colonialism with democracy

India had limited experience with democracy before independence. In 1919 and again in 1935, the British introduced some institutions with limited representation to respond to growing demands from Indian activists. For over half a century, the Indian National Congress "had resounded with countless cries for freedom, equality, and the entire lexicon of democratic rights, civil liberties, and social and economic justice" (Wolpert 2009, 190). Following a long line of leaders, Jawaharlal Nehru demanded both independence from Britain and democratic rights:

> We believe that it is the inalienable right of the Indian people, as of any other people, to have freedom and to enjoy the fruits of their toil and have the necessities of life . . . . We believe also that if any government deprives people of these rights and oppresses them the people have a further right to alter it or to abolish it. The British government in India has not only deprived the Indian people of their freedom but has based itself on the exploitation of the masses. . . . We believe, therefore, that India must sever the British connection and attain *Purna Swaraj* or complete independence. (quoted in Wolpert 2009, 191)

The Indian National Congress adopted Nehru's resolution on January 26, 1930, but independence remained an aspiration rather than a reality.[1] Another influential leader, Mohandas (also called Mahatma or "great soul") Gandhi, further advanced the anticolonial nationalist movement with his effective use of nonviolent resistance tactics. Although Gandhi drew on Indian thought and spirituality, both he and Nehru were lawyers educated in London, familiar with British philosophies and concepts of democracy, and eager to point out the hypocrisies of colonial rule.

The nationalist movement succeeded in toppling colonialism in 1947, and replaced it with a democracy. At the same time, colonial India divided into two parts—a Hindu majority India and Muslim majority Pakistan. This division, known as Partition, led to massive migration and violence in the new border area.[2] Many Hindus and Sikhs left their homes for India, while many Muslims left their homes to go to Pakistan (Menon and Bhasin 1998, 33–38). Despite this migration, Muslims still comprise 13.4 percent of the Indian population today—the third largest population of Muslims in the world (Pew Research Center 2009).[3] For this reason, Indian democracy prioritized religious and cultural diversity and freedoms.

After much research and debate, India's Constituent Assembly completed the democratic constitution in 1950, a comprehensive and detailed constitution still in effect today. Some sections of the constitution were drawn from late colonial era acts, while others were borrowed from foreign constitutions, including those of the United States and Ireland. Crucially, "[A]lthough the Assembly borrowed freely, it fashioned from this mass of precedent a document to suit India's needs. Although the constitution at some point defies nearly all the rules devised by constitutional lawyers for success, it has worked well" (Austin 1999, xix). Thus, the Indian constitution is a unique blend of selective attention to the international community and an abiding concern with maintaining national autonomy.

The Indian constitution is quite detailed, and includes a comprehensive set of freedoms and a commitment to equality. It forbids discrimination on the basis of religion, race, caste, sex, or place of birth (Constitution of India, article 15). The constitution promotes tolerance and accommodation of religious diversity, particularly through measures like distinct civil laws for different religious communities. It also promotes respect for cultural diversity through federal structures, language policies, and educational accommodations. "Directive principles" articulate additional goals, such as equal pay for equal work and environmental protection, although these are not enforceable through the courts and consequently are often not fulfilled in practice (Constitution of India, articles 36–51).

India also inherited some positive legacies from colonial rule, including a functional bureaucracy and a parliamentary system of government. Still, it has found it difficult to shrug off some of the negative bequests. For example, the colonial practice of dismissing or circumventing uncooperative local rulers lives on in President's Rule (Constitution of India, article 356), which enables the central government to dismiss a state government deemed unable to govern in accordance with the constitution. This power has been manipulated for political purposes (Hardgrave and Kochanek 2008, 80–81). However, the Supreme Court has tried to limit this power, most notably with the 1994 S. R. Bommai case, in which it subjected the use of article 356 to judicial review (Dasgupta 2001, 65). More recently, the Supreme Court warned against the arbitrary dismissal of state governors by the central govenrment (Mahapatra 2010).

The low point of Indian democracy was the Emergency (1975–77). During this period, Prime Minister Indira Gandhi and her Congress Party responded to growing discontent and political opposition with repressive measures. Indira Gandhi faced sharp criticism, including the opposition's charges of corruption and authoritarian tendencies and a high court ruling challenging her 1971 election. A Communist-led Naxalite revolt in West Bengal intensified political tensions. In response, Prime Minister Gandhi dramatically curtailed democratic rights, raising the "spectre of internal and external conspiracies against the state" to try to justify her actions (Jalal 1995, 76). She declared a state of emergency, censored the media, arrested thousands of political opponents, limited the role of the courts, and post-poned two elections (Hardgrave and Kochanek 2008, 283–87). These repres-sive measures backfired. When Gandhi held elections in 1977, she and her party were decisively beaten. This suggests that India's democratic institutions ultimately were able to check executive power, and that India's population had become committed to democratic ideals, a key factor in democratic consoli-dation. Indira Gandhi, however, was later reelected, underscoring the grip her political family and the Congress Party had on the Indian electorate.

The Emergency of 1975–77 was a major setback to Indian democracy, but it was a temporary setback. What explains the success of Indian democ-racy? We turn now to assess, in the Indian context, key explanatory variables from the literature on democracy, namely: state institutions, elites, political culture/civil society, social divisions/national unity, economic development, education, and the international context. India's exceptional experience with democracy shows not only that democracy has transformed India, but that India has transformed democracy.

State institutions

British colonization definitely left its mark on India. As Hardgrave and Kochanek (2008, a) note: "On gaining independence, India inherited a highly institutionalized imperial regime." India's robust and slow-moving bureaucracy, which is spread throughout the national and state levels, is one aspect of this colonial heritage. Indeed, the skeleton of India's current government is based upon structures like the Indian Civil Service. Although often credited for facilitating the postcolonial transition, stabilizing the political system, and even helping establish formal democracy, the Indian bureaucracy has faced criticism for some authoritarian tendencies (Bose and Jalal 1998, 204–5).

India's federal system is based on the post-independence reorganization of states along the lines of language, a departure from colonial boundaries. India's executive power lies between the president and the prime minister, which serve as head of state and head of government, respectively. The position of president is one of a figurehead representing the country, with a marginal level of power and influence. In contrast, the prime minister leads the bicameral Parliament, comprised of the Lok Sabha (lower house) and the Rajya Sabha (upper house).[4] The prime minister also advises the president by leading the Council of Ministers. The president is sometimes involved in major decision-making and, "[a]lthough in both theory and practice power has remained concentrated in the hands of the Prime Minister, the advent of hung parliaments and coalition politics since 1989 has enhanced the discretionary powers of the president" (Hardgrave and Kochanek 2008, 69). For example, when no party wins a majority in parliamentary elections, the president invites a party to try to form a coalition of parties to reach a majority. Divided executive power provides India with primarily symbolic leadership by a president, a position that has been held by a woman, a Muslim, and a Dalit (member of a low caste formerly known as "untouchable"), while leaving governmental affairs that are of grave importance to a prime minster. Notably, even this key position of executive power has been held by a woman, Indira Gandhi, and a member of the Sikh religious minority, Manmohan Singh.

A crucial institutional fixture in Indian democracy has been the Election Commission, which has played a pioneering role in ensuring free and fair elections. Through its supervision of parliamentary and state elections, the Election Commission has helped to monitor candidates' conduct during campaigns and to reign in poll-day violence. Its success has varied depending on who has been in charge over the years, but it remains one of India's most trusted political institutions (Rudolph and Rudolph 2001, 159). The Election Commission faces an increasing number of challenges, including the growing number of criminals running for office, out-of-control campaign finance, and corruption.

At the pinnacle of the Indian justice system is the Supreme Court, which presides over all state and lower courts. The Supreme Court holds "original and exclusive jurisdiction" over disputes between states, or between a state and the central government, and serves as an appellate court for cases involving a constitutional question. Indian citizens have the right to petition the Supreme Court directly on matters relating to their fundamental rights under the constitution (Epp 1998, 81). Unlike in the United States, the court's power of judicial review is stated in the constitution, but its scope is not as wide as its American counterpart. For example, the Supreme Court cannot challenge the declaration of an emergency, and such a declaration can limit its ability to protect civil liberties (Hardgrave and Kochanek 2008, 117). Still, the Supreme Court has used its review power in important cases. For example, it has declared constitutional amendments unconstitutional for violating the constitution's "basic structure" (Epp 1998, 82). The Indian Supreme Court's workload is mind boggling. According to its monthly statement for January 2010, it disposed of 8,204 cases during the month, but still had 54,108 pending at the end of the month.[5] This can create problems of delayed justice, a problem that extends to the lower courts as well.

Some Indian traditions of local government have also been important to its democratic success. Some of these local traditions predate colonial rule. Both colonial and postcolonial leaders have periodically tried to revive these practices. For example, Mohandas Gandhi promoted an idealized vision of a highly decentralized democracy made up of village republics. This ideal was, however, ultimately rejected in favor of a more centralized yet federal system (Hardgrave and Kochanek 2008, 131–32). Featuring prominently among these local traditions are the *Panchayats*, or local councils, which represent from one to eight villages (depending on population). *Panchayats* are headed by a leader known as a *sarpanch* or *pradhan*. In addition to these local councils, there are also intermediate and district level councils. The degree to which the *Panchayat* system persisted varied across time and space within India, but in 1992, the 73rd constitutional amendment gave new life to the *Panchayat* system and formalized some of its basic characteristics on a national level (Hardgrave and Kochanek 2008, 134). For example, *Panchayats* play a role in local development policies, and a certain percentage of seats on these councils are reserved for historically disadvantaged and underrepresented groups, including "Scheduled Castes" (or Dalits), "Scheduled Tribes" (certain culturally and often geographically distinct groups), and women.

Elites

Elites were critical in establishing Indian democracy and broadening political participation to the nonelites in society.[6] The Indian National Congress was a nationalist organization emerging under colonialism to fight for more power and, eventually, independence. Although many of its key leaders were from elite or middle class backgrounds, they worked to become a mass-based organization by including women and people from different cultural and class backgrounds. Gradually Congress elites enhanced their legitimacy through public appeals and elections for leadership positions within the organization even before they had gained that right at the national level. Although structural and institutional factors are important, it is impossible to ignore the role of key individuals in the historical development of democracy in India. Some of these individuals were elite by birth and others were propelled into leadership roles through extraordinary circumstances.

Mohandas Karamchand (Mahatma) Gandhi (1869–1948) was a key democratizing influence within and through the Indian National Congress. A lawyer from a middle caste, he was committed to the uplift of lower castes, unity across religious communities, and even women's participation in the movement against colonialism (at a time when such involvement was quite revolutionary). Gandhi is best known for his nonviolent resistance or *satyagraha* strategies, which he developed during his 21 years in South Africa as a means to resist discrimination and stand up for Indian rights as workers and members of the British Empire. When he returned to India, he put these nonviolent tactics to good use against the empire in his native land. For his first nationwide *satyagraha* in 1920, he called for boycotts of "British goods, British courts, British schools, British honors, British employment—in short to withdraw Indian support from the vast, monstrous Machine of Empire until it ground to a halt" (Wolpert 2009, 61). This tradition of nonviolence speeded a relatively peaceful end to colonization and remains a popular tactic of various social movements to this day.

Gandhi's other major contribution to India's democracy was his ability to juggle multiple and competing interests to achieve a unified front for both freedom and democracy. This feat was particularly notable, as the goals of freedom and democracy actually worried several groups in India, both elite and nonelite. Landlords worried about keeping their property. Princes who were allowed to rule princely states through colonial compromises feared losing their powers. Various minority communities, including Muslims and lower castes, were apprehensive about majority rule. Gandhi did his best to allay these fears through a combination of inspiration and tough negotiation (Gandhi 1995, xv–xvi). He articulated his dream for democratic inclusiveness by saying, "If I have my way, the first President of the Indian Republic will be a chaste and brave *Bhangi* [low caste] girl. If an English girl of 17 could become the British Queen and later even Empress of India, there is no reason why a *Bhangi* girl of robust love of her people and unimpeachable integrity of character should not become the first President" (Gandhi 1995, 263). As we have noted, India subsequently has had a female prime minister and a Dalit president. At the same time, Indian democracy has been dominated by certain powerful political families.

For many of its post-independence years, India has functioned as a sort of democratic dynasty, with power passing like a baton from one family member to another. The electorate has always chosen the successor, but family dynasties still matter. Jawaharlal Nehru, Indian National Congress President Motilal Nehru's son, became president of the Indian National Congress prior to becoming the first prime minister of India. From an elite, upper caste family, Nehru made the practice of democracy routine by successfully holding multiple elections until his death in 1964. Although rhetorically committed to socialism and keen on achieving development for all, Nehru's government had the support of landowning elites and engaged in only limited land reforms (Jalal 1995, 45).

After Jawaharlal Nehru's death, his daughter, Indira Gandhi, ruled as prime minister for many years, followed by her son Rajiv Gandhi. Rajiv Gandhi's wife, Sonia Gandhi, could have become prime minister after the 2004 elections, but chose instead to throw her support behind Manmohan Singh. Rajiv and Sonia Gandhi's son, Rahul Gandhi, is a member of Parliament, and their daughter, Priyanka, has been involved in the campaigns of her mother and brother. Although other parties have taken power periodically at the national level and quite often at state and local levels, the Congress Party's historical dominance has been aided by the power and appeal of this remarkable political family. On the one hand, this family provided continuity and a sense of stability in the early years of Indian democracy. On the other hand, elite familial succession is not an ideal democratic pattern. Indeed, many political parties in India lack internal democracy, or fail to follow their own democratic rules when making decisions (Rudolph and Rudolph 2001, 159). Although powerful political families abound in many fully consolidated democracies, such as the Clintons and Bushes in the United States, their dominance is not conducive to a truly competitive system.

The Indian National Congress transformed itself into India's predominant political party, the Congress Party. This organizational continuity aided the transition to democracy, although it led to a system dominated by a single party. In recent decades, political parties based on religion, region, or caste have achieved more electoral success and shifted the nature of political elites in India. Jaffrelot (2003) calls the rise of the so-called Backward Classes (an official term referring to lower and middle castes) in Indian politics a "silent revolution." Noting that political democracy in India did not initially herald social democracy—the notoriously stratified society remained inequitable—Jaffrelot argues that in recent decades lower caste groups have been able to both capture political power and use that power to reform social relations, even in North India, where lower castes had been slower to mobilize (Jaffrelot 2003). Political parties dominated by lower castes, such as the Bahujan Samaj Party, are on the rise, and the Congress Party and the Hindu nationalist Bharatiya Janata Party must increasingly include lower caste candidates or form alliances or coalitions with parties or leaders from lower and middle castes. In short, although India remains highly stratified and dominated by powerful political families, its democracy has benefited from the democratic zeal of key leaders, and the social backgrounds of political elites have shifted and diversified over time.

Political culture and civil society

Many democratic theorists have noted "that the reason why liberal democratic institutions have performed more creditably in India than in many other parts of the formerly colonial world is the strength of its civil social institutions which are relatively independent of the political domain of the state" (Chatterjee 2001, 174–75). Although India has a variety of associations ranging from neighborhood councils to sports clubs, the literature on Indian civil society has drawn attention to the role of associations based on identities such as religion or caste. Such associations do not mimic the types of voluntary associations idealized in Western political theory; yet influential scholars of Indian politics have noted that even religious or caste associations have, under certain conditions, played positive roles in Indian democracy.

In the 1960s, influential work on the "modernity of tradition" challenged prevailing notions in the social sciences that traditional societies would "progress" into Western style democracies, and that religious or caste identities would fade away or retreat into the private sphere (Rudolph and Rudolph 1967). Rudolph and Rudolph's study of "caste associations" showed that even traditional caste groupings, which modernization theorists expected to dissipate with modernity, could be repurposed to serve democratic goals. "In its transformed state, caste has helped India's peasant society to make a success of representative democracy and fostered the growth of political equality" (Rudolph and Rudolph 1967, 11). Caste-based associations and social movements, although not always forces for equality or progressive policies, help explain high political participation rates in India.

More recent work on civil society has focused on the importance of certain types of religious organizations in preventing violence between Hindus and Muslims. For example, Varshney (2002) finds peace is associated with cities that have intercommunal associations, in other words, associations that include both Hindus and Muslims (Varshney 2002, 46). Leftist parties and class-based civil society can also help explain low communal violence in states such as West Bengal and Kerala. For example, Heller (2000) highlights the particularly successful democratic deepening of the state of Kerala, in part due to attention to lower class interests. Attention to the needs of the lower classes has lead to higher literacy rates, per capita newspaper circulation, electoral participation, and vibrant civil society. As Heller notes, "Keralites of all walks of life, it would seem, have an irresistible urge to combine, associate and organize" (Heller 2000, 497). Such social mobilization has strengthened rather than destabilized democracy in Kerala, as "organized societal demands and democratic governance can be mutually reinforcing" (Heller 2000, 486). Lower class and leftist activism through civil society associations and formal political parties has contributed to ideological diversity, party competition, and democratic deepening.

Indian political culture firmly supports democracy as well. Indeed, Nobel Prize winning economist Amartya Sen points out that Indian voters, even those from the poorer classes, rejected Indira Gandhi's Emergency:

> Suppression of basic political and civil rights was firmly rejected, and the Indian electorate—one of the poorest in the world—showed itself to be no less keen on protesting against the denial of basic liberties and rights than it was in complaining about economic poverty. (Sen 1999, 151)

Social divisions and national unity

India is an unconventional case because it has an almost endless number of cross-cutting social and economic cleavages, yet India's constitution is supportive of diversity to the point that it protects and encourages it. India is "socially and culturally the most diverse [country] in the world" (Bhattacharyya 2005, 4). Social divisions in India include class, caste, religion, ethnicity, language and gender. In addition, there is an urban/rural divide, with 29 percent of the population living in urban areas (CIA 2010). Many of these distinctions are cross-cutting; for example, class cuts across religion, resulting in poor Hindus and poor Muslims. Thus a poor Hindu woman, rather than solely identifying with one social category, may share some interests and problems with Hindus, others with poor Indians of any religion or gender, and still others with women of any class or community, while also experiencing some problems unique to her particular social niche. In this way, the very complexity of social divisions can actually help foster a sense of national unity.

Government efforts to address social divisions and promote national unity manifest themselves in numerous ways, including state-based language accommodation, religious personal laws, and political reservation laws benefiting historically disenfranchised groups. India, despite the number of fault lines within its borders, achieved freedom via an extraordinary anticolonial nationalist movement, which laid the groundwork for an ongoing sense of national unity. Committed to Indian nationalism yet familiar with India's key breaking points, "[w]ith remarkable prescience, the framers of the Indian constitution have equipped the Indian state to respond to the demands for linguistic autonomy through the double mechanism of individual and group rights" (Mitra 2001, 58). India's three-language formula includes Hindi as the official language, English as the link language, plus a variety of official state languages. State languages are acceptable for communication with the national government, and multiple languages are routinely taught in schools. In addition, language groups were the key focus of the States' Reorganization Commission, which in 1956 resulted in a reorganization of the federal system along linguistic lines, thus quelling various secessionist demands. Through the three-language policy and the reorganization of the states, "India, that veritable Babel of tongues, managed to contain an issue which at one point seemed to threaten the unity, integrity and indestructibility of the union" (Jalal 1995, 168).

Indeed, later movements demanding their own states within India have moved away from the linguistic rationale. India's newest states—Jharkhand, Uttarakhand, and Chhattisgarh—formed in 2000, did not have a linguistic basis for statehood. In a study of these three states as well as three as yet unsuccessful statehood movements (Telangana, Gurkhaland, and Vidarbha), McHenry (2007, 2) found that "a consistent part of separatist movement identity is being economically disadvantaged," even if economic data does not always support such a claim. For example, the Telangana movement in Andhra Pradesh is demanding a separate state be carved out of parts of Andhra Pradesh, including its capital city, Hyderabad, a technology hub. The main arguments for this separate state are economic, including complaints of government neglect, poverty, unemployment, and lack of irrigation in the Telangana region (Agarwal 2010). Such statehood movements have complex and multiple precipitants and causes, but economic factors are becoming as important as linguistic and cultural social divisions.[7]

As Table 9.1 indicates, India is home to many religious communities. The diversity does not end there, as even the largest religious population, Hindus, is spread out and "regionally specific, plural in beliefs and practices, and divided by castes, and languages" (Bhattacharyya 2005, 4). Scholars are amazed that with such a diverse population in an area "the size of continental Europe, India has, arguably, survived as a developing democracy with relatively low levels of religious and ethnic conflicts" (Singh 2004). A notion of secularism as symmetry, rather than complete separation between religion and the state, shapes its democratic institutions related to religion. The "dominant approach" to secularism in India has been "a basic symmetry of treatment" of various religious communities rather than a "demand that the state must stay clear of any association with any religious matter whatsoever" (Sen 2005, 296).

Table 9.1 Indian Diversity

Major Religious Groups	Major Languages
Hindu 80.5%	Hindi 41%
Muslim 13.4%	Bengali 8.1%
Christian 2.3%	Telugu 7.2%
Sikh 1.9%	Marathi 7%
Other 1.8%	Tamil 5.9%
Unspecified 0.1%	Urdu 5%
	Gujarati 4.5%
	Kannada 3.7%
	Malayalam 3.2%
	Oriya 3.2%
	Punjabi 2.8%
	Assamese 1.3%
	Maithili 1.2%
	other 5.9%

Source: CIA World Fact Book

One attempt to treat religious communities symmetrically and protect religious freedom is India's system of multiple "personal laws." These are civil laws, specific to different religious communities, which govern certain family-related legal matters, such as marriage, divorce, adoption, and inheritance (Jenkins 2009, 920–27). The Indian Constitution calls for the creation of a uniform civil code, but only in the unenforceable "directive principles" section. Critics of personal laws point to the gender inequity in all the various personal law systems, despite some reforms (Parashar 2008, 103–12). Some leaders of religious minority communities are concerned by the prospect of a uniform civil code, for fear it would make it hard to be a fully practicing member of their community or it would be primarily written by Hindus. The meaning of secularism and the future of the civil code continue to spark debates over the future of Indian democracy (Needham and Rajan 2007).

India contains some religiously polarizing groups, such as the Hindutva movement, which seeks an India dominated by the Hindu religion. In India, the proliferation of numerous political parties, including several with an ethnic or regional base, has become a balancing mechanism. For example, the Hindu Nationalist Bharatiya Janata Party (BJP) has been able to take power at the center, but only in coalition with other parties. Its coalition partners have forced the BJP to shelve the more extreme planks of its party platform. Political parties in India, as with any democracy, are a powerful tool of representation and help shape policy to suit public needs. In India, ethnic parties serve as a platform for groups from different states and backgrounds to voice their views.

Many scholars argue "that ethnic diversity is inversely related to the maintenance of democracy," but Kanchan Chandra points out that ethnic parties have helped maintain balance in India; according to Chandra, "A multitude of freely forming ethnic majorities may be a more effective safeguard against the destabilization of democracy than the imposition of constraints on any single one" (Chandra 2005, 235–36). In other words, a system that recognizes and encourages the cross-cutting nature of Indian identities can help prevent their polarization, as Chandra has argued with the example of randomized electoral quotas for women, Scheduled Castes and Tribes, or even other groups state governments choose to recognize as underrepresented (Chandra 2008, 110). In addition, the complex claims of identity-based social movements can shatter polarized categories. For example social movements organized along class, religious, or gender lines have challenged affirmative action categories based largely on caste (Jenkins 2001, 45).

India has political reservations or quotas in the form of reserved legislative seats for Scheduled Castes, Scheduled Tribes and, at the local level, women. Scheduled Castes and Tribes, and, increasingly, another constitutional category known as the "Other Backward Classes" (OBCs) also benefit from reservations in public sector employment and higher education.[8] India's commitment to social justice and equality stems in large part from the key role of Dr. B. R. Ambedkar, who was born into a Dalit caste yet rose to be India's first law minister and the chair of the constitution drafting committee. The Indian constitution prohibits discrimination on the basis of caste and includes equality before the law as a fundamental right. Thus, India has one of the longest standing and most ambitious affirmative action programs in the world (Jenkins 2003).

Granted, it remains possible for smaller minorities to get lost in the plethora of divisions based on religion, caste, ethnicity, language, gender, and more. Progressive laws to further caste or gender equality are not fully enforced or implemented. Policies that reinforce a singular identity, such as religious personal laws that do not heed gender inequalities, have tended to exacerbate identity-based tensions. Yet, dynamic policies, such as randomized electoral quotas for women, Scheduled Castes, and Scheduled Tribes, reflect or even promote cross-cutting identities, benefiting Indian democracy. The Indian system has shown an extraordinary amount of resilience in the face of the social divisions that could threaten its democracy, and a variety of social movements based on caste, class, religion, and gender play a crucial democratic role by continuing to push for the implementation of India's civil and minority rights.

Economic development

Amartya Sen contends that Indian democracy, especially "open discussion, public scrutiny, electoral politics, and uncensored media" have prevented dramatic catastrophes in India, such as famines, but have not led to the end of "endemic poverty" and "persistent deprivation" (Sen 1999, 187). In this sense, Indian democracy has ameliorated but not solved some of India's economic development and resource distribution issues. The impact of the economy on democracy is less clear. India is becoming a major economic power, but in its early years as a democracy and developing economy, India challenged the notion that a certain level of national wealth is a democratic prerequisite. India has moved toward free market reforms and private enterprise, but, again, its early years as a largely state-run economy debunk assumptions that free markets are necessary for a free and democratic polity. Finally, India has a burgeoning middle class, which some consider key to democratic success, but this is a relatively recent development in its democratic history. We will assess the role of national wealth, private enterprise and the middle class in turn.

National wealth

The size of India's economy, not taking into account its large population, has made it an important actor in the international economy. India's total gross national income placed it twelfth out of 210 countries (World Bank 2009). When one accounts for the large size of India's population, however, a different picture emerges. Although India is getting wealthier, its gross national income (GNI) per capita of $1,070 is quite low, ranking 163 out of 210 countries (World Bank 2009). There is no denying that Indians are relatively poor, considerably poorer than citizens of many nondemocracies. Thus, the Indian case challenges a presumed link between national wealth and democratic governance.

Like many other aspects of India, its economy varies from place to place subnationally. India exhibits dramatic regional or state-level differences in the success of capitalist development, and this has influenced democracy. Partly the result of historical factors, this uneven development can also be attributed to decisions of state level economic policy makers, decisions of the central government about the placement of public sector undertakings, and decisions of big business leaders about where to locate and invest (Baru 2000, 214).

What are the implications for India's democracy of the disparities from state to state in economic development? These regional economic disparities have contributed to the rise of regional political parties that have increasingly challenged the hold of national level parties. As Baru notes:

[T]he failure of national political parties and the central government to address the needs of emergent regional business groups encouraged the latter to seek political and material support from state governments and regional political parties. It is not surprising that regional political parties have been most active in States where regional business groups have been more dynamic and assertive. The link between the emergence of regional capitalism and regional parties is too stark to be ignored. (Baru 2000, 226)

Regional political parties certainly increase political competition and the choices available to voters. Still, the increasing necessity to form complex coalitions including regional parties in order to rule at the center is problematic. It can precipitate deadlocks over policies, or exaggerate the power of a small party willing to threaten to pull out of a coalition.

Private enterprise

Indian democracy has functioned under both state-dominated and, later, increasingly privatized economies. Thus the economic freedom variable is not a key determinant of the existence of democracy in this case. Has the shift toward an increasingly liberal, privatized economy improved or strengthened democracy? We will consider the impact on democracy in India of growing inequality, the weak role of trade unions, and the increasing growth of the informal sector of the economy.

In the early years of India's democracy, the economy was characterized by planned industrialization, large public sector undertakings, and a relatively closed economy. With increasing privatization and liberalization in the 1980s and especially the 1990s, India has experienced increases in both economic growth and inequality. In this situation, Aseema Sinha notes that

> widening gaps between rich and poor may impose tensions and stresses on a democratic system in two distinct ways: The rich may seek to make their economic advantaged permanent by subverting democracy in order to seize political power for themselves, and the poor may seek the system's overthrow through violence. . . . [Neither has happened in India] because the rich now enjoy many options outside the state while the poor are too diffuse and divided to mount a full-scale anti-system challenge. (Sinha 2007, 197)

In other words, the rich do not undermine democracy because they have options in the private sector economy, or in other countries, if they become frustrated with the Indian state or its policies for the poor. The poor tend not to identify as a unified class. Thus people at both ends of the economic spectrum continue to work within the democratic system.

Labor unions in India have historically been affiliated with, and even dominated by, political parties (Bhattacharjee and Azcarate 2006, 64). With privatization, Indian industrial and postindustrial development has increased the role of both the old, large Indian business houses and new multinational corporations, and led to a growth in contract labor (Bhattacharjee and Azcarate 2006, 65). Many people in India have worked in the informal economy, but with the recent growth of contract labor, the unorganized labor sector has expanded even more. According to a recent estimate, 93 percent of the total workforce is unorganized labor (Bhattacharjee and Azcarate 2006, 65). Thus the democratic potential of labor unions as associations independent of the state has been limited during the state-controlled economic phase (by their dominance by affiliated political parties), as well as during the privatization phase (by the continuing dominance of political parties as well as the growth of the unorganized sector). Moreover, the growth of the informal sector of the labor force, or the increase of "jobs offered on a temporary, casual, contract, or other flexible basis," may have negative consequences for democracy (Sinha 2007, 203). For example, the decline of the textile industry in the state of Gujarat pushed many unemployed mill workers into informal, sometimes illegal occupations, and some into militantly Hindu political organizations, contributing to deadly riots along religious and caste lines (Sinha 2007, 204).

Tensions due to economic disparities also have been destabilizing. In several Indian states, Naxalite movements fueled by inequities draw on communist ideology and use guerilla tactics and violence rather than elections to try to gain economic or political power. Xenophobic attacks on low wage migrant laborers are a recurring problem in several parts of India, even in cosmopolitan cities such as Pune, a hub in the information technology industry. Such attacks threaten the harmony India has managed to maintain. Increasing economic freedom for some, in the form of policies to increase privatization and liberalization, is accompanied by increasing economic inequalities and uncertainties for many, which can be detrimental to democratic stability. India does not provide much evidence for a link between economic and political freedoms.

The economic variables of national wealth or economic freedom do not seem to explain the success of Indian democracy. Indeed, Atul Kohli has argued that "India's democracy is thus best understood by focusing, not mainly on its socioeconomic determinants, but on how power distribution in that society is negotiated and renegotiated" (Kohli 2001, 1). A third economic variable, the class structure and, in particular, the middle class, may shed light on this question of power distribution and democracy.

Middle class

Despite growing economic inequalities, three mechanisms quell potential backlashes from various classes and preserve democratic stability in India: "[L]eaving (or potential exit) by the elites; leaguing (or collective action) by the losers, and linking (to global patterns of prosperity) by the middle class" (Sinha 2007, 196). Notably the middle class has become more diverse, a "social churning" that helps explain the persistence of democracy despite continuing poverty and growing inequalities. Patnaik notes that India has experienced

> a broadening of the social composition of the bourgeoisie as well as keeping alive hopes of economic betterment among sections of the poor. The co-existence of substantial deprivation on the one hand, with political democracy on the other, has been possible because this deprivation has been accompanied by social flux and upward mobility. (Patnaik 2000, 242–43)

Thus, although inequalities are actually becoming more extreme, the perception of opportunities for social and economic mobility into the middle class helps stabilize the system.

Interestingly enough, a closer look at the Indian middle class debunks assumptions that middle class citizens are the key participants in democracy. Although typically members of the middle class vote in higher numbers than do the poor, in India Jaffrelot (2007) found quite the opposite. The urban middle class no longer votes in large numbers, perhaps because they have the social and material resources to influence people in power directly rather than via the voting both. "For Indian democracy, the real danger lies more in this changing mentality of the elite than in any revolutionary threat from below" (Jaffrelot 2007, 83). Elite complacency and low turnout may simply mean they have the social capital (education, personal connections) to get people in government to respond to their requests or complaints, whereas a poor person's request or complaint is ignored. More worrying, the continuing and growing role of money in politics suggests growing wealth in India could fuel corruption rather than democratic deepening.[9] If it continues, the middle class tendency to bypass democratic institutions means this class, considered so important in the literature on democracy, could do more harm than good.

One must also keep the size of the Indian middle class in perspective. The much vaunted information technology boom has drawn global attention to the new IT-related middle class in many Indian cities. Although the growing middle class is huge in absolute numbers due to India's population of one billion people, it is a small percentage of the overall population. One estimate, the "middle-high" income category used by India's National Council of Applied Economic Research, defines middle class as those earning over 90,000 rupees (about $2,000) per year, a group that constitutes less than a third of India's population (Fuller and Narasimhan 2007, 121). The majority of the population is poor and rural. They are often not able to access the kind of education that would allow them to move into information technology or other middle class jobs.

Education

Despite relatively low rates of literacy and education, democracy has persisted in India. According to the 2001 census, India's literacy rate was 75 percent for men and 54 percent for women. Illiteracy rates are higher in rural areas and among minority populations. India has made some strides in recent years toward enrolling more children in primary schools. Whereas in 2002 the World Bank estimated that 25 million (13 percent) primary school aged children were not in school, an Indian government survey suggested that the number of these children had been almost halved by 2005 (Wu et al. 2007, 120–21).

The people of India are very engaged in politics, and voting rates routinely exceed those in the United States and other countries that have higher education rates. Politicians reach illiterate voters with vivid campaign posters, auto rickshaws outfitted with loudspeakers, and live or recorded speeches. Public discussions of politics are common, helping form a "discerning Indian electorate" despite the educational limitations of many (Bose and Jalal 1998, 204). Voters have the benefit of ballots that feature both names and party symbols, another way to accommodate illiterate voters. Despite the various ways India's campaign seasons and elections allow uneducated voters to participate, the educational divide remains a problem for Indian democracy. Poor, less educated voters may be more easily manipulated or pressured to vote in line with the preferences of local elites, on whom they may depend for their livelihoods. Even if uneducated voters are politically savvy, their lack of quality education can limit their life opportunities and political choices due to patron–client ties, or "clientelism." Landless or nearly landless laborers' dependence on powerful local patrons impedes the freedom to choose one's preferred candidate, as vividly described in Aravind Adiga's satiric but informative novel, *The White Tiger* (Adiga 2008).

India's elite institutions of higher education, such as the Indian Institutes of Technology, are among the best in the world. On the other end of the spectrum are many rural, government primary schools, often lacking resources or adequate instruction. In the words of political scientist Yogendra Yadav,

"You simply do not go to a government school in a village if you can afford not to."[10] Despite the abysmal educational prospects of a significant number of citizens, democratic pressure has not led in practice to universal, mandatory, and free primary education. Constitutional directives and legislation to achieve this goal, including a constitutional amendment making education a fundamental right (passed by Parliament in 2009), continue to fall short. Political scientist Myron Weiner wondered why in India's democracy such low priority was given to solving the problem of millions of uneducated working children. He concluded that social stratification made many middle class Indians unconcerned about educating the children of the poor. Many distinguished between "the child who must be taught to 'work' and the child who must be taught to 'learn'" (Weiner 1991, 188). Illiteracy has not prevented democracy in India but, unfortunately, democracy has not, so far, prevented endemic illiteracy.

International context

Historically, South Asia has experienced a number of foreign invasions, but within the modern context Britain controlled much of India's political development. Following independence, however, domestic factors drove Indian democratic development, not international ones. During the Cold War, India's first prime minister, Jawaharlal Nehru, took a bold step to pursue an international policy of nonalignment, choosing not to formally side with the United States or with the Soviet Union, and becoming an influential leader among a group of other nonaligned nations, including many former colonies. Due to its democratic government and strategic location, the Indian government decision not to take sides allowed it to receive aid from both sides. "While New Delhi's declared policy of nonalignment, supporting neither East nor West, was a potential issue for the US, Washington chose to provide development aid to India despite the latter's reluctance to join any formal alliance" (Muirhead 2005, 1).

India also sought assistance from the international community, including the World Bank and Western governments, for economic development. India was a "prime battleground in the Cold War: as the world's largest democracy, it was a focus of Western support, especially given the alternative example" established in 1949 in communist China (Muirhead 2005, 1). The impact of aid on democracy is less certain, but it did help deal with economic crises that could have destabilized the young democracy, such as the financial crisis of 1958 (Muirhead 2005, 3). Notably, even substantial aid was not able to budge India from nonalignment or, for decades, from its preference for state economic planning and control.

Today, Indian democracy is in some ways influenced by its neighbors. In particular, the relationship between India and Pakistan has had an effect on political parties and elections within India as well as on India's human rights record. The ongoing territorial dispute between India and Pakistan over the northern region of Jammu and Kashmir has been a key issue on the platform of Hindu nationalist parties and has kept both countries on edge. Human rights organizations are critical of rights violations and impunity in the context of this conflict (Amnesty International 2009). Attacks perpetrated in India by groups from Pakistan, such as the attacks on India's Parliament building in 2001 and on the Taj Mahal Hotel and other locations in Mumbai in 2008, contribute to an antiterrorist mindset that could further harm democratic freedoms. People in India have reported their concerns that Indian Muslims may be "arrested on ill-founded suspicions of terrorism" and that counterterrorism measures could undermine human rights (Jahangir 2009, 9–10).

In sum, international influences on Indian democracy were key during the late colonial and postcolonial transitions, but have been kept at bay ever since. Despite some modest international influences, the development of Indian democracy has been a domestic affair. The memory of colonial interventions means sovereignty and autonomy are political priorities.

Conclusions

India's democracy succeeded ultimately because it is *India's* democracy. The state institutions embedded in its remarkable constitution were drawn from constitutions all over the world, redesigned for India, and then frequently amended. Key leaders prioritized the inclusion of all segments of India's vast population in democratic processes and institutions, and the political elites of today include a broad spectrum of society. Indian civil society emerged in some unique forms, such as caste associations, that made sense in this distinct context. Far-reaching measures to encompass and include all groups in the most culturally diverse democracy in the world offered new conceptualizations of key concepts such as secularism and even democracy itself. Efforts to empower historically disadvantaged groups—including lower castes, the poor, and women—have also expanded the stakeholders in the democratic polity. The enthusiastic and often discerning political participation of poor (even poorly educated) citizens and the growing political lethargy of the middle class form a distinct pattern of democratic practice.

India's tendency to remain as autonomous as possible in the international arena extends to its approach to democracy, adopting democratic practices that fit India's goals and context without being pressured into a democratic template that does not meet its needs.

The key to Indian democracy is that Indians made it their own. Yogendra Yadav argues against the idea that democracy is "hardware" to be installed

> The story of Indian democracy can be told differently. . . . It requires that we treat democracy like a language or software that cannot even begin to work without establishing a firm protocol of shared symbols with its users. . . . [T]o have a life, democracy must exist in and through the minds of ordinary people. (Yadav 2001, 37)

Emerging democracies may draw from, or be inspired by, the particular institutions India has developed, but India's most important lesson for the rest of the world is to avoid democratic conformity in favor of democratic innovation and variation tailored to specific times and places.

Additional resources

Two novels provide fascinating insights into key events in Indian political development. Kiran Desai's *Inheritance of Loss* addresses colonialism and its many legacies, particularly some of its tragic consequences. Rohinton Mistry's *A Fine Balance* provides a glimpse of life during the Emergency. Mohandas Gandhi's autobiography, *Gandhi An Autobiography: The Story of My Experiments with Truth*, provides rich insight into one of the most pivotal figures in Indian history. In popular culture, the 1982 film *Gandhi* depicts the Indian independence movement. In a more serious vein, the documentary, *Dynasty: The Nehru-Gandhi Story*, examines the legacy of India's founding fathers, while a UN-Showtime production, *What's going on? Girls Education in India*, features the challenges of contemporary India through the stories of three girls.

Notes

1 India's constitution was enacted on this same day 20 years later, and is still celebrated annually as Republic Day.

2 After the Partition, states within India were also reorganized to better reflect the ethnic and linguistic makeup of India in 1956.

3 Indonesia and Pakistan have the first and second largest Muslim populations in the world.

4 The Lok Sabha, translated as the House of the People, has 543 members, elected directly through universal adult suffrage, and two nominated members. The constitution provides for representation to all 28 states as well as the seven Union Territories. The Rajya Sabha, or the Council of States, is comprised of no more than 250 members, with seats also allocated according to population.

5 http://www.supremecourtofindia.nic.in/new_s/pendingstat.htm (accessed March 11, 2010).

6 For example, while some women were allowed to vote in colonial era elections, after independence universal suffrage ensured all women could vote.

7 The Vidarabha movement to break from Maharashtra also is based largely on the region's failure to thrive within a relatively successful state. The long-standing demand for Gurkhaland is one of several demands for microstates in northeast India, and stems from economic factors as well as a distinct geographic and cultural identity (emphasized and exploited under colonialism).

8 The OBCs are lower, but not Dalit, castes and other disadvantaged groups within non-Hindu communities.

9 Corruption is a growing challenge for Indian democracy. For example, persons becoming rich from illegal mining have bought off public officials in order to continue their mining operations, sometimes stealing publicly owned minerals (Yardley 2010).

10 Author interview with Yogendra Yadav, political scientist at the Centre for the Study of Developing Societies, Delhi, January 12, 2008.

References

Adiga, Aravind. 2008. *The White Tiger: A Novel.* New York: Free Press (Simon and Schuster).

Agarwal, Vibhuti. 2010. "Telangana Statehood Drive Stays Strong." *Wall Street Journal* July 30, 2010. http://blogs.wsj.com/indiarealtime/2010/07/30/statehood-drive-stays-strong-in-telangana/ (accessed August 20, 2010).

Amnesty International. 2009. *Amnesty International Report 2009: State of the World's Human Rights.* London: Amnesty International, http://thereport.amnesty.org/en/regions/asia-pacific/india (accessed March 12, 2010).

Austin, Granville. 1999. *The Indian Constitution: Cornerstone of a Nation.* New Delhi: Oxford University Press.

Baru, Sanjaya. 2000. "Economic Policy and the Development of Capitalism in India: The Role of Regional Capitalists and Political Parties. In *Transforming India: Social and Political Dynamics of Democracy,* edited by Francine R. Frankel, Zoya Hasan, Rajeev Bhargava, and Balveer Arora, 207–30. New Delhi: Oxford University Press.

Bhattacharjee, Anannya, and Fred Azcarate. 2006. "India's New Unionism." *New Labor Forum* 15(3): 64–73.

Bhattacharyya, Harihar. 2005. "Federalism and Regionalism in India Institutional Strategies and Political Accommodation of Identity." Working Paper No. 27, *Heidelberg Papers in South Asian and Comparative Politics.* South Asia Institute, Department of Political Science, University of Heidelberg, http://archiv.ub.uni-heidelberg.de/volltextserver/volltexte/2005/5500/pdf/hpsacp 27.pdf (last accessed September 13, 2010).

Bose, Sugata, and Ayesha Jalal. 1998. *Modern South Asia: History, Culture, Political Economy.* London and New York: Routledge.

Central Intelligence Agency (CIA) World Factbook. India. https://www.cia.gov/library/publications/the-world-factbook/geos/in.html (accessed August 20, 2010).

Chandra, Kanchan. 2008. "Ethnic Invention: A New Principle for Institutional Design in Ethnically Divided Democracies." In *Designing Democratic Government: Making Institutions Work,* edited by Margaret Levi, James Johnson, Jack Knight, and Susan Stokes, 89–113. New York: Russell Sage Foundation.

Chandra, Kanchan. 2005. "Ethnic Parties and Democratic Stability." *Perspectives on Politics* 3: 245–52.

Chatterjee, Partha. 2001. "On Civil and Political Society in Postcolonial Democracies." In *Civil Society: History and Possibilities.*, edited by Sudipta Kaviraj, Sunil Khilnani, 165–78. Cambridge: Cambridge University Press.

Constitution of India. http://indiacode.nic.in/coiweb/welcome.html (accessed March 22, 2010).

Dasgupta, Jyotirindra. 2001. "India's Federal Design and Multicultural National Construction." In *The Success of India's Democracy,* edited by Atul Kohli, 49–77. Cambridge: Cambridge University Press.

Epp, Charles R. 1998. *The Rights Revolution.* Chicago: University of Chicago Press.

Fuller, C. J., and Haripriya Narasimhan. 2007. "Information Technology Professionals and the New-Rich Middle Class in Chennai (Madras)." *Modern Asian Studies* 41(1): 121–50.

Gandhi, Rajmohan. 1995. *The Good Boatman: A Portrait of Gandhi.* New Delhi: Viking.

Hardgrave, Robert L., and Stanley A. Kochanek. 2008. *India: Government and Politics in a Developing Nation.* 7th ed., Boston: Thomson Wadsworth Press.

Heller, Patrick. 2000. "Degrees of Democracy: Some Comparative Lessons from India." *World Politics* 53(4): 484–519.

Jaffrelot, Christophe. 2007. "Caste and the Rise of Marginalized Groups." In *The State of India's Democracy,* edited by Sumit Ganguly, Larry Diamond, and Marc F. Plattner, 67–85. Baltimore: Johns Hopkins University Press.

Jaffrelot, Christophe. 2003. *India's Silent Revolution: The Rise of the Lower Castes in North India.* New York: Columbia University Press.

Jahangir, Asma. 2009. *Report of the Special Rapporteur on Freedom of Religion or Belief, Addendum: Mission to India.* United Nations, A/HRC/10/8/Add.3, http://daccess-dds-ny.un.org/doc/UNDOC/GEN/G09/104/62/PDF/G0910462.pdf?OpenElement (accessed March 12, 2010).

Jalal, Ayesha. 1995. *Democracy and Authoritarianism in South Asia: A Comparative and Historical Perspective.* Cambridge: Cambridge University Press.

Jenkins, Laura Dudley. 2009. "Diversity and the Constitution in India: What Is Religious Freedom?" *Drake Law Review* 57(4): 913–47.

Jenkins, Laura Dudley. 2003. *Identity and Identification in India: Defining the Disadvantaged.* London and New York: Routledge.

Jenkins, Laura Dudley. 2001. Becoming Backward: Preferential Policies and Religious Minorities in India. *Commonwealth and Comparative Politics* 39(1): 32–50.

Kohli, Atul, ed. 2001. *The Success of India's Democracy.* New York: Cambridge University Press.

Mahapatra, Dhananjay. 2010. "SC raps UPA for sacking governors from NDA term." *The Times of India,* May 8. http://timesofindia.indiatimes.com/india/SC-raps-UPA-for-sacking-governors-from-NDA-term/articleshow/5904284.cms (accessed August 19, 2010).

McHenry, Dean E., Jr. 2007. "Is Economic Inequality a Foundation of Separatist Identity? An Examination of Successful and Unsuccessful Movements in India." Paper presented at the Annual Meeting of Asian Studies on the Pacific Coast (ASPAC), Honolulu, June 15–17.

Menon, Ritu, and Kamla Bhasin. 1998. *Borders and Boundaries: Women in India's Partition.* New Delhi: Kali for Women.

Mitra, Subrata K. 2001. "Language and Federalism: The Multi-Ethnic Challenge." *International Social Science Journal* 53(167): 51–60.

Muirhead, Bruce. 2005. Differing Perspectives: India, the World Bank and the 1963 Aid-India Negotiations." *India Review* 4: 1–22.

Needham, Anuradha Dingwaney, and Rajeswari Sundar Rajan, eds. 2007. *The Crisis of Secularism in India.* Durham and London: Duke University Press.

Parashar, Aarchana. 2008. "Gender Inequality and Religious Personal Laws in India." *Brown Journal of World Affairs* 14(2): 103–12.

Patnaik, Prabhat. 2000. "Economic Policy and Its Political Management in the Current Conjuncture. In *Transforming India: Social and Political Dynamics of Democracy,* edited by Francine R. Frankel, Zoya Hasan, Rajeev Bhargava, and Arorar Balveer, 231–53. New Delhi: Oxford University Press.

Pew Research Center. 2009. "Mapping the Global Muslim Population." In Pew Research Center [database online]. 2009 [cited 3/2/2010]. Available from http://pewresearch.org/pubs/1370/mapping-size-distribution-worlds-muslim-population (accessed March 2, 2010).

Rudolph, Lloyd, and Susanne Hoeber Rudolph. 2001. "Redoing the Constitutional Design: from an Interventionist to a Regulatory State. In *The Success of India's Democracy,* edited by Atul Kohli, 127–62. Cambridge: Cambridge University Press.

Rudolph, Lloyd, and Susanne Hoeber Rudolph. 1967. *The Modernity of Tradition: Political Development in India.* Chicago: University of Chicago Press.

Sen, Amartya. 2005. *The Argumentative Indian: Writings on Indian History, Culture and Identity.* New York: Picador (Farrar, Straus and Giroux).

Sen, Amartya. 1999. *Development as Freedom.* New York: Anchor Books.

Singh, Gurharpal. 2004. "State and Religious Diversity: Reflections on Post-1947 India." *Totalitarian Movements and Political Religions* 5(2): 205–25.

Sinha, Aseema. 2007. "Economic Growth and Political Accommodation." In *The State of India's Democracy,* edited by Sumit Ganguly, Larry Diamond, and Marc F. Plattner, 195–208. Baltimore: Johns Hopkins University Press.

Varshney, Ashutosh. 2002. *Ethnic Conflict & Civic Life*. New Haven: Yale University Press.

Weiner, Myron. 1991. *The Child and the State in India*. New Delhi: Oxford University Press.

World Bank. 2009. World Development Indicators Database: [database online]. http://siteresources. worldbank.org.proxy.libraries.uc.edu/DATASTATISTICS/Resources (accessed March 10, 2010).

Wolpert, Stanley. 2009. *Shameful Flight: The Last Years of the British Empire in India*. New York: Oxford University Press.

Wu, Kin Bing, Pete Goldschmidt, Christy Kim Boscardin, and Mehtabul Azam. 2007. "Girls in India: Poverty, Location and Social Disparities." In *Exclusion, Gender and Education: Case Studies from the Developing World,* edited by Maureen A. Lewis and Marlaine E. Lockheed, 119–143. Washington, D.C.: Center for Global Development.

Yadav, Yogendra. 2001. "India's Electoral Democracy, 1952–2000." Paper presented at international symposium, Election Commission of India, January 18, 2001, New Delhi, http://eci.nic.in/eci_ main/Eci_Publications/books/micell/ECI-GJC.pdf (accessed March 8, 2010).

Yardley, Jim. 2010. "Despite a Swirl of Scandals, Mining Bosses Thrive in India." *New York Times,* August 19, 2010. A1, A10.

Hypothesis testing exercise and discussion questions for Section 3

Using the guide below, assess how well the classical theories of democratization explain democratization in Germany, Japan, and India. Be sure to specify the causal mechanisms, or processes by which each independent variable determined the dependent variable. Also, differentiate between the independent variables that caused the emergence of democracy from those that caused its eventual consolidation.

Hypothesis testing exercise

Independent Variables	Evidence from Germany	Evidence from Japan	Evidence from India
Economic development • National wealth • Private enterprise • Middle class • Inequality			
Elites			
Political culture/civil society			
Education			
State institutions			
Social divisions/national unity			
International context			

Section 3: Discussion questions

1 What role do outside powers play in shaping political development in these three cases? Is the role of outside powers typically benign, or even helpful? What leads outside powers to promote democracy in some cases, yet oppose it in others?

2 What are the benefits of inheriting democratic institutions designed by foreign powers? What are the disadvantages? In these three cases, to what extent was democracy a domestic or international affair?

3 In each case, how did elites and average citizens interact with the outside powers?

Section 4
Third Wave of Democracy

With the return of democracy, this monument to Salvador Allende now graces the front of the Ministry of Justice building (Santiago de Chile, Chile).

Photo by Heiner Heine

10

Democracy Interrupted and Restored: The Case of Chile

Mary Fran T. Malone

The Chilean road to democracy is a fascinating one. While Chile enjoyed a long democratic tradition in the mid-1900s, in 1973 a coup destroyed this foundation and established a repressive authoritarian regime. The military dictatorship endured until 1990, when a national referendum led to the return of civilian rule. The 1973 reversal of Chilean democracy challenged conventional theories of democratization. Given its level of economic development and highly literate population, many modernization theorists had expected democracy to thrive in Chile. As O'Donnell (1973) famously pointed out, however, the very processes of economic development can stimulate demand for income redistribution and exacerbate socioeconomic divisions. When these divisions become sharply polarized, some view the military as the appropriate arbiter. As the case of Chile illustrates, the adoption of military governance bears a high cost, not just for democratic governance but for basic human rights.

While Chilean democratization challenges the role of economic development in promoting democracy, it reaffirms the importance of international context, elites, and civil society. However, the Chilean case demonstrates that the importance of each of these factors can fluctuate over time. For example, civil society helped challenge the legitimacy of military rule in the early 1980s, but ultimately took a back seat as elites orchestrated a pacted transition to democracy at the end of the decade.

Chile's early experiences with democracy

Following independence from Spain in 1818, the Chilean experience with democracy was a bit rocky.[1] The new republic strongly favored elites, but these elites disagreed on which constitutional structures would best govern the newly independent nation. Liberals and conservatives clashed, and these skirmishes sometimes escalated into violent uprisings against the government. From independence until the 1930s, Chile experienced periods of limited democracy interrupted by political violence and authoritarian rule. By 1932, however, constitutional order had been restored, proving quite stable until 1973. Indeed, during this time Chile was regarded as the democratic success story of Latin America, its stable democratic tradition standing in marked contrast to the military juntas and political instability that reigned in neighboring countries such as Argentina. Chileans were proud of their democracy and their ability to settle political disputes at the ballot box instead of the battlefield.

Chile was unique in many other respects. Chilean democracy was marked by pluralism, as parties and politicians existed to represent most parts of the political spectrum. This political spectrum was quite wide, ranging from the extreme left to the extreme right. Ideologically, the Chilean public tended to divide into thirds, identifying with the political right, left, and center respectively. The political system accommodated this ideological diversity. For example, as early as the 1930s Chile's large working class was able to voice its grievances through the Socialist Workers' Party (Oppenheim 2007). Overall, Chilean pluralism encouraged citizens to channel their grievances through political parties and processes, rather than resort to violence. Political freedoms were respected, legal norms upheld, and by and large Chile adhered closely to its democratic foundations.

Still, Chile shared some similarities with its Latin American neighbors. Chilean economic development was led by an export-oriented economy, heavily dependent on copper production. Foreign corporations, such as the American company, Anaconda, tended to dominate the copper industry. This economic model led to discontent among the working class, particularly due to the obvious inequalities that existed between the living standards of factory workers and owners. These urban patterns of inequality were replicated in rural areas, where large *latifundios* (plantations) dominated much of rural Chile and led to a great deal of social, economic, and political inequality between the wealthy *patrónes* and the peasants who worked the land. While this pattern of economic development was similar to many countries in Latin America, what distinguished Chile during this time was the strong organizational framework of the lower classes. The organizations of the workers in particular allowed them to pressure political parties to address the living and working conditions of the nation's poorest citizens.

By 1970, such pressure bore fruit. In the presidential election that year Salvador Allende Gossens, a self-proclaimed Marxist, emerged victorious with a razor thin plurality of the popular vote.[2] A former medical doctor, Allende entered politics after witnessing firsthand the effects of poverty on many Chileans, as he treated the sick in the slums encircling the capital city of Santiago. He enjoyed a long career in Chilean politics, and remained committed to democratic norms. Indeed, some critics to the left felt Allende was too cautious and had been on the political stage too long; they were reluctant to choose him as the presidential candidate for the leftist coalition (Winn 1986).

Despite these worries, Allende led his coalition to a slim victory, promising to address the plight of Chile's poorest citizens. An idealist, Allende advocated a "third way" of economic development for Chile. Termed the "Third Path to Socialism," Allende aimed to carve a middle road for economic development, one that would avoid the polarizing models of capitalism versus communism that abounded during the Cold War. Trying to sidestep Cold War alliances, Allende proclaimed Chile would incorporate some elements of socialism into the Chilean democratic tradition.

Allende headed a rather diverse coalition, called Popular Unity (UP). Ultimately, seven political parties formed the coalition, ranging from the extreme left to the center (Oppenheim 2007). Its members originally included workers, peasants, the urban poor, and intellectuals, as well as a few middle class sectors. While ideologically unified around Marxist ideals of economic equality, the coalition members differed radically on strategies for achieving these ideals. Allende and party elites favored carefully control-led economic reforms that relied exclusively on legal channels. The nation-alization of key property areas, price controls, wage increases, and expanded social programs would all be the product of legal, constitutional measures (Winn 1986). Allende's popular base had a very different timetable in mind, however. Particularly for the organized workers' groups, Allende's electoral victory signified the beginning of a new period of history—this was their moment. They did not want to wait for Allende's carefully orchestrated democratic revolution; they wanted to seize their historical moment and redress the inequalities they had endured for so long. As peasants and work-ers began to seize farms and factories, it was clear Allende's popular base of support was pushing him to become more radical in his reforms (Winn 1986).

Democratic breakdown

Allende's economic plan was successful from 1970–71, during which time Chile experienced not only economic growth but also greater income equality. This growth along with equity did not last, however. By late 1971, Allende's economic reforms had alarmed the middle and upper classes, who felt threatened by the rapid pace of reforms and consequently boycotted economic production. The US reacted by imposing an economic blockade, greatly diminishing foreign investment in the Chilean economy. The result-ing economic crisis created even more political instability. Strikes and demonstrations became common as Allende's supporters and opponents clashed in the streets. The Chilean electorate grew sharply polarized, and the political parties were locked in a stalemate. Political elites from all sides of the political spectrum refused to compromise, holding staunchly to their ideological convictions instead of pursuing pragmatic solutions to move out of the political impasse. While Chile had been famous for its long and stable democratic history, by 1973 democracy was in jeopardy.

In June of 1973, the military launched its first attempt to remove Allende forcibly. The coup was not successful, but it further polarized the Chilean electorate. The left became even more determined to support Allende, organizing a series of parades and demonstrations to show their fervent support for their *Comrade Presidente*.[3] The political right, joined by the center, doggedly pursued Allende's ouster. Alarmed at the tanks patrolling the streets of downtown Santiago, and the thousands of demonstrators marching in the streets in support of Allende, the political center felt the situation had spiraled out of control. While Allende himself upheld democratic norms, many worried he could not control his own supporters. This fear led Chileans in the political center to join the right in clamoring for the ouster of Allende and his Popular Unity coalition—forces they viewed as ruining the long political and democratic stability of which Chile had once been so proud.

On September 11, 1973, General Augusto Pinochet led a successful coup against Allende. The coup plotters offered a plane for Allende and his family to flee Chile, but Allende refused and mounted a futile attempt to defend the *Casa Moneda* (seat of government) with approximately forty bodyguards. Allende died in the ensuing battle, along with Chile's democratic tradition. The generals who had organized the coup later appeared on Chilean television, announcing the suspension of all political activity "until further notice." This further notice did not arrive for another 16 years. Immediately upon taking office, General Pinochet emerged as the leader of the group, and launched a campaign to crush the organized working class.

Military rule

Pinochet moved quickly against his opponents. Dubbing popular mobilization and leftist activities "cancers that must be removed," he set the stage for massive human rights violations on a scale unprecedented in Chile. These violations took many Chileans by surprise—their democratic tradition left them ill-prepared for the torture and arbitrary killings orchestrated under the guise of national reorganization. Social forces that supported Popular Unity were labeled "enemies of the state," and thousands were targeted for "disappearance" and torture.[4] Chile was no longer exceptional; it joined many of its South American neighbors in a coordinated campaign to kidnap, torture, and kill those suspected of leftist activity.

In its violent campaign against the left, the military dictatorship had a specific purpose—it aimed to depoliticize Chilean society and change the country's political culture. The junta thought Chile was too politicized, and discouraged political participation. The military dissolved Congress, disbanded political parties, suspended civil liberties, and barred even conservative elites from the political process. Within a year, Pinochet had eliminated most of his opposition and squelched leftist activities.

The reactionary junta was also alarmed at the activist role the state had assumed in the economy under Allende. Pinochet quickly dismantled and reversed Allende's economic plan. To assist Chile's economic restructuring, Pinochet relied upon the "Chicago Boys," a group of Chilean economists trained at the University of Chicago. According to Pinochet, Chile would prosper if technocrats, not politicians, ran the government. Pinochet's technocrats pursued a neoliberal economic agenda, which restricted the role of the state in the Chilean economy. [5] In direct contrast to Allende, under neoliberalism Pinochet promoted a laissez-fare approach to the economy, encouraging privatization and a free market system (Edwards and Edwards 1987). He reversed agrarian reform as well, and returned nationalized property to the previous owners. In this capitalist, laissez-fare economy, Pinochet strongly encouraged citizen consumption. Rather than march in the streets for political beliefs, Pinochet wanted to see his citizens marching to the malls.

Pinochet's economic plan worked well initially, and Chile experienced an economic boom, especially as factory owners renewed production. As Table 10.1 indicates, in the first year of Pinochet's rule the economy recovered somewhat and grew a modest 2.5 percent. By the late 1970s, however, economic growth was quite impressive, reaching over 8 percent. Inflation remained a problem, but reduced substantially by 1978. Pinochet also reversed the downward trend of per capita income, and by 1978 Chileans saw increases in their income levels on average. This strong record of growth did not render Chile immune to the 1982 debt crisis, however, and its reliance on foreign investment made it particularly vulnerable. Economic growth recovered by the mid 1980s, but the debt crisis, for the first time, opened the door to dissent under military rule.

Table 10.1 Economic indicators 1970–90

	1970	1972	1974	1976	1978	1980	1982	1984	1986	1988	1990
GDP per capita6	2209	2304	2172	1929	2186	2494	2272	2288	2506	2773	3072
GDP Growth (%)	2.1	-.8	2.5	3.4	7.5	8.1	-10.3	8.0	5.6	7.3	3.7
Inflation (%)	32.5	74.8	504.7	211.8	40.1	35.1	9.9	19.9	20.6	14.7	26.0

Source: World Bank's World Development Indicators

Even prior to the debt crisis, not all benefited from the economic boom. While the working class and the poor had been the focal point for Popular Unity, under Pinochet they were quickly marginalized. Sweeping reforms eroded labor rights, paving the way for economic growth at the expense of equality (Winn 2004b). In some cases the marginalization of the poor was quite literal, as some residents of the slums surrounding Santiago found themselves forcibly relocated to environmentally less desirable parts of the city. Such relocations made way for wealthier residents to build fine homes in the outskirts, which were not as susceptible to problems of pollution.

Ironically, even though Pinochet had bombed the presidential residence, tortured dissenters, killed opponents, disbanded Congress, and suspended political rights and civil liberties, he did not like to be thought of as a dictator.[7] He viewed himself as the savior of Chile, and his official title was "Supreme Chief of the Nation." He argued that military intervention into Chilean democracy was necessary to save the country from the chaos imposed by Allende and the political left. Pinochet's quest for legitimacy ultimately opened the door to the restoration of democracy, as he held a series of referenda that reintroduced elections into Chilean politics.

Referenda and the constitution of 1980

Pinochet held his first plebiscite in 1978, asking Chileans to either support or oppose his rule. According to the military, 75 percent of Chileans voted in favor of Pinochet's government (Drake 1991). A second referendum in 1980 centered on a new constitution Pinochet had written, which specified a drawn-out transition to civilian government. The Constitution of 1980 is particularly important since this imperfect document eventually served as the basis for democratic restoration. This new constitution contained both permanent and transitory articles. The permanent articles were designed to serve as foundations for a return to civilian government, including provisions that institutionalized military oversight of the civilian government, banned leftist activity, and greatly empowered the executive branch at the expense of the legislature (Oppenheim 2007). The transitory articles, or emergency articles, were viewed as temporary affairs while the nation was still governed by the military. These articles barred legislative elections and party activity for eight years. According to Pinochet's timeline, the transitory articles would remain in effect until a 1988 referendum. If Chileans supported Pinochet in this referendum, he would remain in power until 1997. If Chileans voted against him, new presidential elections would be held in 1989, and a new government would take office in 1990. When the military tabulated the votes of the 1980 referendum, it reported that 67 percent of the public supported the new constitution. Pinochet would rule Chile for another eight years; little did he imagine that the 1988 plebiscite would take place amidst a climate of tremendous domestic and international change.

The fall of Pinochet

Pinochet and his Chicago Boys faced problems with their economic plan in 1982, when an economic crisis racked the country.[8] GDP growth registered at −10.32 percent, and unemployment crept to nearly 20 percent. Ironically, some failing privatized factories faced closure and fell back into state ownership (Winn 1986). These economic problems emboldened dissenters, culminating in the Day of National Protest in 1983. Marking one of the first public displays of protest against the Pinochet dictatorship, this demonstration spawned several other Days of Protest over the next few years. Not surprisingly, Pinochet relied upon repressive tactics to respond to the protests. Consequently, opposition groups began to abandon highly visible marches and demonstrations in favor of collaboration with like-minded political parties and civil society groups. Pinochet's opposition began to coalesce around a victory strategy for the 1988 plebiscite established in the previous referendum.

By 1988, Pinochet faced numerous domestic and international challenges. At 73, he was viewed by many military leaders as too old to hold office for another eight years, and they preferred a pliable civilian candidate. Also, by 1988 the world was about to embark on tremendous change. The end of the Cold War was nearing, and Pinochet's stalwart anti-communist stance was not nearly as valuable to countries like the US as it had been in 1973. Indeed, the US began to distance itself from Pinochet and his human rights abuses, and began to fund his opposition by channeling money through the National Endowment for Democracy.

The prospect of a competitive referendum on Pinochet's rule fueled the opposition, but 15 years of repression had taken their toll. Labor organizations in particular were divided and weakened (Angell 1991). The Socialists stumbled to recover from a major split in 1979, while the Communists became much more radical (Winn 2004a). Consequently, leftist parties experienced both internal divisions as well as greater distance from one another. The center parties, particularly the Christian Democrats (PDC), enjoyed a slightly stronger position and assumed a leadership role during the protests from 1983–88. Even though the opposition parties experienced both internal and external divisions, elites did remember the lessons from their earlier failed attempts to compromise, which led to the fall of democracy in 1973. Also, the nature of the referendum—either a yes or no vote on Pinochet's rule—made it easier for opposition parties to find areas of agreement. Eventually these disparate parties were able to forge a 16-party coalition—*la Concertación por el No* ("Coalition for No") to compete against Pinochet.

Even though the 1988 referendum was held under the auspices of an authoritarian regime, the process was remarkably free and fair. As the self-appointed "savior of Chile," Pinochet was confident he would emerge victorious, and saw little justification for fraud. The military enrolled approximately 92 percent of eligible voters, granted television time to the opposition, and employed foreign observers to monitor the ballot boxes (Drake 1991). The *Concertación* soundly defeated Pinochet, winning 55 percent of the vote to Pinochet's 43 percent. Defeated, Pinochet allowed elections to go forward the following year, and he set to work devising a series of conditions for his gradual withdrawal from Chilean politics. To be sure, Pinochet did warn the opposition that the military would intervene again if it disapproved of the direction taken by the civilian government. Furthermore, since the 1980 constitution served as the foundation of the new regime, Pinochet had the deck stacked in his favor.

Transforming a weak institutional foundation

Since the military had destroyed Chile's democratic tradition in 1973, it was only fitting that democracy would strike back and end 16 years of authoritarian rule through a national election. In 1989, Chileans voted in the first presidential election held since Allende's 1970 victory. Even though civilians had defeated the military at the ballot box, it is important to remember that the Chilean transition to democracy in 1989 was a pacted transition. That is, the military agreed to turn over the reins to a democratically elected civilian government under a series of specific conditions. The military was still quite powerful in 1989 and was negotiating from a position of strength.

Since the 1980 constitution provided a timetable for an eventual return to civilian rule, the military regarded it as the natural blueprint for the new democratic government. Pinochet had written much of the constitution himself to ensure future governments could not tinker too much with his economic and political vision for Chile. Not surprisingly, there were numerous provisions to benefit the military and far right parties and their constituents. While this imperfect document has governed Chile from the 1990 transition to the present, it has not held democratization hostage. Reformers have been remarkably successful at gradually chipping away at the undemocratic elements and biases pervading the constitution, amending the document in 1989, 1991, 1997, 1999, 2000, 2003, and 2005.[9] Each wave of reforms has strengthened democracy, and the implementation of the 2005 reforms is widely considered as the final step in consolidating democratic governance. The incremental nature of these reforms prolonged the process of democratic consolidation, but also promoted consensus among left and right parties on the future direction of Chilean political development.

The *Concertación* began to contest the Constitution of 1980 immediately after its 1988 plebiscite victory, and succeeded in negotiating some concessions from the military government. Reforms made the constitution slightly more palatable, but it still contained numerous undemocratic elements. Power was concentrated in the executive branch, led by a president elected for an 8-year term. The Chilean presidency was powerful vis-à-vis the other branches of government, but the military was able to curb this authority through a variety of institutional mechanisms (Weeks 2003). First, the constitution created the National Security Council (CSN), which in effect had veto power over the president. Since the majority of the CSN was comprised of members of the armed forces, it ultimately institutionalized military oversight of the executive. Furthermore, the military was able to maintain its autonomy by limiting the appointment power of the executive branch: to appoint military commanders, the president could only choose from the top five senior members of each respective branch. The president could not fire any head of the armed forces without approval of the CSN. Taken together, these measures rendered the military an autonomous pillar of government with institutional mechanisms for controlling civilian officials. In addition to these military restraints, the bureaucracy further hampered the president. Pinochet had hand-selected most of the bureaucratic leaders, and in many cases made it impossible for the new president to dismiss these officials.

Institutional design also gave the military and its supporters an upper hand in the legislature. The National Congress consisted of two chambers, the Senate and the Chamber of Deputies. The Senate was the more powerful of the two bodies, and consequently was the focus of constitutional negotiations. After the 1989 reforms, the Senate was comprised of 38 elected senators and nine appointed senators (Weeks 2003). Not surprisingly, Pinochet selected the nine appointed senators, guaranteeing his supporters a voice in subsequent legislation.

The designation of appointed senators tilted the legislature in favor of the right, and the electoral system further exacerbated this bias. Legislative elections for both chambers were held under the unique binomial electoral system. Under this system, each voting district has two seats. Each party or coalition presents two candidates for each voting district. Candidates obtaining the majority among the *two* most voted lists are then elected. In order for a coalition or a party to send both its candidates to the Senate or Chamber of Deputies, it must win more than 67 percent of the vote (Siavelis 1997). Given the realities of ideological orientation in Chile, this electoral system basically guarantees the political right in each voting district a seat as long as it unites behind a single candidate to garner the second highest number of votes. In other words, if the political right comes in second at election time, it is guaranteed half the seats in the legislature. In practice, while approximately one third of Chileans identify with the right, the right tends to control half of the elected legislative seats. In the 1989 congressional elections, the allocation of seats to designated senators and the biases of the binomial electoral system resulted in the right controlling the majority of the seats in the Senate, even though *Concertación* won the majority of the popular vote (Oppenheim 2007).

Initially, the judiciary was also very weak, as Pinochet had appointed the majority of judges. Furthermore, the judiciary was hamstrung by the many undemocratic laws passed by the military government. Most contentious were the amnesty laws. In 1978, the junta passed laws prohibiting the prosecution of military or police officials for human rights violations committed purportedly to protect the internal security of the nation. These amnesty laws remained in effect under the new democratic regime. The Supreme Court initially upheld these laws and refused to prosecute those charged with human rights offenses. The reluctance to investigate and prosecute human rights offenses proved to be a thorny issue throughout the transition to democracy (Lira 2006).

Despite the undemocratic elements, some constitutional measures enjoyed widespread support for their potential to strengthen democratic government by addressing problems of the past. In particular, most Chileans approved of the structure of presidential elections. Under the new system, presidents would be elected by a popular vote for an 8-year term, but with the possibility of a runoff if the leading candidate did not win more than 50 percent of the vote.[10] By requiring the winner to command support from at least 50 percent of the voting population, the electoral system sought to avoid the pitfalls of the Allende presidency. Also, even though the binomial electoral system did bias the legislature in favor of the political right, it also promoted compromise among party elites (Navia 2006). Since only the top two candidate lists earn congressional representation, party elites have a strong incentive to form coalitions with like-minded parties. Indeed, coalition politics has been a hallmark of Chilean democracy from 1990 to the present. This practice of coalition building and the compromises it entails stands in marked contrast to the ideological polarization and stubbornness of party elites during the Allende years (Oppenheim 2007).

Upon taking office, *Concertación* officials pledged to prioritize institutional reform. Their ability to do so was constrained by institutional realities, however. Particularly in the first four years of democratic governance, the military kept a watchful eye over the civilian government, and did not hesitate to stage maneuvers to indicate its displeasure (Hunter 1998). Understandably, the first democratic officials tread cautiously. They put controversial reforms on the backburner for the most part, and began to tackle less sensitive issues to start. Most importantly, *Concertación* officials did not tinker with Pinochet's neoliberal economic model. Instead, the first two presidential administrations concentrated most of their initiatives at the local and regional levels, successfully implementing reforms to decentralize power and introduce elections for local officials.[11]

During these early years, the *Concertación* also succeeded in reforming the judiciary. A series of high profile scandals involving the court system gave impetus to reform efforts, as parties across the political spectrum recognized the serious deficiencies of the justice system. Reforms completely overhauled the justice system and included major revisions of the penal code and the creation of a public prosecutor's office. Most importantly, the National Congress approved a constitutional amendment to expand the Supreme Court from 17 to 21 judges and to establish a mandatory retirement age of 75 (Oppenheim 2007). Mandatory retirements led to the instant dismissal of six judges appointed by Pinochet, which greatly reduced previous biases in the Supreme Court.

The change in the composition of the Supreme Court created a more hospitable environment for the investigation and prosecution of human rights offenders. Almost immediately upon taking office, the *Concertación* had initiated a process of national reconciliation, entailing the investigation of human rights abuses and prosecution of those not covered by the 1978 Amnesty Law. Unfortunately, given the institutional obstacles at the time, human rights offenders were rarely held accountable. Judicial reform made the political climate for investigations much more hospitable, especially since the new Supreme Court rejected the expansive interpretations of the 1978 Amnesty Law rendered by the earlier judges. In 1998, the political landscape changed even more dramatically with the arrest of Pinochet.

In October of 1998, Pinochet had recently retired as head of the army and was enjoying his new post as "Senator for Life." He indicated he would be quite active in senatorial affairs and would assume a leading role in the coalition of right-wing parties. However, Pinochet's legislative career was abruptly cut short when he was arrested in London (while recovering from back surgery) at the behest of a Spanish judge who charged him with the murder of Spanish citizens.[12] While the implications of Pinochet's arrest were not immediately clear at the time, his detention fundamentally altered Chilean politics. His arrest created a political opening for more widespread reform, and his opponents seized the moment to reshape Chile's domestic institutions (Agüero 2003).

Pinochet's arrest brought human rights violations to the forefront of national politics once again. Even though he eluded trial through a series of legal maneuvers, investigations sparked by Pinochet's detention shed new light on the extent to which his regime had murdered and tortured civilians.[13] Pinochet's reputation was further tarnished by new revelations that he and his family had embezzled large sums of money from the public coffers during his rule. The *Concertación* capitalized on these developments and pushed for more investigation and prosecution into human rights offenses, but perhaps the most interesting developments occurred among the military and the right. Leading military officials and party leaders began to distance themselves from Pinochet's legacy and denounced such abuses of power (Agüero 2003). As leading members of the right coalition began to drift to the center, new consensus emerged on the need for institutional reform. Political parties across the spectrum began compromising on a series of initiatives to reform the legislative and executive branches of government, culminating in the sweeping 2005 package of constitutional reforms.

The 2005 reforms swept away most of the atavistic elements inherited from authoritarian rule. All nonelected senators were removed from office, leaving 38 elected members in the Senate. The binomial electoral system remained in place, but it was demoted from constitutional provision to a law, making it easier to change in the future (Borzutzky and Oppenheim 2006). The executive branch also shed the constraints of former military rule. The president now had the power to dismiss and appoint commanders of the armed forces, as is typical in most democracies where the military is usually subordinate to civilian authority (Oppenheim 2007). Also, the CSN's role in government was sharply curtailed; it would now serve only to advise the president.

For most observers of Chilean politics, the 2005 reforms marked the end of the transition to democracy. Current Chilean institutions have shed most of their authoritarian markings, and democratic governance in Chile now resembles that of older, consolidated democracies. With the exception of the binomial electoral system, political institutions are no longer contested.[14] Politicians have agreed upon the rules of the game, and now seek to advance their agendas within this framework.

This examination of political reform puts an interesting twist on the conventional wisdom concerning the role of political institutions in shaping democratic development. As discussed in Chapter 3, theorists have long pointed to the pivotal role institutions play in determining the success of democratization. The Chilean case most certainly does not dispute the importance of institutions; however, while Chile's institutions bore an authoritarian stamp, they were not beyond repair. Chile illustrates that institutions alone do not decide the fate of democratization. In 1990, Chile's institutional inheritance weakened civilian government and severely curtailed the ability of Chileans to select their own leaders. Despite these limitations, elites still found room to maneuver and push for political reform. The evidence from Chile suggests that if elites are committed to democratization, they can overcome many institutional obstacles. The next section examines the roles of elites in more detail.

Elites

The 1990 transition to democracy was the product of elite negotiation (Garretón 1991). Elites on the political center and left were instrumental in contesting Pinochet's rule in the 1988 plebiscite, as well as cobbling together an effective coalition to compete in the 1989 elections (Garretón 1991).[15] Military elites accepted the results of the plebiscite and bargained with the inaugural coalition to reform the Constitution of 1980. Civilian elites on the political right were also crucial to Chilean democratic consolidation, as they were willing to compromise with the *Concertación* to pursue gradual reforms. At critical moments, they also demonstrated they were ready to break with Chile's authoritarian past and carve out a more traditional conservative niche for themselves under democratic auspices.

Center-left elites

Given the dramatic repercussions for their behavior in 1973, most elites were "scared straight" in 1990. They were committed to avoiding the ideological polarization and rigidity that had paralyzed the previous democratic government and opened the door to military intervention (Oppenheim 2007). Most important were the compromises between the Christian Democrats and the Socialists. As the two largest parties, the commitment of their respective elites was crucial to the formation of a strong coalition, the *Concertación para la Democracia*. To form this coalition, elites became less ideological and more pragmatic. The first *Concertación* president, Patricio Aylwin (1990–94) exemplified this strategy of compromise. Once an ardent opponent of Allende and one who refused to compromise to end the political stalemate of 1973, Aylwin now led a multiparty coalition with his former opponents. Together, these coalition partners focused their platform on areas of agreement, centering in particular on the need to reform institutions. This strategy proved remarkably successful, as the *Concertación* won every presidential election from 1990 to 2006.

In addition to the willingness to compromise, the *Concertación* was also very selective in picking its political battles. President Aylwin first set the stage for this strategy. Upon taking office, he vowed not to alter Pinochet's neoliberal economic plan, viewing such a measure as far too controversial. Instead, he pursued a series of smaller reforms (e.g., increases in minimum wage) to offset some of neoliberalism's consequences for Chile's most vulnerable citizens. In addition, Aylwin clearly stated that the focus of his administration would be to consolidate procedural democracy; that is, strip away the undemocratic elements of Chilean political institutions. More contentious questions of substantive democracy (e.g., economic equality) would wait. Indeed, some critics have charged that these issues of substantive democracy have waited far too long, neglected by *Concertación* elites (Frank 2004).

Still, Aylwin did push the envelope on one highly charged issue: human rights. Despite military scrutiny, Aylwin argued that amnesty could not be granted to any individual until the facts of the specific case had been substantiated. Known as the Aylwin Doctrine, this interpretation of the 1978 Amnesty Law opened the door to the first commission to investigate human rights offenses, the Rettig Commission. Upon receiving this commission's report, Aylwin tried to prosecute those not covered by the 1978 Amnesty Law, but backed down when faced with military pressure.[16]

Subsequent *Concertación* presidents followed this path. Eduardo Frei (1994–2000) pursued an even more careful style of governance, focusing on areas of left and right consensus, such as judicial reform. When Pinochet's 1998 arrest forced Frei to respond to the issue of human rights violations, he cautiously established the *Mesa de Diálogo*, or Roundtable Dialogue (during the last year of his presidency), to investigate human rights abuses

(Lira 2006).[17] His successor, Ricardo Lagos (2000–06), pushed a bit farther. Realizing his counterparts on the right were anxious to distance themselves from the growing scandals associated with Pinochet, Lagos led his party to broker the 2005 constitutional reforms that ultimately consolidated democracy in Chile.

Lagos and his allies also made notable progress in the area of human rights. Perhaps most influential was the creation of the Valech Commission, which confirmed there had been widespread systematic torture of approximately 28,000 Chileans. Following the retirement of many former military leaders, a new generation was ready to respond to the Valech Commission's report. Under new leadership, and confronted with such overwhelming evidence, some branches of the military acknowledged their institutional responsibility for human rights abuses, creating a far more hospitable environment for human rights prosecutions.[18]

In 2006, Chile elected its first female president, Michele Bachelet (2006–10). Her personal background offers insight into how Chilean elites have fostered the process of democratic consolidation. Bachelet is the daughter of an air force general who died under torture at the hands of Pinochet's junta. Both Bachelet and her mother were subsequently arrested and tortured as well. Bachelet went on to earn a medical degree, and with the return of democracy became a leading member of the Socialist Party. She served under Lagos as minister of health and later as minister of defense. As minister of defense, she presided over civil–military relations during the Valech Commission's investigations and was instrumental in working with military commanders to press for accountability on human rights issues. Her political agenda prioritized issues of substantive democracy, such as poverty reduction, healthcare reform, and women's rights.

Despite her popularity while in office, Bachelet was unable to bequeath public appeal to the next presidential candidate of the *Concertación*. In the 2010 presidential elections, *Concertación's* hold on power slipped. For the first time since the return to democracy, a candidate from the right, Sebastián Piñera, won the presidential popular vote. Piñera's electoral success illustrates the political evolution of the right, and the alternation of power between political coalitions signals the normalization of Chilean democratic politics.

Right elites

Early in the transition, Pinochet had been a rallying point for the right, but following his arrest and subsequent scandals, he became a political liability.

Pinochet's arrest demonstrated that impunity was not foolproof, and that Chile could not sweep the human rights issue under the rug of amnesty forever. Furthermore, while Pinochet's supporters had sometimes turned a blind eye to human rights violations, their trust in their leader was shaken by a new scandal: corruption. When evidence emerged that Pinochet and his family had misappropriated funds for his own personal enrichment, even staunch supporters began to turn away from their former leader. Upon his death in 2006, he was no longer a force in Chilean politics.

Given these events, the right in Chile has struggled to reinvent itself in order to escape political irrelevance.[19] In the aftermath of the transition, these elites counted on their traditional popular support base—business elites, social conservatives, and military supporters. Historically, these sectors have combined to form one third of the Chilean electorate. Initially, this traditional support base was augmented by the power of designated senators and the binomial electoral system, which gave the right far more political representation proportionate to its support in the population as a whole.

As pressure for reform intensified, the right began to diversify its appeal. On this front, Joaquín Lavín of the Union for Chile made the most progress in the 1999 presidential elections, capturing 47.5 percent of the popular vote in the first round. This far exceeded the right's traditional base of support. Lavín achieved these impressive results by uniting the right around a single candidate, appealing to younger Chileans, and adopting a populist campaign style (Agüero 2003). Lavín largely ignored Pinochet, despite high profile developments in his case during the campaign. When the Valech Commission issued its report, Lavín went even further, publicly stating he would have voted against Pinochet in 1988 had he known the full extent of the human rights abuses (Oppenheim 2007). Lavín's political career illustrates two key points. First, the right also benefits from coalition politics and the compromises it entails, as demonstrated in the 1999 presidential elections. Second, the right is willing to move to the political center in order to compete more effectively in elections. Sebastián Piñera's presidential victory in 2010 clearly illustrates the electoral efficacy of both of these strategies.

Elites have been crucial to the consolidation of Chilean democracy. Across the political spectrum, commitments to gradual reform and consensual politics have made democratization successful, albeit protracted. Indeed, many Chileans have criticized their democracy as too elite-centered. Critics charge that elites have run the show without incorporating civil society and the mass public into their consultations. Furthermore, the possibility of electoral reform raises doubts about the future of coalition politics, as it is questionable whether coalitions will persist in the absence of electoral necessity. Finally, as the political situation has normalized and the raison d'être for the *Concertación* has diminished, it will be interesting to see if the four remaining parties coalesce behind a new platform or go their separate ways, particularly since their defeat in the 2010 presidential elections.

Political culture

Ideologically, on the eve of the transition Chile was still divided into thirds (Navia 2006). At this time, most Chileans on the political right stood by Pinochet. They supported the military intervention and neoliberal economic plan, and some even tolerated the human rights abuses. For these Chileans, Pinochet had saved Chile from chaos and communism. Only after Chile had purged all leftist activity could it resurrect democracy. On the political center and left, Pinochet did not fare so well. While many Chileans in the center supported military intervention initially, they quickly became disenchanted by the longevity of authoritarian rule and the scale of human rights abuses (Oppenheim 2007). On the left, respondents were outraged by both human rights abuses as well as the economic plan that brought growth to Chile, but not necessarily equity.

Throughout the 1990s, while the ideological composition of the electorate was similar to pre-1973 levels, voters were wary of extremist candidates (Agüero 2003). Figure 10.1 illustrates this modified trend. In most consolidated democracies, there tend to be fewer respondents on the ideological extremes (i.e., far left and far right) of the political spectrum; responses tend to taper off when one reaches these "tails" of ideological distribution. As Figure 10.1 indicates, in Chile this is not exactly the case. Most Chileans coalesce in the ideological center, but approximately 10 percent of Chileans still identify with each of the ideological extremes. These survey results demonstrate that while previous ideological patterns are still present in Chile, they are tempered by more moderate voices.

Public opinion data also indicate Chileans are very supportive of democracy. For example, in the 2008 LAPOP survey 66 percent of Chileans stated they thought democracy was the best form of government. Even though the public is very supportive of democracy, it seems this support does not always translate into political activity. While voter turnout is high, null voting, abstention, and nonregistration have increased recently (Carlin 2006). This appears to reflect low levels of interest in politics. Indeed, in the 2008 survey only 19 percent of respondents indicated they had any interest in politics.[20]

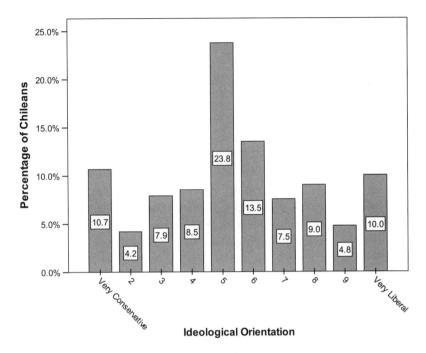

Figure 10.1 Chilean ideological orientation (2008)
Source: Latin American Public Opinion Project (LAPOP 2008)

Thus, it appears that while political culture is very supportive of democracy, lack of interest might impede this support from turning into meaningful political action.[21]

What role has political culture played in Chilean democratization? First, it is important to remember that the first stirrings of protest against authoritarianism in 1983 came from the grassroots. Also, when given the opportunity in 1988, a clear majority of Chileans (55 percent) voiced their support for the restoration of democracy in a pivotal plebiscite. Currently, an overwhelming majority of Chileans states that democracy is the best form of government. This strong support for democracy is coupled by more moderate positioning on the ideological spectrum, suggesting the public is more leery of ideological extremism today than it was in 1973. Still, even though civil society was instrumental in advocating for democracy in the 1980s, in the aftermath of the plebiscite Chilean elites monopolized control of politics. The public's role in democratization was quite small throughout the 1990s, although one could argue that the public's preference for moderate candidates encouraged parties to focus on issues in the political center. For example, evidence from Lavín's campaign indicates that public preferences for moderation encouraged some candidates to compete for votes by drifting to the center. Thus, it appears public support for democracy, coupled with ideological moderation, did strengthen democracy to some extent.

National unity

In 1973, social divisions played a role in the fall of democracy. These divisions were based primarily upon socioeconomic class and led to ideological polarization. Given this history, it is imperative to examine Chilean society today to determine whether such patterns persist.

Chilean society is very homogenous on a variety of indicators. In terms of ethnic composition, 92 percent of the population classifies itself as white or mestizo. This ethnic homogeneity is mirrored in religious identification. Chile is an overwhelmingly Catholic country, with the Church commanding allegiance from 68 percent of Chileans. Another 16 percent of Chileans identify with other Christian religions, particularly Evangelicals.[22] Spanish is the first language for 99 percent of the population. Thus, Chile does not encounter the typical societal cleavages present in many other countries. However, some economic divisions do persist. Inequality was high at the beginning of the transition to democracy, and this gap has remained stable to the present day. For the past 17 years, the poorest 20 percent of the population has held only 4 percent of the national wealth, while the top 20 percent has owned 56 percent (Drake 2004). The labor market is also notably divided into white collar and blue collar occupations. In contrast to the early 1970s, however, these economic cleavages do not appear to be polarizing. Indeed, when asked to what extent they agreed with the phrase, *"Despite our differences, Chileans have many things and values that unite us as a country,"* 83 percent stated they agreed.[23] Such sentiments indicate that there is a strong sense of national unity in Chile. Thus, while socioeconomic cleavages chipped away at national unity in the 1970s, it appears that such tensions have dissipated and are no longer obstacles to democratization.

Education

Table 10.2 provides a snapshot of one measure of education, literacy rates, from 1970–2005. As this table indicates, if education is a necessary prerequisite for successful democratization, it most certainly is not sufficient.

Table 10.2 Literacy rates 1970–2005

	1970	1975	1980	1985	1990	1995	2000	2005
Literacy Rates[24]	88%	90%	91%%	93%	94%	95%	96%	97%

Source: World Bank's World Development Indicators

The Chilean population was extremely well educated in 1970, prior to the collapse of democracy, and literacy rates have increased steadily over time with no connection to the process of democratization. It could be that the theory concerning education needs to be refined, and should assess not just levels of education but the type of education prevalent in each country. Education is a crucial tool for inculcating democratic values in citizens, providing numerous opportunities for political socialization. Therefore, it could be that in order to link education to democratization, one must examine the type of socialization and values latent in countries' educational systems.

Economic development

In his now famous assessment of South America's industrializing countries, O'Donnell (1973) was one of the first scholars to note that economic development does not necessarily promote democratic governance. On the contrary, industrialization can create societal friction and redistributional pressures that undermine democracy and foster political instability. The turmoil of Allende's administration most certainly lends support to O'Donnell's view and questions the conventional wisdom of modernization theorists.

Indeed, the case of Chile underscores the fact that there is little correlation between key economic indicators and democratization. As Table 10.1 illustrates, national wealth (as measured by GDP per capita) remained steady throughout the 1970s and 1980s. Chile did experience economic crises, but was able to weather them without losing its status as a middle income country. Despite steady income levels, democratic development oscillated dramatically during this same time period. There is no relationship between national wealth and democracy; the two have fluctuated independently of each other.

An examination of other economic indicators tells a similar story. High inflation levels in 1973 precipitated regime collapse, and a relatively minor jump in inflation in 1982 unleashed civil society protest against the junta. Based upon this evidence, one could argue that economic crises such as high inflation lead to regime change. In the former case this regime change led to the reversal of democracy, while in the latter it created an opening for the possible restoration of democracy in the future. However, there are no major fluctuations in the inflation rate in the late 1980s and 1990s, when the junta handed over the reins of government and the actual process of democratization began. Consequently, the empirical evidence regarding inflation is a bit tepid. It seems high inflation and regime change coincide in some cases, yet not in others. Most likely, other factors mitigate the relationship between inflation and regime change—such as the ability of elites to show leadership during the economic crisis and forge important alliances with their political peers and/or popular sectors.

Chile confounds additional theoretical perspectives linking economics and politics. In contrast to theoretical expectations, the middle class in Chile historically has not pursued democracy as a means of ensuring its economic security through the rule of law. Indeed, the middle class in 1973 allied itself with the military and supported the overthrow of democracy (Power 2002). In 1983, the protests against dictatorship emerged not from middle class sectors, but from working class sectors such as the copper miners' union. Once working class sectors began the protest movement, most members of the middle class did support the initiatives and in the late 1980s threw their wholehearted support behind the *Concertación*. While such support undoubtedly helped present a united front against military rule in 1989, it is hard to credit the middle class with a causal role in promoting democratization.

Private enterprise

One economic factor has played a role in promoting democratization in Chile: private enterprise. Still, private enterprise has shaped political development through different mechanisms than those envisioned by early democratic theorists. In 1973, perceived threats to private enterprise endangered democracy. Many business owners were angered when their private industries were nationalized under Allende's economic plan, and others feared Allende's working class supporters might begin nationalizing properties on their own (Winn 1986). Many business elites feared the left would become more radical and nationalize all property, thus obliterating private enterprise in Chile. Such fears led them to support the economic boycott and subsequent military coup rather than pursue political compromise.

In the late 1980s and early 1990s, it appears business owners were confident Pinochet's neoliberal reforms were firmly in place and would protect private enterprise. Furthermore, economic elites did seem to want a greater say in government, particularly if they could restrain the left through a series of institutional mechanisms. Negotiations toward democracy did not include discussions about changes to the economic order. Massive economic reforms were off the table, and *Concertación* elites centered their claims squarely on procedural democracy. Weyland (2009) argues that this acceptance of neoliberal economic policy can strengthen democracy, as it reassures economic elites their capital will not be subject to nationalization or even to high rates of taxation. Indeed, Weyland notes "Latin America's economic, social, and political elites are therefore much more secure nowadays than they were during the decades preceding the recent neoliberal wave" (Weyland 2009, 40). Secure elites apparently make happy democrats. As long as democracy is committed to the neoliberal promise, economic elites will support democracy. As Chapter 2 points out, democracy's commitment to neoliberalism is reinforced by international trends that tie aid and investment to the implementation of free market reforms, frequently called the "Washington Consensus." This can produce some tensions that are difficult to resolve. Indeed, Weyland (2009) argues that even as neoliberalism strengthens the viability of democracy as a regime, it simultaneously erodes the quality of democracy by restricting the decision-making abilities of elected officials.

International context

In addition to reinforcing neoliberal principles, the international context has shaped democratization in Chile in many important ways. Indeed, the relationship between international context and democracy dates back to the 1970s, when Chilean democracy found itself in the crosshairs of Cold War politics. Throughout the 1970s, the US intervened heavily in Chilean politics to oppose Allende and later support Pinochet. At the height of the Cold War, the US viewed the election of a Marxist as a dangerous new path toward communism (Smith 2000). Despite Pinochet's human rights abuses, the US saw him as a reliable anti-communist ally and a staunch believer in an open capitalist economy. American opposition to Allende and subsequent support of Pinochet facilitated the 1973 military coup, although it was by no means the decisive factor.

American foreign policy toward Chile changed in the late 1980s. As the Cold War neared its end, Pinochet's support became superfluous, and his human rights offenses became a political liability (Portales 1991). The US began to distance itself from Pinochet, at the same time exerting diplomatic pressure on the junta to allow some political space for the opposition. Leading up to the plebiscite, the US funded the *Concertación*, showering support on the Christian Democrats in particular. Once again, foreign support was influential but not the decisive factor in the political transition. Rather, the changing international context provided new allies for Chilean elites. Domestic forces in Chile were able to tie their political aspirations to powerful allies in the international community, particularly in Washington, to push for democracy.

Evidence from the Chilean case indicates the international context can play a pivotal role in democratization. It would be an overstatement to say the international context has determined political development on its own, but it clearly has shaped the political arena in which domestic forces operate. Just as domestic institutions delineate the political playing field, the international context molds the choices available to political actors. Furthermore, the international arena can provide valuable allies for domestic elites. For example, in the 1970s Chilean elites were able to appeal to US anti-communism concerns to bolster their efforts to oust Allende. In the late 1980s, opposition forces courted American support by framing their struggle against Pinochet as a fight for democracy.

Conclusions

The Chilean case illustrates how democratic theories developed for the first and second wave democracies do not always do justice to the analysis of democracies of the third wave. Most importantly, Chilean democratization demonstrates that the accumulation of national wealth and the creation of a middle class do not explain the reversal or restoration of Chilean democracy. Private enterprise does influence democratization, but not necessarily because elites seek to protect their economic power through democratic mechanisms. Rather, in Chile it is the pledge to promote private enterprise through neoliberal reforms that has garnered the support of business elites.

Chile also indicates how the predictors of democratization vary over time. The international context of the Cold War led the US to support Pinochet's overthrow of democracy in 1973. In contrast, by 1989 the international context was much more conducive to democratization, as the end of the Cold War created new incentives to support democracy and led the US to turn its back on Pinochet. Also, civil society mobilized in the early 1980s to protest for political reform; however, the ultimate push for democratization came from elites. Finally, Chile highlights how a weak institutional foundation need not necessarily imperil democratic development. If a critical mass of elites is committed to protecting democratic governance and upholding democratic norms, authoritarian institutions can be gradually reformed. Committed democrats can overcome authoritarian legacies.

Additional resources

In a superb series of documentaries, Patricio Guzmán offers a front row seat to the tumultuous events of 1973. His three-part series, *The Battle of Chile* (1976), vividly captures daily life amidst political turmoil in Chile prior to the military coup. Part two of this series, *The Coup d'Etat*, portrays the final days of the Allende government and the bombardment of the capital. Equally important for understanding Chilean democratization is Guzmán's later documentary, *Chile, Obstinate Memory*. This latter work captures the pernicious effects of authoritarian rule and depicts the struggle of many Chileans to come to terms with the past. *Chile, Obstinate Memory* does an excellent job of capturing the divisions that persist in Chile, and of how different societal actors perceive very different political realities in the past and present.

Renowned Chilean author Isabel Allende offers excellent insights into Chilean political development in her 1982 novel *House of Spirits*. For contemporary politics, *El Mecurio* is a leading Chilean newspaper with online access, http://diario.elmercurio.com/2010/09/07/_portada/index.htm (accessed September 7, 2010). *The Santiago Times* is an English language Chilean news source, available at www.santiagotimes.cl/ (accessed September 7, 2010).

Notes

1 Chile declared its independence from Spain in 1810, and succeeded in defeating the Spanish militarily in 1818.

2 Allende won by one percentage point, 36.2 percent of the vote. In accordance with Chilean electoral law, Congress ratified Allende's election prior to his taking office.

3 Interestingly enough, Allende's reaction to the attempted coup angered many of his supporters. Given the unconstitutionality of the military's actions, many of Allende's supporters argued that he should declare a state of emergency, even though Congress refused to approve this measure. Allende was reluctant to discard the proper constitutional channels, and thus did not declare a state of emergency. Instead, he planned to hold a plebiscite on his presidency to escape from the political impasse. He intended to announce the plebiscite on September 11, 1973.

4 The "disappeared" or "*desaparecidos*" refers to individuals who were kidnapped by state security forces and then vanished without a trace. Family and friends of these victims typically could not receive any information about the victims and thus felt as if they had simply disappeared from daily life. After the restoration of democracy the fate of many of the disappeared was uncovered through declassified documents and judicial proceedings. However, in several cases victims' fates were never ascertained.

5 This type of regime is called a bureaucratic authoritarian regime, whereby the military is in charge of repressing public dissent in order to allow technocrats leeway to implement the economic policies they deem best. Technocrats use the discretion garnered from such repression to pursue foreign investment in their countries.

6 Reported in constant US dollars based on the year 2000.

7 For Pinochet's own perspective on his rule, as well as his disparaging words for dictators, see Anderson's (1998) interview with Pinochet shortly before his arrest in London.

8 Although the economic crisis hit Chile especially hard, this was not a singular event in the region. Most Latin American countries faced economic crisis during this time as debt default, hyperinflation, and unemployment became common throughout the region. Due to this widespread economic crisis, the 1980s is known as the "lost decade" in Latin America.

9 Cumplido (2006) provides an overview of the many constitutional reforms and their import for Chilean democracy.

10 Presidential term limits have been changed numerous times during the transition to democracy. The original Constitution of 1980 stipulated an 8-year term, but after the transition to democracy this term was reduced to four years for the first civilian president. The law was changed so the second president, Eduardo Frei, could hold office for six years. Frei's successor, Ricardo Lagos, was also elected for six years. By the 2005 elections, however, presidential term limits had once again been reduced to four years.

11 Prior to these reforms, the military government had appointed mayors to lead local governments.

12 Pinochet officially resigned from the Senate in 2002.

13 The first commission to investigate human rights abuses, the Rettig Commission, reported in 1991 that 2,279 people had been killed during military rule. Critics have argued that this figure underestimates the number of those killed, as the fate of many of the disappeared was never ascertained.

14 Electoral reform remains on the political agenda. Reformers have commissioned a series of studies to examine the possibilities of other congressional electoral systems. For an example, see Helgesen (2006).

15 After its 1988 victory, the *Concertación por el No* converted itself into the *Concertación para la Democracia* to present a unified center-left front in the 1989 congressional and presidential elections.

16 Aylwin used the Rettig Commission's report to provide some type of compensation and health services to victims of human rights abuses and their families.

17 Members of the Roundtable Dialogue included military representatives, human rights lawyers, civilians, and representatives of the Catholic Church.

18 The military was far from monolithic in its response to the Valech Commission's report, however. Retired military leaders were outraged and disputed the findings. The navy stated it would "analyze the possibility of someday taking institutional responsibility" (Weeks 2006). Prosecutions were also facilitated by the sweeping changes in the judiciary, the product of earlier judicial reform.

19 The Democratic Independent Union (UDI) and the National Renewal (RN) are two of the most prominent parties on the right with original ties to Pinochet.

20 Respondents were asked, "*How much interest do you have in politics?*" (1) much; (2) some; (3) little; (4) none at all. The figure 19 percent was reached by combining the "much" and "some" categories.

21 Low interest in politics is most likely the result of socialization under the previous authoritarian regime, as well as the legacy of the elitist politics prevalent from 1990 to the present. In the future, this low level of political involvement might pose problems for the quality of democracy in Chile.

22 Sociodemographic information is based upon self-identification in the 2008 LAPOP survey.

23 Responses were coded on a scale of one (complete disagreement) to seven (complete agreement). Thirty-four percent responded with the highest value (7), 28 percent with the second highest (6), and 21 percent ranked their level of agreement as a five. These three responses were added to arrive at 83 percent (LAPOP 2008).

24 Literacy rates are determined through the percentage of the adult population (aged 15 and older) that can read and write.

References

Agüero, Felipe. 2003. "Chile: Unfinished Transition and Increased Political Competition." In *Constructing Democratic Governance in Latin America*, edited by Jorge Domínguez and Michael Shifter. Baltimore: Johns Hopkins University Press.

Anderson, Jon Lee. 1998. "The Dictator." *The New Yorker*, October 19, 1998.

Angell, Alan. 1991. "Unions and Workers in Chile during the 1980s." In *The Struggle for Democracy in Chile, 1982–1990*, edited by Paul Drake and Ivan Jaksic. Lincoln: University of Nebraska Press.

Borzutzky, Silvia, and Lois Hecht Oppenheim. 2006. *After Pinochet: the Chilean Road to Democracy and the Market*. Gainesville, FL: University Press of Florida.

Carlin, Ryan. 2006. "The Decline of Citizen Participation in Electoral Politics in Post-authoritarian Chile." *Democratization* 13 (4):632–51.

Cumplido, Francisco. 2006. "Reforma constitucional en Chile." *Anuario de Derecho Constitucional Latinoamericano*.

Drake, Paul. 2004. "Foreword." In *Victims of the Chilean Miracle: Workers and Neoliberalism in the Pinochet Era, 1973–2002*, edited by Peter Winn. Durham: Duke University Press.

Drake, Paul. 1991. "Introduction." In *The Struggle for Democracy in Chile, 1982–1990*, edited by Paul Drake and Ivan Jaksic. Lincoln: University of Nebraska Press.

Edwards, Sebastián, and Alexandra Cox Edwards. 1987. *Monetarism and Liberalization: The Chilean Experiment*. Cambridge: Ballinger.

Frank, Volker. 2004. "Politics without Policy: The Failure of Social Concertación in Democratic Chile 1990–2000." In *Victims of the Chilean Miracle: Workers and Neoliberalism in the Pinochet Era, 1973–2002*, edited by Peter Winn. Durham: Duke University Press.

Garretón, Manuel Antonio. 1991. "The Political Opposition and the Party System under the Military Regime." In *The Struggle for Democracy in Chile, 1982–1990*, edited by Paul Drake and Ivan Jaksic. Lincoln: University of Nebraska Press.

Georgetown University, Political Database of the Americas. 2005. "Political Constitution of 1980 through 2005 Reforms." http://pdba.georgetown.edu/ (accessed September 10, 2010).

Helgesen, Vidar. 2006. "Options for Reforming Chile's Electoral System." International Institute for Democracy Assistance (IDEA). www.idea.int/elections/upload/chile%20speech%20vidar%20 060424.pdf (accessed September 10, 2010).

Hunter, Wendy. 1998. "Civil–Military Relations in Argentina, Brazil, and Chile: Present Trends, Future Prospects." In *Fault Lines of Democracy in Post-Transition Latin America*, edited by Felipe Agüero and Jeffrey Stark. Miami: North–South Center Press, University of Miami.

LAPOP (Latin American Public Opinion Project). 2008. *Americasbarometer*. www.vanderbilt.edu/ lapop/ (accessed September 10, 2010).

Lira, Elizabeth. 2006. "Human Rights in Chile: The Long Road to Truth, Justice, and Reparations." In *After Pinochet: The Chilean Road to Democracy and the Market*, edited by Silvia Borzutzky and Lois Hecht Oppenheim. Gainesville, FL: University Press Florida.

Navia, Patricio. 2006. "Three's Company: Old and New Alignments in Chile's Party System." In *After Pinochet: The Chilean Road to Democracy and the Market*, edited by Silvia Borzutzky and Lois Hecht Oppenheim. Gainesville, FL: University Press Florida.

O'Donnell, Guillermo. 1973. *Modernization and Bureaucratic-Authoritarianism: Studies in South American Politics*. Berkeley: Institute of International Studies, University of California.

Oppenheim, Lois Hecht. 2007. *Politics in Chile: Socialism, Authoritarianism, and Market Democracy (3rd edition)*. Boulder, CO: Westview Press.

Portales, Carlos. 1991. "External Factors and the Authoritarian Regime." In *The Struggle for Democracy in Chile, 1982–1990*, edited by Paul Drake and Ivan Jaksic. Lincoln: University of Nebraska Press.

Power, Margaret. 2002. *Right-Wing Women in Chile*. University Park, PA: The Pennsylvania State University Press.

Siavelis, P. 1997. "Continuity and change in the Chilean party system—On the transformational effects of electoral reform." *Comparative Political Studies* 30 (6):651–74.

Smith, Peter. 2000. *Talons of the Eagle: Dynamics of U.S.–Latin American Relations (2nd ed.).* New York: Oxford University Press.

Weeks, Gregory. 2006. "Inching towards Democracy: President Lagos and the Chilean Armed Forces." In *After Pinochet: The Chilean Road to Democracy and the Market*, edited by Silvia Borzutzky and Lois Hecht Oppenheim. Gainesville, FL: University Press Florida.

Weeks, Gregory. 2003. *The Military and Politics in Postauthoritarian Chile.* Tuscaloosa: University of Alabama Press.

Weyland, Kurt. 2009. "Neoliberalism and Democracy in Latin America: A Mixed Record." In *Latin American Democratic Transformations: Institutions, Actors, and Processes*, edited by William Smith. Malden, MA: Wiley-Blackwell.

Winn, Peter. 2004b. *Victims of the Chilean Miracle: Workers and Neoliberalism in the Pinochet Era, 1973–2002* Durham: Duke University Press.

Winn, Peter. 2004a. "The Pinochet Era." In *Victims of the Chilean Miracle: Workers and Neoliberalism in the Pinochet Era, 1973–2002*, edited by Peter Winn. Durham: Duke University Press.

Winn, Peter. 1986. *Weavers of Revolution.* New York: Oxford University Press.

11

Poland's Democratic Development

Ewa Golebiowska

On April 10, 2010, Polish president Lech Kaczynski and dozens of Poland's political, military, and intellectual elites died in an airplane crash outside of Smolensk, Ukraine. The sudden demise of the core of Poland's governing elite proved particularly traumatic, as the passengers were on their way to commemorate the seventieth anniversary of the Katyn slaughter of over 20,000 Polish officers by the Soviet secret police during World War II. The trauma was heightened by initial worries that the tragedy could destabilize Poland's young democracy. Very quickly, however, it was clear Polish democracy had passed a major test. Its democratic institutions continued to work as expected despite the devastating loss (Grzymala-Busse and Tucker 2010;

Kulish and Levy 2010). Parliament's marshal, Bronislaw Komorowski, assumed the role of the president ex officio, upholding the legal line of succession. Military officials who perished in the airplane crash were immediately replaced by committees established for this type of contingency. The members of the Polish Parliament who died on the presidential plane were "replaced by the next-highest vote winner from the same party in the electoral region" (Kulish and Levy 2010, 1). The duties of the president of Poland's central bank were immediately assumed by the first deputy president. In accordance with the dictates of Polish law, new elections took place in June. Despite some initial fears and anxieties, it was quickly clear that Poland's governing institutions would function without major disruptions. While tragic for Poles situated anywhere on the political spectrum, the event proved to be a successful test of Polish democracy's stability. There was "no talk of coups, colonels, or emergency measures" (Grzymala-Busse and Tucker 2010).

By many measures, Poland has consolidated its democratic regime. Poland boasts the requisite competitive and free elections, extensive protection of human rights and minority rights, an independent media, and the rule of law. In every national election in the post-1989 period, a peaceful transfer of power has taken place (Millard 1999). No significant setbacks to democracy occurred in the post-communist period. This chapter examines Poland's road to democracy, illuminating the factors that propelled its democratic development.

Historical democratic development

Together with Hungary, Poland spearheaded the process of democratic transition in Eastern Europe. In 1989, Polish opposition representatives met for several months with members of the Communist government during the famous Roundtable Talks in order to discuss economic and political reform (Czubinski 2002). Among other things, the resulting agreement included legalization of the opposition and semi-open elections to the bicameral Polish Parliament. Much to the surprise of the governing coalition and the opposition alike, opposition candidates scored an unexpected victory while those affiliated with the ruling Communist Party suffered a humiliating defeat (Czubinski 2002). The Communists' control crumbled much more quickly than anybody could have predicted. Following the unexpected outcome of the first semi-open parliamentary elections, a free presidential election was scheduled for 1990, and the first completely free parliamentary elections followed quickly in 1991. In every Polish election since 1989, a peaceful transfer of power has taken place between winners and losers.

Poland's early experiences with democracy: "Noble democracy"

Poland was no newcomer to democracy in 1989, however. As early as the 1400s, the Polish nobility successfully pushed for greater economic and political rights (Tworzecki 2002). The nobility acquired the right to elect kings and gradually gained control over the legislative process. Nobility representatives were elected at regional assemblies (*sejmiki ziemskie*) and subsequently represented their regions at an annual national assembly (*sejm walny*). Under "noble democracy," the king enjoyed executive powers and the courts held judicial power, but legislative authority was concentrated in the hands of the nobility. The nobility's control over the legislative process included the absolute veto (*liberum veto*) power that gave any member of the parliament a chance to thwart law-making (Tworzecki 2002). While the so-called noble democracy may be considered Poland's first experiment with some democratic principles, it only extended meaningful political power to one socioeconomic group.

Poland's interwar democracy

In 1795, Poland ceased to exist as an independent country. Partitioned between its Prussian and Austrian neighbors, Poland did not regain its independence until 123 years later, after the end of the World War I. With this newfound independence, Poland experienced a second brief interlude of democratic governance. In the period between the two world wars (1918–39), Poland adopted a constitution that provided a basis for a republican form of government modeled on the French political system, with power concentrated in the parliament. Reborn Poland faced a number of daunting challenges, including extensive war damage and a ruined economy. Its interwar experiment with democracy was not set up to succeed (Curtis 1992). Democratic rule ended in 1926 with a military coup and the assassination of democratically elected President Gabriel Narutowicz, who served for only five days before he was killed by a civilian with ties to the extreme nationalistic movement. For the next decade, a military regime ruled Poland, one best described as having "mixed democratic and dictatorial elements," with popular strongman Jozef Pilsudski at its helm (Curtis 1992). Following Pilsudski's death, his successors made a shift toward open authoritarianism. In short, the attempt to implant democracy in briefly independent Poland did not succeed.

Polish independence was again compromised in World War II. During the war, the Soviet Union and Germany carved up Poland into their respective spheres of influence. Many of the legitimate Polish authorities sought refuge abroad. After the war ended, the Soviets controlled Poland's political development until 1989. Poland became a Soviet satellite, where the Soviets replicated their own economic and political structures. As was the case throughout Eastern Europe, the Soviets reinforced communist economic and political institutions with repression. Most citizens of Poland had no deep-rooted connections to the Soviet model; only repression kept the system in place.

The successful democratic experiment

It is difficult to mark the beginning of Poland's most recent transition to democracy, although the 1989 Roundtable Talks and subsequent semi-democratic elections have tremendous symbolic significance (Millard 1999). In 1989, Poland was like many of its Eastern European neighbors, where democratization filled a sudden political vacuum. Indeed, Ekiert describes the political scene of 1989 as one marked by "the rapid disintegration of existing political institutions, the further aggravation of economic dislocations, [and] the proliferation of various political movements breaking into the political arena" (Ekiert 1991, 287).

How did the political order implode so suddenly? Communism's grip on power had seemed absolute, and its quick demise took most observers by surprise. However, the roots of communism's chaotic crumbling can be traced to the late 1970s, when Poland's economy plunged into a severe crisis. Poland was not unique, as many other countries suffered a similar fate at this time. In Poland, industrial production and foreign trade plummeted together with the gross domestic product. Food prices shot up without a corresponding increase in wages. As a result, strikes became common and spread particularly quickly when word got out that strikers were successful in getting higher wages. The strike in the Gdansk Shipyard in 1980, was of particular significance, in part because Lech Walesa, the future leader of the Polish opposition, became the leader of the strike committee (Czubinski 2002). Walesa channeled such protests into an organized, viable opposition movement. Representatives of various strike committees met in Gdansk in

September, 1980, and formed the national Solidarity trade union organization (NSZZ Solidarnosc), with Walesa as its leader. A new political force, independent of the Communist Party and the government, thus came into being (Czubinski 2002).

It is important to note that Solidarity was not a centralized organization but a federation of regional trade unions. Contrary to its name, Solidarity could more accurately be described as a sociopolitical movement with many ambitions. The movement represented several different factions and ideologies, albeit all were united in their anti-communist stance. The strongest faction in this movement was a social-Catholic bloc, with Walesa as its representative (Czubinski 2002). In addition to his substantial personal charisma, Walesa benefited from the backing of the Catholic Church and Poland's intelligentsia.

The opposition's goals initially focused on reforming the existing political and economic system rather than completely overhauling it; however, the opposition increasingly voiced more and more (not always realistic) demands (Czubinski 2002). For example, Solidarity demanded power to hire factory directors, decide on wage increases, and require that Saturdays remain free from work. Solidarity's membership ranks were rapidly growing, as was the support of many religious and nonreligious organizations. It became difficult for the ruling Communist Party to dismiss the opposition's power. Under a threat of general strike, Solidarity received legal recognition in October of 1980. The ruling party made some additional minor concessions to appease Solidarity and its supporters, but ultimately these concessions failed to address the real problems of the government in power.

Strikes, demonstrations, and the removal of factory directors combined to deepen Poland's economic crisis throughout the 1980s (Czubinski 2002). The dearth of basic goods (e.g., meat, butter, flour, rice, and milk) was one indicator of the depth of the crisis. Empty shelves were a common sight in Polish stores. Basic goods were rationed with food coupons. A food coupon, however, did not guarantee that one could buy any of the basic goods without waiting in long lines, often forming overnight in response to a mere rumor that a delivery of some goods might take place the following day. To get a handle on the situation in the country, the military gradually started to take over control of the government, with generals assuming several key positions.

On December 12, 1981, the government declared martial law. The newly formed Military Committee for National Recovery (WRON), with General Wojciech Jaruzelski as its leader, proceeded to intern opposition activists as well as some former members of the party. In the initial phase, about

6,000 individuals were interned in 41 centers (Czubinski 2002). Thousands of soldiers and police officers, equipped with tanks and other military vehicles, were put in charge of the internment. The following day, television and radio stations kept replaying the announcement and the new rules at regularly scheduled intervals. As a result of martial law, most associations and political groupings, including Solidarity, were banned. Independent newspapers and television stations were closed. Yet, Solidarity was weakened rather than completely destroyed. Much oppositional activity continued illegally under martial law. For example, leaflets, newspapers, magazines, and books were printed, and demonstrations and strikes still took place.

Martial law was finally lifted in July 1982. The government attempted to stabilize the situation in the country and to pursue reform. In spite of the government's efforts, Poland's economic crisis continued. Its national debt continued to grow, in part as a result of foreign loans. In July of 1986, General Jaruzelski was reappointed as leader of the ruling Communist Party to take charge of the situation. Energized by his government's failure to curb the economic crisis, Jaruzelski aimed to reach out to the opposition, and did not crack down on Walesa's expansion of Solidarity's activity. Jaruzelski was joined by a growing number of politicians in the government camp who spoke in favor of reforms and of reaching out to the opposition. While the Communist hardliners vilified the pro-reform forces of their party, events in the Soviet Union were tipping the balance in favor of reform. The selection of the new first secretary of the Soviet Union's Communist Party Central Committee helped the reformers' cause. Mikhail Gorbachev, a relatively young politician, took the reins of the Soviet Communist Party and embarked on a series of reforms that have collectively become known as *glasnost* (openness). Gorbachev came to the conclusion that Soviet domestic and foreign policy had led to crisis, and that reform was needed within the Soviet Union as well as throughout the communist world. He set aside conservative activists and launched a new platform for the party. As part of his new approach, Gorbachev decided to stop interfering in the internal politics of the countries dependent on the Soviet Union (Czubinski 2002). Without the threat of Soviet tanks, the Polish opposition had new room to maneuver.

This extraordinary change in Soviet policy led Poland's Communist Party leaders to embark on their own soul searching and internal reforms. The reform faction, including General Jaruzelski, toyed with the idea of an agreement with the opposition. The diehards staunchly opposed any such negotiations. The opposition itself was also divided on the question of negotiations with the government. Catholic bishops played a crucial role in the opposition's debates about the best way to proceed. The bishops assumed an intermediary role between the government and Solidarity. Ultimately, the pro-reform forces in the government and moderates in the opposition movement got the upper hand and agreed to formally talk to each other. Representatives from the ruling coalition and the opposition met at the so-called Round Table Talks in Warsaw between February 6 and April 5, 1989. The name of the talks comes from the fact that a special, round table was custom-made for the occasion. Interestingly, the participants in the talks only sat at this round table on two occasions: at the beginning and at the end of the talks (Dudek 1997). General Czeslaw Kiszczak and Lech Walesa opened the negotiations, representing the ruling party and the opposition, respectively. While over 400 people took part in the talks, most of the deliberations occurred among three small workgroups charged with discussing economic and social reforms, trade union pluralism, and political reforms (Czubinski 2002).

The agreement that emerged from the talks was far-reaching in its implications. First, Solidarity received legal recognition. Second, a two-chamber parliament composed of the *Sejm* (lower house) and Senate (upper house) would be elected, and the elected parliament would choose the president who, in turn, would choose the government (or the executive branch). Third, a new election law would be established. One hundred representatives were to be democratically elected to serve in the Senate. Limits were placed, in contrast, on the number of seats different political forces would be allowed to assume in the 460-seat Sejm. Opposition forces were allowed to hold up to 35 percent of the seats. Faith-based groups with pro-government leanings (e.g., Polish Catholic-Social Association or *Polski Zwiazek Katolicko-Spoleczny*) could take up to 5 percent of the seats. The remaining 60 percent of the seats were reserved for members of the ruling coalition: Polish United Workers' Party, United Farmers' Party, and Democratic Left Alliance (Czubinski 2002, 323).

Many members of the ruling coalition were dumbfounded by the agreement and saw it as a defeat for their camp. In the June elections, therefore, ruling party candidates did not campaign very hard. Many did not publicly acknowledge their partisan affiliation nor did they campaign on their party's platform (Czubinski 2002, 324). Most opposition candidates, in contrast, saw the election as an opportunity to share power and limit the ruling party's monopoly. They enthusiastically set out to win as many seats as their quotas allowed, focusing especially on the Senate elections, where there was no cap. Their expectations were modest, however, as they did not anticipate a dramatic change in the nature of Poland's political system. In fact, no one predicted the opposition's landslide victory. Opposition candidates won 160 of the 161 seats they were allowed to win in the Sejm and 99 of the 100 seats in the Polish Senate (Czubinski 2002, 325).

While election results proved a major defeat to the ruling coalition's candidates, the Communists did have a consolation prize: they still controlled Poland's army, police, and security forces. This control of coercive institutions led the Communists to feel they were still in charge despite their electoral losses. They assumed they would continue to share power with the opposition in the years to come. The victorious opposition did not necessarily challenge this sentiment, as the sweeping electoral victories had taken it by surprise. The opposition was unprepared for the takeover of power, and still afraid of the reactions of the Soviet Union and/or other members of the Eastern Bloc (such as militarily powerful neighbor, East Germany). Still, the momentum continued, and the opposition's power was further consolidated in the fully democratic elections that followed. The first democratic presidential election, which took place in 1990, delivered victory to the Solidarity candidate, Lech Walesa. The first completely open parliamentary elections followed in 1991 and featured a plethora of political parties vying for representation in the Polish Parliament.

State institutions

Poland's democratic institutions have evolved over time, as a series of constitutional revisions aimed to deepen democratic practices from 1989 to the present. When the Solidarity government formed in the wake of the first semi-open elections in 1989, the constitutional framework for the new Polish state was in flux. To construct the new regime, reformers began by amending the 1952 constitution developed under Stalin. Unlike the original, the amended document no longer spoke of the socialist system, the leading role of the Communist Party, or Poland's alliance with the Soviet Union. Instead, the amended constitution included lofty references to popular sovereignty, political pluralism, and the rule of law (Domagala 2008). The Council of State, a central governing body in communist Poland, was disbanded and replaced with the position of the president (Graczyk 1997). The president had a 6-year term and was endowed with many powers, serving as the head of state and commander in chief (Domagala 2008). The president enjoyed expansive powers in the realms of foreign and defense policy, and exercised considerable power over the other branches of government. For example, the president could object to laws passed by parliament and disband the legislature under some circumstances, as well as select and dismiss the prime minister (Graczyk 1997). A bicameral parliament, composed of the Sejm (lower house) and Senate (upper house), served as the country's legislative body. The constitution accorded lofty status to the Sejm, establishing it as "the highest organ of state power." In addition to legislative powers, the Sejm also had "extensive powers of appointment and it could override decisions of the Constitutional Tribunal" (Millard 1990, 39). Thus, this interim constitution established a strongly centralized semi-presidential system, with many powers vested in both the president and parliament.

This new constitution differed radically from the former communist regime, but was still not fully democratic (Graczyk 1997). Only a part of the government (the Senate) was elected in free elections. A majority of the seats in the Sejm, in contrast, was automatically guaranteed for the Communist coalition. This arrangement sought to preserve the central role of the Communist Party while allowing some role for the opposition. After the 1989 legislative elections delivered a mortal blow to the Communists, the first government was dominated by their political opponents. In light of his party's embarrassing losses, President Jaruzelski did not even attempt to avail himself of many of the tools the amended constitution gave him (e.g., he did not try to dissolve the parliament) (Graczyk 1997). In contrast, his democratically elected replacement, Lech Walesa, was not at all shy about aggrandizing his powers after his 1990 electoral victory. For example, Walesa tried to create a presidential political committee that would essentially shadow the powers of the parliament (Graczyk 1997, 85). After months of conflict between President Walesa and parliament, new parliamentary elections were scheduled in 1991.

Emboldened by their respective presidential and legislative electoral victories in 1990 and 1991, democrats used their new presidential post and parliamentary majority to go further, producing the so-called Little Constitution, which took effect at the end of 1992. While the Little Constitution made several changes to the 1989 Constitution, the latter largely remained in force until the passage of the 1997 Constitution, the foundation for Poland's current institutional framework. The Little Constitution was supposed to address the many challenges of governing Poland during the first three years of democratic transition (Graczyk 1997). During this time, parliament was highly fragmented, rendering decision-making difficult. Parliamentary elections relied on strict proportional representation, which was very democratic on one level as it gave any party a chance to win a legislative seat. On the downside, the system heightened political fragmentation, as it led to the ascension of 29 parties in the Sejm, 13 in the Senate, and a number of independent senators (Millard 1999). The presence of a large number of political parties in the Parliament made coalition-building and governing difficult. To exacerbate matters, the Senate conflicted constantly with the Sejm. Furthermore, the president lacked important powers to deliver on his initiatives, albeit President Walesa was never shy about pushing for changes to enhance the legal bases of his powers (Graczyk 1997).

The Little Constitution's principal objectives were to fix these problems and clarify the relationships among the highest branches of government, dividing power among the legislative, executive, and judicial branches. The Little Constitution did accomplish some of these tasks. For example, it established a 5 percent threshold for individual parties or electoral committees to assume parliamentary seats, which reduced the number of legislative parties and made governing easier. Still, the Little Constitution did not always make clear where the powers of the president and parliament started and ended, inviting conflict over interpretation (Graczyk 1997). While the Little Constitution aimed to decrease the volatility of Polish politics, ultimately it failed in this regard, as indicated by the fleeting governments of prime ministers Jan Olszewski (collapsed in June 1992), Waldemar Pawlak (failed in July 1992 after only 33 days), and Hanna Suchocka (failed in September 1993) (Domagala 2008). By 1993, this heightened factionalism drove President Walesa to dissolve parliament and call for new elections yet again (Millard 1999).

Given the inability of the Little Constitution to promote stability, reformers kept busy. On May 25, 1997, reformers offered a new constitution to the public in a national referendum. The public endorsed the new constitution, which serves as the basis for Poland's current institutional framework (Millard 1999). The new constitution retained many of the previous institutions of the semi-presidential system, but with important modifications. For example, the 1997 Constitution provided for a separation of powers among the legislative, executive, and judicial branches. The bicameral parliament and elected government both retained their legislative powers, and executive power was vested in the elected government composed of the Council of Ministers, with the prime minister at its helm. The president's most important functions include serving as head of state and as supreme commander of the armed forces, as well as having the power to veto legislative acts and make several high level appointments. The new constitution curbed the power of the president, however, mandating cooperation "with the prime minister and relevant ministers" in the areas of foreign and defense policy (Millard 1999, 44–45). Thus, the new constitution strengthened the position of the prime minister at the slight expense of the president. Several judicial institutions, including the Constitutional Tribunal, the Tribunal of

State, and several other courts, also remained intact (Millard 1999). Most importantly, the Constitutional Tribunal has the power to review laws that violate freedoms guaranteed in the constitution.

Elites

Poland's successful transition to democracy relied heavily on three groups of elites. While participants were unaware of it at the time, the Roundtable Talks ultimately set the stage for the democratic transition. These talks included representatives from the three integral elite groups: the governing coalition (PZPR, ZSL, and SLD), [1] the opposition (Solidarity), and the Catholic Church (Dudek 1997). While a total of 452 people took part in the talks, only a handful actually ran the show. The governing coalition saw the talks as a way to incorporate the opposition into the existing political system (Dudek 1997). It certainly did not anticipate a transition to a democratic political system. The Solidarity representatives also had modest expectations. They agreed that the first elections would not be entirely democratic but expected that future elections, starting with those to be held four years later, would be completely open (Millard 1999). Participants in the Roundtable Talks also agreed on an undemocratic selection of Poland's first president, allowing the legislature to choose the president. In short, none of the elites negotiating Poland's initial transition from communism thought they were on the threshold of a full democratic transition. The Communists expected to maintain their dominance while ceding some power to the opposition. The Solidarity representatives aimed to carve a space for themselves in government, but did not anticipate immediate access to full power. The Catholic Church expected to continue to play a central mediating role in the new political system (Millard 1999).

In the immediate aftermath of the first round of the semi-competitive parliamentary elections, it became clear that political change would be greatly accelerated (Dudek 1997). The tremendous success of opposition candidates in the first round of elections opened the door to rapid democratization. The PZPR imploded and dissolved in the aftermath, facilitating the 1990 presidential election of Lech Walesa as Poland's first president. Walesa was committed to democratic reforms and to "sweeping communism out of the cracks and crannies" (Millard 1999, 83). In the economic realm, he was highly supportive of privatization, promising each citizen "100 million *zloty* to invest in privatization" (Millard 1999, 83). While Walesa won, in the process he alienated not only former Communists but also some of his former supporters, who were now organized in the Democratic Union (UD), a party boasting a strong base in the urban intelligentsia (Millard 1999). While he was a skillful revolutionary, Walesa lacked the qualities necessary in a good statesman. For example, he went out of his way to insult and humiliate other politicians (Czubinski 2002). While campaigning for president in 1990, he did not hesitate to use any means necessary to win, including playing an anti-Semitic card against Tadeusz Mazowiecki, Poland's first prime minister. Additional elite divisions took place after the presidential election, as several new political parties geared up for the 1991 parliamentary elections. Thus, the unified Solidarity movement fell apart in the wake of the 1990 presidential election.

Against this fragmented backdrop, President Walesa called for new parliamentary elections in 1993. The ex-Communist parties came to power in a landslide victory. Reinventing themselves under new party labels like the Left Democratic Alliance (SLD) and the Polish Peasants' Party (PSL), the former Communists capitalized on public outrage over the painful economic reforms designed to convert the Polish economy to a free market. The SLD and PSL became the largest parties in parliament. Some observers worried that such electoral victories signaled a return to Poland's communist past. Very quickly, however, it was clear that such fear was unwarranted. The new government did not intend to do away with democracy, the market economy, or diplomatic relations with the West. The new governing post-communist elite proved quite pragmatic and continued to support a capitalist, democratic future for Poland. Revisiting the communist past was not a viable alternative. However, unlike their immediate predecessor, the ex-Communists were committed to easing the social costs of the reforms.

The Polish left further strengthened its political position during the 1995 presidential election (Millard 1999). In this election, a peaceful transfer of power took place, from Lech Walesa, a "symbol of anti-Communist liberation," to Aleksander Kwasniewski, a "symbol of new, modernizing social democracy" (Millard 1999, 91). Kwasniewski proved to be a victor not because he differed from Walesa in his programmatic aims, but because of their differences in values and style. Kwasniewski was a more dynamic and youthful candidate, whereas Walesa was notorious for his verbal and political incoherence (Millard 1999). Also, Kwasniewski triumphed because he succeeded in convincing "more people of his ability to protect social welfare, while rejecting old-style Communist authoritarianism" (Millard, 1999, 93). In the 2000 presidential election, Kwasniewski handily won reelection in the first round.

After the 1997 parliamentary elections, the Polish right scrambled to regroup in order to form a coherent center-right block to maintain the

Walesa electorate. This strategy proved successful, as an offshoot of Solidarity, *Akcja Wyborcza Solidarnosc* (AWS), or Solidarity Election Action,[2] won the 1997 parliamentary elections by an unexpectedly strong showing (Millard 1999). SLD came in second, and a total of five parties won seats in the Sejm. AWS won an absolute majority in the Senate. AWS and Freedom Union (*Unia Wolnosci* or UW, a centrist party) joined forces to form a coalition government. In the 2001 parliamentary elections, the balance of power shifted again to the left, but elites all over the ideological spectrum remain committed to a democratic, capitalist Poland. Divisions emerged over the specific policies of the democratic, capitalist state, and these divisions did occasionally undermine governing coalitions. Still, elites coalesced around the basic principles of democracy and free markets.

Elite divisions over specific policy measures did take their toll, however, and elite factionalism reverberated throughout the electorate. The 2005 parliamentary elections witnessed the lowest rates of voter turnout in the entire post-communist period, with voters unhappy with the available choices (Bonusiak 2008). To the surprise of many, *Prawo i Sprawiedliwosc* (PiS), or Law and Justice, won the election in both the Sejm and Senate. PiS, a party founded by the Lech and Jaroslaw Kaczynski (the Kaczynski brothers), is far right, nationalistic, pro-Catholic, anti-European Union in its political orientations. A more centrist party, *Platforma Obywatelska* (PO), or Civic Platform, came in second. The left suffered a major defeat in these elections, with SLD getting a handful of the seats in the Sejm and no seats in the Senate. There was not much love lost between the two top vote-getters and both decided to wait until the outcome of the 2005 presidential election before forming the new government. In a highly divisive election that, in its runoff, featured Donald Tusk (PO) and Lech Kaczynski (PiS), Kaczynski got the upper hand after sparing no effort to ensure his victory. For example, Kaczynski's supporters circulated rumors that Tusk's grandfather had volunteered to serve in the German army during the World War II. More generally, Kaczynski's campaign was based on exploiting social divisions in Polish society between what they dubbed "liberal" and "solidarity" Poland. At every step of the way, Kaczynski emphasized he was a Polish Catholic while reminding voters that Tusk was a nonbeliever. Much of Kaczynski's and PiS's success in the parliamentary elections was due to the activism of ultra-Catholic forces campaigning on their behalf. For example, a famous Polish priest (or infamous, depending on one's perspective), Father Rydzyk, used his ultranationalist media outlets to promote PiS candidates and besmirch others, especially those affiliated with the PO.

In the aftermath of the divisive presidential election, any plans for a parliamentary PO-PiS coalition were quashed. Instead, PiS decided to form a governing coalition with two extreme right-wing parties: League of Polish Families, or *Liga Polskich Rodzin* (LPR), and Self-Defense, or *Samoobrona* (Bonusiak 2008). Contrary to his earlier pronouncements, the president's twin brother, Jaroslaw Kaczynski, soon accepted the position of Poland's prime minister.

By many accounts, the Kaczynski government detracted from, rather than enhanced, the quality of Polish democracy. Both the president and his brother, with many believing the latter was actually in charge, exhibited authoritarian tendencies. They seemed intent on finding enemies and polarizing society along many different "we vs. they" dimensions. They often used lustration, a discrediting of individuals associated with the prior regime, as a tool to disparage their political enemies.

In foreign policy, the Kaczynski brothers were driven by the premise that "Poland has so far been on its knees and that they were going to help her stand up" (Bonusiak 2008, 239). Thus, they favored confrontation rather than cooperation with Germany and Russia, Poland's historical enemies. The Kaczynski government also had a conflict-ridden relationship with the European Union (EU), refusing to sign the European Union's Charter of Basic Rights. This document spells out important human rights to which members of the European Union subscribe (e.g., human dignity, freedom, and equality). The Kaczynski brothers preyed on fears that the Charter would make it easier for Germans to get Polish property and that it would force Poles to legalize same-sex marriages. All in all, social tensions intensified under the Kaczynski brothers' government, and in many ways, their approach to governing hindered the progress of Polish democracy.

The 2007 parliamentary elections proved to be a referendum on this rather divisive status quo. More voters turned out in these elections than in any other since the 1990 parliamentary elections. The Civic Platform (PO) won a majority of votes in both the Sejm and Senate elections, and ended up forming a governing coalition with the PSL. Thus, while Polish democracy faced challenges under the Kaczynski government, voters returned en masse to register their unhappiness with the status quo.

Political culture and civil society

With the Roundtable Talks, elites opened the door to some democratic practices. Civil society took this opening and pushed the door wide open. Indeed, civil society had long been an important force in Polish politics. Particularly with mass-based movements like Solidarity, disaffected Poles have long used protest as a tool for negotiating economic and political concessions from the communist-era government. Organized protest activity that had started before the fall of communism continued after it fell and also influenced the consolidation of Polish democracy. Hundreds of strikes took place in Poland in 1989 and continued in the years to come. In 1990, for example, farmers' unions were responsible for regional protests and road blockades (Ekiert and Kubik 1999). Transportation workers also organized countrywide protests. In 1991, farmers organized road blockades, strikes, and demonstrations (Ekiert and Kubik 1999). More recently, in May 2006, thousands of people took to the streets in several Polish cities to protest the nomination of ultraconservative and openly homophobic Roman Giertych as Poland's education minister (Ekiert and Kubik 1999).

Once democracy was consolidated, civil society lost its momentum, however. Compared to its fellow EU members, contemporary Poland hosts substantially less protest activity. Poles are also very unlikely to sign petitions compared to most other EU citizens, and are near the bottom in terms of membership in nonpolitical organizations and associations (Ekiert and Kubik 2009). The levels of Polish participation in voluntary associations, parties, trade unions, or religious movements hover around 15 percent of the population (Ekiert and Kubik 2009). Similarly, in recent years only 15–20 percent of the population report activity in their communities or in public meetings (Ekiert and Kubik 2009). Union membership, essentially automatic under communism, has also declined sharply in the postcommunist period (Ekiert and Kubik 2009).

These low levels of civic engagement can spell trouble for the quality of Polish democracy. Civil society successfully challenged communism in the 1980s, but today widespread disengagement from civic and political life characterizes Poles' attitudes and behavior (Paczynska 2005; Tworzecki 2008). Analyses of voting turnout over time demonstrate that Poles have not yet developed a habit of voting. They tend to tune in and out of political participation, with different voters showing up to vote in different elections (Czesnik 2009). Participation in other types of political activities (e.g., contacting officials or signing petitions) has been far lower in Poland than in most of Western Europe (Czesnik 2007; Tworzecki 2008, 48).

While civil society activism has waned in recent times, Poles remain committed to democracy as a form of government. Since the early 1990s, the Center for the Study of Public Opinion (CBOS) located in Warsaw has asked Poles whether democracy is a better form of government than any other political system. Over time, polls demonstrate that a growing majority of respondents agrees democracy is indeed a superior political system (CBOS 2009).

At the same time, a sizable percentage of Poles (hovering at about a third of respondents at any point in time) have endorsed a belief that undemocratic rule can sometimes be superior to democratic governance. Still, while most Poles support democracy in the abstract, throughout the democratic transition a majority of Poles has expressed dissatisfaction with the functioning of democracy in Poland. The number of dissatisfied survey respondents has been on the decline in the last few years, however (CBOS 2009).

The question of whether Poles are supportive of democracy can be assessed using other yardsticks as well. For example, we can examine Polish support for key democratic norms and values, such as public support for the rights of political minorities. While a majority of Poles embrace democracy as a preferred form of government, commitment to specific democratic norms, such as the rights of political dissenters, is substantially less than uniform (Golebiowska 2006). A majority of survey respondents agree, for example, that "radical and fringe groups should not be allowed to demonstrate, that freedom of speech does not include the right to expound fringe political views, and that foreigners who do not like the Polish form of government should not be allowed to live in Poland" (Golebiowska 2006, 236). Such findings indicate that a significant number of Poles hesitate to extend fundamental democratic rights and liberties to groups or individuals they may dislike.

In addition to lackluster support for the rights of political minorities, Polish public opinion data reveal that another key democratic norm, tolerance, is also lacking. For example, Polish society shows a continuing legacy of negative attitudes toward Jews in Polish society and politics. While Jews comprise a minuscule amount of the population in Poland, public opinion surveys consistently report that close to 50 percent of Polish respondents have rated Jews on the "dislike" end of commonly used liking scales, with almost a quarter giving Jews the lowest possible rating in 2006 (CBOS 2006). Existing cross-national comparisons of anti-Semitism in Europe, in addition, demonstrate that levels of anti-Semitism are among the highest in Europe, and are on the rise (Anti-Defamation League 2007; Krzemiński 2004; Pew Global Attitudes Project 2008). While Jews are rated lower than some two dozen other ethnic and national groups, the levels of Poles' dislike for other ethnic minorities living in Poland are also considerably high.

The issue of gay rights has also been very controversial in Poland, particularly once Poland's accession to the EU politicized the issue. Gay Poles' rights to participate in public life were vehemently attacked within months of Poland's accession to the EU. Several major cities banned gay rights parades, including Warsaw, where a proposed parade was banned by (future

Polish president) Lech Kaczynski in his capacity then as mayor (O'Dwyer 2010). Furthermore, gays suffer from discrimination in employment, housing, and health care (O'Dwyer 2010).

Social divisions and national unity

While this has not always been the case, Poland is today one of the most ethnically and religiously homogeneous countries in the world. Before World War II, Poland boasted a highly diverse population. In the 1930s, for example, a third of Poles declared a non-Polish ethnicity (Bajda, Syposz, and Wojakowski 2002). The country's ethnic profile changed dramatically during and after the war as a result of the massacre of Jews and Roma, mandatory and voluntary migration of Germans, Byelorussians, and Ukrainians, and assimilation policies directed at other minority group members (Golebiowska 2004). The result of such upheaval is a homogenous population. Recent estimates place the number of ethnic Poles living in Poland at about 98 percent of the population, with small groups of ethnic Germans, Byelorussians, Ukrainians, Roma, Lithuanians, Slovaks, Russians, and Jews (Wilczak 2002). An overwhelming majority of Poles (about 95 percent) identify as Catholic. Still, this homogeneity has not rendered ethnicity irrelevant. Ethnicity has emerged as an important factor in elections, where rumors about candidates' ethnicities have been the principal vehicle for unleashing ethnic prejudice in electoral campaigns in post-communist Poland. For example, while Jews are only a tiny minority in Poland,[3] anti-Semitism has been used as a political card in Polish elections in the post-communist period (Gebert 1991; Golebiowska 2008).

Ideological divisions have also emerged as potent political forces in democratic Poland. Differences in religiosity, not religious affiliation, have fueled these ideological divisions, as the more-religious have been clashing with the less-religious over such issues as religious education in public schools, regulation of abortion, or Poland's relationship with the Vatican (Grabowska and Szawiel 2001). Indeed, far right groups gained widespread political legitimization in the late 1990s thanks in large part to the support of ultrareligious Catholics (Starnawski 2003). These groups have propagated a restrictive conception of national identity that prizes Polish ethnicity and Catholicism at the expense of other ethnicities and religions. In short, religiosity-based cleavage in Polish post-communist politics has oftentimes detracted from, rather than enhanced, democracy in Poland.

Economic development

Economic development has been closely intertwined with democratization, but not in the manner classic democratic theorists would predict. Instead, the failure of communism to bring economic prosperity to Poland helped discredit it as a viable form of governance. Soviet recognition of the need for market reforms underscored a grim reality—the communist economic model was sinking fast in the late 1980s and early 1990s, and free market reforms appeared to be the only viable lifeboat. The Cold War had long promoted two rival models of economic development: communism vs. capitalism. With communism on the brink of collapse, most Polish democrats saw capitalism as the only alternative. The appeal of capitalism was heightened by the proximity of the EU, which boasted vibrant economies and abundant consumer goods under democratic, capitalist regimes. Democracy and capitalism appeared to move in tandem and were widely viewed as the ticket to a better economic and political life. Polish elites made a conscious choice to introduce political and economic reforms simultaneously (Orenstein 2001).

As Poland began the transition to democracy, the economy was in deep crisis, marked by "falling production, profound shortages, rising external debt, and deterioration in social services" (Millard 1999, 143). The budget deficit was sky-high and prices approached hyperinflation. In 1989 and 1990, for example, inflation rates reached 264 percent and 586 percent respectively (Secretariat 2000). Unemployment rates in the early years of Poland's democratic transition rose rapidly, as the rate of unemployment grew from less than 7 percent in 1990 to over 16 percent in 1993 (Secretariat 2000). In response, strikes erupted all over the country. The new democratic government had to confront the economic crisis head-on and do it quickly, implementing radical free market reforms. On January 1, 1990, a team of Polish economists and foreign advisers introduced an economic reform strategy known as Poland's "shock therapy." Shock therapy provided for a rapid and painful transition to a free market economy. Its main components included balancing the country's budget, control of inflation, conversion of the Polish *zloty*, limitations on wage growth, liberalization of trade and prices, curtailment of trade subsidies, and privatization (Orenstein 2001).

Under shock therapy, the standard of living of the majority of Poles plummeted. Public outrage over the reforms' effects translated into anger with the Solidarity government. The 1990 presidential election "turned into an early referendum on the progress of the transition" (Orenstein 2001, 37), but presidential candidate Lech Walesa was able to sidestep public anger by blaming the prime minister for the economic crisis. Once reelected, however, Walesa continued the reforms. Future governments tempered Walesa's approach and remained committed to free market reforms while at the same time attempting to ease the social costs of the country's economic transition. This approach was facilitated by the stabilization of key economic indicators by the mid-1990s, such as unemployment and inflation.

What made free market reforms so appealing, despite their cost? How did these reforms influence democratization? Here, private enterprise played an important role, but again, in a different way than classic democratic theory suggests. In communist Poland, private enterprise was virtually non-existent. Given the imminent collapse of the communist economy by 1989, private enterprise appeared to be a viable means of salvaging the Polish economy. Promoters promised privatization would modernize the economy, stimulate economic growth, reduce unemployment, improve Poles' standards of living, and provide a foundation for the creation of the middle class. Privatization was also propelled by expectations from the European Union prior to Poland's accession to the EU community (Dempsey 2010).

Privatization also became an important incentive for many former Communists to embrace democracy. The process of transitioning from state-owned to privately owned enterprises was often plagued with extensive corruption. The prevalence of corruption worked to the advantage of Communist elites, who were often able to leverage their political power during this process and transform that power into economic power under the new democratic, capitalist state. The promise of private enterprise converted former Communists into ardent capitalists and subsequent democrats.

The toll of privatization reforms eroded the power of one of democracy's former champions, however. Contrary to the theoretical expectations of democratic theorists, the working class, not the middle class, led much of the drive for democracy. Indeed, 45 years of communist rule impeded the development of a middle class, as one of the ideological tenets of communism is the basic financial and social equality of all people (Weltrowska 2002). In the absence of a true middle class, the working class actively pursued political reform, organizing strikes and protests particularly under the auspices of Solidarity. The political and economic transformations of the 1990s shook the country's social structure, however (Bonusiak 2008). The working class that formed the heart of Poland's social structure under communism, and was instrumental in stimulating the sweeping changes of 1989, lost its importance under the new system (Bonusiak 2008). Still, these economic and political transformations did foster the creation of the Polish middle class, despite persistent problems of inequality.

Twenty years after the simultaneous transition to democracy and capitalism, it is clear Poland has successfully liberalized its economy and fully transitioned from a centrally planned economy to a free market one. Despite their initial drop in the early 1990s, real net wages and living standards have been on the rise in post-communist Poland. Average assessments hide the great polarization of wealth that has come to characterize Polish society. Still, contemporary Poland has one of the most successful economies in post-communist Europe. During the global financial crisis of 2008, Poland did not plunge into a recession, as did many of its EU counterparts (Dempsey 2010). It managed to post a rise in gross domestic product even at the height of the economic crisis, and was expected to enjoy positive growth in the near future (Dempsey 2010).

Education

Poland's communist education system served up heavy doses of indoctrination, but it also succeeded in maintaining high levels of education throughout the population. On the eve of democratization, Poland's adult literacy rate was 98 percent (UNDP 1990). Thus, the new democratic system inherited a highly educated population. Still, like many other parts of Polish society, the post-communist education system (including schools, students, parents, teachers, and principals), had to be transformed to fit the new realities of a democratic society (Hejwosz 2009).

Democrats recognized the need for educational reform early on, but ten years elapsed before meaningful reforms were implemented. Reformers aimed to increase the number of Poles graduating from high school, equalize educational opportunities, and improve the quality of instruction to include not only information but also the development of skills and character (Winiarski 2005). The school financing system was transferred to local governments and the number of teachers was significantly reduced. Reformers developed new educational programs and updated textbooks to reflect the realities of the new political system (Czubinski 2002). Communist propaganda and occasional outright lies had to be excised from textbooks (Winiarski 2005). Conversely, omissions of important events and players in Polish history had to be integrated or reintegrated into the new textbooks. In contrast to communist-era educational approaches emphasizing rote memorization, the new educational programs prioritized creative thinking and understanding.

These reforms were so controversial that they spurred particularly intense protests when initially announced (Czubinski 2002). Once enacted, however, these reforms have had positive implications for education. Historically, only a relatively small number of adults have had the opportunity to attend college, but the number of students enrolled in institutions of higher education has almost quintupled from 1990 and 2006 (Bonusiak 2008). The improvements in educational attainment and quality have had salutary consequences for Polish democracy. For example, the well-educated tend to have greater tolerance for diversity, be it ethnic or religious, as well as higher levels of support for the rights of political dissenters (Golebiowska 2004, 2006, 2009).

International context

The international context has long shaped Poland's political development, and the 1989 transition to democracy is no exception. First, democratization processes in Poland's Eastern European neighbors helped propel Poles' quest for freedom. In 1989, Poland was part of a cohort of countries dismantling communist practices and replacing them with democratic ones. Democratization processes began in Hungary even before the Roundtable Talks began, and subsequent events in Poland mirrored those in Czechoslovakia, East Germany, Romania, and Bulgaria. In this climate, the push for reform in Poland picked up additional momentum (Dudek 1997).

Second, internal changes within the Soviet Union also advanced the Polish cause. When Soviet leader Mikhail Gorbachev unveiled his domestic reforms of *glasnost* (political openness) and *perestroika* (economic restructuring), he triggered grassroots movements calling for economic and political reform throughout the Eastern Bloc. Even more importantly, Gorbachev's decision to stop interfering in the internal politics of Eastern Europe emboldened Polish opposition and gave Poland's Communist Party leaders an incentive to reform (Czubinski 2002). The absence of Soviet tanks created space for reformers.

The European Union also deserves credit for promoting democracy in Poland. Joining the EU became one of the most important goals of Polish foreign policy in the post-1989 world. Poland's leaders saw the integration of Poland into the European Community (termed "Coming back to Europe") as an important means for facilitating Poland's economic and political transition. Poles hoped they would receive significant economic aid from their alliance with the EU (and they have) to help complete their economic, political, and technological transformations (Domagala 2008).

Pre-accession conditions also helped, as Poland was expected to stabilize its political situation and strengthen democratic institutions before it could even enter into negotiations regarding accession (Domagala 2008). Member countries are expected to establish the rule of law, guarantee human rights and respect for minority rights, and allow political pluralism. For example, EU pressure facilitated the formal codification of legal protections for Poland's ethnic, national, and religious minorities (Bajda, Syposz, and Wojakowski 2002; Malicka 2004). Still, in some instances Poland's relationship with the EU has had unanticipated consequences for democracy. For example, Poland's accession initially strengthened some antidemocratic movements that saw accession as a threat to Poland's independence (Kolarska-Babinska 2003).[4] Indeed, in June 2006, the European Parliament noted a significant rise of racial intolerance and xenophobia in Poland (Domagala 2008).

Conclusions

Twenty years after representatives of Poland's then-ruling Communist Party and its political opposition sat down to negotiate some measure of political and economic reforms, most people would agree that Poland today has a consolidated democracy. Poland's success reaffirms some conventional wisdom of democratic theory. Major changes in the international context opened the door for democratic reform. Elites and a highly educated civil society took advantage of this opportunity and played a crucial role in the transition to democracy. Democracy advocates inherited some authoritarian institutions, but these features did not derail democratization. Rather, as elites across the ideological spectrum agreed on the basic tenets of democratic governance, authoritarian practices were whittled away and institutions were reformed to promote good governance. Finally, economic development featured prominently in Poland's democratic transition, but played its role quite differently than democratic theorists might predict. The belief that private enterprise was the only viable means to salvage the economy and bring about a better quality of life swayed potential authoritarians into the democratic camp.

Additional resources

CNN's 1998 24-part documentary, *Cold War*, provides an excellent account of the demise of communism in Eastern Europe and its aftermath, particularly in parts 23 and 24. Archival footage and interviews provide important insights into the work of both elites and civil society. For contemporary coverage of Polish politics, see one of Poland's largest and most influential daily newspapers, *Gazeta Wyborcza* (*Electoral Gazette*), available online at www.gazeta.pl/0,0.html.

Notes

1 PZPR or Polish United Workers' Party (*Polska Zjednoczona Partia Robotnicza*), ZSL or United People's Party (*Zjednoczone Stronnictwo Ludowe*), and SLD or Left Democratic Alliance (*Sojusz Lewicy Demokratycznej*).

2 This was an alliance of Solidarity and approximately 20 small right-wing parties.

3 Estimates vary depending on the source. The most recent national census (2002) estimates the number of Jews to be only around 1,000. Ethnic group representatives claim a much more significant presence.

4 Representatives of these reactionary forces were even elected to the European Parliament. Maciej Giertych, later an LPR candidate for Polish president, gained notoriety for his openly anti-Semitic remarks while serving in the European Parliament (Domagala 2008).

References

Anti-Defamation League. 2007. "ADL Survey in Six European Countries Finds Anti-Semitic Attitudes Up: Most Believe Jews More Loyal to Israel than Home Country" (accessed on September 12, 2010). www.adl.org/PresRele/ASInt_13/5099_13.htm.

Bajda, P., M. Syposz, and D. Wojakowski. 2002. "Equality in law, protection in fact: Minority law and practice in Poland." In *Diversity in Action: Local Public Management of Multi-Ethnic Communities in Central and Eastern Europe*, edited by Anna-Mária Biró and Petra Kovács. Budapest: LGI Books.

Bonusiak, Wlodzimierz. 2008. *Trzecia Rzeczpospolita (Third Republic) (1989–2007)*. Rzeszow: Wydawnictwo Uniwersytetu Rzeszowskiego.

CBOS (Center for the Study of Public Opinion). 2006. Data file.

CBOS report. Feb 2009. "Opinie o Funkcjonowaniu Demokracji w Polsce." (Opinions about the Functioning of Democracy in Poland). www.cbos.pl/SPISKOM.POL/2009/K_020_09.PDF (accessed on July 20, 2010).

Curtis, Glenn E. 1992. "Poland: A Country Study." *Washington: GPO for the Library of Congress*. http://countrystudies.us/poland/14.htm (accessed on September 12, 2010).

Czesnik, Mikolaj. 2009. "Voter Turnout Stability—Evidence from Poland." *Polish Sociological Review* 1(165): 107–22.

Czesnik, Mikolaj. 2007. *Partycypacja Wyborcza w Polsce: Perspektywa Porownawcza*. (Political Participation in Poland: Comparative Perspective) Warsaw: Wydawnictwo Naukowe Scholar.

Czubinski, Antoni. 2002. *Historia Polski 1864–2001. (History of Poland 1864–2001)*. Wroclaw: Ossolineum.

Dempsey, Judy. 2010. "Renewed Push for Privatization in Poland." www.nytimes.com/2010/05/24/business/global/24iht-rdbeurpol.html?_r=1&ref=privatization (accessed May 23, 2010).

Domagala, Arkadiusz. 2008. *Integracja Polski z Unia Europejska. (Poland's Integration into the European Union)*.Warsaw: Wydawnictwa Akademickie i Profesjonalne.

Dudek, Antoni. 1997. *Pierwsze Lata III Rzeczpospolitej 1989–1995. (First Years of the Third Republic 1989–1995)*. Krakow: GEO.

Ekiert, Grzegorz. 1991. "Democratization Processes in East Central Europe: A Theoretical Reconsideration." *British Journal of Political Science* 21: 285–313.

Ekiert, Grzegorz, and Jan Kubik. 2009. "Civil Society in Poland: Case Study." Paper presented at the *International Conference: The Logic of Civil Society in New Democracies: East Asia and East Europe*. Academia Sinica, Taipei, June 6–7, 2009.

Ekiert, Grzegorz, and Jan Kubik. 1999. *Rebellious Civil Society: Popular Protest and Democratic Consolidation in Poland, 1989–1993*. Ann Arbor: University of Michigan Press.

Gazeta Wyborcza. 2006. "Protesty przeciw Ministrowi Edukacji Romanowi Giertychowi–Raport. (Protests against Education Minister Roman Giertych – A Report)" http://wyborcza.pl/1,76842,3351386.html (accessed on May 17, 2010).

Gebert, K. 1991. "Rola Antysemityzmu (The role of anti-Semitism)." In *Bitwa o Belweder (The Battle for Belweder)*, edited by M. Grabowska and I. Krzemiński, Warsaw: MYŚL.

Golebiowska, Ewa A. 2009. "Ethnic and Religious Tolerance in Poland." *East European Politics and Societies*, 23(3): 371–91.

Golebiowska, Ewa A. 2008. "Norm evolution in Polish society and politics." Unpublished manuscript.

Golebiowska, Ewa A. 2006. "Poles' Support for the Rights of Political Dissenters." *Polish Sociological Review*, 2(154): 231–42.

Golebiowska, Ewa A. 2004. "Religious Tolerance in Poland." *International Journal of Public Opinion Research*, 16(4): 391–416.

Grabowska, Miroslawa, and Tadeusz Szawiel. 2001. *Budowanie Demokracji: Podzialy Spoleczne, Partie Polityczne, i Spoleczenstwo Obywatelskie w Postkomunistycznej Polsce. (Building Democracy: Social Divisions, Political Parties, and Civic Society in Postcommunist Poland)*. Warsaw: Wydawnictwo Naukowe PWN.

Graczyk, Roman. 1997. *Konstytucja dla Polski: Tradycje, Doswiadczenia, Spory. (Constitution for Poland: Traditions, Experiences, and Conflicts)*. Warsaw: Fundacja im. Stefana Batorego.

Grzymala-Busse, Anna, and Joshua Tucker. 2010. "Transitions: The Unlikely Triumph of Polish Democracy." *The New Republic online*, April 12, 2010

Hejwosz, Daria. 2009. "System Oswiaty w Polsce po 20 Latach—Under Construction. (Poland's Education System after 20 Years—Under Construction." www.liberte.pl/spoeczestwo/612-reformaszkolnictwa-wyszego-w-polsce-krok-w-dobrym-kierunku.html (accessed on September 12, 2010).

Kolarska-Babinska, Lena. 2003. "The EU Accession and Strengthening of Institutions in East Central Europe: The Case of Poland." *East European Politics and Societies* 17(1): 91–98.

Krzemiński, I., ed. 2004. *Antysemityzm w Polsce i na Ukrainie: Raport z Badań (Anti-Semitism in Poland and Ukraine: A Research Report)*. Warsaw: Wydawnictwo Naukowe Scholar.

Kulish, Nicholas, and Clifford Levy. 2010. "Poland Mourns Nation's Loss, but Begins to Rebuild." *The New York Times*, April 11, 2010.

Malicka, Agnieszka. 2004. *Ochrona Mniejszosci Narodowych—Standardy Miedzynarodowe i Rozwiazania Polskie. [Protection of National Minorities—International Standards and Polish Approaches]*. Wroclaw: Wydawnictwo Uniwersytetu Wroclawskiego.

Millard, Frances. 1999. *Polish Politics and Society*. London: Routledge Studies of Societies in Transition.

O'Dwyer, Conor. 2010. "From Conditionality to Persuasion? Europeanization and the Rights of Sexual Minorities in Postaccession Poland." *Forthcoming in Journal of European Integration*.

Orenstein, Mitchell. 2001. *Out of the Red: Building Capitalism and Democracy in Postcommunist Europe*. Ann Arbor: The University of Michigan Press.

Paczynska, Agnieszka. 2005. "Inequality, Political Participation, and Democratic Deepening in Poland." *East European Politics and Societies* 19(4): 573–613.

Pew Global Attitudes Project. (2008). "Unfavorable Views of Jews and Muslims on the Increase in Europe." http://pewglobal.org/reports/display.php?ReportID=262 (accessed on September 12, 2010).

Secretariat. 2000. "Poland: Evolution of Major Economic Indicators from 1989 to 1998." In *The Polish Experience of Transition: Accomplishments and Problems*. Round Table held on June 7, 1999 at the Palais des Nations, Geneva, Switzerland. United Nations Economic Commission for Europe: Geneva/New York.

Starnawski. 2003. "Nationalist Discourse and the Ultra-Conservative Press in Contemporary Poland: a Case Study of Nasz Dziennik." *Patterns of Prejudice* 37(1): 65–81.

Tworzecki, Hubert. 2008. "A Disaffected Democracy? Identities, Institutions, and Civic Engagement in Post-Communist Poland." *Communist and Post-Communist Studies* 41: 47–62.

Tworzecki, Hubert. 2002. *Learning to Choose: Electoral Politics in East-Central Europe*. Stanford: Stanford University Press.

United Nations Development Program (UNDP). 1990. "Human Development Indicators 1990". http://hdr.undp.org/en/media/hdr_1990_en_indicators1.pdf (accessed on August 11, 2010).

Weltrowska, Justyna. 2002. "Economic Change and Social Polarization in Poland." *European Urban and Regional Studies* 9(1): 47–52.

Wilczak, J. 2002. "Kto Ty Jestes? (Who Are You?)" *Polityka* 16 (2346).

Winiarski, Jozef. 2005. "Reforma Systemu Edukacji w Zderzeniu z Praktyka Szkolna. (Educational system reform in Poland in conflict with educational practice)" www.wychowawca.pl/miesiecznik_nowy/2005/09–2005/01.htm (accessed on September 12, 2010).

Photo by author of the Khulumani Support Group, an apartheid survivors' group, at the launch of an art exhibit at the Slave Lodge, Cape Town, in July 2006. Khulumani is one of the organizations that make up South Africa's thriving civil society.

12

South Africa's Miraculous Transition to Democracy

Emily Rodio

South Africa's transition to democracy is often called miraculous. For decades, a repressive, racist oligarchy ruled the country, privileging the white minority population at the expense of the impoverished black majority.[1] This racial system, known as *apartheid*, created the world's most systematically segregated society and became synonymous with massive human rights violations. The regime clung to power despite an organized, domestic resistance that eventually swelled to a global antiapartheid movement. Finally, in 1990, resistance leader Nelson Mandela triumphantly walked out of his prison cell to begin negotiations for a new democratic system. In 1994, South Africa held its first ever inclusive, multiparty, democratic elections. South Africa's successful transition to democracy defies its history of division and challenges many classic theories of democratization. This chapter demonstrates the pivotal role of the international community, civil society, and key elites in South Africa's political transformation.

The apartheid state

South Africa's apartheid system and unique racial dynamics were rooted in its history of colonialism. Indigenous African populations had long inhabited the region, and in 1652 the Dutch East India Company brought the first white settlers to South Africa, establishing the Cape Colony in present day Cape Town. The Dutch also brought slavery to Cape Town, transporting slaves from India and southern Asia. South Africa's modern Coloureds are of mixed race, the descendents of the indigenous blacks, Dutch, and slave populations. In 1806, the British took over the Cape Colony, and continued ongoing Dutch battles with indigenous black populations.

To escape skirmishes with the British, the Dutch began a mass movement out of the Cape Colony into the interior part of the state, later glorified as the "the Great Trek" of the 1830s. By this point, the Dutch had developed culturally into a unique white-African population, known as the Afrikaners or Boers. The Afrikaner trek eastward resulted in the establishment of two independent Boer republics and strained Boer-black relations as white settlers moved deeper and deeper into indigenous territory. Tension among the British, the Afrikaners, and the blacks escalated with the discovery of diamonds in 1867 and gold in 1884. The competition for these resources resulted in the suppression of the indigenous black population. After the British triumphed over the Dutch in the Boer Wars, South Africa went on to become a dominion of Great Britain in 1910.

At this point, the first formal steps toward political apartheid emerged. While English-speaking whites and the Afrikaners disagreed politically in the aftermath of the Boer Wars, they were unified in their desire to protect white interests. In 1913, the whites-only "democratic" government passed the Native Lands Act, which declared that blacks could only own land in designated "reserves." These reserves amounted to 7 percent of South African land (Butler, Rotberg, and Adams 1978). A policy of "Civilized Labor" followed the Land Areas Act, which institutionalized a system of favoritism for white workers by forbidding blacks to join unions and setting a rigid color bar for skilled labor. Additional pieces of legislation followed, slowly solidifying segregation in all aspects of life.

World War II challenged this pact between English-speaking whites, represented by the South African Party (SAP), and Afrikaners, mobilized under the National Party (NP). English-speaking whites were eager to fight alongside the British, while the Afrikaners prioritized neutrality. Eventually, South Africa joined the Allies and fought against the Axis. Despite Allied victory, the SAP's power declined as South Africa struggled to recover economically after the war.

In 1948, the NP emerged victorious in the so-called Black Peril election, playing on white fears over increasing black urbanization and the industrialization of the war period. Once in power, the NP instituted the formal system of apartheid or "apartness," a system of complete political, social, and economic segregation. As Thompson (2000) explains, apartheid advocated "separate development," whereby South Africa's four "racial groups" (White, Coloured, Indian, and African) would develop to the best of their abilities through separation. The "African" racial group was further divided into ten distinct ethnic groupings. Apartheid deemed the white racial group superior, and therefore best-suited to determine all policy for the other groups. Not surprisingly, white interests prevailed.

To institute apartheid, the NP passed a series of laws in the early 1950s, creating two forms of apartheid: petty and grand. Petty apartheid separated all aspects of public and private life by race. For example, the 1949 Immorality Act and the 1950 Prohibition of Mixed Marriages Act banned marriage and sexual relations between whites and other racial groups. The 1953 Reservation of Separate Amenities Act segregated public spaces, vehicles, and services according to race. Grand apartheid went even further, organizing the territorial division of South Africa along racial and ethnic lines. Grand apartheid sought to separate "white South Africa" from what it called black "homelands." The 1950 Population Registration Act, the organizational basis for grand apartheid, required that every South African be categorized by racial group and subgroup. On this foundation, the Group Areas Act of 1950 formalized residential segregation, extending the existing "reserves" of the 1913 Native Lands Act to create ten compulsory black "homelands" or "Bantustans."[2] Grand apartheid assigned members of each racial group to a homeland, where they were given citizenship. The homelands constituted only 13 percent of South Africa's land (the least desirable), and contained approximately 75 percent of the population (Butler, Rotberg, and Adams 1978). The establishment of such segregation required the mass relocation of peoples. To accomplish this, the apartheid regime undertook "forced removals" of blacks from their homes, as witnessed in the infamous cases of Sophiatown, Johannesburg, and the multiracial District Six, Cape Town.

The apartheid state sought to ensure its existence in two significant ways: education and dehumanization. The 1953 Bantu Education Act created a centralized educational system for blacks, which became a resource-deprived system to foster the creation of submissive, manual workers. The educational system also furthered the apartheid strategy of "divide and conquer" by requiring that each homeland be instructed in the local language. In addition, apartheid sought to systematically dehumanize the black population by depriving them of basic freedoms and imposing an atmosphere of constant fear. For example, passbooks were a mandated identification system that recorded one's race, ethnicity, employment, and travel permissions. Passbook raids and the bureaucratic difficulties of keeping one's book "in order" created a degrading system.

The resistance movement

South Africa's resistance movement predates the formal inauguration of apartheid in 1948. Early opposition organizations include the African National Congress (ANC), the Congress Youth League (CYL), the South African Indian Congress (SAIC), the Pan Africanist Congress (PAC), and the South African Communist Party (SACP). These groups formed in the early twentieth century, growing organizationally and structurally to respond to increasing repression. From the early twentieth century until the 1960s, antiapartheid resistance was a peaceful, cross-racial resistance movement relying on policies of passive resistance (e.g., boycotts, strikes, and civil disobedience campaigns). For example, to protest apartheid the 1949 Program of Action and May Day Strike and 1951 Defiance Campaign utilized civil disobedience and work stoppages. Both campaigns resulted in the arrest of thousands and drew the attention of the international community, particularly the United Nations. In 1955, 3,000 representatives from resistance organizations gathered at the Congress of the People's national meeting to draft and sign the Freedom Charter, a document calling for a nonracial South Africa with political, social, and economic rights for all.[3] White South African groups also joined the resistance, such as the Black Sash, an organization of white women who often protested outside parliament.

The apartheid regime responded to growing resistance with ever harsher repression. In 1956, the government charged 156 leaders of the resistance movement with treason, successfully cutting off communication between the leadership and the masses for five years before acquitting all of them (Mandela 1994). New legislation empowered the government to declare a state of emergency and ban resistance organizations. In 1960, the government responded to a peaceful anti-passbook campaign in Sharpeville and Langa townships with gunfire; police killed 69 people, most of whom were shot in the back as they were running away. The government then banned the ANC and PAC under the Unlawful Organization Act of 1960. The 1962 Sabotage Act, 1963 General Law Amendment Act, and 1967 Terrorism Act further expanded police powers to draconian levels. Powers of detentions without warrant expanded just as access to lawyers and trials was curtailed.

The deaths at Sharpeville spurred the resistance movement to engage in guerilla warfare and sabotage against the government. The ANC and PAC each created armed wings, *Umkhonto we Sizwe* (MK) and *Poqo*, respectively. In 1963, a raid on MK's headquarters led to the arrest of key ANC leaders, including Nelson Mandela. The Rivonia Trial, named after the headquarters of the raided MK, resulted in guilty verdicts and life sentences for eight resistance leaders. In his famous "Statement from the Dock" at the Rivonia Trial, Mandela brought international attention to the horrors of apartheid.

The turning point

In 1976, the Soweto Uprising marked the turning of the tide against the apartheid regime. In response to the Afrikaans Language Decree, which required that half of all school subjects be taught in Afrikaans (seen as the language of the oppressor), new student organizations like the South African Students' Organization (SASO) responded with a mass march in Soweto (South West Township) outside Johannesburg. The police responded brutally, killing and injuring students. The protest in Soweto triggered a year-long violent uprising that spread to the rest of South Africa. Thousands of youth fled South Africa to train with MK and Poqo in camps throughout Southern Africa.

The already repressive apartheid regime turned even more brutal in Soweto's aftermath. First, it banned all student organizations, including SASO, and declared illegal all forms of outdoor meetings.[4] The apartheid regime also sought to silence the leaders of resistance, as it had done to the previous generation with the Treason and Rivonia Trials. In 1977, Steve Biko, the charismatic leader of SASO, was killed in police custody. On a larger scale, the new prime minister, P. W. Botha, initiated a policy aptly called "Total Onslaught, Total Strategy." Botha argued that communists, both domestic and international, were conspiring to seize power in South Africa in a "total onslaught." As such, South Africa needed to respond in kind with a "total strategy." The government initiated a full military buildup, including: compulsory conscription for all white males, the creation of a state arms industry, and active raids on "communist" leaders in exile. South Africa, in essence, became a militarized state.

At the same time, the Botha government also engaged in reform, lessening some of the petty apartheid laws and extending greater freedoms to the Coloured and Indian communities in an attempt to curry favor. In 1983, Botha's government wrote a new constitution, which created a presidential democracy and established a Tricameral Parliament comprised of three racially classified houses: a House of Assembly for whites, a House of Representatives for Coloureds, and a House of Delegates for Indians.[5] While each house had control over its "own" affairs, in reality, the white House of Assembly retrained control over all major issue areas. The blatant absence of a black house of parliament led to a substantial backlash from the resistance community. As Alexis de Tocqueville appropriately warned over a century before, "the most perilous moment for a bad government is when it seeks to mend its ways" (cited in Sparks 1995).

To respond to the 1983 Tricameral Parliament, the antiapartheid resistance movement formed the United Democratic Front (UDF), a nonracial alliance of some 400 national, regional, and local organizations. In 1984, the UDF initiated massive "township revolts," rendering the townships ungovernable. In 1985, the government issued a state of emergency, using its extensive powers to arrest, interrogate, search, detain, censor, and use force. The South African Defense Force (SADF) patrolled townships, and the country appeared on the cusp of civil war.

Negotiations: Secret and public

Throughout the 1980s, secret negotiations to end apartheid commenced in South Africa and throughout the world. In South Africa, the government transported Nelson Mandela, leader of the ANC and MK, from Robben Island to prisons in the Cape Town area so that he could engage in secret talks. In his autobiography, Mandela chronicles 47 meetings with Hendrik Jacobus Coetsee, the minister of justice, while still a prisoner (Mandela 1994). In 1989, Mandela even met secretly with President Botha. Secret negotiations on a political transition occurred simultaneously in places like London, Senegal, Zimbabwe, and Switzerland. Exiled leaders of the ANC, such as Oliver Tambo, met with members of the white South African government, academic community, business community, and even the

Broederbond, the secret Afrikaner organization whose members effectively controlled apartheid in South Africa.

By the end of 1989, the government began making public steps towards dismantling apartheid. After President Botha suffered a stroke, President F. W. de Klerk took office. In his first address to Parliament on February 2, 1990, de Klerk lifted the ban on resistance organizations and the ANC, freed Nelson Mandela and other political prisoners, and committed the South African government to negotiations for a democratic system. Eight days later, Nelson Mandela walked out of the gates of Victor-Vester prison to domestic and international applause.

Over the next four years, South Africa's government and the resistance movement negotiated the terms of a new democratic government. The Convention for a Democratic South Africa (CODESA I and II) provided a framework for multiparty talks from 1991–94. At CODESA, the parties agreed the convention would draw up an interim constitution, which would serve as the basis for the final constitution to be written by the newly elected government. During CODESA, there were numerous setbacks. Violence between black parties, such as the ANC and Inkatha Freedom Party (IFP), threatened the negotiation process. The revelation that the apartheid government was the mysterious "third force" funding and prodding the IFP further jeopardized talks.[6] While elites struggled over a 4-year period to construct a new democratic government, an estimated 14,000 people were killed due to political violence (Truth and Reconciliation Final Report, vol. 2, 1998). Ultimately the violence did not derail democracy, however, and negotiations successfully created an interim government, setting the stage for the future multiparty, majority rule system.

Transition to democracy

In 1994, South Africans elected Nelson Mandela to the presidency in the country's first multiparty, multiracial, democratic elections. Since then, South Africa has become an established electoral democracy with substantial rights protections. Indeed, the South African constitution boasts one of the world's most extensive bill of rights, protecting speech, expression, press, and labor while prohibiting discrimination. South Africa's long history of resistance bequeathed a thriving civil society and culture of protest to the new democracy. However, democracy still faces stiff challenges. Apartheid's legacy includes an enormous inequality of wealth and high levels of poverty. The ANC's domination has also led to corruption, even alleged claims against current president, Jacob Zuma. In addition, South Africa's rates of violent crime and HIV/AIDS infections are among the highest in the world. Finally, even with reconciliation efforts, divisions persist among races, as well as between South Africans and immigrants.

Despite current problems, largely due to apartheid's legacy, South Africa has successfully transitioned to democratic governance. How exactly was this transition achieved? What best explains South Africa's radical move from racial oligarchy to liberal democracy? Several traditional theories of democratization, particularly those highlighting economic factors and education, do not do justice to the South African case. However, as the following sections explain, key changes in elites, civil society, national unity, and international context culminated in South Africa's transition.

State institutions

When the new, post-apartheid government came to power in April 1994, it eliminated the state institutions affiliated with the old apartheid regime. However, the pacted nature of South Africa's transition allowed the outgoing National Party to have a substantial voice in the structure of the new democracy. As neither the apartheid government nor the resistance movement achieved a full "victory" in the internal struggle, both groups had enough power to shape the transition and the new government. The resulting power-sharing government, the Government of National Unity (GNU), ultimately limited and structured the permanent, majority-rule government. Still, the South African case cautions against overly deterministic interpretations involving state institutions. State institutions most certainly set the stage for democratic governance, but elites and civil society still had room to operate.

The negotiations from 1990–94 largely hinged on one key issue: whether South Africa would be a power-sharing or a majority-rule democracy. The outgoing apartheid regime wanted to retain as much power as possible in a power-sharing government that reserved seats and positions for the opposition, which would soon include the NP. The ANC, on the other hand, wanted a clear majority-rule government that would allocate seats and positions on the basis of electoral results. Joe Slovo of the SACP salvaged negotiations from numerous roadblocks by proposing a "sunset clause" that created a Government of National Unity (GNU), or a power-sharing arrangement, for the first five years. After this period, power-sharing gave way to a system of majority rule. In addition, CODESA, the nonelected, multiparty negotiating forum, produced the interim constitution that would serve as the foundation for a final constitution.

The interim constitution outlined the structure of both the government of national unity and the final majority-rule government. It included a bicameral legislature, comprised of the National Assembly and Senate. Citizens elect their 400 National Assembly representatives through a system of proportional representation, with a low threshold for party inclusion. The National Assembly in turn elects the president and head of state. The Senate originally formed the upper legislative house, and included 90 representatives (ten from each of the nine newly established provinces).[7] Under the interim constitution, these 490 legislators also formed the Constitutional Assembly (CA), charged with drafting the final constitution within the span of two years. For approval, the final constitution required a two-thirds parliamentary majority and certification by the Constitutional Court.

The results of the 1994 election gave the ANC a clear majority—62 percent of the popular vote. With 20 percent of the votes, the NP came in second, followed by the IFP with 10 percent. The Freedom Front, the right wing umbrella Afrikaner Party, garnered a paltry 2 percent. Given the power-sharing arrangement, the Cabinet of the GNU included twelve ANC representatives, six NP representatives, and three IFP representatives. In addition, Thabo Mbeki (ANC) and F. W. de Klerk were appointed deputy presidents. The presence of the National Party in the executive power of the new democracy was part of the grand compromise, the sunset clause, which allowed for a power-sharing arrangement until the next election in 1999.

The interim constitution also made provisions for the judiciary, which had been debilitated under apartheid. These provisions included the Constitutional Court, to ensure parliamentary legislation would be consistent with the constitution. The Constitutional Court did not hesitate to exercise its newfound judicial independence, rejecting the first draft of the "final constitution" for failing to uphold the 34 required constitutional principles of the interim constitution.

The GNU and interim constitution set the institutional foundation for democratic governance, but the GNU itself and the final constitution were not overly limited by that foundation. First, the GNU changed substantially in May of 1996 when the NP withdrew to formally pursue the role of opposition. With this, the NP relinquished its right to cabinet seats in the power-sharing government. Second, the final constitution substantially expanded the Bill of Rights of the interim constitution, providing additional safeguards for individual rights, such as the equality clause (stipulating equality both in law and in impact) and protection from discrimination in both the public and private sphere. The newly elected government was not restricted by the more limited protections the NP had favored in the interim constitution.

South Africa's new democratic system is a clear antithesis of its apartheid predecessor. The proportional representation electoral system allows for many voices and parties, and the constitution provides for extensive rights and protections. At the same time, however, the institutional design of proportional representation has contributed to ANC dominance. Consolidated democracies require the peaceful transition of power from one party to another, and at this point, South Africa has yet to see an opposition party gain the presidential office. In sum, the pacted negotiation shaped the institutional makeup of South African democracy, but this course was not irrevocable. Actors, particularly elites, had room to maneuver within this institutional framework.

Elites

Generally speaking, theories of political science shy away from focusing heavily on specific individuals. However, the case of South Africa illustrates exactly how much influence individuals can have on political development, as particular elites played a major role in South Africa's democratic transition. While many of the world's academics and observers predicted the outbreak of civil war in South Africa, key leaders instead negotiated a pacted transition. Most theories of elite-fostered transitions focus on political parties or groupings, and these most certainly did play an important role in South Africa's transition. However, particular individuals warrant special attention, as it is difficult to properly understand South Africa's transition without the examination of two key players: Nelson Mandela and F. W. de Klerk.

As a leader of the ANC and MK, Mandela shaped the resistance struggle. However, his imprisonment in 1963 and his resulting inability to communicate directly with the resistance elevated him to new heights domestically and internationally. His legend grew in his absence. By the time of his release in 1990, Mandela had reached almost cult-personality proportions. Mandela could have used his impassioned following for personal gain, solidifying his power and hold on the reins of government. He could have chosen to continue the armed struggle, to "drive the white man into the sea," as many whites feared. He could have sought revenge on the white population. Instead, he came out of prison voicing a message of unity and reconciliation. In addition, after one term in office, Mandela did not run again. Had Mandela had the drive for personal gain, such as that of Robert Mugabe in neighboring Zimbabwe, the state of South Africa could be very different today.

F. W. de Klerk's individual decisions also shook South African politics. From a prominent Afrikaner family with a history of high-ranking NP political appointments, de Klerk was deeply ingrained in apartheid ideology. Yet, upon assuming power in 1990, he took major steps toward democratic transition. Today, it is well known that no one had access to de Klerk's 1990 monumental address to Parliament before he gave it (Sparks 1995). No one knew exactly what de Klerk had planned. When de Klerk spoke, he declared:

> [T]he Government will accord the process of negotiation the highest priority. The aim is a totally new and just constitutional dispensation in which every inhabitant will enjoy equal rights, treatment and opportunity in every sphere of endeavor—constitutional, social and economic. . . . The Government accepts the principle of the recognition and protection of the fundamental individuals rights which form the constitutional basis for most Western democracies.[8]

Had P. W. Botha remained in power, or had a different member of the NP gained the presidency, the transition may not have occurred when it did (if at all).

Today's elites have been shaped by apartheid and the battle against it, and have struggled to adapt to the new post-apartheid period and its challenges. While the ANC continues to win supermajorities in elections, it must also confront many of the challenges facing resistance-turned-political party organizations. Most importantly, resistance organizations are unified forces confronting an "external" enemy; this overshadows the differences of factions within the organization. Once this enemy is defeated, however, factional differences surface. While Mandela unified the ANC from 1994–99, cracks began to surface in 1999, under two individuals: Thabo Mbeki the "technocrat" and Jacob Zuma the "man of the people."

Elected president in 1999, Thabo Mbeki represents the technocratic wing of the ANC. At the age of 20, Mbeki went into exile, where he received advanced degrees and traveled the world pressuring governments to aid the resistance movement. After Mandela's release, Mbeki returned to South Africa after 28 years abroad. Mbeki's presidency is best known for two programs: "African Renaissance," which adopted the neoliberal reforms of the

Washington Consensus, and "Black Economic Empowerment," which aimed to address apartheid's legacy of economic inequality. Mbeki's tenure was also marred by his policies on HIV/AIDS, where he aligned with the denial camp and resisted the use of antiretroviral drugs (Dugger 2008).

In a dramatic turn of events, Mbeki was forced from office in September 2008, seven months before national elections. He was ousted by the more populist wing of the ANC, led by Jacob Zuma, who had defeated Mbeki in the 2007 party leadership elections. In response, Mbeki supporters broke from the ANC and created the Congress of the People (COPE), which won 7 percent of the vote in the 2009 election. Zuma's populist camp of the ANC has powerful backers, including the Congress of South African Trade Unions (COSATU), the SACP, and the left-wing CYL. While Mbeki represents the elite, exiled, and educated population, Zuma represents the uneducated, "in the trenches" masses. Zuma left school after completing the equivalent of fifth grade, joined the ANC, MK, and SACP, and served ten years on Robben Island with Nelson Mandela. After his release, he went into exile in Mozambique and Zambia, where he led the underground resistance movement.

Zuma is a vibrant, charismatic figure who stands in sharp contrast to Mbeki's technocratic style. Yet while Zuma is extremely popular with the majority population, controversy dogs him. South Africa's elite crime-fighting unit, the Directorate of Special Operations, brought charges against Zuma for corruption in a controversial arms deal. After almost five years of investigation and numerous court decisions, investigators finally dropped the case. However, many people (including Archbishop Tutu), question Zuma's innocence, and claims of judicial compromise have emerged.

The NP also sought to transform itself in the new democratic system, taking great pains to distance itself from its apartheid past. Yet, after winning only 2 percent of the vote in the 2004 elections, the freshly named New National Party disbanded in 2005. The main opposition party, the Democratic Alliance (DA), gained momentum after winning 17 percent of the national vote and control of the Western Cape Province (the only province not controlled by the ANC) in 2009. The DA, under the leadership of Helen Zille, receives support primarily from the white and Coloured populations. It advocates a classical liberal agenda supporting small government, individual freedoms, neoliberal economics, and greater local control over policy.

Elites have exerted enormous influence over South Africa's democratic destiny. The post-transition environment has ushered in a new generation of elites, changed traditional internal party dynamics, and altered cross-party alliances. Contemporary elites face considerable challenges constructing new identities and strategies. The greatest remaining challenge is the dominance of the ANC and its tolerance of corruption. The consolidation of democracy, as measured by the turning over of power to a new party, will not occur if the ANC remains one umbrella party.

Political culture

In addition to elites, civil society has also played an important role in South Africa's democratic transition. Organizations like the ANC, SACP, SASO, and UDF were able to harness the power of civil society in the struggle against apartheid. For decades, civil society unleashed campaigns that eventually forced the government to the negotiating table. Though the apartheid regime held the weapons, government offices, finances, and education, it proved no match for the civil society movement.

In the post-apartheid period, civil society also faced the challenge of reshaping its political mission. Dismantling apartheid was no longer the target. Instead, civil society needed to learn to negotiate democratic processes to address the myriad of issues affecting South Africans, such as education, development, health, and jobs. The new democratic government, comprised of many members from the resistance movement, created a legal and political environment conducive to civil society engagement. For example, it created a Directorate for Non-Profit Organization position in government. This new environment, combined with a strong history of civic engagement, has produced a thriving civil society. Recent studies find this sector of South African society is growing in size and influence, with approximately 100,000 organizations to date (Swilling and Russell 2002).

In addition, South Africa's political culture is very supportive of democracy and its institutions. According to the 2008 Afrobarometer public opinion survey, 67 percent of South Africans believe democracy is preferable to any other type of governing system, up from 60 percent in 2000 (Afrobarometer 2009). South Africans demonstrate their support for this system of governance by turning out to vote in high numbers. In 2009, voter turnout was 77 percent of registered voters (Independent Electoral Commission South Africa 2009). This statistic is comparable to other sub-Saharan democracies, such as Namibia and Botswana, and on par with Western democracies like Great Britain and Germany.

South Africans have internalized the norms of democratic governance, but they still express frustration with the actions of government, particularly as they relate to service delivery. Support for government action is highest at the national level (where, under federalism, policies are broader and more abstract), with 73.1 percent of South Africans expressing "a great deal" or "quite a lot" of confidence in the national government (Institute for Justice and Reconciliation 2006). At the local level, however, where many of the national government's policies are actually put into action (or not), South Africans are less confident. Service delivery in the areas of housing, electricity, water, land reform, and education has lagged substantially behind government goals. Apartheid left generations of South Africans uneducated and lacking skills, with the majority of the state's wealth concentrated in the hands of the minority white population. Many see the government as moving too slowly and too inefficiently to correct these imbalances. With an unemployment rate of 24.3 percent and slow delivery of services, many predict that confidence in government institutions will decline as the initial joy of the new democracy wears off (South African StatsOnline 2010).

National unity

Apartheid purposefully polarized every possible cleavage in South Africa's very diverse society, exploiting racial, ethnic, and linguistic differences. Figure 12.1 illustrates the racial breakdown of South African society. Though the black African population makes up 79 percent of the population, it is divided into many ethnic groups, such as Xhosas, Zulus, Sothos, Tswanas, Tsongas, and others. Linguistically, South Africa has 11 official languages, including English, Afrikaans, and nine tribal languages spoken by the black population.

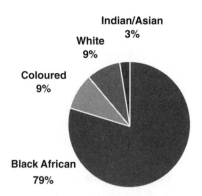

Figure 12.1 South Africa's racial and ethnic groups (*Source*: Statistics South Africa 2009)

Race relations were a focal point during the transition to democracy and continue to be an area of concern. During the transition, Nelson Mandela called for a multiracial, "rainbow nation," where all South Africans could be proud of their individual racial and ethnic makeup, while at the same time taking pride in their South African nation. In an effort to mend relationships among races, the new democratic government established the Truth and Reconciliation Commission. Headed by Nobel Peace Prize winner Archbishop Desmond Tutu, the commission sought to heal the divisions of the country and restore "human and civil dignity" by revealing and confronting the crimes of the apartheid era. The commission heard the testimony of both victims and perpetrators, granted amnesty to perpetrators in exchange for full disclosure, made recommendations for how to reconcile the country in the long term, and granted reparations to those who suffered most under apartheid. In its final report, the commission identified the apartheid system as a crime against humanity.

The commission was a great experiment in social healing. For some, it was a key piece of the transition's success. Without it, many believe South Africa would have been unable to move forward, weighed down by the denial of apartheid and steep racial divisions. For others, the commission was a "witch hunt" that unequally targeted the Afrikaner population and failed to investigate the crimes of the MK and other guerilla groups. While the debate on the commission's effectiveness continues, it has come to be seen as a model for other states transitioning to democracy in the wake of massive human rights violations.

The statistical evidence of improvements in South Africa's race relations is mixed. The Institute for Justice and Reconciliation's 2006 Reconciliation Barometer found that 87.7 percent of the population agrees apartheid was a crime against humanity, therefore accepting the narrative of the Truth and Reconciliation Commission (Institute of Justice and Reconciliation 2006). It also found that South Africans demonstrate high levels of nationalism and patriotism for the South African state. Yet, evidence of increased interracial trust and interaction is not promising. Recent surveys found "more than half of South Africans, or 56 percent, indicated that they never communicate informally with people from other groups on an average day" and that "almost 40 percent of South Africans believe that people from groups other than their own are untrustworthy" (IJR 2006). In addition, key events of racial discord often gain national media attention, further hampering racial relations. For example, a video of abuse of black workers by white students at the mostly Afrikaner Free State University reignited anger and distrust in 2007.

South Africa's ethnic and racial problems are not limited solely to the South African citizenry. Xenophobia has become a significant problem in the country, as evident in the May 2008 attacks on foreigners that swept across the country, killing 60 people and displacing 100,000 (Plaut 2008). The South African army was deployed to suppress the violence, and the United Nations High Commissioner for Refugees constructed temporary refugee centers throughout South Africa. While this bout of violence was quelled, many warn that xenophobic sentiments are on the rise.

In all, overcoming the social divisions exacerbated by apartheid is a difficult task. In many ways, South Africa is confronting these divisions directly, through means such as the Truth and Reconciliation Commission. In other ways, the divisions of South Africa will persist so long as the economic divisions created and fostered by apartheid are not addressed.

Economic development

Apartheid was more than a system of racial segregation. It was an economic system based on the cheap, exploited labor of blacks. Under apartheid, the minority white population had one of the highest standards of living in the world, while the majority black population suffered immensely (Thompson 2000). The white minority-run economy was a protected system of import substitution and state-owned enterprise, which adopted policies that advanced the white worker.[9] Sixteen years after its demise, apartheid's inequality persists, and South Africa's economy remains one of the world's most unequal.

When the democratic government came to power in 1994, many assumed the new black-dominated government would adopt socialist and redistributive economic policies. Indeed, the most prominent actors in the resistance movement had espoused such beliefs. After the intense negotiations of the democratic transition, the new government embraced a free market capitalist model, while at the same time trying to address the legacy of apartheid. Two major economic plans underscore the state's commitment to free market capitalism: the Reconstruction and Development Plan (RDP) and the Growth, Employment, and Redistribution Program (GEAR). The RDP combined infrastructure development (e.g., housing, water access, and electricity) with neoliberal policies of trade liberalization. GEAR adhered more narrowly to neoliberal principles: privatization, free trade, reduction in state economic intervention, and foreign direct investment.

The results of these reforms are mixed. South Africa's economy has grown at an average rate of 4.1 percent from 1997–2007 (*Economist* 2009), and as

Table 12.1 Economic indicators 2000–08

	2000	2005	2007	2008
GDP growth %	4.1	3.5	3.8	2.0
GDP per capita	2,961	5,050	5,770	5,565
Inflation %	4.7	4.9	5.4	8.1

Source: World Bank's World Development Indicators and United Nations Statistical Division

Table 12.1 demonstrates, this growth has translated into a steady rise in GDP per capita. In addition, South Africa has attracted substantial foreign direct investment, with a 38 percent increase from 2004 to 2005 (South African Institute of Race Relations 2008). Yet, South Africa's growth is mainly isolated within the white population and the newly formed black upper class. The economy remains highly unequal, and poverty persists. With one of the world's most unequal economies South Africa has a Gini Index of .65 (CIA 2005).[10] Over 40 percent of the population lives in poverty (Schwabe 2004). The government's efforts to improve infrastructure and increase basic services have fallen behind the growing need. For example, while the government has built 2.8 million homes for the large portion of the population that lives in informal settlements, millions more are needed and informal settlements are increasing rather than decreasing (BBC 2009). Also, whites still own the majority of the land, and land reform efforts have seen only 5 percent of white farmland transferred to blacks, despite a government goal of 30 percent transferred by 2014 (*Economist* 2008). In addition, unemployment averaged 24.5 percent from 1995 to 2006, with limited opportunities for the largely uneducated and unskilled black population (*Economist* 2009). For most black South Africans, economic life under the new democratic government sees little to no improvement over that of apartheid.

Post-apartheid economic indicators clearly demonstrate that democracy has not improved the lot of many South Africans. Theories of democratization focus on the reverse argument, however, aiming to determine whether economic factors influence democratization. Did the accumulation of national wealth, the creation of a middle class, or private enterprise contribute to the fall of apartheid and rise of democracy? The evidence from the South African case indicates the answer is a resounding "No."

First, there is no relationship between the accumulation of national wealth and democracy in South Africa. In the post–World War II period, South Africa's economy experienced steady growth at rates of 4.9 percent from 1946–74, fueled by import substitution policies and high gold prices

(Lowenberg 1997). However, starting in the 1970s, domestic and international factors began to make the apartheid system unsustainable. Domestically, apartheid's educational policies resulted in a shortage of skills, and the domestic security costs of repressing resistance sapped the economic resources of the state. The international context exacerbated domestic constraints on the economy, particularly the 1973 oil crisis. Furthermore, South Africa's dependence on foreign capital made it vulnerable to the economic sanctions of the international community. Sanctions and divestment contributed to a sharp drop in the value of the South African currency (the rand), and the ultimate decline of the South African economy by the 1980s. From 1974–87, growth of real GDP averaged 1.8 percent, and in the late 1980s and early 1990s growth rates were negative (Lowenberg 1997). Therefore, it was a fall in national wealth that precipitated the transition to democracy. The collapse of the South African economy was a key factor that forced the apartheid regime to the negotiating table.

Second, there is no relationship between the creation of a middle class and political reform in South Africa. South Africa's extreme levels of inequality have shaped society into two primary economic classes: a small, rich population and a vast, poor population. At the time of apartheid's demise, South Africa's middle class was negligible, if not nonexistent. More importantly, the poor and working classes provided the forces for the resistance and democracy movements. Once in power, the democratic regime did seek to create a black middle class through the Black Economic Empowerment (BEE). However, critics charge that BEE has only produced an elite black upper class, mockingly called "BEE-llionaires." Over time, BEE may help blacks achieve ownership and control of South Africa's economy, but to date the middle class numbers are small, and consequently not a major force for democracy.

South African democracy is also not the product of economic freedom or private enterprise. Under apartheid, private enterprise was generally restricted to the white population, which favored limiting protective policies that furthered white labor. For example, the strict racial color bar retained skilled and managerial positions for whites and demanded that no black ever hold a position superior to whites. The apartheid regime supported nationalized, state-owned industry in the areas of armaments, steel, energy, and mining in order to keep wealth in the hands of whites. Therefore, although demands for democracy grew, state control of industry was substantial, leaving limited room for private enterprise.

In sum, traditional theories linking economic development to political transition have no credence in the case of South Africa. Wealth, a middle class, and private enterprise did not play a role in creating democracy.

However, whether these three elements will play a role in sustaining democracy now established is an important question for exploration.

Education

Many theorists argue that an educated population is a necessary prerequisite for democracy, particularly given the nature of the participatory political system. The case of South Africa questions this conventional wisdom. Mandela himself tackled this issue in a television interview with journalist Brian Widlake in 1961. Briefly emerging from hiding to promote his cause of universal franchise, Mandela quickly responded to Widlake's question about the educational levels of black South Africans:

> We have a large number of Africans who are educated and who are taking part in the political struggles of the African people, [but] the question of education has nothing to do with the question of the vote. . . . [T]he people can enjoy the vote even if they have no education. Of course, we desire education and we think it is a good thing, but you don't have to have education in order to know that you want some fundamental rights, that you have got aspirations or claims. It has nothing to do with education whatsoever.[11]

Mandela's view runs counter to some theoretical expectations. Democratization scholars like Seymour Lipset have found strong correlations between educational indicators (e.g., national level literacy rates) and levels of democracy.[12] The South African case highlights the inadequacy of this approach. As Table 12.2 demonstrates, the population as a whole became increasingly literate under apartheid. However, the Bantu education system severely restricted education for black South Africans. Theories linking education to democracy overlook the pernicious effects education can have when opportunities for socialization are twisted to create a subservient workforce en lieu of engaged democratic citizens.

The Bantu education system purposely aimed to curtail the ability of blacks to think critically in the way required for democratic governance. Hendrick Verwoerd, South African Minister of Native Affairs, architect of Bantu education, and prime minister from 1958–62, famously stated, "[T]here is no place for [the Bantu] in the European community above the level of certain forms of labor. . . . What is the use of teaching the Bantu child mathematics when it cannot use it in practice?" (quoted in Lapping 1988). With this foundation, not surprisingly the South African educational system was highly unequal, with government per child expenditures on white education reaching 16 times the amount spent on black education (*Economist* 2010).

Table 12.2 Literacy rates 1970–2007

	1970	1980	1990	2000	2008
Literacy Rate	69.7	76.1	81.2	85.2	88

Source: UNESCO Institute for Statistics

The Bantu education system created two "lost generations." The first lost generation learned only what the apartheid government deemed useful for unskilled labor. In reaction, the second lost generation emerged after the Soweto Uprising and boycotted schooling, seeking "liberation before education." This second generation was furthered by the Black Consciousness Movement headed by Steve Biko, which encouraged the youth to seek pride in black identity, culture, and history and to liberate itself from the mental, as well as physical, oppression of whites. Interestingly enough, while education did not create democracy advocates, the apartheid-imposed Bantu education and educational centers galvanized the larger resistance movement. For both generations, the Bantu education system produced an uneducated population, and became a focal point of resistance.

Under democracy, South Africa has sought to address the educational imbalances of the past and undo generations of Bantu education. The constitution grants each individual the right to education, no matter what age a citizen may be. However, despite spending a greater percentage of GDP on education than the United States, South Africa has seen little success in the area of educational reform (*Economist* 2009). "Of the one in four black South Africans who took matric maths [matriculation exams] in 2008, only 39 percent passed (despite a lowly passmark of just 30 percent), compared with 98 percent of whites; 28 percent of whites achieved a score of at least 80 percent, compared with just 2 percent of blacks" (*Economist* 2010). Substantial reform is still necessary to equalize the educational system, which in turn will contribute to a more equal economic society.

International context

The international context is crucial for understanding South Africa's ultimate transition to democracy. Indeed, the international context had long shaped South African political development, as the apartheid regime originally relied heavily on the global divisions of the Cold War to sustain itself. The regime capitalized on anti-communist sentiment to garner international support (particularly from the United States) for its apartheid policies. By painting opponents as communists, the NP was able to manipulate the foreign policy of the United States and its allies against the resistance movement. For example, the NP crafted legislation like the Suppression of Communism Act, which defined communism broadly as any oppositional movement, and granted increasing powers to the South African government to limit such opposition. The labeling of opponents as communists yielded success domestically and internationally. For example, in the 1960s the NP branded Nelson Mandela a terrorist, and the United States upheld this designation, placing him and other leaders of the banned ANC on its terrorist watch list. Mandela and ANC leaders remained on this list until 2008. Economic motives frequently underpinned the willingness of some countries to follow the lead of the apartheid government. Labeling the apartheid opposition as communist allowed the United States and its allies to sidestep the problematic nature of the apartheid government and to sustain their profitable economic relations with South Africa.

By the late 1980s, however, the impending collapse of the Soviet Union took the wind out of this manufactured anti-communist crusade. As communism ceased to be of concern in the international community, the apartheid regime flailed. In the absence of a communist threat, the government could no longer argue that the resistance movement was seeking anything but democratization. In this way, the international context of the end of the Cold War created a window of opportunity for democratization.

Even prior to the end of the Cold War, key elements of the international community actively fought against apartheid. To complement domestic antiapartheid organizations, a global movement challenged apartheid on many fronts. On a global scale, and in a way not seen before, an international movement formed against the apartheid regime. In the post–World War II period, a new equality and human rights framework was constructed via the United Nations Charter, which called for a series of international declarations and treaties for equal and universal human rights. Yet, as this new frame was building, South Africa's system of apartheid was solidifying. As a result, some parts of the world community began to take steps against this pariah regime.

Economically, countries passed sanctions and trade embargoes on the apartheid regime. As early as 1964, India passed a comprehensive embargo on South Africa. Other states followed suit with restrictions on air travel and the disruption of trade. In 1977, the United Nations imposed an arms embargo on South Africa. In the same year, many corporations independently adopted the Sullivan Principles, which demanded that international companies mandate racially neutral policies in all operations, particularly those in South Africa. In the 1980s, a grassroots movement began on university campuses, where students demanded their universities end all investments in apartheid South Africa. For example, protests (which often included the construction of shantytowns on university property) were successful in compelling several universities to divest from South Africa.[13] Grassroots efforts reached national governments when the United States Congress passed the Comprehensive Anti-Apartheid Act in 1986, imposing economic sanctions on South Africa even over the veto of President Ronald Reagan. As a result of such sanctions, many lenders called in their loans to South Africa, inflation rose, and the value of the South African currency dropped sharply .

The economic arm was only one aspect of the global antiapartheid movement; there was also a large social, cultural, and political wing of the movement. Politically, many countries severed diplomatic ties with South Africa, and the United Nations established the United Nations Special Committee against Apartheid in 1962, after the Rivonia Trial. A cultural boycott existed for all South African products, including art and music. Perhaps the most visible form of such resistance occurred in the realm of sports, where the International Olympic Committee banned South Africa from Olympic competition in 1962. The next year the International Federation of Football Associations (FIFA) followed, suspending South Africa from international soccer competition. Under the banner of the call to "Free Mandela," massive protests erupted throughout the world. In all, there was a worldwide global movement for the end of apartheid that manifested itself in global protest, sanctions, and suspensions, which together branded South Africa as a pariah state.

South Africa is a key case to demonstrate the tremendous impact the international context can have on a domestic political transition. While it is not the only factor, the international context, particularly the end of the Cold War and the global antiapartheid movement, significantly influenced the collapse of the apartheid regime and the construction of a democratic state. While we can only postulate the counterfactual, it is evident that South Africa's transition may not have occurred when it did without the end of Cold War-without the end of the Cold War, as well as, as well as enormous pressure from state and nonstate actors.

Conclusions

While FIFA had banned apartheid South Africa from international soccer competitions in 1963, in 2010 it selected a democratic South Africa to host the World Cup. Today, South Africa is an established, electoral democracy with substantial political freedoms and rights protections. It has a particularly strong institutional design, a healthy balance of powers among the branches of government, and the opportunity for diverse representation through a proportional representation system. Its strong history of apartheid resistance has created a thriving civil society, and the population has internalized the norms of democratic governance.

Yet, major challenges confront the young democracy. First, dramatic inequality and high poverty rates pose the biggest threat to the state, accompanied by the interconnections between race and class. The population is beginning to express its frustration with the lack of improvement under the new democracy. Economically, most South Africans have seen little change in their economic position. The growing fear for many is that the masses will switch their allegiances to any political system that produces a change for the better, whether or not that system is democratic. Further perpetuating the issue is the high crime rate. South Africa is notorious for soaring violent crimes rates, including murder, rape, and carjacking.

The second major problem concerns the dominance of the ANC and its connection to corruption. Winning elections by supermajorities has contributed to corruption within the ranks of the ANC, and high-profile scandals have greatly tainted the state of democracy and trust in the government. Zuma's case in particular leaves many questions unanswered. Did his supporters influence justices? Why were charges dropped just weeks before the national elections in 2009? Were the charges initiated by the Mbeki camp to discredit Zuma? Lingering questions about Zuma's guilt or innocence have led many to ask whether he will become Africa's next "Big Man," by refusing to relinquish power after his term has ended.

Third, South Africa has one of the highest rates of HIV positive persons in the world. Recent studies find that 10.9 percent of the population over the age of two is living with HIV/AIDS (UNAIDS 2008). Government policy under the Mbeki presidency greatly contributed to the epidemic in South Africa, when health ministers denied the relationship between HIV and AIDS and proposed the use of traditional medicine over antiretroviral drugs. Since coming to office in May 2009, President Zuma has taken steps to combat the spread of HIV/AIDS by announcing an expansive government policy to provide antiretroviral drugs to a greater portion of the population. Whether this will be enough to turn the tide is still unknown.

In all, there are many significant challenges, and they do have the potential to erode the quality of democracy in South Africa. Despite years of progress, South Africa shares many similarities with other third wave democracies. Only time will tell whether South Africa can address these challenges within a democratic framework, and truly become the "miracle" case that so many hope it will be.

Additional resources

Several books provide powerful accounts of the fight against apartheid and the struggle for democracy. Particularly noteworthy are Nelson Mandela's *Long Walk to Freedom*; Pumla Gobodo-Madikizela's *A Human Being Died that Night: A South African Woman Confronts the Legacy of Apartheid*; and Mark Mathabane's *Kaffir Boy: The True Story of a Black Youth's Coming of Age in Apartheid South Africa*. In film, *Have you Heard from Johannesburg?*, directed by Connie Field (Clarity Films) offers a riveting account of the global antiapartheid movement through seven documentaries. Some popular films also do a good job of portraying the harsh realities of apartheid and the work of the resistance movement, such as *Cry Freedom*.

Notes

1 This analysis keeps with the general practice of using the term "black" to refer collectively to black Africans, Coloureds, and Indians.

2 The term "Bantu" refers to the linguistically related people of sub-Saharan Africa. During the years of apartheid, the National Party and the apartheid regime referred to black South Africans as Bantus.

3 The Congress of the People was a national meeting where many resistance groups across the ideological spectrum met to discuss plans for a democratic South Africa. The groups participating included: the African National Congress, the South African Indian Congress, the Coloured People's Congress, and the South African Congress of Trade Unions.

4 The practice of banning was a common act of the apartheid government that limited the physical movements, associations, and statements of individuals or groups. For example, banned individuals could not publish writings or speeches in newspapers, meet with more than one person at a time (including family members), or leave particular geographic areas.

5 With the change in the structure of democracy from parliamentary to presidential, Prime Minister Botha became President Botha in 1983.

6 As part of the apartheid regime's "divide and conquer" strategy, the regime sought to create tensions between the ANC and the IFP. In particular, the regime funded and prodded the IFP into violent interactions with the ANC by promising the IFP leadership control over historically Zulu lands. This strategy also had the intention of fostering "black on black" violence to prove to South Africans and the rest of the world that blacks were not capable of running a country.

7 The Senate was later replaced by the National Council of Provinces.

8 De Klerk's entire speech from February 2, 1990 can be found at: www.info.gov.za/speeches/1996/101348690.htm

9 Import substitution industrialization (ISI) is an economic development policy that seeks to reduce a developing state's dependence on imports and instead foster the growth of domestic industry. The government helps channel growth in industry through tariffs and subsidies. In addition to South Africa, ISI was the dominant policy in Latin America in the 1950s and 1960s.

10 The Gini coefficient measures the inequality of income distribution within a country. Its scale ranges from zero to one, with zero representing complete equality and one representing complete inequality.

11 Mandela's first television interview with Brian Widlake on May 21, 1961, is available online: www.mg.co.za/article/2009–07-17-mandela-in-video (accessed July 21, 2010).

12 Literacy rates are typically measured as the percentage of the population over the age of 15 that can read and write

13 Such protests erupted across campuses like Hampshire College, Stanford University, Michigan State University, and Columbia University.

References

Afrobarometer. 2009. "Summary of Democracy Indicators, South Africa 2000–2008." www.afrobarometer.org (accessed September 10, 2010).

BBC News. 2009. " 'One House, One Vote' for South Africans." April 21, 2009.

Butler, Jeffrey, Robert I. Rotberg, and John Adams. 1978. *The Black Homelands of South Africa: The Political and Economic Development of Bophuthatswana and Kwa-Zulu.* Berkeley: University of California Press.

Central Intelligence Agency (2005). *World Factbook.* www.cia.gov (accessed September 10, 2010).

Dugger, Celia W. 2008. "Study Cites Toll of Aids Policy in South Africa." *New York Times.* November 25, 2008.

Economist. 2010. "South Africa's Education System: No One Gets Prizes." January 14, 2010.

Economist. 2009. *Pocket World in Figures, 2009 Edition.* London: Profile Books, Ltd.

Economist. 2008. "The Promised Land: Land Reform is Going too Slowly in South Africa." April 24, 2008.

Independent Electoral Commission South Africa. 2009. www.elections.org.za (accessed December 1, 2009).

Institute for Justice and Reconciliation. 2006. "Sixth Round: SA Reconciliation Barometer Survey 2006." www.ijr.org.za (accessed September 10, 2010).

International Institute for Democracy and Electoral Assistance. www.idea.int/ (accessed July 2010).

Lapping, Brian. 1988. *Apartheid: A History.* Boulder: Paladin Books.

Lowenberg, Anton D. 1997. "Why South Africa's Apartheid Economy Failed." *Contemporary Economic Policy* 15(3): 62.

Mandela, Nelson. 1994. *Long Walk to Freedom: The Autobiography of Nelson Mandela*. New York: Little, Brown, and Company.

Plaut, Martin. 2008. "South Africa: Behind the Violence." BBC News. June 4, 2008.

Schwabe, Craig. 2004. "Fact Sheet: Poverty in South Africa." Human Sciences Research Council. Pretoria, South Africa.

South African Institute of Race Relations. 2008. South Africa Survey: Economy. Braamfontein, SA: South African Institute of Race Relations

South African StatsOnline. 2010. "Latest Key Indicators." <www.statssa.gov.za> (accessed January 1, 2010).

South African Truth and Reconciliation Final Report. 1998. "Volume 2." Statistics South Africa. 2009. "Mid-year Population Estimates 2009." www.statssa.gov.za (accessed September 10, 2010).

Sparks, Allister. 1995. *Tomorrow Is another Country: the inside Story of South Africa's Road to Change*. Chicago: The University of Chicago Press.

Swilling, Mark, and Bev Russell. 2002. "The Size and Scope of the Non-profit Sector in South Africa." Graduate School of Public and Development Management (P&DM), University of the Witwatersrand and The Centre for Civil Society, University of Natal.

Thompson, Leonard M. 2000. *A History of South Africa*. New Haven: Yale University Press.

UNAIDS. 2008. "2008 Report on the Global AIDS Epidemic." www.unaids.org (accessed September 10, 2010).

Hypothesis testing exercise and discussion questions for Section 4

Using the guide below, assess how well the classical theories of democratization explain democratization in Chile, South Africa, and Poland. Be sure to specify the causal mechanisms, or processes by which each independent variable determined the dependent variable. Also, differentiate between the independent variables that caused the emergence of democracy from those that caused its eventual consolidation.

Hypothesis testing exercise

Independent Variables	Evidence from Chile	Evidence from Poland	Evidence from South Africa
Economic development • National wealth • Private enterprise • Middle class • Inequality			
Elites			
Political culture/civil society			
Education			
State institutions			
Social divisions/national unity			
International context			

Section 4: Discussion questions

1 To what extent does the nature of the democratic transition affect the subsequent quality of democratic governance? How does the balance of power at the end of the authoritarian era shape the new democratic regime?

2 To what extent does the institutional structure of the new democratic regime affect the quality of democratic governance? If the new democratic regime inherits some authoritarian elements, does this inevitably weaken the quality of

democratic governance? Does the initial institutional structure of the new democracy constrain political actors?

3 How have these three third wave democracies addressed human rights violations that occurred under authoritarian rule? How do these three cases differ from those of the second wave democracies in this respect? How do amnesty laws, truth and reconciliation commissions, and human rights trials shape democratic governance?

Section 5
Conclusion

Among the protesters in Tahrir Square, Cairo, February 1, 2011.
Photo: Timothy Kaldas

An Egyptian flag waves above protesters calling for an end to Hosni Mubarak's rule in
Egypt, Tahrir Square, Cairo, February 1, 2011. Photo: Timothy Kaldas

13

Authoritarian Regimes and Democratic Demands in the Middle East

Jeannie Sowers

The end of 2010 and early months of 2011 saw a wave of protest sweep across the Middle East and North Africa. In December, sustained protest in Tunisia forced President Zine al-Abidine Ben Ali, who had ruled for 23 years, into precipitous exile in Saudi Arabia. In late January, a campaign of largely peaceful street protest across Egypt induced the military to ease out long-standing president Hosni Mubarak after eighteen days. Faced with mounting demonstrations and strikes, Egypt's Mubarak disappeared from public view after 30 years in power and three televised addresses insisting he would not relinquish office.

The escalating cycles of street protest, repression by security forces, and the eventual refusal of the army to shoot mounting numbers of demonstrators echoed patterns that produced rapid regime breakdown in Iran in 1978–1979 and in East Germany and other Eastern European communist governments in 1989. The abrupt departures of the old rulers in Egypt and Tunisia, or revolutions as the protesters have termed them, have sparked similar urban demonstrations and uprisings across the Middle East and North Africa. As of this writing, military and security forces have sought to quell protest in Iran, Bahrain, Libya, Jordan, Yemen, and Algeria. These protesters include a large number of youth—in countries where the median age is between 25 and 30 years old—and seek to replace aging leaders presiding over sclerotic authoritarian regimes. The protesters demand more representative, democratic political systems as well as better economic opportunities and basic civil liberties.

One of the most widespread slogans used in Egypt's street demonstrations made clear that protesters were not simply seeking a replacement of Mubarak but an end of authoritarian rule more generally. Thousands marched through the streets of Cairo, Alexandria, Suez and other cities chanting "The people . . . want . . . the fall of the regime!" (*al-sha'ab . . . yureed . . . isqaat al-nizaam*). This slogan and its variations soon became staple features of protests in Benghazi, Amman, Algiers, Sana'a, and Manama. In Iran, protesters chanted in rhymed Persian slogans for the Supreme Leader Ali Khamenei to step down, linking their demands to the uprisings in Egypt and Tunisia: "Bane Ali, Mubarak, now it is Seyed Ali (Khameni)'s turn" and "Dictator flee! Take a look at Mubarak!" (Arang Keshavarzian, pers. comm., February 20, 2011).

It is not yet clear whether the more violent crackdowns in Iran, Bahrain, Yemen, Algeria, and most especially Libya, will quell dissent or provoke greater popular anger. Bahrain's Sunni ruling family, for instance, facing a mobilized Shi'ite majority, may seek to negotiate a limited democratic bargain that preserves the monarchy rather than face escalating internal and external criticism. In Libya, however, where Col. Qaddafi sought to remake the country in his idiosyncratic image for 43 years, violence has reached a scale unseen in Tunisia or Egypt. Qaddafi unleashed the army and the air force, ordering pilots to fire on protesters in cities below. Libyan diplomats outside the country publicly criticized this decision, and two air force pilots took their planes and defected to Malta, but others reportedly obeyed orders. As of March 2011, opposition rebels held the eastern part of the country, while Qaddafi ruthlessly stamped out opposition in Tripoli.

For Tunisia and Egypt, with their autocrats ousted, the difficult challenge begins of translating aspirations for democracy into viable democratic institutions. In this process, the vested interests of many within existing authoritarian institutions will come into play, and none more importantly than that of the military. Egypt's military sought neutrality during the height of the demonstrations, publicly vowing it would not fire on protestors, but not intervening to protect them from attacks by government-organized thugs, plainclothes security forces, and mobs. As a result, at least 684 people were killed and 5,500 injured across the country, according to a coalition of Egyptian human rights groups (Al Desoukie 2011).

When the military formally asserted control with Mubarak's departure, it promised to reform the constitution and hold elections for a civilian-led government in 6 months. However, as of this writing, the military had not devised a participatory process to revise the constitution, or indicated when it would lift the despised Emergency Laws. In Tunisia, political change has gone forward a few more steps. An interim government includes some members of the opposition, though it is under heavy criticism for retaining senior technocrats from Ben Ali's tenure. The government has also allowed prominent opposition leaders to return from exile, particularly Rashid Al-Ghannushi, leader of Tunisia's moderate Islamic party, *al-Nahda*, banned under Ben Ali's rule.

While the scale and scope of these protests was stunning, urban and labor protests have been escalating since the mid-2000s across the region. Egypt and Tunisia both saw significant increases in protest campaigns, labor actions, and public sector strikes. Urban protest erupted in Tehran in 2009 over rigged presidential elections. Recurrent urban demonstrations rocked Beirut, pitting Hizballah and its allies against the rival political coalition led by Sa'ad Hariri. The ongoing strikes, marches, and demonstrations that have characterized popular uprisings in the Palestinian territories, which intensified in the periods 1987–1993 and 2000–2005, brought the Arabic term for uprising, *intifada*, into mainstream use in the international media. These protests in turn echoed earlier periods of urban unrest. The late 1970s and early 1980s saw a significant wave of urban protest across the Middle East, which eventually subsided as regimes intensified repression, extended subsidies for basic commodities, and promised political reform.

The protests of 2010–2011 saw activists making greater use of new social media (Facebook, Twitter, and blogs) to coordinate protest and provide eyewitness accounts of unfolding events for domestic and international audiences. Al Jazeera and some private satellite stations carried nonstop coverage of the protests, making the propaganda beamed out over state-owned media channels self-defeating, as the contrast revealed just how limited state control of information had become. As important in sustaining protest, however, were "older" forms of social communication, from telephone landlines to dense informal networks that organized to protect neighborhoods and provide medical relief and supplies to protesters.

Just as protest is not new to the region, neither is the demand for democratic governance. As this chapter shows, Middle Eastern elites and mass movements have long articulated demands for constitutions, parliaments, and elections. Modern public opinion polls reflect these democratic preferences. They consistently show that significant majorities favor democratic government. To give but one example, in a 2006 survey of Jordan, Palestine, Morocco, and Kuwait, the Arab Barometer found that 86 percent of respondents agreed with the statement that "despite drawbacks, democracy is the best system of government," while 90 percent felt that "having a democratic system of government in our country would be good" (Jamal and Tessler 2008). Cross-regional comparisons from the World Values Survey indicate that support for democracy in the Arab world is as high or higher as in other world regions (Jamal and Tessler 2008).

It is much too early to say whether the recent largely peaceful mass protest movements will bring substantive democratization to the Middle East. The region acquired a reputation for authoritarian permanence when the much-heralded third wave of democratization largely bypassed it during the 1990s. Nevertheless, the Middle East is not without its democracies. One of the few transitions from dictatorship to a system of electoral competition -and endemic civil violence- came through the 2003 American-led invasion of Iraq (Sluglett 2007). Turkey (intermittently since 1950), Israel (since 1948), and Lebanon (intermittently since 1926) have met minimal procedural standards for democratic governance, where power rotates according to the results of elections that are relatively fair and inclusive. The substantive democratic character of these states, however, has been bedeviled by fundamental conflict over who is included in the nation-state, producing endemic conflicts with regional as well as domestic dimensions. And lastly, a handful of relatively free elections in the Palestinian National Authority have been sporadic precisely because the Israeli-Palestinian "peace process" has produced no substantive movement toward a viable Palestinian state. Increasingly authoritarian practices by the Palestinian Authority, the international isolation of Hamas in Gaza, and ongoing Israeli settlement and land expropriation in the West Bank undermine possibilities for meaningful elections in the fragmented, stateless pieces of Palestinian territory.

The majority of states in the Middle East and North Africa do not meet even thin procedural definitions of democracy. Many states conduct some semblance of elections and allow national parliaments some scope, but these processes are not yet constitutive of political outcomes. Instead, most regimes have consistently manipulated elections and limited contestation, thereby perpetuating political systems most accurately classified as authoritarian.

If popular support exists for democratic government, why has democratization eluded much of the region to date? In this chapter, I argue that we can explain the consolidation and persistence of authoritarian rule in the Middle East without invoking the flawed notions that Arab political culture or Islam is intrinsically authoritarian. As elsewhere, religious, communal, and cultural identities and movements have often become politically salient in the Middle East. Yet these processes are broadly comparable with those in other developing countries.

If we look at past and present trends, we find that authoritarian rule has been fostered and sustained by factors all too common in developing countries in the post–World War II period. In reviewing the extant literature on democratization, Geddes (2009) argues that the causal factors facilitating democratization or durable authoritarianism change over time. For third-wave transitions to democracy, Geddes argues that elite calculations about whether to democratize can be analyzed in terms of: (a) regime type, or how state institutions link rulers with ruled; (b) the extent of state control over the domestic economy; and (c) changes in the international geopolitical and economic context (Geddes 2009). These three broad categories of analysis have infused much of the comparative research on authoritarianism and democracy in the Middle East.

This chapter reviews some of the most significant contributions in this literature, showing how international influences, patterns of economic development, and the evolution of state-society relations have shaped the strategies of authoritarian rulers and the possibilities for opposition. Until recently, these three factors created mutually reinforcing, interlocking obstacles to democratization in the Middle East and North Africa. As this chapter shows, however, domestic and regional politics are changing rapidly, creating new prospects for political change and, potentially, democratization.

One of the most challenging aspects of understanding political development in the Middle East and North Africa is accounting for the significant diversity of political regimes, domestic economies, and international influences within the region. The family rule systems in the Arabian Peninsula have different origins (and different consequences for democratization) than the presidential authoritarian systems found in Tunisia, Egypt, Algeria, and Syria. The region is further characterized by great divides in wealth and poverty. Per capita GDP in the oil-exporting countries of the Persian Gulf averages approximately $26,000, while in the more populous, larger countries it ranges from $6,800 in Turkey to $1,260 in Egypt (World Bank 2010). While the analysis here focuses on broad commonalities in political

experience, this approach cannot do justice to the many important particu-
larities and variations within the region.

Colonial rule and emergence of modern nation-states

The late nineteenth century to World War II

International intervention and the construction of centralized state institutions went hand in hand in most of the Middle East. For much of the nineteenth century and the first half of the twentieth, Britain and France were
the dominant powers in the region. They established direct and indirect
forms of colonial rule in North Africa, Egypt, and the eastern Mediterranean
as the power of the Ottoman Empire, centered in Istanbul, waned.

While this period is often portrayed as one of political stagnation, significant movements for constitutional reform emerged in the Ottoman heart-
land (contemporary Turkey) as well as in Persia (modern-day Iran) under
the Qajar dynasty during the late nineteenth century (Gelvin 2008). Political
reformers and protesters called for popularly elected parliaments and a
written constitution to constrain the power of the ruler. European social
theorists from Montesquieu (1689–1755) to Marx (1818–1883) to Weber
(1864–1920) had popularized the notion of "Oriental despotism," a trope for
absolute power and unfettered indulgence. Yet within the heartlands of the
"Orient" itself—the Qajar and Ottoman empires—movements for political
reform obtained formal constitutions and the formation of parliaments.
These, however, were periodically suspended in subsequent decades as part
of ongoing struggles for power between rulers, urban political elites, and
other social forces.

Meanwhile, on the peripheries of the Ottoman Empire, European powers
took control. The footprint of colonialism was deepest and most prolonged
in North Africa, or the *Maghreb* as the western part of the region is termed
in Arabic. Direct colonization by French settlers (*colons*) of Algeria began in
1830 and lasted until 1962, when after a protracted and bloody revolt
Algeria became one of the last states in the region to achieve independence.
French rule began in Tunisia in 1881 and Morocco in 1912. In Libya, Italian
colonization and a brutal military occupation began in 1912, killing large
numbers of Libyans and forcibly relocating most of the indigenous population.

Farther east, the Russians and British carved out spheres of influence in Iran, centered on control of new oil fields. The British embarked on a long period of bitterly resented presence in Egypt by the late nineteenth century, focused on control of the Suez Canal as a key transit route for Britain's empire in South and East Asia.

In the aftermath of World War I, Britain and France famously redrew the boundaries of the *Mashreq*, the eastern Arab provinces of the Ottoman Empire, into the modern states of Iraq, Jordan (then Transjordan), Palestine (until 1948), Syria, and Lebanon. These newly created nation-states were placed as "mandates" under British or French control by the newly created League of Nations, until these countries were deemed fit for independence by their colonial rulers. These mandates, however, did not correspond with previous Ottoman administrative jurisdictions (based on control of prominent cities) or the wishes of the local inhabitants. This was made abundantly clear by the findings of an American fact-finding delegation, the King-Crane Commission, sent by President Wilson in 1917 to ascertain the wishes of the local people in "Greater Syria" about how they should be ruled. Henry King and Charles Crane met with "442 delegations representing people from all walks of life, such as municipal and administrative councils, village chiefs, and tribal *shaykhs*. They received farmers and tradesmen, and representatives of over a dozen Christian denominations, Sunni and Shiite Muslims, Jews, Druze, and other minority groups. They met with eight different women's delegations [and] collected 1,863 petitions, with a total of 91,079 signatures" (Rogan 2009, 160).

The commission reported that the local population overwhelmingly desired self-governance under a constitutional monarchy. By the end of World War I, then, nationalist movements in the eastern part of the Middle East clearly expressed the desire for representative, local political institutions. Specifically, the commission reported that the delegations wanted an independent Greater Syria, an American presence if necessary rather than British or French control, and limitations on Zionist immigration and land purchases in Palestine, which the vast majority of the local population saw as an integral part of the *Mashreq* (Rogan 2009, 162). In the 1917 Balfour Declaration, however, the British government promised the emerging Zionist movement its support in establishing a "national home for the Jewish people" that would not "prejudice the civil and religious rights of existing non-Jewish communities in Palestine." King and Crane observed that the Balfour Declaration was clearly at odds with nine-tenths of public opinion in Palestine and Greater Syria. Thus were laid the seeds of the conflict between Israel, the Palestinians, and the Arab states. Meanwhile, the King-Crane report, submitted to the Paris Peace Conference by the American delegation, was not made public until three years later (Rogan 2009, 162).

With the exception of the King-Crane Commission, American contact with the region remained limited largely to tourism and Christian missionary activity. For most Americans, nationalist political struggles in the Middle East were remote. Instead, visions of the region were mediated by mass cultural productions—travel accounts, postcards, religious tracts, and novels. Through the lens of "the Holy Land," these productions often depicted the region as backward and undeveloped because of long centuries of Muslim (i.e., Ottoman) rule. As Edward Said argued, these portrayals also drew on long-standing tropes in European cultural and scholarly productions, in which the "Orient" was viewed as despotic, irrational, fascinating, and erotic (Said 1978). After World War II, Hollywood films increasingly elaborated on these and other images of the region (McAlister 2001).

As elsewhere in the developing world, colonial rule was highly unpopular. Local revolts against colonial powers were protracted, violent, and costly for local populations. Those areas where colonial rule began earliest faced the first organized opposition movements and guerilla armies. Abd al-Qadir's guerilla forces in Algeria delivered a series of defeats to the French during the 1830s and 1840s, resulting in two peace treaties demarcating independent Algerian territory and administration before the French pursued a scorched-earth policy in the Algeria countryside that left civilian casualties estimated in the hundreds of thousands (Rogan 2009, 115–19). Similarly, widespread revolts spanning cities and countryside erupted against British rule in Egypt (1919), Iraq (1920), Syria (1925), and the Palestinian Arab populations in mandatory Palestine (1936–1939). Between 1921 and 1925, Berber forces in the Moroccan Rif mountains, led by local magistrate turned rebel leader Abd el-Krim, decimated the Spanish army and then inflicted a series of defeats on French imperial forces (Rogan 2009, 221–24).

These revolts were put down with the sustained use of violence and collective punishment, targeting villages, tribes, and cities as well as insurgent forces. For instance, only when the combined forces of France and Spain "imposed a complete blockade to starve the Rifis into submission" did Abd el-Krim in Morocco surrender (Rogan 2009, 224). Prolonged armed conflict strengthened the role of the armed forces and internal security forces in newly formed states. Reliance on the devastating use of airpower, for instance, defined the British response to tribal uprisings in Iraq (Dodge 2003). The routine use of violence to suppress political dissent thus quickly became a defining feature of the emerging Iraqi state, long before Saddam Hussein consolidated power (Tripp 2000).

Colonial rulers, like later authoritarian leaders, did not rely simply on repression, though this was a crucial tactic. Britain, for instance, created two types of governing institutions to facilitate indirect control. The first was colonial support for family dynasties (Owen 1992). The British either created new monarchies (namely the Hashemite dynasties in Jordan and Iraq), or supported indigenous ruling families through assistance and treaties, as in Saudi Arabia and the "Trucial" states of the Gulf, where various kinship groups had long controlled seaports crucial to trade. Alongside family rule, the British established weak parliamentary systems in which landed conservative elites generally held sway. The authority of local parliaments and ruling dynasties was, however, limited by direct colonial control over diplomatic relations, fiscal affairs, and other similar "reservations." This was the case with parliaments in Jordan, Lebanon, Iraq, Syria, Sudan, and Egypt. In Egypt, a tripartite system of colonial rule evolved that combined direct administrative oversight by Britain on key domestic and foreign policy decisions, a weak monarch dependent on British support, and a weak parliamentary electoral system. Thus, colonial powers and centralizing local dynasties alike sought to limit the effectiveness and scope of parliamentary authority in favor of centralizing executive power. The dominance of executive control, concentrated in the capital city, is a common facet of authoritarian rule across much of the region, with the exception of weakly centralized states such as Lebanon and Yemen.

The advent of mass politics

In the more urbanized and industrialized parts of the Middle East, popular classes in both rural and urban areas increasingly joined in formal political life during the interwar period. The 1920s and 1930s saw the emergence of a number of mass-based movements that called for an end to colonial rule and for more authentic and representative governments. Middle Easterners marched in the streets, organized political parties of all sorts, voted in elections (where given the chance), and waged rebellions against colonial rule. Many were imprisoned, executed, and exiled in the process. The names given to emerging mass-based political parties revealed claims for sovereign and representative government: *Istiqlal* (Independence) in Morocco; the *Destour* and *neo-Destour* (Constitution and New Constitution) in Tunisia; and the *Wafd* (Delegation, originally to the Paris Peace Conference after World War I) in Egypt.

As in Europe and elsewhere, the proliferation of political parties during this period reflected diverse and often polarized ideological stances based on significantly different material interests and political visions. In Iraq, Iran, Egypt, and elsewhere communist parties were active among industrial workers in textile plants, oil installations, and ports. Socialist and fascist parties mobilized urban youth and rural constituencies. These parties highlighted the inequality and injustices of concentrated land holdings, grave income inequalities, and rigid class systems that limited economic mobility. Conservative parties, representing landed elites and tribal leaders, continued to win significant numbers of parliamentary seats through the distribution of patronage in rural areas.

New movements also emerged that meshed some of the mass-mobilizing tactics of political parties with calls to renew the centrality of Islam in public and political life. The most prominent of these emerging groups was the Muslim Brotherhood (*Al-Ikhwan Al-Muslimeen*), first founded by the schoolteacher Hassan Al-Banna in 1928 in the British-controlled Suez Canal zone in Egypt. The Brotherhood expanded rapidly during this period until it was formally banned in 1948, after which it continued to organize. Today, it remains a potent oppositional movement in Egypt.

Consolidation of authoritarian regimes post World War II

Party systems and elite bargaining

With the exhaustion of the European powers in the trauma of World War II, and continued nationalist protest, colonial rule gradually came to an end. The two decades following the war saw the emergence of independent regimes across the Middle East and North Africa. Many of these quickly moved from fragmented parliamentary systems to authoritarian rule under single parties, monarchs, or presidents. This shift toward authoritarian rule was common to many newly decolonizing states throughout Africa and Latin America. Convergence to authoritarianism rather than democracy was not a foregone conclusion, however.

As Angrist (2006) highlights, in Tunisia, Algeria, and South Yemen, single dominant parties headed by nationalist leadership quickly consolidated power in the aftermath of independence. In these countries, deeply entrenched colonial rule had excluded local elites from substantive participation in parliaments. Angrist argues that local elites thus turned to building mass mobilizing parties as other avenues of participation were closed, and used these parties to consolidate control over parliament and governmental institutions. The result was the rapid construction of presidential authoritarian systems with dominant government-supported parties.

Egypt, Syria, and Iraq also evolved into presidential authoritarian systems with dominant single political parties, but the process was more protracted and polarized (Angrist 2006). This period of unstable, factionalized multiparty politics ended only with military coups, as was seen also in Latin America, sub-Saharan Africa, and East Asia, where factionalized elite conflict culminated into military takeovers. For the Arab countries, several factors made this outcome more likely. For the countries surrounding Palestine, the 1948 defeat of the Arab armies by the new Israeli army marked a turning point, as the disastrous defeat thoroughly discredited nascent parliamentary systems. Urban protest, assassinations, and escalating civil violence became commonplace.

Young nationalist army officers took advantage of disintegrating public order to overthrow existing parliamentary-monarchical-colonial regimes, perceived by many citizens as corrupt, ineffectual, and elitist. In Syria and Iraq, these army officers belonged to a relatively small party known as the *Ba'ath*. Both Saddam Hussein in Iraq and Hafez al-Assad in Syria would later expand and use the political apparatus of the *Ba'ath* to eventually control state institutions. In doing so, they ultimately created personal dictatorships.

Only Turkey, which had never experienced colonial rule, evolved into a competitive electoral system, though even here the military intervened successively. Ataturk's party of urban professional elites, the Republican People's Party (RPP), faced a series of coordinated challenges in the provinces from commercial and agricultural elites who had long resisted centralizing, secularizing government initiatives (Angrist 2005). These networks of provincial elites supported a series of parties that challenged the dominance of the RPP. In 1950, the RPP finally allowed a free and fair election, convinced that the opposition had moderated key policy stances, and reassured by its own increased capacity to secure votes at the local level (Angrist 2005). The military still intervened intermittently in politics, however, dismissing parliamentary governments in 1960, 1971, and 1980, and appointing new civilian successors.

In Morocco, Jordan, Saudi Arabia, and the small Persian Gulf states, the consolidation of authoritarian rule did not involve the overthrow of monarchies but rather their persistence. In these countries, family dynasties succeeded in holding on to power despite recurrent opposition. In Morocco, for instance, the king joined the nationalist *Istiqlal* party in mobilizing against French control; when the French departed, the monarch consolidated his position at the expense of the nationalist party. In the Gulf, in the absence of mass-based parties, ruling families arranged for external protection by shifting gradually from British security guarantees to those offered by America.

Within the Gulf monarchies, however, significant differences emerged in the levels of institutionalized representation of the populace in parliament (Herb 2005). The elected parliaments of Kuwait, Jordan, and Morocco have relatively strong constitutional powers, but their political party systems are not well developed. Saudi Arabia and the United Arab Emirates have no elected parliaments or elections at any level, though calls for reform are increasing. In the small states of the Gulf, parliaments exist, but with weak constitutional powers and virtually no development toward cohesive political parties (Herb 2005, 186).

Domestic political economy and class structure

New military regimes and modernizing monarchies in the Middle East enacted a variety of popular measures to increase support even as they dismantled and constrained the scope of parliamentary government. They emphasized improving the material lot of middle class and poor citizens who had seemingly gained little under conservative parliamentary parties and monarchies. In their interventions in the domestic economy, Middle Eastern regimes fit the postwar development patterns in most decolonizing regions. Developing countries embraced state-led development strategies, in light of the success of Japan, Germany, and the Soviet Union in accelerating industrialization through significant state intervention and control.

Authoritarian regimes in the Middle East rapidly expanded central state bureaucracies to promote state-led development, undertaking programs of land redistribution, expansion of educational opportunities, and job creation (particularly in growing public bureaucracies). As throughout Africa, state control over key agricultural crops facilitated the financing of public expenditures, which over time resulted in the stagnation of agricultural sectors and rural incomes. State control over unions, professional associations (syndicates), and other forms of civil society also expanded through government supervision, registration, and restrictions on private and foreign financing.

Egypt led the way under Gamal Abdel Nasser's military junta. Between 1952 and 1966, the regime nationalized all private banks, insurance companies, most shipping companies, construction companies, transportation, utilities, and many industrial companies. The capital market was closed. Elite Egyptian and resident minority communities with significant investment in the economy fled the country. Through nationalization, the share of the private sector in GDP fell from 85 percent to 56 percent (Waterbury 1983, 160). The government increasingly used price controls, subsidies, and central planning to administer the economy, and promised public sector employment to every university graduate. State-led industrialization initially produced high growth rates, estimated at 7 percent per year, but, as in other countries, by 1966 these policies produced negative growth rates (Metz 1991).

The expanding role of the state in economic production and social regulation shaped class structures and state-society relations in ways that arguably hindered prospects for democracy. As Chapter 3 explains, prominent scholars have pointed to the historic linkage between the growth of a middle class and the demand for greater representation. Barrington Moore best captured this argument with his famous phrase "no bourgeoisie, no democracy" (Moore 1967). In a similar vein, others argue that the incorporation of the working classes into political life was pivotal to the creation of modern social democracies (Rueschemeyer, Stephens, and Stephens 1992).

In the Middle East, however, neither middle classes nor working classes were in a position to demand democratic openings (Bellin 2002). Many middle-class professionals were employed in government ministries and other public sector entities, constituting what Luciani (2007) termed a class of "scribes" and Waterbury (1983) described as a "state bourgeoisie." Most industrial workers were also similarly dependent upon the state, as state-owned enterprises dominated the industrial sectors and workers unions were essentially corporatist institutions established and run by government ministries.

The "dependence" of the middle and working classes on state employment was complemented by the growth of informal networks that linked private business actors with state officials. While often categorized as "corruption," these networks also meant more individuals had a stake in evolving forms of authoritarian rule. Some of these networks involved the highest levels of the regime, linking high-ranking officials, businessmen, military officers, and party leaders, but they could also be found systemically down through levels of public bureaucracies and private enterprises. The result was what Waterbury (1983) termed a "public-private symbiosis," in which boundaries blurred between the state and other forms of economic and political activity.

Despite the expansion of state ownership and informal networks linking public and private sectors, however, the vast majority of Middle Easterners were still employed in the small- and medium-scale private sector, in commerce, agriculture, and services. These enterprises were typically family-owned and sought to avoid entanglements with the state. This "petite bourgeoisie" would form much of the support for various Islamic movements and parties that later emerged (Fischer 1982).

The international economy and rentier states

The dependency of citizens on state employment and state-provided subsidies expanded with the influx of oil revenues into the region. The age of petroleum that flourished after World War II had profound consequences for the durability of authoritarian rule in much of the Middle East. The discovery of vast oil fields in Iran, the Arabian Peninsula, and North Africa in the decades before the war greatly enhanced the geostrategic importance of the Middle East. The "light crude" of the Gulf was cheaply and readily accessible compared to other petroleum reserves. Nowhere was this more the case than in Saudi Arabia, with the largest known oil reserves of any Middle Eastern country. The US government soon followed private American oil companies in helping the al-Saud family build the rudiments of a modern state, ensuring in the process that the largest oil producer in the world became a staunch American ally (Vitalis 2007). In recent decades, technological innovations enabling the distribution and consumption of natural gas have further cemented the region's central position in the global energy system.

For much of the twentieth century, oil exploration, production, refining, and distribution was controlled by a cartel of largely British- and American-owned multinational firms (the "Seven Sisters"). The rapid increase in the global postwar consumption of oil generated increasingly large profits for multinational oil firms, which paid royalties to ruling families in return for long-term concessions to oil fields. The creation of locally owned and controlled oil companies was thus a long-standing demand by nationalist parties and leaders in Iran and Iraq, one that multinational firms and their governments resisted. When popularly elected Iranian Prime Minister Mossadeq nationalized the Anglo-Iranian Oil Company in 1951, multinational firms boycotted Iranian oil, successfully shutting off the main source of revenue for the government. This measure contributed to the downfall of

Prime Minister Mosaddeq, as did the intervention of the US and British secret services in organizing a coup and restoring the Pahlevi monarchy in the person of the Shah's son, Mohamed. It was not until 1970 that the young military officer Muammar al-Qadhafi, having overthrown the local monarchy, successfully nationalized the oil sector in Libya, setting a precedent other oil-producing states were quick to follow.

Along with maintaining a reliable supply of fossil fuel, American policy makers saw the growing power and influence of the Soviet Union as their most significant global challenge. As left-leaning army officers and nationalists came to power through military coups d'etat in Egypt, Iraq, and Syria, the United States consolidated alliances with conservative monarchies in Jordan, Iran, and Saudi Arabia. Throughout the cold war, the United States offered pro-Western regimes in the Middle East access to US arms and economic assistance as it sought to isolate and contain states it considered too pro-Soviet.

These cold war policies, however, produced a number of internal contradictions. Nowhere was this clearer than in American relations with Iran. After decades of American military assistance to the Pahlevi monarchy in Iran as a bulwark against Soviet influence, the 1979 Iranian revolution unexpectedly overturned this "pillar" of American foreign policy. The Iranian revolution ushered in a new form of authoritarian rule for the Middle East. Rule by leading Shi'ite clerics was constitutionally enshrined, while the authority and effectiveness of parliament were increasingly circumscribed. With the passing of the charismatic founding leader, Ayatollah Khomeini, the regime gradually morphed into factionalized rule among competing clerics and populist leaders with competing institutional bases (Keshavarzian 2005).

Most foreign observers inaccurately considered prerevolutionary Iran stable, in part because it could draw on extensive revenues from the sale of oil and the receipt of foreign military aid. In 1970, an Iranian economist published an influential article describing the adverse effects of oil revenues on economic development in Iran (Mahdavy 1970). His study of Iran as a "rentier state," that is, a state relying heavily on the export of natural resources as a principal source of income, helped many scholars explain the persistence of authoritarian rule in the Middle East.

Rent from oil, foreign aid, and other external sources helped sustain authoritarian rule by providing funds directly to the incumbent regime. Oil revenues financed patronage networks and the rapid expansion of state welfare functions in oil-exporting states. The upshot, many scholars argued, was that rulers were freed from bargaining with social groups over the extraction of direct income taxes and therefore from popular demands for

representation to constrain fiscal demands. Inverting the slogan "no taxation without representation," the argument could be summed up as "no
taxation, no representation" (Beblawi 1990; Chrystal 1995; Karl 1997; Luciani
2005). Other scholars pointed out that although Middle Eastern regimes
relied heavily on indirect rather than direct taxation, these arrangements
characterized other developing countries that had nevertheless transitioned
to democracy (Waterbury 2001).

Oil revenues also had a profound impact on non–oil-exporting states of
the region. Beginning in the 1970s, booming yet volatile labor markets in
construction and infrastructure projects attracted workers and middle-class
professionals from around the Middle East to the Gulf. Wages sent back to
home countries (remittances) soon became the largest source of foreign
exchange for labor-exporting countries like Egypt. Migrants returning from
the Gulf also brought exposure to a more literal, fundamentalist version of
Islam officially supported in Saudi Arabia, which prompted broader changes
in public culture and religious practice. The increase in oil wealth also fueled
expansive lending to poor countries throughout the Middle East and the
rest of the developing world. Many poor countries took on levels of debt
they proved unable to repay, prompting fiscal crises and various types of
economic restructuring.

Economic and political restructurings: Precursors to democratization? 1974 to the present

Market reform and domestic political economy

By the late 1970s, the non-rentier states in the Middle East had taken on
extensive debt and could no longer afford to provide employment in the
public sector. Subsidies on basic commodities and fuel also imposed heavy
costs on state budgets. Egypt and Tunisia were among the first to embark on
programs of *infitah*, or reopening of the economy to private investment and
market reforms. As with structural adjustment programs elsewhere, governments tried to reduce budget deficits, restrain inflation, stabilize the currency, and restore creditworthiness by negotiating reform packages with
the International Monetary Fund. Cuts in food and fuel subsidies sparked

popular unrest and riots in some countries, including Egypt in 1977. Middle Eastern governments also embarked on more fundamental restructuring of their economies, liberalizing trade regimes, privatizing state-owned enterprises, and establishing regulatory frameworks for banking, credit, and stock markets.

Thorough economic reform potentially threatened the regimes' systems of governance as well as ordinary citizens' dependence upon state employment and subsidies. Consequently, reforms were often undertaken in piecemeal fashion, and largely benefited well-connected business elites and state officials.

Along with 'crony capitalism', market reform tended to result in in greater income inequality and greater numbers living in poverty. After the oil-fueled high growth rates of the 1970s, Arab countries posted negative rates of growth per capita in the 1980s due to declining oil revenues and relatively high population growth rates. However, over time ongoing economic restructuring produced an increasingly diversified and vibrant private sector alongside increasing economic inequality. By the 1990s, in countries with decades of market reform (e.g., Turkey, Egypt, and Tunisia), the majority of economic activity was firmly back in the hands of the private sector, even as symbiotic relationships persisted with state authorities.

In "rentier" states, the recycling of oil revenues in construction, finance, tourism, and commercial activities helped create sizeable well-capitalized business sectors (Luciani 2005). These elite business groups have increasingly played a governance role, setting policy agendas through parliamentary representation and business associations (Moore 2004). Gulf business groups increasingly have a regional economic impact through foreign direct investment in agriculture and other sectors in neighboring countries (Sowers forthcoming). As the "elite cartels" of the early decades of economic reform continue to diversify, they may well produce a "discussion on rules and rights that will inevitably point to progressively increasing participation" in countries with sufficiently large and diversified private sectors (Luciani 2007, 173).

Social movements and "non-movements" in the Middle East

As the state withdrew from key areas of economic activity through economic reform, popular participation in community associations and non-state forms of service provision increased. Some of these associations and organizations articulated an explicitly Islamic worldview. The message or call (*daw'a*) of Islamist organizations typically emphasized personal and social reform (*islah*) in the service of the larger Muslim community. Across the Middle East, there was a broad renewal of interest in Islamic practices, dress, and community mobilization during the 1990s. The Islamic trend found supporters in new business elites, educated but underemployed middle- and lower-class youth, middle-class professionals, small artisans, traders, and provincial elites.

Some scholars argued that these movements benefited from state failures to provide basic services, address corruption, and safeguard human rights in rapidly urbanizing areas. In Egypt, for instance, Islamist organizations built networks of parallel institutions in urban, popular (*sha'abi*) neighborhoods, on the periphery of formal politics (Wickham 2002). These institutions provided concrete social services—child care, health care, banking, local neighborhood improvement projects, and income assistance to the needy—along with new ideological frameworks for adherents. Hizballah followed a similar strategy in mobilizing Shi'ite communities in the southern suburbs of Beirut in Lebanon, as did Hamas in the Gaza Strip from the 1980s until it took power in the early 2000s.

Political-religious mobilization, however, was not the dominant means by which most ordinary citizens sought to make ends meet or engage in political life. As Bayat (2010) argues, scholarly work on social movements as intentional forms of organization obscures how the quotidian coping mechanisms of urban populations have reworked urban space and the provision of basic services. Bayat shows how through strategies of "quiet encroachment," families and individuals sought access to housing, tapped into water and sanitation services, and pursued small- and micro-scale economic activity in informal and unregistered enterprises (Bayat 2010).

These strategies of survival and coping reflect the dire economic and social conditions that characterize poor urban neighborhoods of the Middle East. Urbanization rates in the Middle East are among the highest in the world, averaging 4 percent per year over the past two decades (Sims et al. 2008). Rapid urbanization is in part a function of rapidly growing population rates, averaging around 2.1 percent per year between 1990 and 2003 (Sims et al. 2008). Unemployment rates, caused by a "youth bulge" in population, inadequate education, and resource-intensive rather than labor- and knowledge-intensive development strategies, make the lack of jobs the most pressing issue for Middle Eastern youth.

As elsewhere in the developing world, most growth in urban housing and employment development has been in the "informal" sector, in physical spaces outside planned infrastructure development and in unregistered enterprises. In the Middle East, such informal or unplanned areas constitute 20 to 40 percent of urban areas (Sims et al. 2008). In Egypt, between 45 and 60 percent of urban populations live in informal areas (Sims et al. 2008, 1). In Greater Cairo, where an estimated 20 million inhabitants make it the largest urban agglomeration in the Middle East or Africa, residents of informal areas are estimated to account for 65 percent of the total urban population (Sejourne 2009, 17).

With the shrinking of public services and rapid expansion in urban areas, urban and labor protests have become a common feature of political life in much of the region, long before the dramatic events of 2010 and 2011. Protest in countries like Egypt spanned professional organizations, political currents, unions, government employees, farmers, students, and other groups. These actors engaged in myriad forms of peaceful protest, including strikes, boycotts, petitions, demonstrations, and vigils. Much of the protest focused on demands central to livelihood, such as payment of overdue wages by public and private companies. Other demands have challenged the key means used by incumbent authoritarian regimes to control political organizing. Among the repeated demands by striking Egyptian workers, for instance, is the right to form unions independent of state control (Shehata 2010; Beinin and el-Hamalawy 2009). Protests focused on issues such as pollution, lack of public services, and water scarcity are also intensifying, given the grave impacts of these issues on human health, family well-being, and economic productivity (Elmusa and Sowers 2009).

Political reform and electoral competition

From the 1990s to the present day, regimes have restructured the political rules of the game alongside the economic rules. Authoritarian governments sought to dampen internal and external criticism by establishing the façade of multiparty elections. Most of these elections were manipulated to ensure that the government's favored party maintained majorities in parliament and other elected institutions (e.g., professional associations and clubs). With governments maintaining and expanding legal restrictions on political activity and civil associations, some scholars characterized the 1990s as a period of political "de-liberalization" (Kienle 2001). With the exception of Jordan and possibly now Tunisia, most countries in the Middle East ban religiously based parties, such as the Muslim Brotherhood, from contesting elections. These restrictions have been partially circumvented in Egypt in the past, however, by running "independent" candidates with well-known Brotherhood connections or by allying with legally recognized opposition parties.

The 1990s civil conflict in Algeria offered a sobering illustration of the perils of simply excluding such parties from electoral competition. The Algerian regime began liberalizing the political system in the early 1990s, allowing competitive elections. The National Liberation Front (known often by their French acronym as the FLN) had been the dominant party since Algerian independence. The principal challenger party was the Islamic Salvation Front (FIS), which won local elections by a large margin in 1990. With the FIS poised to win legislative elections in 1991, the army took power in early 1992 and engaged in a massive crackdown on the party. The FIS fragmented into smaller, more radical groups, in some cases aided perhaps by covert assistance from Algerian security forces (Le Sueur 2010). Violence and atrocities committed by underground Islamist militias and the Algerian military resulted in hundreds of thousands of civilian deaths before a cease-fire was arranged in 1997 and an accord signed in 1999 (Le Sueur 2010).

Cautious, gradual, and structured inclusion (rather than rejection) of Islamist parties can produce different outcomes. In Turkey, the Islamist Justice and Development Party (AKP) won an overwhelming majority in parliament by 2007. By 2010, the prime minister and president were both drawn from the ranks of the AKP. The AKP made some early and significant strides in addressing some of the most difficult and exclusionary aspects of the adamantly secularist, rigidly ethnonationalist founding ideology of the Turkish republic. These included some accommodation of Kurdish demands for linguistic and cultural expression. In part, the AKP was motivated by its desire, waning in recent years, to further Turkey's accession to the European Union. Of course, Turkey has had some form of democratic practice for much of the period since 1950. This has arguably moderated the ideological stances of political parties and habituated the military to limit its interventions.

Only recently have some authoritarian regimes in the region extended the staging of elections to encompass some of the highest positions in the land. Egypt conducted its first presidential election in 2005. The government reported that the incumbent, Hosni Mubarak (in power since Anwar Sadat's assassination in 1981), had won 88.6 percent of the official vote. The government, however, limited a number of eligible candidates from running, engaged in a variety of tactics to deter voters and manipulate outcomes, and, in a move reminiscent of Putin's Russia, shortly after the election imprisoned the runner-up, Ayman Nour, on charges of corruption. The single most decisive verdict on the illegitimacy of this presidential 'election' came from ordinary Egyptians, however, as most of them simply refused to vote. Very low voter turnout reflected the citizens' assessment that the regime would not allow serious competition for presidential office.

International influences: The "war on terror" and the Iraq war

At the end of the cold war, rising expectations that the Middle East would finally escape the machinations of great powers interested in oil and strategic real estate were short-lived. US policy toward the Middle East since the end of the cold war has been characterized by several fundamental continuities as well as some significant shifts. Consistent priorities under successive administrations have included the security of oil acquisition from the Persian Gulf by Europe, Asia, and the United States; arms sales to "friendly" regimes; the primacy of the special relationship with Israel; and the use of political pressure, economic sanctions and incentives, and threats of military intervention toward what the United States views as "rogue regimes."

In the aftermath of the 9/11 Al Qaeda attacks on the United States in 2001, discussions about counterterrorism quickly veered into broader concerns about the absence of democracy in the Middle East as a "root cause" of terrorist movements. The 9/11 attacks prompted the United States to strike against the Taliban regime in Afghanistan, which was harboring Osama Bin Laden and jihadist networks. At the same time, neoconservatives advocated waging a preemptive war on Saddam Hussein's regime in Iraq, ostensibly because of his possession of weapons of mass destruction.

The George W. Bush administration argued that an American-led construction of a new democratic regime in Iraq would serve as a catalyst for other regimes in the region to democratize. Many scholars familiar with the region, however, argued that an American invasion and occupation of Iraq, however short-lived, would dim prospects for regional democratization, harden anti-American sentiments in much of the region, and might or might not succeed in democratizing Iraq.

Wars in Afghanistan and Iraq were accompanied by a series of US measures in Africa and the Middle East to strengthen the US military and intelligence presence for activities against various kinds of radical terrorist networks. The United States redeployed most its forces out of Saudi Arabia (which ironically was one of Bin Laden's early demands) and into the smaller oil-exporting countries of the Persian Gulf. It also expanded security guarantees and governmental cooperation with these states, including Qatar, Bahrain, the United Arab Emirates (UAE), and Kuwait.

The wars in Afghanistan and Iraq committed the United States to nation building on a scale it had never before attempted in the region. Official statements about a new US commitment to promoting democracy raised expectations from publics across the Middle East. Fearing US pressure, long-standing authoritarian regimes in Egypt and Saudi Arabia undertook superficial political reform (such as Egypt's presidential election). The Arab world soon perceived the commitment to democracy promotion as hollow, however, as long-standing US patterns of cooperation with undemocratic regimes reasserted themselves amid the mounting political and fiscal costs of the Iraq war and the uncertainty associated with the outcomes of democratic reform. These factors made any serious pressure for democratic reform by the United States on friendly yet autocratic regimes, such as Egypt, Kuwait, Bahrain, the UAE, and Saudi Arabia, evaporate.

Two wars and continued US silence on the situation of Palestinians made many Arabs skeptical of American intentions in the region. A 2010 public opinion poll taken in Jordan, Egypt, Lebanon, Morocco, Saudi Arabia, and the UAE found 85 percent of respondents had a "somewhat unfavorable" or "very unfavorable" view of the United States, even as they ranked it among the top countries in the world for freedom and democracy among its own people. When asked to rank what two steps would most improve their view of the United States, 54 percent chose an Israeli-Palestinian peace agreement, 45 percent chose a withdrawal of forces from Iraq, 43 percent supported stopping aid to Israel, and 35 percent chose withdrawing American bases and military forces from the Arabian Peninsula (Telhami 2010).

Conclusion: Developmental challenges and prospects for democratization

To explain the persistence of authoritarian rule in the Middle East, and understand prospects for democratization, this chapter argues that we must examine international influences, patterns of economic development, and state-society relations. From the colonial period through postwar consolidation of authoritarian regimes, these factors have not been conducive to democratization. Yet as the outpouring of protest in 2011 has shown, the stasis of "old" authoritarian regimes is becoming increasingly untenable in the face of dizzying economic and social change. The urban and rural landscapes of the Middle East have been profoundly transformed in the six decades since World War II through population growth, rapid urbanization, and energy and industrial infrastructures. These physical changes have mirrored equally dramatic social changes such as rapid reductions in infant mortality and increases in literacy rates. More young people are educated but face limited employment opportunities, from narrow economic reform strategies as well as a series of devastating civil and interstate wars that have limited foreign investment and undermined human development. Movements, parties, and social movements invoking a range of national and religious motifs intersect with local, concrete concerns about lack of jobs, inadequate public services, access to basic needs, and significant poverty. Given limited (and polluted) water resources, emerging environmental threats such as climate change exacerbate human insecurity (Zawahri, Sowers, and Weinthal 2009).

The balance of economic and political power within the region is shifting, as is the region's external orientation. The dramatic oil price increases that began after 2002 and the resulting flows of wealth to the oil-exporting states of the region, have exacerbated a gap between the oil-rich and oil-poor states in the region. Oil exporters with small indigenous populations and large expatriate workforces have significantly more economic clout in the Middle East than do the more populous oil-poor states, which have historically served as the political and economic centers of the region (Luciani 2007). If the Egyptian revolution successfully creates more transparent, accountable governance, we may see some re-assertion of its traditional regional importance.

While the United States will maintain significant military and economic ties with the Middle East, trends suggest a gradual re-engagement of the region with Turkey, India, China, and Europe. Energy sales and investment opportunities are strengthening the linkages between the oil-rich portions of the Middle East and China, India, Russia, and the rest of industrializing Asia. Given that Russia has been moving away from democratic and competitive politics and China has avoided it, these new orientations might be expected to provide additional external support for incumbent authoritarian regimes. However, the most significant factor shaping prospects for democratization in the near future will be the staying power of popular protest, or "people power." If protesters can sustain their demands through large-scale mobilizations, authoritarian regimes will be increasingly forced to make substantive concessions or follow the paths of ousted presidents Mubarak and Ben Ali.

Democratization processes are protracted and subject to frequent reversals and erosion. As many third-wave transitions to democracy founder or return to forms of semi-authoritarianism, the Middle East no longer seems particularly exceptional (Waterbury 2001). Clear movement toward more institutionalized, robust forms of democratic practice often become apparent only in hindsight (Heydemann 2007, 37). As Heydemann observed, paraphrasing Adam Przeworski, if many developing countries are characterized by poor capitalism and militarized democracies, then future developments in many Middle Eastern states will not seem exceptional (Heydemann 2007).

Additional resources

For up-to-date analysis of developments based on research in the field, see the Middle East Research and Information Project (www.merip.org) and the periodic reports by the International Crisis Group (www.icg.org) and Human Rights Watch. There are also many English-language newspapers and news outlets from the Middle East on the web. Some major sources include:

- *Al Masry Al Youm* (Egypt, English), www.almasryalyoum.com/en
- *Al Jazeera*, English edition, http://english.aljazeera.net
- *The Daily Star* (Lebanon, English), www.dailystar.com.lb

Bloggers are an increasingly important part of public debate in the Middle East, as are Facebook pages, and authoritarian governments take them seriously. Egypt and Iran, for instance, have imprisoned several young bloggers on charges of "defaming the state." One well-known English-language blog is the Arabist, run by Issandr Amrani (http://www.arabist.net/). One of best-known Facebook pages involved in coordinating protest in Egypt was "We are all Khaled Said" (http://www.facebook.com/home.php#!/elshaheeed.co.uk). Established to commemorate a young man beaten to death in Alexandria by two policemen in June 2010, the site was dedicated to exposing the routine torture and inhumane treatment experienced more broadly in Egypt. In one of the pivotal moments of the Egyptian uprising, the young Google employee Wael Ghoneim revealed he had created the site from the United Arab Emirates, where he worked. During an emotional, heartfelt TV interview, done two hours after he was released from a 12-day secret detention by Egypt's Interior Ministry, his passionate and at times tearful defense of the protesters as loyal, patriotic Egyptians reportedly motivated many to join the protest in Cairo's Tahrir Square the next day.

There is a wealth of fascinating films and documentaries that explore political and social change in the Middle East. Iran, Egypt, and Turkey all have significant numbers of filmmakers and production companies, and the region attracts talented documentary filmmakers as well. Some better-known works, and some lesser-known but well worth watching, include:

- *Children of Heaven*, Majid Majidi, 1997, Iran
- *Bab El-Oued City*, Merzak Allouache, 1994, Algeria
- *Chronicle of the Years of Embers*, Mohamed Lakhdar-Hamina, 1975, Algeria
- *Alexandria Trilogy, Youssef Chahine, 1978–89, Egypt*
- *Budrus*, Julia Bacha, 2011, West Bank/Palestine, documentary
- *Gaza Strip*, James Longley, 2002, documentary

References

Al Desoukie, Omnia. 2011. "Rights group: Egypt's revolution death toll more than 680". AlMasry AlYoum, www.almasryalyoum.com/node/346094 (last accessed March 9, 2011).

Angrist, Michele Penner. 2006. *Party Building in the Modern Middle East*. Seattle: University of Washington Press.

Angrist, Michele Penner. 2005. "Party Systems and Regime Formation: Turkish Exceptionalism in Comparative Perspective." In *Authoritarianism in the Middle East: Regimes and Resistance*, edited by M. Posusney and M. Angrist. Boulder: Lynne Rienner.

Bayat, Asef. 2010. *Life as Politics: How Ordinary People Change the Middle East*. Stanford: Stanford University Press.

Beblawi, Hazem. 1990. "Rentier States in the Arab World." In *The Arab State*, edited by G. Luciani. Berkeley: University of California Press.

Beinin, Joel, and Hossam el-Hamalawy. 2009. "Strikes in Egypt Spread from Center of Gravity." *Middle East Report Online*, www.merip.org/mero/mero050907.html (last accessed September 7, 2010).

Bellin, Eva Rana. 2002. *Stalled Democracy: Capital, Labor, and the Paradox of State-Sponsored Development*. Ithaca, NY: Cornell University Press.

Chrystal, Jill. 1995. *Oil and Politics in the Gulf: Rulers and Merchants in Kuwait and Qatar*. Cambridge: Cambridge University Press.

Dodge, Toby. 2003. *Inventing Iraq: the Failure of Nation-building and a History Denied*. New York: Columbia University Press.

Elmusa, Sharif, and Jeannie Sowers. 2009. "Damietta Mobilizes for Its Environment." *Middle East Report Online*, www.merip.org/mero/mero102109.html (last accessed September 7, 2010).

Fischer, Michael M. J. 1982. "Islam and the Revolt of the Petit Bourgeoisie." *Daedalus* 111 (1):101–25.

Geddes, Barbara. 2009. "Changes in the Causes of Democratization through Time." In *The SAGE Handbook of Comparative Politics*, edited by T. Landman and N. Robinson. Thousand Oaks, California: Sage Publications.

Gelvin, James L. 2008. *The Modern Middle East: A History*. New York: Oxford University Press.

Herb, Michael. 2005. "Princes, Parliaments, and the Prospects for Democracy in the Gulf." In *Authoritarianism in the Middle East: Regimes and Resistance*, edited by M. Posusney and M. Angrist. Boulder: Lynne Rienner.

Heydemann, Steven. 2007. *Upgrading Authoritarianism in the Arab World*. Washington, D.C.: Saban Center for Middle East Policy, Brookings Institution.

Jamal, Amaney, and Mark Tessler. 2008. "The Democracy Barometers: Attitudes in the Arab World." *Journal of Democracy* 19 (1):97–110.

Karl, Terry Lynn. 1997. *The Paradox of Plenty: Oil Booms and Petro-States*. Berkeley: University of California Press.

Keshavarzian, Arang. 2005. "Contestation without Democracy: Elite Fragmentation in Iran." In *Authoritarianism in the Middle East: Regimes and Resistance*, edited by M. Posusney and M. Angrist. Boulder: Lynne Rienner.

Kienle, Eberhard. 2001. *A Grand Delusion: Democracy and Economic Reform in Egypt*. London: I. B. Tauris.

Le Sueur, James D. 2010. *Algeria Since 1989: Between Terror and Democracy, Global History of the Present*. New York: Palgrave Macmillan.

Luciani, Giacomo. 2007. "Linking Economic and Political Reform in the Middle East: The Role of the Bourgeoisie." In *Debating Arab Authoritarianism: Dynamics and Durability in Nondemocratic Regimes*, edited by O. Schlumberger. Stanford: Stanford University Press.

Luciani, Giacomo. 2005. "Oil and Political Economy in the International Relations of the Middle East." In *International Relations of the Middle East*, edited by L. Fawcett. New York: Oxford University Press.

Mahdavy, Hussein. 1970. "The Patterns and Problems of Economic Development in Rentier States: The Case of Iran." In *Studies in Economic History of the Middle East*, edited by M. A. Cook. London: Oxford University Press.

McAlister, Melani. 2001. *Epic Encounters: Culture, Media, and U.S. Interests in the Middle East, 1945–2000*. Berkeley: University of California Press.

Metz, Helen, ed. 1991. *Egypt: A Country Study*. Washington, D.C.: Library of Congress Federal Research Division.

Moore, Barrington. 1967. *Social Origins of Dictatorship and Democracy: Lord and Peasant in the Making of the Modern World*. Boston: Beacon Press.

Moore, Peter. 2004. *Doing Business in the Middle East: Politics and Economic Crisis in Jordan and Kuwait*. Cambridge: Cambridge University Press.

Owen, Roger. 1992. *State, Power, and Politics in the Making of the Modern Middle East*. London and New York: Routledge.

Rogan, Eugene. 2009. *The Arabs: A History*. New York: Basic Books.

Rueschemeyer, Dietrich, Evelyne Huber Stephens, and John D. Stephens. 1992. *Capitalist Development and Democracy*. Oxford: Polity Press.

Said, Edward W. 1978. *Orientalism*. 1st Vintage Books edition. New York: Vintage.

Sejourne, Marion. 2009. "The History of Informal Settlements." In *Cairo's Informal Areas: Between Urban Challenges and Hidden Potential*, edited by R. Kipper and M. Fischer. Cairo: Deutsche Gesellschaft für Technische Zusammenarbeit.

Shehata, Samer S. 2010. *Shop Floor Culture and Politics in Egypt*. Albany: State University of New York Press.

Sims, David, Ahmed Eiweida, Same Wahba, and Catherine Lynch. 2008. *Arab Republic of Egypt: Urban Sector Update*. Washington, D.C.: The World Bank.

Sluglett, Peter. 2007. "The Ozymandias Syndrome: Questioning the Stability of Middle Eastern Regimes." In *Debating Arab Authoritarianism*, edited by O. Schlumberger. Stanford: Stanford University Press.

Sowers, Jeannie. Forthcoming. "Institutional Change and Environmental Governance in the Middle East: Water and Authority in Egypt." In *Comparative Environmental Politics*, edited by P. Steinberg and S. VanDeveer. Cambridge: MIT Press.

Telhami, Shibley. 2010. 2010 Arab Public Opinion Poll. Washington, D.C.: Brookings Institution.

Tripp, Charles. 2000. *A History of Iraq*. Cambridge: Cambridge University Press.

Vitalis, Robert. 2007. *America's Kingdom*. Stanford: Stanford University Press.

Waterbury, John. 2001. "Democracy Without Democrats? The Potential for Political Liberalization in the Middle East." In *Democracy Without Democrats?* edited by G. Salame. New York: I. B. Tauris & Co. Ltd.

Waterbury, John. 1983. *The Egypt of Nasser and Sadat*. Princeton: Princeton University Press.

Wickham, Carrie Rosefsky. 2002. *Mobilizing Islam: Religion, Activism, and Political Change in Egypt*. New York: Columbia University Press.

World Bank. 2010. Development Indicators, http://data.worldbank.org/ (last accessed September 7, 2010).

Zawahri, Neda, Jeannie Sowers, and Erika Weinthal. 2009. "The Politics of Dirty Water: The Linkages between Security and Water Quality in the Middle East." Paper Presented at the Water and Security Workshop, International Studies Association Annual Meeting, New Orleans, LA.

USAID has facilitated democratic elections in places like rural Guatemala.
Photo courtesy of USAID/Maureen Taft-Morales

USAID has funded community culture centers, such as this center in Parwan Province, Afghanistan, to provide information about how to use the new legal system
Photo courtesy of USAID

14

The Promotion of Democracy: Actors and Methods

Dinorah Azpuru

Democracy promotion, an attempt to bring democracy to the rest of the world, has long featured prominently in the rhetoric of Western democracies. Until recently, however, such rhetoric was empty. The United States, for example, throughout the nineteenth century frequently justified expansionist activities under the pretext of democracy promotion. Indeed, democracy promotion became the rallying cry for acquiring Oregon, annexing Texas, and invading Mexico. For the past two decades, however, international democracy promotion efforts have been far more earnest. The end of the Cold War created a new opening for the advanced industrial democracies, as they launched more sincere efforts to bring democracy to the rest of the world, particularly the developing countries. Such efforts have taken on a variety of forms and have had different impacts, depending largely on the region of the world in which they are employed. This chapter examines these contemporary efforts to promote democracy, particularly the methods, actors, and recipients. It also weighs in on current debates about democracy promotion, such as what kind of democracy is being promoted and what motivates the promoters. Given the central role of democracy promotion in the foreign policies of developed democracies, it is crucial to understand its scope and methods, but also the reservations and criticisms this practice has evoked.

What is democracy promotion?

According to the Bush Administration, one of the goals of the 2003 American invasion of Iraq was to rid the country of a dictator who had oppressed his people for almost a quarter of a century and install a democratic regime. Unlike other controversial objectives and dubious justifications, replacing an authoritarian regime with a democratic one was sold to the American public as a worthy effort, one that nonetheless has been harshly criticized (Carothers 2007). Iraq painfully illustrates the difficulties of democracy-building through invasion.[1] Even though the US occupation in Iraq is the most famous (or infamous) action of democracy promotion in recent years, the use of force to promote democracy is the least common type of democracy promotion, and it was certainly not the first effort to spread democracy around the world since the end of the Cold War.

Burnell and Randall (2008, 283) identify three different approaches to promoting democracy: conditionalities, democracy assistance, and use of force. The use of force has been largely discredited as a tool for democracy promotion, but the other two approaches have been widely used in a variety of cases with varying degrees of success. The first approach applies democratic and human rights conditionalities to the receipt of development aid and trade concessions. Conditionalities can bring about some improved democratic practices, but is largely ineffective when a determined opposition regime is in place. The second approach, the provision of direct technical, financial, material and symbolic support for democracy programs (i.e., democracy assistance) can have a stronger impact, although long-term sustainability is still problematic. For example, critics such as Levitsky and Way (2005) argue that increased levels of linkage between established democracies and democratizing countries—such as economic, geopolitical, social, communication and transnational civil society links—can have a greater impact on democracy promotion than democracy assistance.

These three approaches demonstrate that the term democracy promotion refers to a diverse group of measures aimed at establishing, strengthening, or defending democracy in a given country. These measures can range from diplomatic pressure to development aid conditionality, sanctions, and even military intervention. While the term democracy promotion is broad, the term democracy assistance is far more specific. Democracy assistance refers to a particular way of promoting democracy through the provision of funding or technical assistance to governments, institutions or other actors in civil society working toward the establishment or strengthening of democracy in a certain country (Azpuru et al. 2008). Carothers (2007) calls democracy assistance the "silent side" of democracy promotion; given its prevalence, democracy assistance, is emphasized in this chapter.

Democracy promotion, and more specifically democracy assistance, is part of the foreign aid packages advanced industrial democracies give developing countries. However, these types of foreign aid are very different from "development aid," which is geared toward helping countries in different areas of socioeconomic development.[2]

What type of democracy is currently promoted?

The industrial democracies of the world began serious programs of democracy assistance at the end of the Cold War. Since the early 1990s, the United States and the countries of the European Union have significantly expanded expenditures in programs designed to advance democracy in other countries (Youngs 2008, Azpuru et al. 2008). The timing of these programs has much to do with concerns about security and the fight against communism during the Cold War (particularly in the United States), when these issues took precedence over concerns about democracy abroad.[3] After the end of the Cold War, once the East–West rift was largely overcome, several actors engaged in democracy assistance efforts. The United States, the European Union countries, and several international organizations focused on the promotion of a dual transition around the globe under the umbrella of the "Washington Consensus" (Burnell and Randall 2008).[4] This entailed the transition from centralized economies to free-market economies and the transition from authoritarian regimes to democratic regimes. The increase in democracy promotion/assistance efforts also coincided with the third wave of democratization.

Given the linkage between economic and political transitions, contemporary democracy assistance programs have focused on promoting what Diamond (1999, 15) calls "liberal democracy," styled after the prevalent model of democracy in the West. Under liberal democracy, priority is given to free and fair competitive elections, protection of individual rights, and mechanisms to hold government officials accountable. While both the European countries and the United States promote liberal, Western-style democracy, they differ significantly in their approaches. Carothers identifies two distinct overall approaches to assisting democracy: the political and the developmental (Carothers 2009, 5). The political approach focuses on the promotion of elections and political liberties and directs aid at political institutions and processes (elections, political parties, and politically oriented civil society groups). The developmental approach, in contrast, has a wider scope. It is based on a concept of democracy that includes concerns about equality and justice and sees democratization as a slow process of change, intertwined with economic and social development. This approach is inclined to use indirect democracy-promotion activities such as supporting local-level projects. Carothers indicates that American and European democracy assistance programs incorporate elements of both approaches, but claims that US democracy aid emphasizes the political approach, whereas the European democracy assistance programs emphasize the developmental approach (Carothers 2009, 13). Canada is another major contributor in the field of democracy assistance and tends to follow the European model, thus favoring a developmental approach.

How is democracy assistance distributed?

We noted above that the main providers or donors of democracy assistance are the advanced industrial democracies, including the United States and Canada in the Western Hemisphere, and several members of the European Union, such as the United Kingdom, Sweden, Germany, Spain, and the Netherlands (Youngs 2008). Other countries, however, also provide democracy assistance, such as Japan, Taiwan, and Norway (which is not part of the European Union). Even some relatively new democracies, such as Poland and South Africa, have joined in the effort to promote democracy abroad (Burnell 2007, 636), but these tend to confine their support to countries in geographic proximity to themselves.

It is important to note that governments of donor countries do not necessarily channel their democracy assistance directly to the recipient country. Certainly, a good portion of democracy aid is given bilaterally, but there are other means and sources of transferring this aid.

International global organizations, such as the United Nations,[5] or regional organizations, such as the European Union and the Organization of American States (OAS), also provide what is called multilateral democracy assistance to countries with emerging democracies. These aid programs also are employed in defense of democracy when it is threatened in those countries.[6] The advantage of multilateral democracy promotion is that the assistance is not seen as politically motivated, as can be the case when provided unilaterally by countries such as the United States. For this reason, donor countries often choose to channel special democracy assistance funding through the multilateral agencies, in what is called "multi-bi" assistance.

Public democracy assistance can also be channeled through private nonprofit organizations. International nongovernmental organizations (NGOs) from donor countries are often the carriers of democracy assistance and implement programs in the field. Some NGOs also conduct fund-raising campaigns among the public in donor countries, but typically such funds are more often used for development or humanitarian assistance, not for democracy aid. In the United States the most important nonprofit organization is the National Endowment for Democracy (NED).[7]

Finally, political parties in developed democracies often provide support for ideologically akin political parties in developing democracies. This aid is generally channeled through Western political parties' foundations or institutes in countries such as Germany, Sweden, the Netherlands, and the United States. These foundations often receive substantial funds from their respective governments.

Box 14.1

Kindred Spirits: Political Parties and Democracy Promotion

In Germany, the Konrad Adenauer Foundation supports parties around the world that share Christian Democratic principles. The other major German foundation is the Friedrich Ebert Foundation, which supports Social Democratic parties. There are, however, other foundations: the Friedrich Naumann Foundation (which supports liberal parties), the Heinrich Böll Foundation (which supports green parties), the Hans Seidel Foundation, and the Rosa Luxemburg Foundation.

In the United States the International Republican Institute (IRI) and the National Democratic Institute for International Affairs (NDI) promote the values of the Republican and the Democratic parties abroad.

The distribution of democracy assistance does not follow a set pattern. Countries across different continents have been recipients of democracy aid of different types and channeled through different means. Still, the geographic distribution of aid has somewhat followed the path of the third wave of democratization. The trailblazers of the third wave in the early 1980s, mainly the Latin American countries, were the first recipients of American and European democracy assistance. The Eastern European countries followed close behind as they broke from communism in the 1990s. Countries in other continents continents have received aid in accordance with their levels of democratization and the rapport they may have with donor countries. Youngs (2008) notes that European countries tend to focus on promoting democracy in Sub-Saharan Africa (where many countries are former colonies), but the pattern varies from country to country. The United States distributes democracy assistance more evenly across different continents, emphasizing some countries when they require it more (i.e. Haiti in the mid 1990s and 2000s) or where the United States has strategic interests (i.e. Iraq and Afghanistan).

Box 14.2

Promoting Democracy in Haiti: A Fairly New Policy

The United States several times changed its policy toward democracy in Haiti in the twentieth century. It occupied Haiti for almost 20 years (1915–34) with the purpose of protecting American interests and preventing Germany from establishing a base on the island during World War I. Although Haitians held public office, US authorities were fully in charge (Keen and Haynes 2004, 531). When the US marines left, instability plagued the island until Francois Duvalier was elected in 1957.

Duvalier was succeeded by his son Jean-Claude; they established a harsh dictatorship that lasted for almost 30 years (1957–86). The Duvaliers counted on US support during their time in office, as they formed part of the group of "friendly dictators"—staunch American allies who opposed communism (Smith 2007). After the ouster of Jean-Claude Duvalier in 1986 and the subsequent end of the Cold War, the policy of the United States has been to strongly support the establishment of democracy in Haiti (as everywhere else in Latin America). The United States first supported the writing of a new constitution for Haiti and helped in the construction of a reliable electoral system on the island.

The first president of the new democratic era in Haiti, Jean-Bertrand Aristide, was elected in December 1990 with the strong backing of the United States and other Western nations. This backing did not, however, shield him from military ouster less than a year after taking office. The international community exerted pressure for a return to democracy without much success; finally, after threatening military action, the Clinton administration was able to negotiate a peaceful return to democracy. In September 1994, the United Nations authorized "Operation Uphold Democracy," which permitted the peaceful entry of US forces to restore democracy on the island. Aristide returned to power and served until the end of his original term in February 1996.

After Aristide, René Préval was elected president and served his full term. Aristide was elected again in 2000, but the opposition boycotted the elections. Aristide's second term in office was marked by allegations of corruption, violence, and human rights violations. After months of instability, Aristide left the country in February of 2004, claiming that he had been kidnapped by the United States and forced into exile in Africa. An interim government was established in Haiti until new elections were held in 2006. The former president, René Préval, was elected again and remains in office as of early 2011, with elections scheduled for March, 2011.

Since 2004, an 8,000-strong United Nations Stabilization Mission, MINUSTAH, has been present in Haiti. The original purpose of the mission was "to restore a secure and stable environment, to promote the political process, to strengthen Haiti's government institutions and rule-of-law-structures, as well as to promote and to protect human rights."[8] After an earthquake devastated the island in January 2010, however, the mission has expanded its scope to focus almost exclusively on recovery and reconstruction efforts. The United States has fully supported MINUSTAH's operations and has provided significant support for this mission.

The case of Haiti shows how difficult it is to build democracy abroad, particularly in a country without a long history of democracy. Between 1990 and 2005 the United States provided $281 million in democracy assistance through the United States Agency of International Development (USAID), the American government's major donor agency for democracy assistance. Haiti is the country in the Western Hemisphere that has received the largest amount of bilateral democracy aid from the United States (in addition to aid received from other donors, including the United Nations). Democracy, nonetheless, remains fragile. It was fragile even before the earthquake and it is now even more at risk. The United Nations envoy to Haiti, Edmond Mulet, declared in June 2010 that "Haiti's struggling democracy is in jeopardy if millions of earthquake survivors' lives are not improved. . . . The longer that the victims continue living in precarious conditions, the more they will have reason [for] discontent. That discontent can be manipulated for political ends." (*Boston Globe*, June 2, 2010)

Methods: How is democracy assistance targeted?

As with other types of foreign aid, donors providing democracy assistance at the bilateral or multilateral levels, or even at the level of private nonprofit organizations, can choose how they will provide that aid. Aid can be given as either direct financial assistance to certain programs (reimbursable or nonreimbursable), as a donation or loan of equipment (i.e. computers) or through technical assistance (direct assistance from specialized personnel from donor countries to local institutions or organizations).

Who manages the aid once it is received depends greatly on the type of program. In most cases, the authorities of recipient countries have to approve any bilateral or multilateral democracy assistance provided by foreign governments, but they do not necessarily have to manage it. Donors can provide aid directly to civil society organizations or local NGOs and often choose to do so when faced with high levels of corruption in the government of the recipient country. International NGOs have more leeway and can often provide aid to local NGOs without the consent of the recipient government.

Both donors and recipients have an interest in assessing what kind of aid can best boost democracy. Unfortunately, this question can be difficult to answer due to a lack of reliable data on the democracy assistance provided to emerging democracies. Youngs (2008) notes that, in the case of European donations, democracy assistance projects are merged into broader development projects, making it difficult to ascertain exactly how much is invested in democracy aid.

The lack of data availability was also a problem with assessing American democracy assistance until USAID commissioned a study to evaluate democracy assistance for the 15-year period from 1990 to 2005.[9] Azpuru et al. (2008) make a detailed analysis of the amount of democracy assistance USAID has provided, the geographical distribution of aid, and the efficacy of different types of assistance. The total investment (in year 2000 US dollars) during that period was approximately $8.47 billion. Figure 14.1 documents the exact distribution of this assistance by geographic region: Latin America and the Caribbean received most of the democracy financing (approximately 20 percent of the total), followed closely by Eurasia, the Mediterranean and Africa.

Figure 14.2 shows, by sector, the amounts the United States has provided to countries around the world between 1990 and 2005. USAID divides democracy assistance into four different areas: rule of law, civil society,

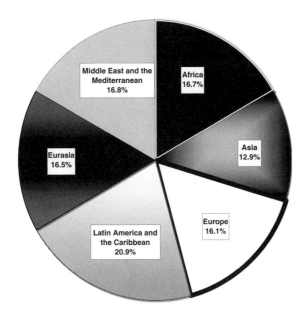

Figure 14.1 Distribution of total USAID democracy assistance by region, 1990–2005 (*Source*: Azpuru et al. 2008)

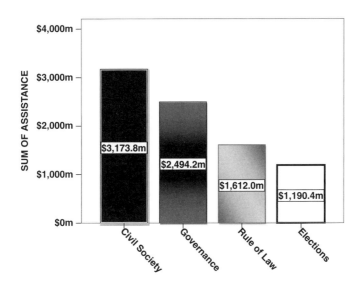

Figure 14.2 Worldwide US democracy assistance by sector (1990–2005) (*Source*: Azpuru et al. 2008)

elections, and governance. Rule of law includes supporting legal reforms, improving the administration of justice, and increasing citizens' access to justice. Civil society includes the support for nongovernmental groups, such as human rights monitoring organizations, civic education groups, media groups, business and labor federations, and others. Elections include programs of voter education and voting promotion, technical and financial support for local electoral commissions, monitoring of the fairness of elections, and political party development. Governance applies to a number of issues related to the functioning of democratic institutions, which include anticorruption activities, decentralization, strengthening local government, effective policy implementation, and improvement of civil–military relations. As figure 14.2 illustrates, most USAID democracy assistance has targeted civil society programs. Perhaps, surprisingly, the least amount of aid was channeled to elections.

When is intervention most successful?

One of the major questions among donors of democracy aid is when to intervene in a given country. At what point is democracy aid a positive contribution to the democratic process, and when can it actually have reverse effects? One would think that promoting or aiding democracy is always a positive thing to do, but some scholars have questioned the timing of such outside interventions. Some critics contend that forcing quick democratization in countries that have deep-rooted ethnic divisions may trigger violence between those groups (Paris, Newman, and Richmond 2009). Others have noted that transforming failing or failed states into democracies is particularly difficult (BMZ 2006). Sometimes donors can decide when and how to intervene to promote democracy: at gunpoint, through a negotiated peaceful transition to democracy, or through a slow process of regime change. Regretfully there is no preestablished model of since success depends on many domestic and international factors. In recent years, most donor countries have chosen the path of slow regime change, aiding democracy from abroad in a gradual way, mostly through democracy assistance.

In other cases donors have to step in when democracy emerges suddenly from within as a product of mass pressure, such as in Egypt in February 2011. Yet the larger question remains: under what conditions and at what stage of political development does a recipient country profit from democracy assistance? By and large, evidence suggests it is best to provide democracy assistance to countries that have already embarked on political reforms, where the government is receptive to the idea of democratization. Democracy assistance can be provided to countries where a semiauthoritarian or fully authoritarian regime is in place, but in these cases the aid is not channeled through the government, and instead through civil society organizations that are seeking to achieve regime change and are often underground. There are several challenges and risks with this option. On the one hand, civil society groups or excluded political parties receiving outside help may be persecuted by the authoritarian regime. The leadership of these groups may be decimated, which in the future may affect the chances of an effective transfer of power to new leaders. Also, it is not always clear that opposition forces will behave in a democratic way once the transition has occurred. It is also possible that circumstances could lead opposition groups to engage in violent actions against the authorities, in which case the funding of the international community for democratic, peaceful change loses its original purpose. Democracy aid to countries with authoritarian or semiauthoritarian regimes is certainly the most controversial, and the authorities of the recipient country are likely to be enraged by outside intervention in their country's political process. They may break diplomatic relations with the country that is allegedly supporting the opposition, and may also retaliate in other ways.

Does democracy assistance work?

Democracy assistance has become one of the cornerstones of foreign policy for many developed democracies, including the United States. Nonetheless, there remain many unanswered questions concerning the promotion of democracy as a foreign policy goal. For example, is democracy assistance effective? Does it work? This question features prominently in debates on democracy assistance. The public in donor countries may question the goal of democracy assistance in the first place, wondering whether it works or is just a waste of effort and money. Few studies have empirically tackled this question at the global level, but one study has assessed whether US democracy assistance has a positive effect on democratization. Seligson et al. (2009) report that American democracy assistance provided in the period 1990–2005 had a positive effect on democratization. Relying on statistical analysis that allowed the authors to control for other factors, Seligson et al. (2009) found democracy assistance makes a difference.[10] Countries that received more US democracy assistance were likely to be more democratic. The topic is still open to debate and further research, but this initial finding is encouraging.

Still, there are those who claim that even if such aid promotes democracy, it is a liberal kind of democracy, culturally biased toward the West. Furthermore, some claim democracy programs tend to be partial and to favor groups that are pro-Western or oligarchic (Robinson 1996). Others argue that democracy assistance fosters dependency and corruption among locals (Moyo 2010).

So far the critics have been outnumbered by the supporters of democracy assistance, but it is unclear whether such assistance will continue at the top of the foreign policy agendas of developed countries in the near future. Ironically, while the use of force is the least common type of democracy promotion, it is the most prominent, and democracy promotion in general may be judged by the outcome of US efforts to bring about democracy in Iraq and Afghanistan.

Box 14.3

Changes in US Democracy Promotion after September 11, 2001

The terrorist attacks of 9/11 have had contradictory affects on US democracy promotion efforts. In the years immediately prior to the attacks of 2001, the United States had begun to rely primarily on diplomatic and monetary tools to promote democracy. For example, the US worked within organizations such as the OAS to strengthen democratic norms and caution countries pursuing undemocratic options (Azpuru and Shaw 2010). The United States also promoted democracy through public diplomacy, as in public speeches and meetings leading US officials touted the importance of democratic reform. More tangibly, the United States established the Democracy and Governance Office under the auspices of USAID. Through this office, the US aimed to strengthen democratic institutions by funding the four areas of democracy promotion: rule of law, civil society, elections and political processes, and governance.

This trend initially appeared promising, but the attacks of 9/11 legitimized a more confrontational approach to democracy promotion. In the high profile cases of Afghanistan and Iraq, the United States argued that military invasion was necessary to promote democracy and reduce the appeal of terrorist elements. American military operations in these countries have not met with global approval, however, and US democratization efforts have been tarnished by accusations of imperialism (Carothers 2006). Furthermore, some authoritarian states have used the threats of terrorism and Islamic fundamentalism as justification for curtailing civil liberties and political rights in their own countries. Thus, the "war on terror" has provided impetus for restricting democratic practices rather than enhancing them (Carothers 2006, Dalacoura 2005).

Still, the US has continued to increase its funding of democratization through USAID, targeting countries of geopolitical importance in particular. In the year following the terrorist attacks, American investment in democracy promotion jumped to $26.54 million in Afghanistan and $32.45 million in the Middle East and Northern Africa. Indeed, the United States increased its investments in democracy promotion across the board from 1990–2002, spending more than five times as much on democracy promotion in 2002 as it did in 1990. It is crucial to remember, however, that the domestic operating environments of the Middle East are very different than those of Latin America and Eastern Europe. In the latter regions, US investment takes place within the context of nascent democracies, while in the Middle East such investment tends to occur in an authoritarian political context. The events of early 2011 in Tunisia and Egypt, as well as other Middle East countries, pose a challenge for donors regarding the best way to provide democracy assistance to countries that do not have a history of democracy. Also, it is important to keep in mind that Middle East states may exhibit divergent reactions to US overtures, depending upon their status as "friends" or "foes" of the United States (Dalacoura 2005).

Additional resources

To see democracy promotion and its challenges "live," Laura Poitras' documentary, *My Country, My Country*, depicts international efforts to hold the first elections in Iraq after the overthrow of Saddam Huseein post-occupation . This documentary provides a glimpse behind the scenes, as international observers and domestic participants talk about their expectations of, and frustrations with, the process.

Notes

1 The invasion began in March 2003, and the authoritarian regime of Saddam Hussein was toppled on April 9, 2003. As of August 2010, after seven years, the United States was in the process of pulling out of Iraq.

2 In addition to development aid and democracy aid, the most common types of foreign assistance are humanitarian aid and financial aid.

3 This does not mean Western democracies ignored democratic ideals throughout the Cold War or before that. Azpuru and Shaw (2010) note that the ideal of promoting democracy and

freedom around the world has been part of the rhetoric of US foreign policy since the days of President Woodrow Wilson, but that in practice real efforts to promote democracy did not begin until the Cold War was over.

4 The Washington Consensus was an agreement among developed democracies to promote a model of free-market economy on the economic side and a model of liberal democracy on the political side. It was called the Washington Consensus because the agreement was reached by international organizations based in Washington D.C., such as the World Bank and the International Monetary Fund.

5 At the United Nations, the Department of Political Affairs, through its Electoral Assistance Division, provides electoral assistance to countries around the world. Other UN entities, such as the United Nations Development Program (UNDP), also work on electoral or other democracy promotion activities in the field.

6 The OAS, for instance, adopted the Inter-American Democratic Charter in 2001, in which member states made the commitment to take measures to defend democracy in the Americas whenever it is under threat. The OAS often sends election observation missions to countries that hold elections in the Western Hemisphere, and sends emergency missions to countries where the democratic process is interrupted or at risk. For many years the OAS had a specific administrative unit, called the Democracy Promotion Unit. Nowadays, it has a Political Secretariat that oversees several departments engaged in advancing democracy in the hemisphere, including the Department of Electoral Cooperation and Observation, the Department of Sustainable Democracy and Special Missions, and the Department of State Modernization and Good Governance.

7 The NED was founded in 1983 and receives public funding from the US government. The NED, in turn, channels these funds to other American foundations that carry out democracy promotion activities. Its funding, however, is rather small in comparison with the amount spent in democracy assistance by the US government through USAID.

8 See the MINUSTAH's homepage: www.un.org/en/peacekeeping/missions/minustah (accessed September 10, 2010).

9 The database comprises 44,958 records that capture the composition of USAID budgets worldwide for specific activities in all sectors over the years 1990–2005. The dataset contains the most extensive and finely grained quantitative information ever compiled on USAID expenditures. Part of the data was initially compiled by John Richter at USAID and the database was later expanded by Andrew Green, a USAID Democracy Fellow, in 2004–05. The database includes those funds allocated by USAID to democracy assistance and development programs. The study was made possible by a grant from USAID to the Academic Liaison Office of Vanderbilt University, in partnership with the University of Virginia and the University of Pittsburgh. The data and reports generated from that data are available at: www.pitt.edu/~politics/democracy/democracy.html.

10 The authors used common measures like Freedom House and Polity IV as dependent variables to measure changes in the democratic status of countries around the globe.

References

Azpuru, Dinorah, and Carolyn Shaw. 2010. "The United States and the Promotion of Democracy in Latin America: Then, Now and Tomorrow." *Orbis (A Journal of World Affairs)* 54(2): 252–67.

Azpuru, Dinorah, Steve Finkel, Aníbal Pérez-Liñán, and Mitchell A. Seligson. 2008. "Trends in Democracy Assistance: What Has the U.S. Been Doing?" *Journal of Democracy,* (19)2: 150–59.

BMZ (Federal Ministry for Economic Cooperation and Development, ed.). 2006. *Transforming Fragile States–Examples of Practical Experience.* Germany: NOMOS.

Boston Globe. "UN Rep: Haiti Democracy Depends on Reconstruction," June 2, 2010. www.boston. com/news/world/latinamerica/articles/2010/06/02/un_rep_haiti_democracy_depends_on_ reconstruction/ (accessed September 10, 2010).

Burnell, Peter. 2007. "Promoting Democracy." In *Comparative Politics,* edited by Daniel Carmani. Oxford: Oxford University Press.

Burnell, Peter, and Vicky Randall. 2008. *Politics in the Developing World.* Oxford: Oxford University Press.

Carothers, Thomas. 2009. "Democracy Assistance: Political vs. Developmental." *Journal of Democracy* 20(1): 5–19.

Carothers, Thomas. 2007. *U.S. Democracy Promotion During and After Bush.* Washington, D.C.: Carnegie Endowment for International Peace.

Carothers, Thomas. 2006. "The Backlash against democracy promotion." *Foreign Affairs* 85(2):55–68.

Dalacoura, K. 2005. "US democracy promotion in the Arab Middle East since 11 September 2001: a critique." *International Affairs* 81(5): 963.

Diamond, Larry. 1999. *Developing Democracy, Toward Consolidation.* Baltimore: The Johns Hopkins University Press.

Keen, Benjamin, and Keith Haynes. 2004. *A History of Latin America.* 7th Edition. Boston: Houghton Mifflin Company.

Knack, Stephen. 2004. "Does Foreign Aid Promote Democracy?" *International Studies Quarterly* 48(1), 251–66.

Levitsky, Steven, and Carolyn M. Way. 2005. "International Linkage and Democratization." *Journal of Democracy.* 16(3): 20–34.

Moyo, Dambisa. 2010. *Dead Aid: Why Aid Is Not Working and How There Is a Better Way for Africa.* New York: Farrar, Straus, and Giroux.

Organization of American States website, www.oas.org/en/about/our_structure.asp (accessed August 30, 2010).

Paris, Ronald, Edward Newman, and Oliver P. Richmond, eds. 2009. *New Perspectives on Liberal Peacebuilding.* New York: United Nations University Press.

Robinson, William. 1996. *Promoting Polyarchy: Globalization, US Intervention, and Hegemony.* Cambridge: Cambridge University Press.

Seligson, Mitchell A., Steven E. Finkel, and Aníbal Pérez-Liñán. 2009. "Exporting Democracy, Does it Work?" In *Is Democracy Exportable,* edited by Zoltan Barany and Robert Moser. Cambridge: Cambridge University Press.

Smith, Peter H. 2007. *Talons of the Eagle: Dynamics of US–Latin American Relations.* 3rd Edition. Oxford: Oxford University Press.

United States Agency for International Development website, www.usaid.gov/ (accessed August 30, 2010).

Youngs, Richard. 2008. "Trends in Democracy Assistance: What has Europe Been Doing?" *Journal of Democracy* 19(2): 160–69.

Hypothesis testing exercise and discussion questions for Section 5

Using the guide below, explain how the independent variables listed below have shaped political development throughout the Middle East. Be sure to examine not just the variables, but also the causal mechanisms linking these independent variables to political development.

Hypothesis testing exercise

Independent Variables	Role in the Region
Economic development • National wealth • Private enterprise • Middle class • Inequality	
Elites	
Political culture/civil society	
Education	
State institutions	
Social divisions/national unity	
International context	

Section 5: Discussion questions

1 How do the processes of political development in the Middle East differ from the historically long process of democratic evolution in places like Great Britain and Switzerland? Will protest movements, economic reform, and political liberalization foster democratic practices? Why or why not?

2 In light of the problems of many third wave democracies, particularly those that struggle to uphold democratic principles in practice as well as on paper, how might we expect democratization to unfold in the Middle East? What similarities

and differences might we expect to see when we compare the Middle East to third wave experiences with democratization?

3 Given the events in the Middle East in early 2011 and what we know about democracy promotion, what are some of the challenges that the United States and other Western democracies face in helping build democracy in that region?

Afterword
Mary Fran T. Malone

In December of 1990, the first free and fair elections in Haitian history declared Jean-Bertrand Aristide president. Given Haiti's legacy of dictatorship, political instability, violence, and foreign intervention, observers within Haiti and around the world hoped these elections would usher in a new era. Winning two-thirds of the vote, Aristide assumed office with an unprecedented mandate, attesting to the appeal of his platform of dramatic social change (Stotzky, 1997). Despite this popular appeal, Aristide's domestic opponents were formidable and his hold on power tenuous; after less than a year in office a military coup forced him into exile and General Raoul Cédras was installed as dictator. The 1991 coup doused the hopes of Haitians and the international community.

On the eve of the first free and fair elections in 1990, Haiti had the ignominious title of the poorest nation in the Western Hemisphere, with the highest levels of income inequality. Approximately 76 percent of Haitians lived in poverty, and only 39 percent had access to safe water. Less than half of the adult population could read and write.[1] Against this backdrop, political instability exacerbated already poor economic conditions and jeopardized the ability of international organizations to provide humanitarian aid, to say nothing of the prospects for economic or political growth. Haitians began to flee the country in the thousands, many of them on makeshift rafts headed for the United States. At one point, the U.S. Coast Guard was intercepting two thousand Haitian refugees a day on the open seas (Smith, 2000).

Roundly criticizing the 1991 coup and the ensuing human rights violations, the international community led efforts to resolve the crisis diplomatically. When these efforts failed, the United States, with UN backing, led a coalition that persuaded the military regime to abdicate shortly before the invasion arrived in September 1994. Aristide resumed the presidency, backed by a series of UN peacekeeping missions, which aimed to stabilize the political situation, reduce public insecurity, and build the institutional infrastructure for democratic governance.

These peacekeeping missions did succeed in holding democratic elections in 1995, with subsequent elections in the late 1990s and early 2000s. At the national level, these elections resulted in the peaceful handover of power from one president to the next (Stotzky, 2002). Still, much of this progress was superficial, and did not reflect substantive change to the foundations of Haiti's political system. The superficial nature of reform in Haiti became glaringly obvious in the wake of the 2000 presidential elections, in which Aristide and his Lavalas Party declared victory amid accusations of fraud and voter intimidation. According to the UN, voter turnout in these presidential and parliamentary elections was a paltry 10 percent, and the opposition contested the results (UNDPO, 2010). Despite international efforts to mediate the crisis, tensions between Aristide and his opponents mounted, culminating in an armed insurgency in February 2004. The international community threatened Aristide with sanctions, and he was eventually spirited out of the country. With the assistance of UN peacekeepers, new elections were held in 2006. Over 50 percent of registered voters trudged to the polls and elected former President Réne Préval. Despite some unrest, observers were cautiously optimistic that President Préval's victory, with 51 percent of the popular vote, would usher in a new, more prosperous era for Haiti. Unfortunately this optimism was short-lived, as political infighting, the dissolution of the electoral council, and alleged assassination attempts derailed the 2007 senate elections (Associated Press, 2009). The political environment was not conducive to new elections until April of 2009, when UN soldiers and international observers appeared to outnumber the few voters going to the polls (Associated Press, 2009).

The consequences of this political instability became painfully clear on January 12, 2010, when an earthquake destroyed large parts of Haiti and claimed approximately 200,000 lives. Side by side with coverage of the devastation, the media highlighted the pervasive problems of corruption and poor leadership that have historically plagued Haiti, with headlines like "In Quake's Wake, Haiti Faces Leadership Void," "Government Struggles to Exhume Itself," and "Haiti PM fears government collapse."[2] While the earthquake galvanized the international community into action to provide humanitarian relief, the issue of governance also surfaced quickly. The task of rebuilding Haiti is daunting, and if history is any indication, both the international community and domestic politicians will be hard pressed to build a functioning system of governance that can start to address the needs of the people.

The story of Haiti illustrates why the study of democracy is so important. Theories of democracy have captured the attention of scholars since the time of Aristotle, but the answer to the question "What causes democracy" is of urgent practical import in places like Haiti. The international community has insisted that the democratic experiment continue, using sanctions and peacekeepers in an effort to keep Haiti on the democratic path. Still, time and time again, democracy has faltered, and with dire consequences. To avoid the piling of mistake upon tragic mistake, it is imperative to identify what factors will lead to the creation of a sustainable democratic government. If one grand theory of democratization eludes us, then, at the very least, knowledge of the democratic development of a wide group of diverse cases can offer a series of lessons. If we are serious about breaking cycles of political instability, these lessons need to be tailored to countries like Haiti.

Given the practical import and ramifications of our testing of democratic theory, we also need to think very carefully about the way in which we test these theories. Scholars must decide how to test the theoretical relationships between their independent and dependent variables. For example, should we examine the political development of a small number of cases in great depth? Or, should we rely upon the statistical analysis of many cases? This book uses a most different systems approach, which allows us to look at democratic success stories and identify the factors they share. There are a variety of other approaches, however. For example, a most similar systems approach would take the opposite track, and look at a group of countries that share many similar independent variables (e.g., economic development, experiences with colonization) and see why they differ on the dependent variable, democracy.[3] For example, a most similar systems approach has been employed in Central America to determine why Costa Rica adopted democratic governance in the 1950s, while the other countries remained mired in dictatorship until the 1990s. Single country case studies explore political development in one particular case. For example, Dominguez (2003) provides an in-depth examination of Cuba to explain why democracy remained elusive even after the fall of the Soviet Union in 1991. At the opposite extreme are large N quantitative studies, which seek to examine as many countries as possible and test the major theories of democracy through statistical analysis.

These different methodologies should be viewed as complementary rather than competitive, as multiple methodologies can provide rigorous tests of the different theories of democratization. Indeed, while this book relies upon the most different systems approach, students may wish to complement that approach with their own independent study of democratization, relying upon one of the other methodologies. By relying upon multiple methodologies, students, scholars, and practitioners can illuminate the ways in which different variables, and their interactions with one another, can lead to successful democratic governance. This is not just good social science, it is also a way in which theories of comparative democratization can be properly generalized for countries like Haiti, where their insight is sorely needed.

Notes

1 Data on poverty and literacy rates are from the World Health Organization's (WHO) Division of Emergency and Humanitarian Action (EHA) https://apps.who.int/eha/trares/hbp/haiti/indic. htm (last accessed March 15, 2010). Data on access to potable water are from the United Nation's Human Development Report 1995 (UN HDR 1995).

2 These are sample headlines of articles appearing in the *New York Times* in the month following the earthquake.

3 Both the most different systems (MDS) and most similar systems (MSS) are based upon John Stuart Mills's method of difference and method of agreement.

References

Associated Press. "Few Vote in Haiti After Clash in City." The *New York Times*. April 20, 2009.

Domínguez, Jorge. 2003. "Why the Cuban Regime Has Not Fallen." In *Cuban Communism 1959–2003 11th edition*, edited by Irving Horowtiz and Jaime Suchlicki, 435–442. New Brunswick, NJ: Transaction Publishers.

Smith, Peter. 2000. *Talons of the Eagle: Dynamics of US-Latin American Relations (Second Edition)*. New York: Oxford University Press.

Stotzky, Irwin P. 2002. "Democracy and International Military Intervention: The Case of Haiti." In *Democracy and Human Rights in Latin America*, edited by Richard Hillman, John A. Peeler, and Elsa Cardozo DaSilva. Westport, CT: Praeger.

Stotzky, Irwin P. 1997. *Silencing the Guns in Haiti: the Promise of Deliberative Democracy*. Chicago: University of Chicago Press.

United Nations Department of Peacekeeping Operations (UNDPO) 2010. United Nations Stabilization Mission in Haiti (MINUSTAH) Background Report. www.un.org/en/peacekeeping/missions/minustah/background.shtml (last accessed March 15, 2010).

Index

Page numbers in **bold** denote boxes, figures, photographs and tables.